The ULTIMATE Guide to
Hawaiian Reef Fishes
Sea Turtles, Dolphins,
Whales, and Seals

John P. Hoover

Mutual Publishing

ISBN-10: 1-56647-887-1
ISBN-13: 978-1-56647-887-8
Library of Congress Cataloging-in-Publication Data

Hoover, John P., 1944-
   The ultimate guide to Hawaiian reef fishes sea turtles, dolphins, whales, and seals / John P. Hoover.
      p. cm.
   Includes index.
   ISBN 1-56647-887-1 (softcover : alk. paper)
   1. Coral reef fishes--Hawaii--Identification. 2. Coral reef fishes--Hawaii--Pictorial works. I. Hoover, John P., 1944- Hawaii's fishes. II. Title.
   QL636.5.H3H66 2008
   597.09969--dc22

Design by John P. Hoover
Cover photo by Mike Roberts
Back cover dolphin photo by Michael S. Nolan

Fifth Printing (updated), June 2013
Sixth Printing (updated), August 2014
Seventh Printing, November 2016
Eighth Printing (updated), February 2019
Ninth Printing, August 2021
Tenth Printing (updated), February 2022
Eleventh Printing (updated), March 2023

Mutual Publishing, LLC
1215 Center Street, Suite 210
Honolulu, Hawai'i 96816
Ph: (808) 732-1709
Fax: (808) 734-4094
Email: info@mutualpublishing.com
www.mutualpublishing.com

Printed in South Korea

Other Books by the Author

Hawai'i's Fishes
A Guide for Snorkelers and Divers
Second Edition

Hawai'i's Sea Creatures
A Guide to Hawai'i's Marine Invertebrates
Revised Edition

Hawai'i's Underwater Paradise

A Pocket Guide to Hawai'i's Underwater Paradise

Hanauma Bay
A Marine Guide to Hawai'i's Most Popular Nature Preserve

Reef Fish Hawai'i
A Waterproof Pocket Guide

Rainbow Reefs
Images from Hawai'i's Underwater Paradise

CONTENTS

INTRODUCTION

This comprensive guide to Hawai'i's marine vertebrate animals is based on my book *Hawai'i's Fishes, a Guide for Snorkelers and Divers,* but contains more species, more pictures, and more stories—in short, it's an upgrade. Although *Hawai'i's Fishes* remains in print and continues to satisfy the basic needs of fish watchers in the Islands, I have long wanted to create a larger, more complete reference. There is so much more to say! Almost daily I get questions from readers who are seeing species they can't identify, or who want information on marine mammals, or strange behaviors they have observed.

To satisfy these advanced snorkelers and divers—and those who want to be—I have doubled the size of the original book by adding over a hundred new fishes, over 500 extra photos, entire chapters on Hawai'i's whales, dolphins, seals, sea turtles, and sea snakes, dozens of first-hand accounts of encounters with marine animals, and a wealth of information on how all these animals eat, live, and reproduce.

Crammed with stories, picture galleries, and over 150 fascinating sidebars, this book takes the concept of a fish ID guide to a whole new level. Enjoy!

ACKNOWLEDGMENTS

This book could never have been written without the scholarship and research of numerous scientists and writers, all far more knowledgeable than myself. Among these John E. Randall and Bruce C. Mundy stand out for their works specifically on Hawaiian fishes. Books by Margaret Titcomb and Mary Kawena Pukui were indispensible for Hawaiian cultural information. John L. Earle, Pauline Fiene, and Cory Pittman contributed invaluable comments and corrections. George Balazs, Brenda Becker, William Gilmartin, Thea Johanos, Marc Lammers, and David Mattila helped me with the marine mammal and reptile chapters. I am greatly indebted to  all these professionals who have spent their lives advancing our knowledge of the sea.

Thanks also go to the snorkelers and divers who contributed their stories and observations. Wherever possible I have mentioned them in the text. I am particularly grateful to Michael S. Nolan for his marine mammal photographs and to Mike Severns for pictures of rare Hawaiian fishes, as well as to Keoki Stender, David R. Schrichte, Kendra Ignacio, Jerry Kane, Mike Roberts, David B. Fleetham, and all the others whose images appear in these pages.

Final thanks go to my dear wife, Marcia, without whose loving encouragement and support no books would have been written.

Fisher's Angelfish (p. 2)

For a list of books and other materials used in the preparation of this volume, please visit my website www.hawaiisfishes.com.

ISOLATION and ENDEMISM

Hawai'i is a wonderful place to watch marine life, not only because of the warm, clear water but because about 25 percent of Hawaiian fish species are endemic—they occur nowhere else. Few locations compare with Hawai'i in number of unique fish species, and none has more. Why? How did our fishes originally get here? Where did they come from? Let us take a closer look.

The Hawaiian Islands are the tops of a dramatic under-

Sunrise Basslet, a rare Hawaiian endemic (p. 160)

sea mountain range stretching 1,500 miles from Kure Atoll in the northwest to the island of Hawai'i in the southeast. This range rises from great depths and, discounting tiny Johnston Atoll to the south, is separated from all others by distances of more than 1,000 miles. Sometime in the past, the ancestors of all Hawaiian shallow-water marine species must have crossed this gap, which is far greater than the distances between any other Pacific islands and their nearest neighbors.

Scientists believe that most tropical marine life—even that of the remote Caribbean—originated near what is now Indonesia and the Philippines. More marine species are found in these ancient seas than anywhere else, and the number decreases markedly as one moves away. Shallow-water animals and plants spread slowly from this "center of dispersal," moving from island to island or along the shores of continents. When they reached the great oceanic gaps, some managed to cross.

Although large ocean-going fishes could swim these distances, how did small reef fish cross them? They did not swim, they drifted. Most fish begin life as minute larvae which are carried varying distances by ocean currents before settling in a suitable habitat to mature. If there is no suitable habitat, they perish.

The ancestors of Hawai'i's shore and reef fishes drifted in as larvae. But only species with long-lasting larval stages made it; those with short larval stages died before they arrived. Ocean currents did not move them fast enough. Distance acted as a natural filter.

Crossing the gap, of course, was only the first challenge. Having arrived in Hawaiian waters, a species still had to find favorable habitat and suitable food. Lacking these it would not survive. To reproduce, it had to arrive in numbers sufficient for males and females to mature at the same time and find each other. Because of these winnowing effects, far fewer marine species occur in Hawai'i than in Indo-Pacific locations such as French Polynesia, Micronesia, Australia, Thailand, or even far-away East Africa. Indeed, whole groups of animals common in those areas are absent from the Hawaiian shallow-water fauna.

Among the fishes that never reached Hawai'i, for example, are the colorful anemonefishes, found almost everywhere else in the tropical Indo-Pacific. Anemonefishes never reached Hawai'i because their larval stage lasts only about a week. Moray eels and surgeonfishes, on the other hand, drift as larvae for months and are here in abundance. As might be expected, the number of inshore fish species in Hawai'i above depths of 600 ft. (about 680 species) is considerably less than the number found in other Pacific locations such as Micronesia (1,400), or the Philippines (2,000).

Isolation, however, has worked two ways. Although impoverishing Hawai'i's fauna on the one hand, it has enriched it on the other. The great distance between Hawai'i and other islands made possible the emergence of many new species. The occurrence of unique species in a limited geographical area is called **endemism**.

About 25 percent of Hawaiian fish species are endemic. Few places have a comparable percentage. Easter Island—also greatly isolated—is one; the Red Sea region—isolated not by distance but by geology—is another. Isolation encourages endemism because species populations are small, localized, and easily affected by genetic changes. Favorable mutations quickly become established, the organism becomes better adapted to its environment and, given enough time, may evolve enough distinct characteristics to separate it from its ancestors. Most Hawaiian endemics have a "sister species" elsewhere in the Indo-Pacific from which they evolved, or with which they share a common ancestor. (In some cases, the sister species itself has also become established in the Islands and now co-exists with its related endemic species; see p. 69.) Those few endemics that do not have a sister species are called "relicts" because their evolutionary line has apparently died out elsewhere in the world (see p. 7).

In isolated regions like Hawai'i, endemic species are often the most successful and numerous representatives of their families, probably because they are the most perfectly adapted to local conditions. Examples are the Milletseed Butterflyfish and the Saddle Wrasse, two of our most abundant reef fishes.

Some Hawaiian endemics, however, are unusual around the main islands. The Yellowbar Parrotfish and the Lined Coris, for example, are uncommon to rare, while the Hawaiian Black Grouper and the Masked Angelfish are almost never seen. These and others like them probably

evolved in the older, cooler Northwestern Hawaiian Islands at a time when the main islands we know today did not exist. Adapted to lower temperatures, they have not done well in warm waters further south. This theory is born out by their relative abundance at the northwestern end of the chain and the fact that some of these species can be found around the main islands only in cool deep water beyond the reach of sport divers.

Because endemism is such an important and interesting feature of Hawaiian fishes, the names of endemic fishes in the species accounts to follow are printed in red.

The Flame Wrasse is one of Hawai'i's most spectacular endemic fishes (p. 332)

Coral reefs in Hawai'i are poorly developed in comparison to other parts of the tropical Pacific. Water temperatures are too low to favor vigorous coral growth, and the dispersal factors which have limited the number of fish species have also limited the number of corals, most especially the colorful soft corals, which are almost entirely absent from our waters. The reefs of the main islands are almost all fringing reefs, built up directly on the sides of the islands. The enormous barrier reefs with enclosed lagoons so common elsewhere in the Pacific occur in Hawai'i only in the northwestern atolls.

Hawaiian shores offer a variety of habitats. The surge zone where sea meets land is characterized by cliffs or large smooth boulders and scanty coral growth. There is ample algae and seaweed here for fishes agile enough to survive the turbulence and crashing waves. Surge zone specialists include some algae-eating surgeonfishes, damselfishes, and blennies. Large dense schools of feeding Convict Tangs are often seen here, as well as resting aggregations of silvery flagtails.

Further from shore is the shallow reef, extending to a depth of about 30 feet. Here, turbulence is less severe, coral is more abundant, and variety of life is greater. Colorful wrasses, triggerfishes, and butterflyfishes feed on small crustaceans and invertebrates, and schools of parrotfishes and surgeonfishes graze on algae. Hawkfishes perch within branches of coral, ready to strike, while goatfishes probe for food in sandy patches and channels. Under ledges and in caves, big-eyed nocturnal squirrelfishes and soldierfishes wait for darkness, while the mysterious, sticklike Trumpetfish stalks its prey and the Longnose Butterflyfish swims upside down on the ceiling. The dominant corals in the shallow reef zone are Cauliflower Coral *(Pocillopora meandrina)* and Lobe Coral *(Porites lobata)*. Hawaiian Cleaner Wrasses often set up their cleaning stations near large Lobe Coral heads where fishes, large and small, line up to be serviced, some coming in from deep water. This is the realm of the snorkeler and shallow diver, and at least half of the fishes described in this book can be seen here.

The deeper reef, starting at about 30-40 ft and subject to little wave action, is typically home to large beds of Finger Coral *(Porites compressa)*. Pygmy angelfishes, juvenile surgeonfishes, and small, colorful wrasses seek refuge here, while plankton-eating damselfishes hover in the water above and schools of goatfishes waiting for nightfall hang motionless, like curtains suspended in midwater. This is the realm of the scuba diver and advanced snorkeler.

The dropoff zone, characterized by steep slopes and perpendicular walls, is a habitat preferred by plankton eaters, such as Pyramid and Pennant Butterflyfishes, and sometimes anthias. Many of the other reef fishes can also be found along the walls, but the excitement along the dropoff comes from the occasional visits of large pelagic or open-ocean fishes, such as manta rays, large **ulua** (jacks), and sharks. At the base of the dropoff a rubble zone is home to yet other interesting fishes, such as the Flame Wrasse and the Curious Wormfish. The dropoff and rubble zones are almost exclusively the domain of the diver, although occasionally the top of a wall is accessible to snorkelers.

Other habitats include shallow, protected lagoons, home to mullets, ladyfishes, stripeys, and gobies, open sand, which which can harbor a surprising amount of fish life such as razor wrasses, flatfishes, and gurnards, and of course blue water, where whales and dolphins are seen..

Hawai'i's underwater landscape, while not offering the lush exuberance of Indonesia or the Caribbean, has a spare beauty of its own in which unique and colorful fishes are the prime attraction.

CLASSIFICATION and NAMES

The world has roughly 23,000 fish species, 120 marine mammals, and 70 marine reptiles. All are classified into a hierarchy of evolutionarily related groups known as **classes**, **orders**, **families**, and **genera**. Genera are separated into individual **species**.

The **class** is the broadest grouping. Mammals comprise the single class Mammalia and reptiles, the class Reptilia. There are two classes of living fishes in this book: the ancient cartilaginous fishes (sharks, rays, skates, and chimaeras) and the more modern bony fishes.

One level down, the **order** is a grouping of broadly similar animals within a class. All whales and dolphins belong to the order Cetacea within the class Mammalia. All eels belong to the order Anguilliformes within the class Osteichthyes (bony fishes). Perchlike fishes belong to the order Perciformes. Other examples of orders are:

Wedgetail Triggerfish juvenile (p. 317)

all scorpionfishes (Scorpaeniformes), or all tubemouthed fishes such as pipefishes, seahorses and cornetfishes (Syngnathiformes).

Families are composed of closely related animals within an order. Dolphins, for example, belong to the family Delphinidae within the order Cetacea, moray eels comprise the family Muraenidae, within the order Anguilliformes, and goatfishes form the family Mullidae, order Perciformes. The fish portion of this book is organized alphabetically by families. The names of families always end in "...**idae**."

Within families are even more closely related groups known as **genera** (singular: **genus**). Finally, each genus is divided into **species**, the lowest unit of classification. (Occasionally, however, species are split into two or more subspecies.)

The formal, scientific names of animals and plants consist of two parts: the genus and the species. This "binomial nomenclature," invented by the great Swedish naturalist Linnaeus (1707-1778), is used in the naming of all living organisms. In print, the genus is always capitalized while the species is entirely in lower case, as in *Gorgasia hawaiiensis*. Both are italicized.

Binomial scientific names are often, but not always, composed of descriptive Latin or Greek words. *Gorgasia* (named for the Gorgons, mythical Greek monsters with hair of snakes) is a genus of garden eels within the conger eel family *Congridae*. The species name *hawaiiensis* indicates precisely which garden eel we mean, in this case, the Hawaiian Garden Eel. Following the two-part name is the name of the biologist or biologists who first formally described the species and the year in which the description was published. Thus we have: ***Gorgasia hawaiiensis* Randall and Chess, 1979**. The authorship is considered part of the full scientific name. Parentheses around the author's name indicate that the genus originally assigned by the author has been changed.

It often happened (especially in the last century when communication was poor) that two or more scientists, working in different parts of the world, each "discovered" and named fishes of the same species. Confusion resulted, with some fishes receiving a dozen or more published scientific names. The rules of scientific nomenclature state that, within certain limits, only the first published name for a species is valid. Later names are known as "synonyms." Great progress has been made in recent years toward sorting out synonyms and valid names. That work is still going on, and some of the scientific names in this book will undoubtedly be revised in the future. Similarly, older books may use a scientific name different than the one given here. If you need to correlate an older name with the current one, the website fishbase.org can be helpful.

Scientific names can be intimidating to nonscientists. They look difficult and hard to pronounce, and they frequently do not connect in any obvious way with the actual plant or animal. Nevertheless, if one wants to communicate precisely about plants and animals, scientific names have no substitute. This book tries to make the scientific names more meaningful by providing translations whenever practical.

Common or popular names present another dilemma. A single fish species can have half a dozen popular names, varying from country to country or even region to region within a country. In some parts of the United States, but not Hawai'i, scientists have attempted to standardize the English names of fishes, as has been done for birds and molluscs. This is a worthy goal, although it sometimes results in names which few people use. This book attempts to solve the problem by giving alternate common names wherever practical.

In the Hawaiian language fish names are rich and detailed. Fishing was an important part of life in old Hawai'i, with many connections to other activities. Different varieties of sugar cane, taro, or sweet potato, for example, often shared names with fishes. The Hawaiians had as many as four or five different names

Black Triggerfish · **humuhumu-'ele'ele**

for a single fish species, designating different stages of its growth. Sometimes fish names had parallel meanings important in ceremony and magic.

Hawaiian fish and plant names were often in two parts, a general name coupled with a specific descriptor (similar to the genus and species of a scientific name). Thus **humuhumu** (triggerfish) and **'ele'ele** (black) join to form **humuhumu-'ele'ele**, the Black Triggerfish (*Melichthys niger*). Unfortunately, by the time anyone thought to record Hawaiian fishing lore much of the old culture and knowledge had been lost. In many cases only the general name has survived. Although secondary descriptive names have been recorded, we often do not know exactly to which species they refer. Many Hawaiian names remain in common use, especially for the more important food fishes. Translations have been provided wherever practical.

WHAT IS A FISH?

Surprisingly, there is no precise answer. Originally, "fish" meant any animal that spends its entire life in the water. (It is still used that way in the words "jellyfish," "starfish," "cuttlefish," etc.). Today, however, when we say "fish" we usually mean any of several types of aquatic animals that have gills throughout life, a backbone of some sort, and (generally) a streamlined body with fins.

Thompson's Anthias (p.163)

This is probably as good a place as any to mention that the plural of "fish" depends on use. Many scientists and educators use "fishes" when referring to individuals of more than one species, and "fish" when referring to individuals of a single species. Sometimes the distinction seems unnecessary. In this book, I try to use "fishes" only as a synonym for "species of fish." Thus there are over 20,000 fishes (i.e. species of fish) in the world, thousands of fish in a school (all the same species), and billions of fish in the sea (species doesn't matter).

Scientists who study fish are called ichthyologists. Through study of fossils, ichthyologists have determined that we are in a golden age of fish. There are probably as many or more fish species living today than at any time in the Earth's past! And more are being discovered every year.

Fish are important. They are the oldest and largest group of vertebrate animals. They are ancestral to all others, and make up slightly more than half the total number of vertebrate species. Scientists believe that the terrestrial vertebrates—reptiles, birds, and mammals—descended from fishes that evolved to live on land. (Curiously, some of these land animals returned to the sea millions of years later to become our present-day sea turtles, sea snakes, seals, dolphins, and whales.) Not only are fish the most diverse and species-rich of the vertebrates, they are also, perhaps surprisingly, among the easiest to observe for anyone with a mask, snorkel and fins.

Oriental Flying Gurnard · **loloa`u** (p. 164)

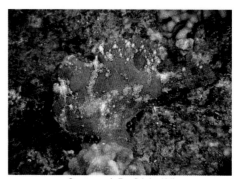
Commerson's Frogfish (p. 134)

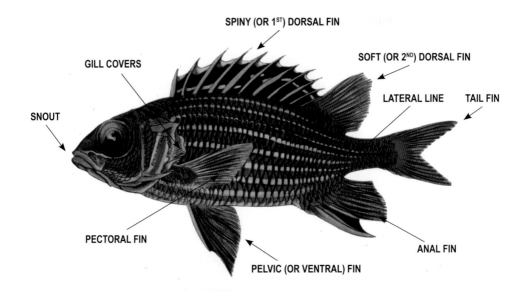

SPINY (OR 1ST) DORSAL FIN

SOFT (OR 2ND) DORSAL FIN

GILL COVERS

LATERAL LINE   TAIL FIN

SNOUT

PECTORAL FIN

ANAL FIN

PELVIC (OR VENTRAL) FIN

FISH ANATOMY

Ichthyologists usually work from preserved specimens and perform their identifications in the laboratory, typically by counting fin spines, scale rows, teeth, and the like, and by examining the structure of other parts such as the gills. For the purposes of this book, such refinements are not necessary. The shapes, sizes, and color patterns of live fish are usually enough for identification in the field.

It is difficult, however, to describe the characteristics and colors of fish species without elementary knowledge of fish anatomy. One must at the very least know the names and locations of the principle fins, such as the dorsal or pectoral fins. For this purpose a self-explanatory diagram is included. Wherever possible, common rather than scientific words are used, i.e. "tail fin" for "caudal fin" and "base of tail" rather than "caudal peduncle." Another distinction is useful: "stripes" are horizontal while "bars" are vertical. The "lateral line" is a sense organ running lengthwise along the upper side roughly from the gill covers to the base of the tail fin. Often visible as a faint line, it detects vibrations in the water.

Bandit Angelfish · one of Hawaiʻi's most striking endemics · Palea Point, Oʻahu. 50 ft. (p. 8)

Colorful and appealing, angelfishes are enduring favorites of fish watchers around the world. In most of the Indo-Pacific and in the Caribbean, a close encounter with a big showy angelfish can be the high point of a dive. Often unafraid, these fishes will turn to face their admirers, displaying to full advantage their gorgeous fins and colors. Although large angelfishes do not occur in Hawaiʻi, small, shy "pygmy angels" of the genus *Centropyge* are common.

Pygmy angelfishes spend most of their lives in the coral or under ledges, seldom venturing far from cover. They are rarely seen by snorkelers, and are easily overlooked by divers. One species, Potter's Angelfish (p. 4), is common enough, but most divers have probably never seen a Fisher's Angelfish or a Flame Angelfish (next two pages). Fewer still have seen the exquisite Japanese Angelfish (p. 4), which occurs in our area only in the Northwestern Hawaiian Islands. Perhaps rarest of all is Nahacky's Angelfish (p. 6), a Johnston Atoll endemic known in Hawaiʻi from a single stray collected near Hōnaunau on the Big Island in 1988.

Most pygmy angelfishes live in social units usually consisting of a male, 1-4 mature females, and sometimes several immature fish. Generally, they begin their lives as females. The only way to become male is to mature as a female, then change sex. Only the largest, most dominant female in a group undergoes this transformation. Fishes with a female-to-male socio/sexual life history (and there are many) are known as "haremic protogynous hermaphrodites." Pygmy angels feed on algae, diatoms, and detritus (decaying organic matter).

Not all Hawaiian angelfishes are pygmies. The larger Bandit Angelfish swims in the open and is so striking in appearance that it can be spotted immediately, even from a distance. The Masked Angelfish also swims openly, but is common only in the Northwestern Hawaiian Islands. Finally, the large and fantastically patterned Emperor Angelfish *(Pomacanthus imperator)* is known in Hawai'i from a single specimen caught in 1948 and some recent sightings of juveniles, all evidently strays. Angelfishes are popular aquarium fishes. Specimens imported from outside Hawai'i, such as the Lemonpeel Angelfish *(Centropyge flavissimus)*, Semicricle Angelfish *(Pomacanthus semicirculatus)*, and Regal Angelfish *(Pygoplites diacanthus)*, are occasionally released by irresponsible aquarists or fish importers, but are not known to be reproducing in Hawaiian waters.

Angelfishes all have a large backward-pointing spine on the gill cover. Their scientific family name, Pomacanthidae, reflects this, combining *poma* ("cheek") and *acanthus* ("spine"). Of the approximately 90 known angelfish species worldwide, five occur regularly in the main Hawaiian Islands. Three are endemic, and none have Hawaiian names.

a) typical female ▲   b) unusual female color variant ▼

c) male ▼

FISHER'S ANGELFISH
Centropyge fisheri (Snyder, 1904)

These small angels are orange-brown with a dark smudge above the pectoral fin. The tail fin is pale and transparent. Males, orange-brown washed with blue, sport alternating blue and black stripes on the rear margins of the dorsal and anal fins. These fish can be common in Finger Coral *(Porites compressa)* and rubble at depths greater than about 50 ft. Few divers notice them, however, as they are fast-moving and stay close to cover. On O'ahu look for Fisher's Angels on the deeper Wai'anae dives. On Maui they are common at Molokini Islet. On the Big Island's Kona coast they can be seen on most steep outer slopes. On rare occasions they hybridize with Potter's Angelfish. The species has been successfully bred in captivity. The name honors California zoologist Walter K. Fisher (1878-1953), who pioneered the study of Hawaiian echinoderms around the turn of the century. Fisher's Angelfish was long considered endemic to Hawai'i. In 2004 the species was broadened to include two previously distinct species, *C. flavicauda and C. acanthops,* from the tropical Pacific and Indian oceans. To about 3 in. Indo-Pacific. Photos: (a) Hōnaunau, Hawai'i. 90 ft. (b) Ho'okena, Hawai'i. 60 ft. (c) Kepuhi, O'ahu. 70 ft.

a) male

FLAME ANGELFISH *Centropyge loricula* (Günther, 1874)
    These beauties are bright red, with 4-6 dark vertical bars on the body and blue trim on the rear fins (more pronounced in males). The bars evidently reminded someone of a lady's corset, for that is the meaning of the species name. Uncommon in Hawai'i (except perhaps along the Kona coast of the Big Island), they live in small haremic groups, often in stands of Finger Coral *(Porites compressa)* or along rocky walls and ledges, sometimes as shallow as 5 or 10 ft. Wherever you find them, they are likely to stay in the same place and can be visited repeatedly. Single individuals are also encountered from time to time. If mates of their own species are unavailable, these may, on rare occasions, spawn with the more abundant Potter's Angelfish (see p. 6). Skilled aquarists have successfully bred Flame Angels in captivity. Aquarium specimens spawn daily around sunset and wild ones probably do the same. To 4 in. Pacific Islands, from the Great Barrier Reef to Hawai'i. Photos: (a) Magic Island, O'ahu. 30 ft. (b) Ka'ohe Bay, Hawai'i. 40 ft. (c) Kepuhi, O'ahu. 70 ft.

b) male

c) young female

Flame Angels from outside Hawai'i often have thicker, more irregular black bars than Hawaiian specimens, and tend to be orange between the bars and at the base of the tail. Hawaiian Flames are known for their more intense and uniform red coloration, but they can vary. The male at left, above, has a bit of the orange color common in non-Hawaiian flame angels, while the young female at right is reminiscent of an interesting variant found in the Marquesas Islands, French Polynesia, which has few or no dark markings except for the black blotch behind the gill covers.

3

JAPANESE ANGELFISH
Centropyge interrupta (Tanaka, 1918)

In bright sunlight, the oranges and blues of this fish are stunning. Males have more blue on the head than females and the rear margins of their soft dorsal and anal fins are blue with horizontal black markings. In Hawai'i, Japanese Angelfish occur only in the northernmost islands of the archipelago, perhaps only at Pearl and Hermes Reef, Midway, and Kure. Like Potter's Angelfish, they live in small haremic groups of a male and several females. At Midway, they are not uncommon along ledges and dropoffs at depths of about 80 ft. In addition to algae and detritus, they feed on the feces of plankton-eating damselfishes and anthias, and are usually found where these are abundant. They have been successfully bred in captivity. To about 6 in. Southern Japan, Taiwan, and the Northwestern Hawaiian Islands. Photo: Midway Atoll. 110 ft.

male

male

POTTER'S ANGELFISH *Centropyge potteri* (Jordan & Metz, 1912)

The only commonly-seen angelfish in Hawai'i, Potter's Angel is rusty orange on head and back, darkening to bluish black on much of the lower side. The entire fish is covered with irregular vertical gray-blue lines. The edges of the rear fins are striped horizontally with bright blue and black. Males have more dark pigment and more blue on the fins than females, and their bodies are slightly more elongate. Some individuals are much darker than others. These fish can be hard to see without scuba, but adventuresome snorkelers on O'ahu might find them off the cliffs at Kawaihoa (Portlock) Point, where for some reason they are frequently in the open. Big Island snorkelers can see them at Hōnaunau or Kealakekua Bay in only a few feet of water. Divers, of course, will see them almost anywhere, peering from the coral and darting from one hiding place to the next. The name honors Frederick A. Potter (1874-1961), director of the Waikīkī Aquarium from its founding in 1903 until 1940. To 5 in. Endemic. Photo: Magic Island, O'ahu. 25 ft.

female ▲   male ▲

Potter's Angels live in pairs or in small haremic groups consisting of a male and several females, usually in clear water at depths of 10-400 ft. under ledges or on reef slopes with plenty of shelter holes. One researcher ranked them among the 10 most frequently seen fishes in such areas. They feed on detritus and algae. Although they inhabit a specific territory, they do not defend it from other algae-eating fishes. A male, however, does defend his harem and breeding territory from other males. The pair above (female at left) occupy a crevice off Mākua, O'ahu, at a depth of about 100 ft.

Rare blue-black color variant, presumably male, from 195 ft. off Kona, Hawai'i. Aquarium photo by Hiroyuki Tanaka.

What female could resist the gaze of this soulful male?

Potter's Angels rarely leave the shelter of the reef, but this bold female regularly ventures out to eat algae from the shells of nearby resting turtles. "Five Graves," Maui. 40 ft.

Juvenile. Pūpūkea, O'ahu. 30 ft.

Potter's Angelfish reproduction

Potter's Angelfish spawn around dusk, generally over the highest outcropping in their territory. Reproductive activity is most frequent from December through May and may peak during the week before a full moon. Dr. Philip Lobel recorded an entire session on film. About one hour before sunset a male approached a female, swimming with a distinct vertical undulating motion. Stopping above her he erected his dorsal and anal fins, fluttered his pectoral fins, turned partially on his side, and drifted slowly upward as he fluttered. When the female did not follow, he darted back down and swam around her with the undulating motion again, swooping up and down. Courtship continued until the female responded. By this time both fish had intensified their orange coloration and were producing audible clicks and grunts. The male then swam to a prominent outcropping and rose above it about 3 ft., the female following. She darted back prematurely the first few times, but the male, continuing his display, finally enticed her to remain

in midwater, where he approached her from underneath, nuzzling her vent with his snout until she released a single burst of eggs. Simultaneously, he released his sperm, then both darted for cover with the female chasing the male and nipping at his tail fin. Soon after, the two hid themselves for the night. Photo: Richard Pyle.

Hybrid angelfish

When two similar species share habitat, one rare and one common, the stage is set for hydridization. If the rare fish cannot find a mate of its own species, it may make do with the available similar species. The angelfish and butterflyfish families are particularly susceptible to hybridization. The fish at left is the result of a "mixed marriage" between a Potter's Angelfish and a Flame Angelfish. Such hybrids may mate successfully with other fish, resulting in second generation hybrids. Photo: Richard Pyle.

NAHACKY'S ANGELFISH
Centropyge nahackyi Kosaki, 1989

In 1987, Randall Kosaki discovered this gorgeous fish at Johnston Atoll, where it is not uncommon at depths of 80 ft. or more on gently sloping outer reefs. It is dark blue-brown with a yellow tail base, abdomen, and head. The top of the head (nape) is marked with iridescent blue bars interspersed with black. Kosaki named it after his friend Tony Nahacky, who in 1988 had caught a single individual of the same as-yet-unknown species off Hōnaunau, Hawaiʻi, at 115 ft. The fish was not seen again in Hawaiʻi until 2011, when Gerard Newman found on at 150 ft. off Hōnaunau. In 2013 the author photographed another off South Point at 100 ft., and in 2021 Stacy Swanke found one off Oʻahu at 180 ft. (see video by Brian Greene on YouTube). With only 4 confirmed sightings, this is easily Hawaiʻi's rarest angelfish. To about 3 in. Endemic to Johnston Atoll.

Randall Kosaki

a) male ▲   b) female ▼   c) female mask variations ▼

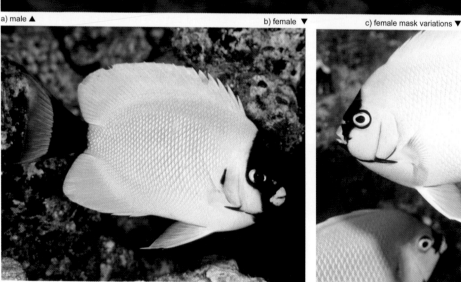

MASKED ANGELFISH *Genicanthus personatus* Randall, 1975

Around the main Hawaiian Islands these angelfish usually occur below 200 ft. Very rarely, small females settle out in shallower water, as when a pair appeared at Molokini Islet, Maui, at 70 ft. in April, 1997. Hard core fish enthusiasts, including the author, flew over from Honolulu to see them, but they vanished after about a month. In the cooler northwestern chain Masked Angelfish are not uncommon and can be seen in as little as 40 ft. They feed on plankton near dropoffs or other areas of high relief, often well off the bottom. Females are snow white with a black "mask" over the eyes. The size and shape of the mask varies considerably (see photo above, at right). Males are white rimmed with orange and have a golden yellow mask; their tail fin lobes are prolonged into streamers. Males sometimes darken to blue-gray, perhaps when displaying aggression. Resembling no other angelfishes, Masked Angels are considered a relict species. They have been bred in captivity at the Waikīkī Aquarium. The species name means "masked." To about 10 in. Endemic. Photos: (a) Midway Atoll. 60 ft. (b) Molokini Islet, Maui. 70 ft. (c) Midway Atoll. 45 ft.

BANDIT ANGELFISH *Apolemichthys arcuatus* (Gray, 1831)

A bold black band, like a robber's mask, passes through the eyes and along the body of these distinctive fish, giving them their common name. They are gray with tiny white spots above the band, and white below. Typically unafraid, Bandits will sometimes swim over to investigate divers. On Kaua'i and in the Northwestern Hawaiian Islands they are common enough that snorkelers sometimes see them. Further south they are encountered less frequently, usually at scuba depths, and most often on the windward sides of the islands. Unlike other Hawaiian angelfishes, Bandits swim in the open, are usually paired, and feed heavily on sponges. Because of their diet they probably taste bad, and the striking color pattern could well be a warning to predators, as well as a means for mates to track each other. Juveniles, which have a masklike black band covering most of the chest, head, and upper side, are secretive and rarely seen, usually below 150 ft. Bandit Angelfish fare poorly in captivity, but master-aquarist Frank Baensch successfully bred a pair in 2006 (see one of his juveniles below, at right). The species name means "bent like a bow," referring to the slightly arched black band. To 7 in. Endemic. Photos: (top) Palea Point, O'ahu. 50 ft. (bottom left) Mākua, O'ahu. 40 ft. (bottom right) aquarium photo by Frank Baensch.

juvenile   Frank Baensch

8

Bandit Angelfish feed mostly on sponges (lower left), but will take other foods when the opportunity arises. The above individual was following a foraging Blackstripe Coris, presumably to seize stray food items it might uncover. (Could the amazing resemblance between the two endemics be completely accidental?) The fish at lower right was feeding on Hawaiian Sergeant eggs along with Milletseed Butterflyfish and other opportunists. Cleaning activity is described at the bottom of the page. Photos: (above) Midway Atoll. 50 ft. (below left) Five Fathom Pinnacle, Ni'ihau. 80 ft. (below right) Moanalua Bay, O'ahu. 70 ft.

First down the mooring line at 'Ewa Pinnacles, I descended into a school of about 30 Island Jacks milling around the bottom. I noticed a Bandit Angelfish moving among them, apparently "cleaning." Other divers coming down the line scattered the jacks, but at the end of the dive, as the divers ascended, the jacks returned and approached the angelfish (which was one of a pair) as it foraged on the bottom. One or two jacks would present themselves broadside and the angelfish would swim up and nip at their sides or fins. Other jacks appeared to be waiting their turn. I called my buddy over to witness the behavior, which he did. However, when he attempted to get closer for a photo, the jacks and the angelfish retreated. At this point we were running out of bottom time, so we followed the other divers up the line.
- John Earle

BARRACUDAS
(Sphyraenidae)

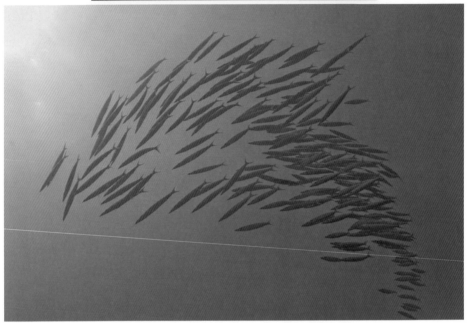

Heller's Barracudas · **kaweleʻā** · Hanauma Bay, Oʻahu. **50 ft.** (p. 12)

Lean, fast, and powerful, barracudas have reputations as predators second only to sharks. They are elongated and almost cylindrical in cross section, with a pointed, protruding lower jaw, two dorsal fins spaced widely apart, and a forked or emarginate tail. The mouth, often held slightly agape, is full of sharp teeth. One species, the Great Barracuda, attains about 6 ft. with a weight of about 100 lbs. and is reported to strike at speeds of almost 40 ft. per second. When they feed, barracudas often cut their prey in two then circle back to eat the pieces. Sharks do the same thing. Both lack the expandable mouths common to other fish predators, such as groupers, which facilitate swallowing prey whole.

The reputations of dangerous marine predators rise and fall. Sharks, for example, were downplayed in the early 1900s when many scientists thought them stupid and cowardly. At the same time barracudas were widely regarded as fearless and liable to strike without warning. One authority even claimed that barracudas were responsible for most "shark" attacks. Today the pendulum has swung to the other side: sharks are treated with respect and caution, while barracudas are seldom considered a threat.

Barracuda attacks, although rare, can cause serious injury. At least two incidents have been recorded in Hawaiian waters, both to Maui fishermen and both in the 1960s. One man, repeatedly slashed on the leg by a six-foot barracuda while throw-net fishing, subsequently underwent five hours of surgery. The other required 255 stitches to close his wounds.

A study of 29 reported barracuda attacks in the United States between 1873 and 1963 confirmed nineteen. Most occurred in murky water or as a result of deliberate provocation. Reasons often advanced for unprovoked attacks include the victim splashing about in the water or wearing bright flashing jewelry that the barracuda might interpret as the flash of silver scales. It is also possible that a small fish being chased by a barracuda could seek shelter under or behind a human in the water, resulting in the human being hit instead. Although a small degree of uncertainty is always present, thousands of snorkelers and divers swim with barracudas each year without problems.

Actually, there is more danger in eating barracudas than in being eaten by them; high on the food chain, these fish often accumulate high levels of ciguatera fish toxin, which causes abdominal pain, nausea, vomiting and strange neurological symptoms such as reversal of hot and cold. Ciguatera poisoning can be fatal.

Snorkelers and divers in Hawai'i occasionally encounter barracudas, either in schools or as individuals. They usually keep their distance and soon disappear into the gloom. Out of perhaps 20 species worldwide only three occur in the Hawaiian Islands, one quite rare.

GREAT BARRACUDA · **kākū** · *Sphyraena barracuda* (Edwards, 1771)
The largest of the barracudas and the one most frequently implicated in attacks on humans, this species is silvery, often with small black blotches irregularly placed on the lower side. The large tail fin is mostly black with pale tips. The second dorsal fin can also be black. Smaller specimens may have about 20 indistinct bars. These powerful predators occur alone or in small groups and are often found in shallow water close to shore, especially in early morning or late afternoon. They typically hang almost motionless over the reef, ready to strike when an opportunity arises. The hot water outfall at Kahe Point Beach Park, O'ahu, is a good place to look for them. As top predators, large barracudas are often ciguatoxic; it is risky to eat them. They grow to about 5½ ft., but are usually half this size in Hawai'i. Large individuals tend to increase in girth rather than length. The name "barracuda" originates in South America. This fish occurs in both the Indo-Pacific and Atlantic; the two populations will likely be declared separate subspecies, or even separate species, in the future. Photo: Hanauma Bay, O'ahu. 10 ft.

Fisherman's friend

A remarkable partnership has long existed between Hawaiian fishermen and certain large Great Barracudas, tamed by hand-feeding and carefully trained to help catch **'ōpelu**, *or Mackerel Scad (p. 184). The fisherman summons his barracuda, or* **'ōpelu mama**, *by pounding rhythmically on the bottom of his wooden boat. Rising from the deep, the barracuda follows the boat until a suitable school is found. Next, the fisherman lowers a large circular net and chums the* **'ōpelu** *with cooked grated squash while the barracuda circles the canoe, driving the fish into a tight ball underneath where they can easily be caught. Before carefully raising the bulging net, the fisherman tosses his helper a well-earned reward. This remarkable tradition continues on the island of Maui, although fishermen complain that their valuable* **'ōpelu mama** *are sometimes caught by commercial fishing charters. "Please write about the* **mama**," *implored one fisherman to a newspaper reporter, "and tell people that they should be respected."*

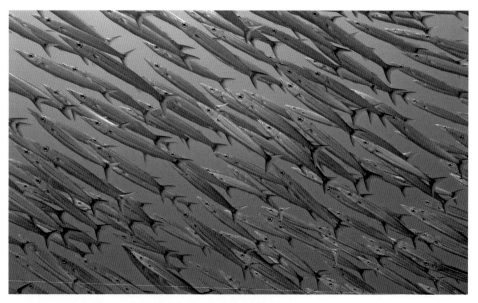

HELLER'S BARRACUDA · **kawele'ā** · *Sphyraena helleri* Jenkins, 1901

The Hawaiian name means "long and bright," an apt description. Slender and silvery, these barracudas have a broad blue stripe running the length of the body. They hunt by night and rest in beautiful, tight schools above the reef by day. In ancient Hawai'i it was said of a confusing situation: "The **kawele'ā** have taken the bait and tangled the lines." The species name honors American zoologist Edmund Heller (1875-1939). Heller often accompanied President Theodore Roosevelt on fishing trips, and in 1909 went with him on safari. Later the two wrote *Life Histories of African Game Animals.* To about 2 ½ ft. Central & Western Pacific. Photo: "Five Graves," south shore Maui. 20 ft. (see also p. 10)

BLACKFIN BARRACUDA *Sphyraena qenie* Klunzinger, 1870

These barracudas rest by day in almost stationary schools which may occupy the same locations for years, usually in current-prone areas. They are silvery gray with about 18 darkish vertical bars and a black margin on the tail fin. Rare in Hawai'i, the species is known so far from only a few locations, including South Point, Hawai'i, and off Lāna'i. The species name *qenie*, derived from an Arabic word, was pronounced "queenie" by English speakers. Unhappy with this, C.B. Klunzinger, who named the species in 1870, tried to change the official spelling to "kenie" in 1884, but to no avail; the first published name is the only official name recognized today (see p. 272). To about 4 ½ ft. Indo-Pacific and Eastern Pacific. Photo: Arno Atoll, Marshall Islands.

BIGEYES
(Priacanthidae)

Bigeyes are red or silvery nocturnal fishes oval in outline, with deep, narrow (compressed) bodies, fine scales, upturned mouths, and large dark eyes. During the day they often remain under ledges and in caves, often seemingly asleep. At night they emerge to feed on planktonic animals high in the water column. Their eyes are extremely reflective—a dive light pointed in their direction will reflect back in a laser-like beam. In rare years the endemic Hawaiian Bigeye appears in enormous numbers close to shore. This happened off Oʻahu and Kauaʻi in 2002, and off Kauaʻi in 1965. Something similar occurred in late January of 1891, about the time when King Kalākaua died in San Francisco. According to contemporary newspapers a multitude of red fish were observed schooling in Puʻu Loa (Pearl Harbor). Red was a royal color in old Hawaiʻi and such an event was considered to foretell the death of a chief. Bigeyes are known in Hawaiian as **ʻāweoweo**, which also means "glowing red." (The caldera atop Mauna Loa, which during eruptions often holds a lava lake, is named **Mokuʻāweoweo**.) Hawaiʻi has two shallow-water bigeyes, both pictured here. Two more occur in deep water, including the "giant **ʻāweoweo**" *(Cookeolus japonicus),* which attains 20 in.

COMMON BIGEYE · ʻāweoweo
Heteropriacanthus cruentatus
(Lacepède, 1801)
[Glass-Eye]

Bright red to silvery, or displaying a blotchy mixture of the two (usually while resting), these fish can switch colors rapidly. The trailing edge of the tail fin is slightly convex. There are often faint dark spots on the dorsal, anal and tail fins. Solitary, they almost always hide under ledges or in caves by day. The species name means "bloody," the Hawaiian name "glowing red." To about 12 in. Found in all tropical seas. Photos: (top) Portlock Point, Oʻahu. 30 ft. (bottom) Pūpūkea, Oʻahu. 40 ft.

a) adult

HAWAIIAN BIGEYE · ʻāweoweo
Priacanthus meeki Jenkins, 1903

These fish have a <u>tail fin with a slightly concave trailing edge.</u> Their color varies from red to pink to silvery white, and there is often a <u>series of faint dark spots along the lateral line.</u> Unlike the Common Bigeye, they will form schools and often congregate in the open by day some distance from shelter. Like many endemic fishes, they are most abundant in the cooler Northwest Hawaiian Islands. Around the main islands they are uncommon except during and after rare bloom years when juveniles and subadults (ʻ**alalauā**) become superabundant. The species name honors American ichthyologist Seth Eugene Meek (1859-1914). To about 12 in. Endemic. Photos: (a) Portlock Point, Oʻahu. 25 ft. (b) Midway Atoll, 30 ft. (c) Pūpūkea, Oʻahu. 30 ft.

b) adult ▲

c) subadults ▼

BLENNIES
(Blenniidae)

Scarface Blenny · **pāo`o** · Hawaiian endemic · Pūpūkea, O'ahu. 30 ft. (p. 17)

Blennies are small, elongated, mostly bottom-dwelling fishes typically seen in tide pools or peering from holes or crevices in the reef. Their alert eyes, doleful expressions, and curious antenna-like filaments (cirri) make them favorite close-up subjects of underwater photographers. Blennies are often confused with gobies, a similar family of small bottom-dwellers. Blennies have one long dorsal fin whereas gobies have two, and blennies tend to back into their holes tail-first, while gobies share a predilection for head-first entry.

Blennies divide easily into two groups: bottom-dwellers and free swimmers. The former (most blennies) typically have blunt heads and subsist primarily on algae and detritus scraped from the rocks with their wide mouths. Poor swimmers, they lack air bladders and sink as soon as they stop moving. When out of their holes they generally rest on rock or coral.

The free-swimming fang blennies (also called sabertooth blennies) have narrow heads and are carnivores. Possessing air bladders, they swim openly and retreat to their holes only at night or when threatened. Their lower jaws bear a set of curved fangs used primarily for defense. If taken by a larger fish, a fang blenny will bite the inside of its captor's mouth and be spat out unharmed. In some non-Hawaiian species the fangs are venomous. These venomous species are often mimicked by yet other blennies.

Many fang blennies feed exclusively on mucus or bits of scale scraped or nipped from the sides of larger fishes. Sometimes called "hit-and-run blennies," these tiny predators make sneak attacks on their larger hosts, sometimes relying on mimicry to approach within striking distance. Most remarkable, perhaps, is the Mimic Blenny *(Aspidontus taeniatus)*, an almost exact double of the common Bluestripe Cleaner Wrasse of the Indo-Pacific *(Labroides dimidiatus)*. The mimic even swims with the wrasse's curious up-and-down dancing motion. When a fish approaches the blenny to have its parasites removed, it loses a bit of skin or scale instead. Although neither of these fishes occurs in Hawai'i, the endemic Ewa Fang Blenny often mimics juvenile Hawaiian Cleaner Wrasses.

The blenny family includes over 300 species. The ancient Greeks knew these fishes as *blennos*, the source of our modern name. The general Hawaiian name is **pāo'o**. In ancient times these fishes figured in many legends and for some families were **'aumākua** (the embodiment of ancestors). Most blennies lay eggs in nests on the bottom and have a short larval stage, thus many Hawaiian species are endemic. Several others are believed to have been introduced, including the Ferocious Blenny, *Omobranchus ferox*, recently found in the lower reaches of Hālawa Stream, O'ahu. Of the fifteen blennies known from Hawai'i, ten are described below. Among those omitted are the Squiggly Blenny *(Cirripectes quagga),* which is small and seldom noticed, and the endemic Ebony Blenny *(Enchelyurus brunneolus),* which lives inside dead coral and is never seen alive.

BULLETHEAD BLENNY · pāo'o
Blenniella gibbifrons
(Quoy & Gaimard, 1824)

These blennies are common on shallow, wave-washed reef flats. Light greenish-brown, mottled and barred with darker brown, they blend in well with the substrate. Males have blue-white spots on the sides and sometimes blue throats (seen during winter and spring, probably breeding coloration); females have red spots on the head. A slender unbranched tentacle above each eye distinguishes this species from the similar Marbled Blenny (next page), which has branched tentacles. The eyes and forehead bulge out slightly, conferring both common and species names (the latter meaning "humped front"). To about 5 in. Indo-Pacific. Photos: Hanauma Bay, O'ahu. 1-2 ft.

male nuptial colors ▼

female ▼

16

MARBLED BLENNY · pāo'o
Entomacrodus marmoratus
(Bennett, 1828)

This blenny feeds on detritus and algae along surf-swept benches and shallow rocky shores where turbulence is moderate to strong, retreating into cracks and crevices to avoid big waves. It probably occurs no deeper than about 3 ft. To escape predators it can leap from ledges to the sea then skip and skitter across the rough foamy water for distances of at least 10 ft. At night it sometimes rests on ledges a few inches above the water, perhaps to avoid predation. The color is light greenish with darker spots and bars. Light vertical streaks cross the mouth. To about 6 in. Endemic. Photo: Makapu'u, O'ahu. (Keoki Stender).

Keoki Stender

STRASBURG'S BLENNY · pāo'o
Entomacrodus strasburgi
(Springer, 1967)

Although common on some shallow rocky bottoms subject to moderate wave action, this small blenny is seldom noticed. It scoots about on the substrate almost too quickly to be seen, and when at rest blends well with its environment. It occurs down to about 6 ft. Females have a large pale pinkish patch behind the eye. Males, somewhat darker, have a similar olive-colored patch. The name honors ichthyologist Donald W. Strasburg (1924-2008), University of Hawai'i graduate and longtime student of Hawaiian blennies. To about 2 in. Endemic. Photo: Pohoiki, Hawai'i. 6 ft.

female

SCARFACE BLENNY · pāo'o
Cirripectes vanderbilti (Fowler, 1938)

Dark overall, with red scarlike marks on the head, these blennies are often seen peering from crevices or resting in the open on rocky substrate at depths of less than about 30 ft. Approached, they quickly take cover. The red marks, more intense in some individuals than in others, may vary according to sex. The species is named for Mr. and Mrs. George Vanderbilt of Philadelphia, wealthy sponsors of a 1937 scientific expedition to the Pacific. This blenny is closely related to the Red-Speckled Blenny (*C. variolosus)* of Micronesia and the South Pacific. To almost 4 in. Endemic. Photo: Pūpūkea, O'ahu. 30 ft. (The similar Squiggly Blenny, *C. quagga*, shares similar habitat. Slightly smaller, it lacks red "scars," has small light spots, and is much too quick to photograph!) (see also p. 15)

male in nuptial colors guarding white egg patch ▲

GARGANTUAN BLENNY · **pāoʻo** · *Cirripectes obscurus* (Borodin 1927)
The largest blennies in Hawaiʻi, these are dark overall with bright pinpoint-like spots speckling the head and body, especially toward the front. During the spawning season (January through March) males develop splendid red heads and yellow pectoral fins. Although not uncommon in the shallow surge zone along steep rocky shores down to about 20 ft., these blennies are infrequently seen. To find them, pick a super-calm day and look along shore under overhangs and in crevices, especially in surge channels that you wouldn't normally dream of entering. The endemic Hawaiian Rock Damselfish (p. 80) often lives nearby. The species name means "dark." To about 7 in. Endemic. Photos: Makapuʻu, Oʻahu. 10 ft.

female ▼

a, b) males ▲▼

c) female ▼

SPOTTED CORAL BLENNY · **pāoʻo ʻo kauila** · *Exallias brevis* (Kner, 1868) [SHORTBODIED BLENNY; LEOPARD BLENNY]

These large, appealing blennies often sit motionless on or near living coral (usually Lobe Coral, *Porites lobata*). They are densely covered with clusters of hexagonal spots (reddish in males, brown to yellow in females) and have a sail-like dorsal fin which they raise when aroused. Feeding exclusively on living coral, they leave small mouth marks ("blenny kisses") all over the reef. However, they are seldom seen feeding; they spend 90 percent of the typical day just sitting in the open (the lower left photo is a typical pose). At spawning time, males clear a small patch of coral or rock on which females lay their bright yellow eggs (see next page). Egg color suggests a possible noxious substance. The male guards the eggs 6-9 days until they hatch. Roving females may spawn with numerous males, and nest sites can contain eggs deposited by more than one female. The cute juveniles (p. 20), white with gold-brown spots shelter between branches of Cauliflower Coral and are seen most frequently in the summer months. Spotted Coral Blennies are unsuitable for aquariums because of their food requirements. The species name means "short." To 6 in. Indo-Pacific. Photos: (a) Kahe Point, Oʻahu. 20 ft. (b) Lānaʻi Lookout, Oʻahu. 30 ft. (c) Pūpūkea, Oʻahu. 25 ft.

Spotted Coral Blennies in Hawaiʻi differ behaviorally from those elsewhere in the Indo-Pacific in that they commonly sit out in the open. Outside Hawaiʻi, they seldom do this, instead sheltering within branching corals almost continually. In Hawaiʻi only juveniles do this.

a) male and female spawning (note male nuptial coloration) ▲

Marjorie L. Awai

b) male fighting colors ▲

c) juvenile ▼

Spotted Coral Blenny reproduction

Dr. Bruce Carlson, Director of the Waikīkī Aquarium from 1986 to 2002, studied Spotted Coral Blennies to exhaustion. Males and females, he reports, have their own territories and come together only when spawning, which occurs year-around usually between 10 am and 1 pm. Males clear a nesting site on live coral, dead coral, or bare rock, usually in a place exposed to some current or surge. Roving females initiate courtship by entering a male's territory and sitting motionless several feet from the nest site. The male swims to her, then rapidly turns and leads her to the nest. Over a period of about one hour she lays a clutch of bright yellow eggs, a few at a time. The male fertilizes them as they are laid. When finished, the female leaves and the male guards the eggs until they hatch in 6-9 days, at night. Females may spawn every 3-4 days, often with different males. Males may spawn daily with different females, whose adjacent egg patches he guards simultaneously. (Eggs of different ages are distinct because they change color as they mature, becoming dark yellow, olive-green, then silvery before hatching.) The larvae are pelagic. Males can assume two subtle color changes. During spawning they darken their spots and widen the white interspaces, creating a conspicuous contrasting pattern (top photo). Confronting a rival, they darken the white interspaces, turning their body brick red and their head golden brown (middle photo). Photos: (a) Hanauma Bay, O'ahu. 20 ft. (Marjorie L. Awai) (b) Kahe Point, O'ahu. 20 ft. (c) Pūpūkea, O'ahu. 30 ft.

HAWAIIAN ZEBRA BLENNY · **pāoʻo** · *Istiblennius zebra* (Vaillant and Sauvage, 1875) [Jumping Jack, Rockskipper]

Anyone who pokes about the rocky seashore is familiar with these engaging fish. Their bodies vary from smart blue-black to charcoal or brownish gray with indistinct bars (hence the name). They become mottled when feeding in shallow water or when alarmed. Adults have a row of tiny bright blue spots under the eye. A crest and two tentacles (longer in males) adorn the head, but collapse entirely when out of the water. Common in calm pools above the high tide line, these fish swim with lateral undulations like little eels, their pectoral fins folded back along their sides. With the same motion, they may wriggle almost out of the water to bask in the sun. If alarmed (they can spot a potential predator as much as 50 ft. away) they can leap, slither, and skip a surprising distance over the rocks, somehow knowing in advance the location of the next pool. They can even leap while swimming, sometimes 2 ft. above the surface! It is possible that these fish are evolving toward an amphibious existence. They feed almost entirely on organic detritus that accumulates on the rocky sides and bottoms of their pools. To 7 in. Endemic. Photos: Makapuʻu, Oʻahu. Splash pools.

male nuptial colors ▼

Zebra Blenny reproduction

Spawning occurs throughout the year but probably reaches a peak in spring and early summer. Large breeding males develop light yellow-tan cheek patches which brighten when they chase intruders and fade completely when they leave their territories. Smaller males and females are not territorial. Typically, a male prepares a nest in a crevice then performs vertical loops to attract a female. The female cements up to 10,000 eggs to the crevice walls. The male fertilizes them then guards them until hatching (about two weeks). The larvae go to sea for an unknown period of time returning to pools when they are about ½ in. long.

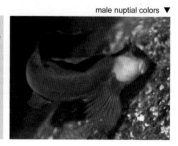

female

MANGROVE BLENNY
Omobranchus obliquus (Garman, 1903) [Roundhead Blenny]

Easily identified by its oblique markings, this blenny is known locally only from O'ahu, where it was likely introduced, perhaps in the 1950s. It occurs only in the most protected locations, such as in Kāne'ohe Bay, where it lives on piers, pilings, buoys, and mangrove roots. Males, slightly larger than females, have a yellow chin and yellow pelvic fins. Several other blennies have been introduced to O'ahu. One, the Tasselled Blenny *Parablennius thysanius,* has occurred in the vicinity of the Kāne'ohe Bay Yacht Club since the 1970s. To almost 2 in. Indo-Pacific. Photo: Coconut Island (Moku o Lo'e), Kāne'ohe Bay, O'ahu, 2 ft.

Erin Baumgartner, who studied Mangrove Blennies at the Hawai'i Institute of Marine Biology, reports that these blennies have a dominance hierarchy with regard to refuge holes. Dominant males oust other males from refuges near theirs, although they tend to ignore smaller fish. (Small fish either hide from or avoid dominant fish by swimming out into the water around them.) Male-to-male aggression usually takes the form of chasing, although occasional fights occur. In a fight, the combatants begin by facing one another and moving back and forth. If one does not give in, they sit flank to flank, usually head to tail, and push against one another. If neither gives way, biting begins. Fish usually bite one another on the back, in front of the dorsal fin. During one fight, Baumgartner observed a large male seize another male by the nape of the neck and give him a body slam.

Ewa Fang Blenny ▼　　　　Gosline's Fang Blenny ▼　　　　(see next page) ▶

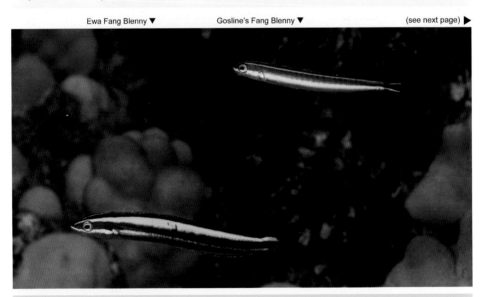

The Ewa Fang Blenny and Gosline's Fang Blenny, both pictured above, make sneak attacks on larger fish to feed on scales, skin, and mucus. They both benefit by their resemblance to harmless juvenile Hawaiian Cleaner Wrasses (p. 339), which approach larger fish to clean them. The Ewa Fang Blenny, however, has an alternate color pattern of orange or reddish brown with narrow blue stripes that does not resemble the cleaner wrasse, and there is evidence that individuals can change from one pattern to the other at will. What advantage might the more conspicuous color pattern confer? Perhaps it serves as warning coloration. If a predator tries to eat a fang blenny, the blenny bites the inside of its captor's mouth with special defensive fangs on the lower jaw (thus the name "fang blenny") and the predator usually spits it out. If the fang blenny is conspicuously colored, the predator is more likely to recognize it the next time and leave it alone.

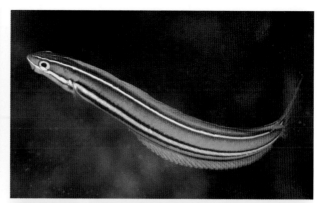

EWA FANG BLENNY
Plagiotremus ewaensis (Brock, 1948)

This colorful fang blenny varies from black to orange to reddish brown, usually with two dark-edged blue horizontal stripes. It feeds on the scales, skin, and mucus of larger fishes. Its mouth, underslung like that of a tiny shark, contains two long fangs used only for defense. Small individuals, often black with a wide upper blue stripe, mimic juvenile Hawaiian Cleaner Wrasses (p. 339) to more easily approach their prey. If you see one of these blue ones, a small Cleaner Wrasse is probably nearby. Many divers have been nipped by these little fish (usually on the leg), but they do no harm. If chased, the blenny usually backs tail first into an abandoned worm snail hole, leaving only its colorful head sticking out. Look closely and you will see it grinning at you. Named for the 'Ewa district of O'ahu. To 4 in. Endemic (with a sister species, *P. rhynorhyncos* elsewhere in the Indo-Pacific). Photos: (top 3) Mākua, O'ahu. 25-30 ft. (bottom) Pu'u 'Olai, Maui. (see also previous page)

GOSLINE'S FANG BLENNY
Plagiotremus goslinei (Strasburg, 1956) [SCALE-EATING BLENNY]

Slightly smaller than the species above, and not as colorful, this fang blenny is greenish yellow on the back and light underneath, often with a bluish midbody stripe. The habits of the two are similar and the resemblance is probably not coincidental. Named for ichthyologist William A. Gosline, Professor of Zoology at the University of Hawai'i from 1954-1971, and co-author of the *Handbook of Hawaiian Fishes* (1960). To 2 ½ in. Endemic (with a sister species, *P. tapeinosoma* elsewhere in the Indo-Pacific). Photo: Pūpūkea, O'ahu. 25 ft. (see also previous page)

Blenny quiz

Plagiotremus goslinei

Exallias brevis

Blenniella gibbifrons

Entomacrodus marmoratus

Did you hear about Blipper?

Istiblennius zebra

24

BOARFISHES
(Pentacerotidae)

Boarfishes, or armorheads, are a small family of unusual fishes with narrow, deep bodies and heads encased in bone. About eleven species are known; two occur in Hawai'i but only one is likely to be seen by divers.

WHISKERED BOARFISH *Evistias acutirostris* (Temminck & Schlegel, 1844)   [WHISKERED ARMORHEAD]
    Rarely seen except off Kaua'i and in the Northwestern Hawaiian Islands, these odd fish are dark brown with five yellowish white vertical bars and a yellow, sail-like dorsal fin which is always extended. The snout projects forward. There are bristles or whiskers under the "chin." The forehead is steep with a lump in front of the eyes. Boarfishes shelter by day, typically in small groups, under overhangs or in caves at depths of 60 feet or more and are exceptionally easy to approach. At night they feed on brittle stars, probably using the "whiskers" to detect their prey. The species name means "sharp snout." These fish prefer cool subtropical waters, occurring in Japan, Hawai'i, Lord Howe Island, and northern New Zealand (where they often occur in large schools). To about 2 ft. Photo: "Fish Bowl," south shore Kaua'i. 60 ft.

BONEFISHES and LADYFISHES
(Albulidae, Megalopidae)

Bonefishes and Ladyfishes (order Elopiformes) are related to eels and considered among the most primitive of the bony fishes. They have slender silvery bodies, a single dorsal fin, and a deeply forked tail. Both inhabit shallow protected areas with sandy or silty bottoms and are well known as hard-fighting game fishes. One ladyfish and two bonefish species occur in Hawaiian waters. None are common in Hawai'i, probably because of habitat degradation and overfishing. Bonefish flesh is full of small bones, hence the common name.

SHORTJAW BONEFISH · 'ō'io · Albula glossodonta (Forsskål, 1775)
    Bonefishes are long, slender, silvery fishes with a forked tail and a single dorsal fin. They have prominent scales and an underslung mouth adapted for feeding on bottom-dwelling organisms. They live over sand, often in shallow lagoons or along protected shores, but will also enter deeper water. This is the commoner of the two Hawaiian species. Good places to see it are Hanauma Bay, O'ahu, and Honolua Bay, Maui. While feeding, bonefish are sometimes followed by jacks, which snatch up tidbits they uncover. (Similarly, bonefish occasionally hang around snorkelers and waders, probably to take advantage of disturbances they might cause.) To about 2 ½ ft. Indo-Pacific. Photo: Hanauma Bay, O'ahu. 3 ft.

Keoki Stender

LONGJAW BONEFISH · 'ō'io · Albula virgata Jordan & Jordan, 1922
    The Longjaw Bonefish is almost identical in appearance to the species above, but has a hard-to-see yellow spot at the base of the pectoral fin. It usually occurs in schools, and has a jaw that is very slightly longer in relation to the head. Once common, these fish are rarely seen today. To about 2 ½ ft. Endemic. Photo: Waimea Bay, O'ahu. 60 ft. (Keoki Stender)

In olden times Hawaiians prized bonefishes for their flavor and gave them different names according to the stage of growth. Finger length fish were pua 'ō'io, those of forearm length were 'amo'omo'o, adults were 'ō'io, a word that also meant the soft flesh of the coconut (which resembled the soft mashed flesh of the bonefish), and a kind of braid or plaiting, such as in hatbands, which resembled the backbone of the fish.

LADYFISH · **awa ʻaua** · *Elops hawaiensis* Regan, 1909 [HAWAIIAN LADYFISH; TENPOUNDER]
Ladyfish are long, lovely inhabitants of sandy lagoons, protected bays, estuaries, and sometimes even the lower reaches of streams. Silvery with a golden tinge, they typically form slow moving or semi-stationary schools by day and, like many carnivores, disperse to feed at night. More slender than mullets, which may occur in the same habitat, they have one dorsal fin (mullets have two), and do not swim at the surface. The mouth is at the tip of the snout, and not underslung as in the bottom-feeding bonefishes (also likely to occur in the same habitat). Ladyfish can easily be seen at Hanauma Bay, Oʻahu, but are absent or have been fished out at most other dive and snorkel spots in the Islands. Though long considered endemic to Hawaiʻi, this species is now known to occur throughout much of the Indo-Pacific. To 2 ft. Photos: Hanauma Bay, Oʻahu. 5-15 ft.

27

BOXFISHES
(Ostraciidae)

Spotted Boxfish male · **moa** · Mākua, Oʻahu. 30 ft. (p. 30)

Boxfishes (or trunkfishes) are completely encased in rigid armor plate; only their fins, eyes, and mouths are movable. Although usually square in cross-section, some are triangular, pentagonal, hexagonal, or even round. Their hard, protective carapace (composed of fused polygonal plates derived from scales) may bear a few thornlike spines on the back, corners, or lower edges. Boxfishes with long forward-pointing spines above the eyes are called cowfishes. Most boxfishes, when stressed, can secrete a toxic slime from the thin layer of skin covering the carapace. The principal poison (ostracitoxin) is not known to affect humans, but a captured boxfish kept in a small container or aquarium can poison itself as well as any other fish kept with it. (Filtering with activated charcoal can remove the toxin.) Some boxfishes have evolved conspicuous patterns of spots which possibly serve to warn predators of their toxicity. Mature males are often more colorful than females. It is not yet known whether the color change results from sex-reversal, as in wrasses and parrotfishes, or whether the change occurs when immature males become adults.

Most boxfishes live in haremic groups with several females inhabiting a single territory defended by a male. Except when courting or spawning, they tend to be solitary, poking about the reef picking at sponges, tunicates, worms, small crustaceans, and algae. Some species squirt water at the sandy bottom to uncover small creatures (see p. 31). While foraging, these awkward-looking fishes propel themselves primarily with their pectoral and anal fins. If alarmed, they fold their pectoral fins back and bring the tail fin into play. The bottom of the rigid carapace acts as a lifting surface during bursts of speed. Surprisingly, boxfishes are good swimmers and can easily outdistance a human.

Boxfishes belong to the order Tetraodontiformes, which includes other odd creatures such as porcupinefishes, triggerfishes, and the bizarre Ocean Sunfish *(Mola mola)*, the largest bony fish in the world. Their family name comes from the Greek *ostrakon* ("shell" or "potsherd"). In old Hawaiʻi they were known generally as **pahu** ("box" or "drum"). Of the five species occurring regularly in Hawaiʻi, only the four described here are likely to be seen by snorkelers or divers.

THORNBACK COWFISH
makukana; pahu
Lactoria fornasini
(Bianconi, 1846)

In addition to its pair of forward-pointing "horns," this species sports a thornlike spike in the center of the back and two backward-pointing spines under the tail fin, one on each side. It is light tan with dusky areas and light blue lines or spots which intensify in males during spawning. The hexagonal or pentagonal plates forming the carapace are particularly evident in this species. It occurs most often over mixed rubble and sand. To about 5 in. Indo-Pacific. Photo: Kawaihoa (Portlock) Point, O'ahu. 30 ft.

SPINY COWFISH · makukana; pahu
Lactoria diaphana
(Bloch & Schneider, 1801)

Uncommon in Hawai'i, this fish resembles the species above but attains twice its size. It lacks blue markings and bears one or more small outward-pointing spines on the ridges of the upper sides, usually on either side of the central thorn. Large specimens have rounded, convex bellies. It is pelagic in Micronesia but lives a settled, bottom-dwelling life in southern Japan and Hawai'i. It is possible that two species are involved. To about 10 in. Indo-Pacific and Eastern Pacific. Photo: Hanauma Bay, O'ahu. 40 ft.

Boxfish love

Ichthyologist Phillip Lobel, working on Johnston Atoll, recorded that Hawaiian Spotted Boxfish (which also occur at Johnston) spawn in the late afternoon or early evening. A male, whose territory usually encompasses those of several females, initiates courtship by circling and nudging one of his females. If she responds, the two swim side by side for a time before rising 6 ft. or more above the bottom, the male leading. Assuming a side-by-side position with tails together and heads facing slightly apart, one or both make a low pitched humming sound lasting about 6 seconds while releasing their gametes. When done they dash back to the bottom where the male begins courting another female. At such times other males may attempt to "sneak" a spawn or disrupt the proceedings; fights are common, the rivals ramming each other with their armored bodies creating audible bumps and sometimes producing a short buzzing sound. Whitley's Boxfish and Thornback Cowfish spawning behavior is similar. The spawning sound of the latter is a high-pitched hum, probably produced by the male. Photo: Hālona Blowhole, O'ahu. 30 ft.

29

a) male ▲

b) male color variant ▼

c) female ▼

SPOTTED BOXFISH · **moa; pahu**
Ostracion meleagris
Shaw & Nodder, 1796

This is Hawai'i's most common boxfish. Females, and perhaps juvenile males, are blackish brown covered on all sides with small white spots. Mature males have dark blue sides with black spots which sometimes have a few gold centers. Their heads and tails are adorned with gold trim, and there is a diffuse light patch under the eye. Spotted Boxfish live in small haremic groups, typically one male and several females, and forage alone within their home ranges for sponges, worms, tunicates, and other small bottom-dwelling invertebrates. Males defend territories against other males. The species name means "guineafowl" (a bird native to Africa covered with light spots). To about 6 in. Indo-Pacific and Eastern Pacific. Photos: (a) Pūpūkea, O'ahu. 25 ft. (b) Makapu'u, O'ahu. 25 ft. (c) Hanauma Bay, O'ahu. 15 ft.

Spotted Boxfish males in the Indo-Pacific outside Hawai'i have many gold spots on their sides, but Hawaiian males typically lack these. Because of this, the local population has been given the subspecies name Ostracion meleagris camurum. But males with scattered gold spots do occur here, and the "Hawaiian" color form also occurs in the Eastern Pacific. For these reasons, and because the subspecies concept is currently out of fashion, the name camurum is rarely used.

Boxfishes as submarines

Despite their ungainly appearance, boxfishes are fast swimmers with good endurance—as anyone who has chased one can testify. The Hawaiian Spotted Boxfish has a sophisticated body shape that is unusually stable and well-controlled when moving through the water. Researchers have found that the boxfish's complex fin movements are just as energy-efficient as those of a flexible, seemingly better-streamlined fish swimming at a comparable speed. Amazingly, the "awkward" boxfish is now serving as a model for advanced submarine design! Engineers especially admire its ability to "turn on a dime" because current mini-subs require the space of several hull lengths to complete their 180-degree turns. The boxfish has also inspired an experimental Mercedes-Benz car with extremely low wind resistance which gets 70 mpg .

a) male ▲   b) female ▼   Jerry Kane

WHITLEY'S BOXFISH · pahu
Ostracion whitleyi Fowler, 1931

Females (and perhaps immature males) of this uncommon boxfish are golden brown with cream spots and a wide cream band along the side which may contain brown spots or markings. Mature males, quite rare in Hawai'i, especially above about 100 ft., are blue with white spots on top and black-edged white lines framing the sides. The underside is marked with an unusual pair of large dark round spots. How these fish reproduce in Hawai'i with so few males is a mystery. The species is restricted to the Central Pacific and most abundant in the Marquesas Islands, where the large blue males are common. Females from the Marquesas and Society Islands bear numerous small brown spots on the underside and also in the lateral white band. Named for Australian ichthyologist G.P. Whitley (1903-1975). To about 5 in. Photos: (a) YO-257 wreck, off Waikīkī, O'ahu. 110 ft. (Jerry Kane) (b) Kawaihoa (Portlock) Point, O'ahu. 30 ft. (blowing sand to uncover prey)

Experiments with boxfish toxin

Experiments with ostracitoxin show that its action is similar to toxins produced by "red tides" and certain echinoderms. Fishes placed in seawater containing ostracitoxin from Hawaiian Spotted Boxfish generally died in 15-60 minutes, whereas most invertebrates were unaffected or slightly affected. Out of the 18 fish species tested, only the Spotted Boxfish itself and a pearlfish (which lives within sea stars and sea cucumbers, see p. 64) showed significant resistance, but even they eventually perished. Active ostracitoxin cannot be extracted from the tissues of dead boxfishes, thus it appears that the toxin is created or activated during secretion. Perhaps this protects the boxfish from its own toxin. Even so, frozen dead boxfish and cowfish fed to captive sharks (genus Carcharinus) were rejected after the sharks took them in their jaws. However, a captive Tiger Shark (p. 266) ate the dead boxfishes without hesitation. Secretions from two additional Hawaiian species, the Thornback Cowfish and the Spiny Cowfish, were found to be similar but less toxic than Spotted Boxfish secretions, but in separate experiments Whitley's Boxfish produced more potent toxin than the Spotted Boxfish.

BUTTERFLYFISHES
(Chaetodontidae)

Ornate Butterflyfish · **kīkākapu** · almost always in pairs · Mākaha, Oʻahu. 30 ft. (p. 44)

If there were a typical coral reef fish, it would probably be a butterflyfish. Brightly colored (often in yellow) pairs of these delicate creatures are a common sight as they flit among the undersea gardens. Their disklike bodies, like artists' palettes, display hues and patterns that are obviously meant to be noticed.

While most other fishes have evolved to blend with their environment, the butterflyfishes have done the opposite. What advantage do they gain? They are spiny and make a prickly mouthful—is their appearance a warning? They travel in pairs and may mate for life—is it for recognition? Whatever the reason—if there is a reason—these fishes delight and inspire all visitors to their undersea realm.

With their disk-shaped bodies, butterflyfishes are well suited for maneuvering through narrow spaces; though they might seem easy targets for predators, they can quickly move out of reach. To further confuse their foes, most species have a dark bar through the eye, effectively disguising it. Some go one step further, displaying a false eyespot near the tail. Depending on the species, butterflyfishes feed on small invertebrates, plankton, coral polyps, and occasionally algae, often using their snouts to probe into crevices. Although they have long-term, possibly permanent mates, butterflyfishes offer no parental care to their young. As with most fishes, eggs are released into the water; after hatching, the larvae drift with the plankton for weeks or months.

Butterflyfishes display a variety of social arrangements. Many, especially coral-eating species, form long-lasting pairs that defend feeding territories. Some species form harems or schools; a few are solitary. Many butterflyfishes, especially coral-eating species, follow set, predictable paths within their territories or home ranges, feeding briefly on certain coral heads then moving on. They repeat the pattern throughout the day. Occasionally they visit distant parts of the reef, perhaps to spawn or avoid predators, but always return home to resume their rounds.

Butterflyfish spawning is seldom witnessed by divers. Elaborate or long-lasting courtship displays are not needed because mates generally stay together. Those species that have been studied tend to spawn at dusk during the week preceding a new or full moon. Typically, 30-45 minutes before sunset the male starts to follow the female closely, stimulating her vent area with his snout until she is ready to release eggs. Both then make a short upward rush, broadcasting their gametes simultaneously. Other males may attempt to join in at the last moment.

Some scientists use coral-eating butterflyfishes as "indicator species" for assessing the long-term health of coral reefs. Because they are conspicuous and normally remain in their territories for years (8-10 years is typical), declining numbers, migration, or behavioral changes are easy to spot and could serve as early warnings of environmental degradation.

In old Hawai'i, butterflyfishes had several general names. Those called **kīkākapu** ("strongly prohibited") are described in several chants as sacred. Others were **lauhau** ("leaf of the **hau** tree") or **lauwiliwili** ("leaf of the **wiliwili** tree"). There were specific names as well, but it is no longer clear to which species they referred.

Anatomically, butterflyfishes are characterized by small, brushlike teeth. The family name, Chaetodontidae, is a combination of *chaeto* ("hair") and *dentis* ("tooth"), the first syllable often pronounced to rhyme with "key." Of the approximately 130 butterflyfish species, 23 occur regularly in the Hawaiian Islands. Five of these are endemic, but two (the Hawaiian Brownbanded Butterflyfish, *Roa excelsa,* and the Orangemargin Butterflyfish, *Prognathodes basebei*) live at depths greater than 300 ft. and are omitted here. The Double-Saddle Butterflyfish *(Chaetodon ulietensis)*, a common reef fish elsewhere in the Pacific, is known in the Islands from only two specimens, evidently strays.

Milletseed Butterflyfish · **lauwiliwili** · feeding on damselfish eggs · Hanauma Bay, O'ahu. 40 ft. (see p. 41)

a) adults ▲   b) juvenile ▼

THREADFIN BUTTERFLYFISH · **kīkākapu** · *Chaetodon auriga* Forsskål, 1775
    These handsome fish have a whitish body that darkens to gold in back and is marked with sets of fine right-angled diagonal lines. One of the soft dorsal spines is elongated into a threadlike filament; below it is a black spot. Juveniles lack the filament and have a larger black spot. These large omnivores are strongly paired. Common but not abundant, they occur on all parts of the reef and are one of the few butterflyfishes that forage over sand. They feed primarily on sessile (attached) and sand-dwelling invertebrates and defend a large feeding territory against members of their own species. The species name means "charioteer," probably because of the whiplike dorsal filament. To about 8 in., reportedly reaching its greatest size in Hawai'i. Indo-Pacific. Photos: (a) Molokini Islet, Maui. 15 ft. (b) Hale'iwa, O'ahu. 2 ft.

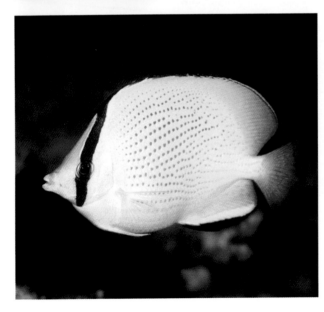

SPECKLED BUTTERFLYFISH
Chaetodon citrinellus Cuvier, 1831
    Uncommon in the main Hawaiian Islands, this butterflyfish is pale yellow speckled with darker spots. It has a black margin on the anal fin and a dark bar through the eye. (The similar and more common Milletseed Butterflyfish, p. 41, lacks black on the anal fin and has a black spot at the base of the tail.) Speckled Butterflyfish swim in pairs and usually occur in 20 ft. or less. On O'ahu look for them off Waikīkī and in the artificial lagoons at the Ko'olina Resort. On Maui they are sometimes seen at Olowalu. The species is reported to be common at French Frigate Shoals, in the Northwest Hawaiian Islands. Outside Hawai'i, it is one of the most common Indo-Pacific butterflyfishes, especially on reef flats. The species name means "citrus." To about 5 in. Indo-Pacific. Photo: Magic Island, O'ahu. 15 ft.

SADDLEBACK BUTTERFLYFISH
kīkākapu

Chaetodon ephippium Cuvier, 1831

These striking butterflyfish are bluish gray with a bold black saddle rimmed in white. The snout and throat are saffron, balanced by a bright orange bar at the rear of the soft dorsal fin. A pugnacious-looking lower jaw juts forward and a long dorsal filament trails behind. Strongly paired, they occur both in shallow inshore waters and on clear outer reefs. Because their home range is large they are sparsely distributed; seeing a pair is always a treat. Saddlebacks subsist largely on coral polyps and often fail to eat in captivity. The species name means "saddled." To 8 in. Western and Central Pacific. Photos: (above) Hanauma Bay, O'ahu. 30 ft. (opposite) Barge Harbor, Lānai. 50 ft. (below) Faga'alu, Samoa, 5 ft.

juvenile   Keoki Stender

a) adult ▲

BLUESTRIPE BUTTERFLYFISH · **kīkākapu** · *Chaetodon fremblii* Bennett, 1829

Uniquely patterned, this butterflyfish has narrow blue stripes running diagonally along a yellow body. It is one of only two butterflyfishes with no eye camouflage at all. Individuals can be common in shallow water, especially around patches of sand or smooth bottom between boulders and coral. Its social arrangement is haremic, unusual among butterflyfishes: males defend a territory containing one to four females. Females within the male's territory defend smaller territories against other females. Pairs have been observed spawning around dusk during the week preceding a full moon in February and March. Unless courting or spawning, however, males and females rarely swim together or pay much attention to each other. They eat mostly algae and sand-dwelling polychaete worms. Hawaiian endemics usually have a sister species elsewhere in the Pacific, but in the case of the Bluestripe Butterflyfish, you have to go all the way to Africa's east coast to find its only probable relative, Blackburn's Butterflyfish *(C. blackburni)*. To 6 in. Endemic. Photos: (a) Mōkapu Rock, Moloka'i. 30 ft. (b) Kahe Point, O'ahu. 25 ft. (c) Hanauma Bay, O'ahu. 40 ft.

b) juvenile ▼

c) displaying to eel (see also p. 114) ▼

Instead of fleeing from a potential predator, a butterflyfish often turns broadside to it, or even beats its tail in its enemy's face. Sometimes it lowers its head, erects its dorsal spines, and faces the predator. During these actions it may change color. ▶

BLACKLIP BUTTERFLYFISH
Chaetodon kleinii Bloch, 1790
[BLUEHEAD BUTTERFLYFISH]

This small species is mostly dull yellow-brown with a pale head and a dark bar through the eye. The dark bar becomes bluish on the forehead in strong light. Faint spots, one on each scale, give a softly speckled appearance. In Hawai'i these fish feed primarily on plankton off the face of the reef in clear water, usually in pairs, occasionally in small groups. They rarely school, appear sometimes to defend a territory, and occasionally clean Manta Rays (see p. 237). In other parts of the Indo-Pacific these fish have a diffuse pale bar down the center of the body and are reported to subsist largely on soft corals (which are almost absent in Hawai'i). To 5 in. Indo-Pacific. Photo: *Mahi* wreck, O'ahu. 60 ft.

LINED BUTTERFLYFISH · kīkākapu
Chaetodon lineolatus Cuvier, 1831

As large as dinner plates, these handsome fish are marked with distinct dark vertical lines on an almost white body. The dorsal, anal, and tail fins are bright yellow. Uncommon and difficult to approach, they typically occur in areas of rich coral growth, almost always in pairs, and can be found both in shallow snorkeling spots and along outer reefs. Occasionally they gather in schools, perhaps to spawn. Like another large butterflyfish, the Threadfin, they probably defend a large territory against others of their species. The species name means "lined." Attaining a length of 12 in., these are the largest of their family and may reach their greatest size in Hawai'i. Indo-Pacific. Photo: Hanauma Bay, O'ahu. 20 ft.

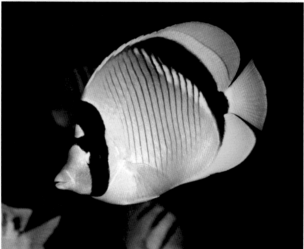

An unusual school of Lined Butterflyfish, perhaps preparing to spawn. Kahalu'u Beach Park, Hawai'i. 8 ft.

37

RACCOON BUTTERFLYFISH · **kīkākapu** · *Chaetodon lunula* (Lacepède, 1803)

The face of this fish, with its masked eyes and white curved bar, resembles that of its namesake, the American mammal. The body, orange-yellow with diagonal brown stripes, darkens to brownish on the upper sides. A broad dark bar bordered in yellow runs diagonally back behind the white curved bar, and there is a dark spot at the base of the tail. Juveniles, which live in tide pools, are brighter yellow with a large false eyespot above the base of the tail. By day these fish often rest in large semi-stationary aggregations that frequent the same locations year after year. Sometimes they patrol the reef in schools, but it is not uncommon to find them in pairs or as single individuals. They do not appear to be nocturnal, as some authors suggest. The species name means "crescent." To 8 in. Indo-Pacific. Photos: (top & below right) Hanauma Bay, Oʻahu. 15 ft. (below left) Makapuʻu, Oʻahu. Tide pool.

juvenile ▼

Most butterflyfishes conceal their eyes. Dark bars or masks are typical, but sometimes a dark head or body does the trick. In addition, about half of all butterflyfish species display a conspicuous false eye spot somewhere near the tail, a pattern especially common in juveniles. Evidently, concealed eyes and false eyespots are highly confusing to predators, for butterflyfishes are rarely found in their stomachs. Furthermore, the bright, contrasting color patterns of butterflyfishes might serve as warning coloration. A predator that failed a few times to catch a butterflyfish, might recognize the conspicuous colors and not bother next time. This would explain why butterflyfishes, instead of fleeing when encountering a potential predator, often pause and turn sideways (see pp. 36, 114). If this is true, the name "butterflyfish" is particularly apt. Terrestrial butterflies, such as the brightly colored Monarch, often make undesirable prey—they taste bad or are poisonous. Conspicuous colors make them easy to recognize and avoid, and everybody wins.

Victoria Martocci

I've been watching the behavior of a school of Raccoon Butterflyfishes off Lāna'i for years. When I lead a group of divers through a certain lava tube, we exit approximately 60 ft. away from a big Hawaiian Sergeant nesting area where the Raccoons are usually hovering in a loose school. Upon seeing divers, the Raccoons rush (I mean swim FAST) away from the Sergeant nests toward us. They swim within inches of my mask, then begin to swim away from me, toward the nests. If I do not follow immediately (which I don't always, in an attempt to keep the Raccoons on their toes), they will circle back toward my face and repeat, attempting to lure us toward the nesting damsels. (It distinctly reminds me of a matador's cap and the bull he is trying to entice.) When we swim over the nests, the damsels will often abandon their eggs, giving the Raccoons a 'free meal.' The Raccoons will also attempt this luring technique with the large Bluefin Trevally when they are nearby. When the damsels aren't nesting, the Raccoons do not school together. – Victoria Martocci

OVAL BUTTERFLYFISH · **kapuhili** · *Chaetodon lunulatus* Quoy & Gaimard, 1825

These exquisite, richly colored fish are apricot gold set off with purple-gray lines and tinges of burnt orange on the anal fin. They prefer areas of lush coral growth along protected shores and almost never inhabit exposed reefs. Pairs spend about 90 percent of their time together, feed almost exclusively on polyps of living coral (they eat most species), and defend a permanent feeding territory against other Oval Butterflyfish. Because of diet, they cannot be maintained in home aquariums. The species name (confusingly similar to that of the Raccoon Butterflyfish, p. 38) derives from the Latin *lunulus*, meaning "crescent." The Hawaiian name means "person with many taboos." This is one of the few butterflyfishes to have a specific Hawaiian name. Perhaps it was considered especially sacred. To 5 ½ in. Central and Western Pacific (with a similar species, *C. trifasciatus*, in the Indian Ocean). Photo: Hanauma Bay, O'ahu. 30 ft.

Tails up!

Observing Oval Butterflyfish in Okinawa, Shinji Yabuta found that they perform a "tail-up" display both to their own permanent mates and toward rivals in territorial disputes. In this display, a fish lowers its head, raises its tail, and shows its side to the other fish. In doing so, it spreads its anal and soft dorsal fins, revealing the conspicuous white band on the latter. Yabuta deduced some simple behavior rules that explain this seemingly contradictory behavior. Rule 1: perform tail-up when approached by another individual. Rule 2: perform tail-up when another individual performs tail-up. Rule 3: If another individual neither approaches nor performs tail-up, then attack. To explain: When one member of a pair loses visual track of its partner for a time, the next individual it encounters might or might not be the partner. If it's not the partner, then it's an enemy and should be attacked. But what if the first fish is unsure? In that case, it performs "tail-up." If the other fish performs tail-up, both have a bit of extra time to recognize each other, or not. Usually they do. If they don't, one flees or they fight. Yabuta found that 70 percent of potentially dangerous attacks were averted by a simple tail-up display.

Romantic getaway

For most butterfyfishes, the best place for spawning is a place where strong currents can quickly carry the fertilized eggs out to sea and away from egg-eating reef fishes. However, Oval Butterflyfish often live in protected bays away from currents. What to do? In Okinawa, Shinji Yabuta discovered that at dusk around the full or new moon pairs of Oval Butterflyfish migrate some distance to an area of reef swept by offshore tidal currents. Here they establish a small temporary territory, spawn, and "camp out" overnight, returning to their feeding territory in the morning.

MILLETSEED BUTTERFLYFISH · **lauwiliwili** · *Chaetodon miliaris* Quoy & Gaimard, 1824 [LEMON BUTTERFLYFISH]

Hawaiʻi's most abundant butterflyfish, these are lemon yellow with vertical lines of dark spots. Although single individuals are sometimes encountered, these fish typically school and are often seen high in the water feeding on plankton. Opportunistic, they can also feed directly off hard substrate, taking fish eggs, algae, and small bottom-dwelling organisms. Individuals will even pick parasites from other fish. Milletseeds readily swarm around divers and snorkelers, especially at sites where they have been hand fed (but see next page). The Frenchmen who named them thought their vertical lines of dark spots resembled seeds of millet. To 6 ½ in. Endemic (with a sister species, *C. guntheri,* in the Western Pacific). Photos: (above) Mākua, Oʻahu. 50 ft. (below, feeding on Hawaiian Sergeant eggs) Hanauma Bay, Oʻahu. 40 ft. (opposite) Mākua, Oʻahu. 25 ft.

juvenile ▲

Why follow divers?

Schools of Milletseed Butterflyfish are often attracted to divers and may follow them for long distances. (In the photo above they were following the photographer.) This can happen even in remote areas where they have never seen humans. Perhaps the behavior evolved because of another large, dark, swimming mammal, the Hawaiian Monk Seal. Although seals are no longer common around the main Hawaiian islands, the fish and the mammal certainly coexisted here for millions of years and still do in the Northwestern Hawaiian Islands. Why would the fish be attracted to seals? Milletseed Butterflyfish love feasting on the eggs of Hawaiian Sergeants (p. 67), which are laid on bare rock in conspicuous purplish red patches and fiercely guarded by the male. Although male Sergeants will attack and drive away egg-raiding fish, they seem to be thrown off balance by the approach of something big, like a foraging monk seal (or a diver). This momentary "blink" creates an opportunity for the waiting Milletseeds, which immediately dive in to enjoy a high-fat, high-protein feast. Humans have now replaced monk seals as the most common mammals on reefs, and, if this theory is correct, the Milletseeds haven't missed a beat—they just follow the humans. Raccoon Butterflyfish engage in similar behavior (see p. 39).

Individual Milletseeds occasionally establish cleaning stations much like Hawaiian Cleaner Wrasses (p. 339), where they apparently remove parasites and/or dead tissue from other fishes that seek their services.

Cleaning Sharpnose Mullets at Hanauma Bay. 5 ft.

Cleaning Hawaiian Bigeyes at Portlock Point. 30 ft.

MULTIBAND BUTTERFLYFISH
kīkākapu
Chaetodon multicinctus Garrett, 1863

These small butterflies are light tan covered with brown dots that coalesce to form four or five vertical bars. Almost always tightly paired, they are a common sight throughout the Islands, probing and picking at the corals upon which they feed. Like other coral-eating butterflyfishes, they take only a few nibbles from a colony and then move on, minimizing damage to their food source. Cauliflower Coral *(Pocillopora meandrina)* and Lobe Coral *(Porites lobata)* are their favorites. They will also feed on other corals and defend their feeding territory from other coral-eating butterflyfishes. Pairs have been observed spawning around dusk during the week preceding a full moon in February and March. Zoologists have probably written more papers on the Multiband than on any other butterflyfish because it is convenient to study. The name means "many bands." To 4 in. Endemic (with a sister species, *C. punctatofasciatus,* in the Western and Central Pacific). Photos: Hanauma Bay, O'ahu. 20-40 ft.

Researchers Janis and John Driscoll observed Multiband, Fourspot, and Ornate butterflyfishes for a period of seven months off Kona, Hawai'i. They found that all three species formed monogamous pairs, and that of the three, Multiband Butterflies spent the most time together. Fourspot and Ornate pairs had longer separations and fewer meetings. All three occupied territories that they defended from others of their own species, but actual fights were uncommon as pairs knew where the boundaries were and generally avoided each others' territories. A full year after completion of the study, the Driscolls revisited all their sites and found the territories and their owner pairs essentially unchanged.

juvenile ▼

ORNATE BUTTERFLYFISH
kīkākapu
Chaetodon ornatissimus Cuvier, 1831

Among the most beautiful of reef fish, these butterflies are cream with black bars on the face and graceful orange lines running diagonally along the body, which is mostly rimmed in black. Strongly paired, they subsist exclusively on live coral and maintain home territories within which they roam freely. Other butterflyfish species are tolerated, but those of the same species are driven away. They will prey on most coral species and are probably the least specialized of Hawai'i's coral-eating butterflyfishes. Instead of picking individual polyps, like the Multiband Butterflyfish, they scrape the coral, removing many polyps in each pass. They also consume considerable quantities of coral mucus. Even so, they do not seem to harm the reef. Because of diet, these gorgeous fish are unsuitable for aquariums. To 8 in. Central and Western Pacific, with scattered records from the Indian Ocean. Photos: Mākaha, O'ahu. 25 ft. Mākua, O'ahu. 30 ft.

Evelyn F. Cox studied five species of coral-eating butterflyfishes at six different locations in Hawai'i, recording their foraging ranges and even counting feeding bites. Ornate Butterflyfish fed on the broadest range of corals (10 species) and showed little preference between them. Multiband Butterflyfish strongly preferred Cauliflower Coral (Pocillopora meandrina), as did Fourspot Butterflyfish. Teardrop Butterflyfish strongly preferred Rice Coral (Montipora capitata) and other members of the genus Montipora, while Oval Butterflyfish ate mostly corals of the genus Porites (Lobe Coral and Finger Coral). Curiously, in laboratory aquariums Oval Butterflies preferred Cauliflower Coral. Perhaps their feeding behavior on the reef is influenced by competition from other coral-eating butterflyfishes.

FOURSPOT BUTTERFLYFISH

lauhau · *Chaetodon quadrimaculatus*
Gray, 1833

Despite both the common and scientific names, only two white spots are visible on these fish. (To make four, the spots on both sides must be counted.) Their bodies are dark brownish black above, becoming orange-yellow below, with a yellow tail and a yellow head and the usual dark stripe through the eye. They subsist largely on polyps of Cauliflower Coral *(Pocillopora meandrina)*, but also eat other invertebrates and algae. At some sites their diet consists mostly of algae. Common on reefs where their preferred coral grows, they form long-lasting monogamous pairs and defend a feeding territory against others of their species. Because of their coral diet they do poorly in aquariums. To 6 in. Known only from the islands of the Pacific. Photos: Hanauma Bay, O'ahu. 15-30 ft.

Tom Hourigan's studies of Fourspot and Multiband Butterflyfish at Puakō, Hawai'i revealed a division of labor between the sexes. In both species, males assumed most of the territorial defense, allowing females to feed more. Females, he speculates, need the extra nutrition in order to produce plenty of eggs.

Moon children?

Studying Fourspot Butterflyfish at Puakō, Hawai'i, Thomas J. Hourigan found that these fish tend to follow a 24-hour lunar cycle, feeding most actively when the moon is above the horizon, day or night, and resting at other times, often under ledges. During the full moon, for example, he found them to rest all day and feed all night, while at the new moon the opposite was true. However, where the pugnacious Hawaiian Gregory restricted their daytime feeding, they sometimes moved permanently to the night shift. This lunar foraging behavior does not seem to occur everywhere.

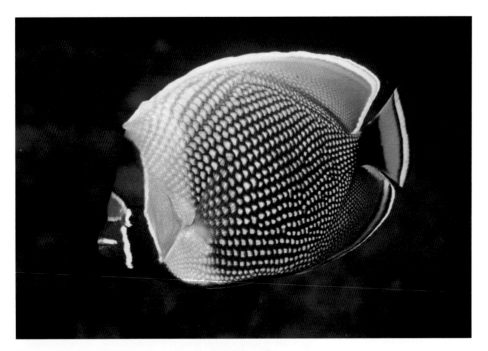

RETICULATED BUTTERFLYFISH *Chaetodon reticulatus* Cuvier, 1831

Combinations of white, cream, and gray with black markings give these elegant fish a quiet beauty all their own. They travel in pairs and are usually fairly approachable. In Hawai'i they are seen most often along the Kona coast of the Big Island in relatively shallow clear water; elsewhere they are unusual. On O'ahu a pair or two are sometimes encountered at Pai'olu'olu Point near the outer entrance to Hanauma Bay. Although uncommon in Hawai'i, they are among the most abundant butterflyfishes in other Central Pacific locations, such as the Marshall Islands and parts of French Polynesia. Feeding primarily on a variety of living corals, they are difficult to maintain in captivity. Both the common and scientific names mean "netlike" or "meshlike," referring to the pattern on the sides. To 7 in. Central and Western Pacific. Photos: (above) Hanauma Bay, O'ahu. 15 ft. (below) "Pinetrees," Kona, Hawai'i. 20 ft.

TINKER'S BUTTERFLYFISH
Chaetodon tinkeri Schultz, 1951

Beautiful and rarely seen, Tinker's Butterflies are a treasured find in Hawai'i. Divided on the diagonal into white and black, they sport gold on the dorsal and anal fins and a gold bar through the eyes. These fish prefer depths of 150 ft. or more, and often occur where black corals grow. Subadults are occasionally found at about 100 ft. Tinker's Butterflies are unafraid of divers. Valuable as an aquarium export and easy to catch, they are now rare at sport-diving depths. (Enlarging our system of marine parks might ensure that more divers could enjoy seeing these fish.) Tinker's Butterflyfish was once considered endemic to Hawai'i, but similar fishes occur in the Marshall and Cook Islands, and probably elsewhere, and it's not clear where the species lines should be drawn. Other closely-related deep-dwelling species occur in Guam, the Marquesas, Palau, Kiribati, and the Philippines. The name honors Spencer W. Tinker (1909-1999) who first discovered these fish in 1949 from fish traps set at 90 ft. off Nānākuli, O'ahu. Tinker headed the Waikīkī Aquarium from 1940-1973 and wrote several books on marine life, including the classic *Fishes of Hawai'i*. To 5 ½ in. Central and Western Pacific. Photos: Hawai'i. 140 ft., 70 ft.

Keoki Stender

CHEVRON BUTTERFLYFISH
Chaetodon trifascialis
Quoy & Gaimard, 1825

Although common throughout most of the Indo-Pacific, this species lives and breeds in Hawai'i solely in the vicinity of French Frigate Shoals in the northwestern chain, the only area within the Hawaiian archipelago where table corals of the genus *Acropora* grow abundantly. Chevron Butterflyfish feed mainly on these corals and cannot survive long without them. Rarely, juveniles settle out around the main islands, and may grow to a length of several inches or more before perishing for lack of adult food. Adults are territorial and pugnacious, usually defending one or two large heads of table coral against all competitors. To about 7 in. Indo-Pacific. Photo: French Frigate Shoals. 50 ft. (Keoki Stender)

TEARDROP BUTTERFLYFISH
lauhau · *Chaetodon unimaculatus*
Bloch, 1787

These yellow and white beauties are immediately recognizable by the dark upside-down "teardrop" on the side. In larger specimens the downward-pointing line fades, leaving a round black spot. They occur individually, in pairs, or in small groups and feed mostly on encrusting rice corals of the genus *Montipora*. Blunt snouts and strong jaws enable them to nip off bits of the stony skeleton to get at the tissue inside. They also eat algae and small invertebrate animals. Individuals occupy large, overlapping home ranges. They do not defend territories or have permanent partners. The species name means "one spot." To about 8 in. but usually smaller. Indonesia to Hawai'i. (The similar *C. interruptus* occurs in the Western Indian Ocean.) Photos: (top & below) Palea Pt., O'ahu. 15-30 ft.

Feeding on Blue Rice Coral *(Montipora flabellata)* at Hanauma Bay, O'ahu.

48

COMMON LONGNOSE
BUTTERFLYFISH [FORCEPSFISH]
lauwiliwili nukunuku ʻoiʻoi
Forcipiger flavissimus
Jordan & McGregor, 1898

This fish and its look-alike on the next page have come to symbolize the exotic beauty of the coral reef. Their long probing snouts, bristling dorsal spines, and intense yellow color are almost unmistakable. The more abundant of the two, this species has a slightly shorter snout. It frequents walls, ledges, and overhangs, often swimming upside down on the ceiling, and feeds on a variety of invertebrates using its long jaws to grasp and tear off pieces. The tube feet of echinoderms and the "fans" of tube-dwelling polychaete worms are typical fare. By comparison, its cousin on the next page has tiny jaws and preys mostly on small shrimps, which it swallows whole. In the Hawaiian language **lauwiliwili** ("leaf of the wiliwili tree"), **nukunuku** ("beak"), and **ʻoiʻoi** ("best," or "sharp") combine to make the longest of all Hawaiian fish names. The scientific name might be translated as "extreme yellow." To 7 in. Indo-Pacific and Eastern Pacific. Photos: Lānaʻi Lookout, Oʻahu. 25 ft.

Subsisting on different organisms, the Common Longnose and the very similar Big Longnose (following pages) are able to share habitat without competing. The Common Longnose, however, feeds on a wider variety of prey and can apparently tolerate more surge and water movement. For these reasons it occurs in a wider range of habitats. It is, in fact, the most geographically widespread of all butterflyfishes, ranging from East Africa and the Red Sea to Mexico's Pacific coast.

49

Jay Schwartz

Longnose cleaning station

On rare occasions, Common Longnose Butterflyfish (previous page) will act as cleaners. The fish above and its mate (not visible) have learned that trumpetfish often carry hordes of small crustacean parasites, probably caligoid copepods, which are apparently too big for Hawaiian Cleaner Wrasses to eat. Setting themselves up in business, these fish have attracted almost more customers than they can handle. This unusual photo was taken by Jay Schwartz off Kona, Hawai'i. A Common Longnose Butterflyfish cleaning a Sleek Unicornfish has also been photographed off Kona.

A mixed pair of Big Longnose Butterflyfish (next page). Hōnaunau, Hawai'i. 40 ft.

BIG LONGNOSE BUTTERFLYFISH
lauwiliwili nukunuku ʻoiʻoi
Forcipiger longirostris
(Broussonet, 1782)
[RARE LONGNOSE BUTTERFLYFISH]

This fish is slightly larger than its near twin on the previous pages, and has a longer snout. It is most easily identified by the lines of fine dots on its chest and behind its pectoral fins. Its long snout terminates in a tiny round mouth with almost no "notch" at the tip, whereas the tip of its look-alike's nose has a noticeable cleft between the jaws. Another difference is the shape of the gill cover, which is slightly more angular in the Big Longnose. Occasional individuals of this species turn completely blackish brown except for a yellow spot at the base of the pectoral fin. This color variation is apparently unrelated to sex or reproduction. Seeing these black phantoms on the reef for the first time is always a bit of a shock. The Big Longnose Butterflyfish specializes in plucking small crustaceans, mostly shrimps, from between branches of coral or from narrow spaces in the reef. Inserting its already long snout into a crevice, it shoots it out an additional half inch to engulf its prey! Prey is swallowed whole, never bitten or torn. In the Hawaiian Islands, the Big Longnose prefers sheltered leeward coastlines or deeper areas where Finger Coral *(Porites compressa)* predominates. But wherever it occurs, the Common Longnose occurs also; a sharp eye is needed to differentiate the two. The best place to see the Big Longnose, especially in its interesting dark form, is along the Kona Coast of the Big Island. Here it often pairs with a mate of the same color, although black and yellow individuals also occur together. The dark color variant is unusual both in other parts of Hawaiʻi and in the Indo-Pacific as a whole. The Hawaiian and scientific names mean "long-beaked." Originally collected during Cook's third voyage to the Pacific, this was the first of many new fish species to be described from Hawaiʻi. **Lauwiliwili** ("leaf of the **wiliwili** tree,") **nukunuku** ("beak") and **ʻoiʻoi** ("best," or "sharp") combine to make the longest of all Hawaiian fish names. To 8 in. Indo-Pacific. Photos: (top) Hanauma Bay, Oʻahu. 30 ft. (dark form) Kealakekua Bay, Hawaiʻi. 20 ft.

PYRAMID BUTTERFLYFISH
Hemitaurichthys polylepis
(Bleeker, 1857)

These handsome schooling butterflyfish are usually found near steep dropoffs, sometimes in large numbers, preferring headlands and points exposed to plankton-bearing currents. The head, dorsal, and anal fins are golden yellow (the upper head washed with brown) and the side is marked with a truncated pyramid of solid white. These beautiful fish sometimes rise almost to the surface to feed; if alarmed they dive as one toward the bottom. In most areas they are absent, but where they occur they are usually abundant and remain year after year. Big Island snorkelers can usually find them in shallow water at Hōnaunau, on the Kona Coast of the Big Island. Often the school contains a few Thompson's Butterflyfish too (next page). The species name means "many scales." To 6 in. Western and Central Pacific. The brown heads of Hawaiian specimens are noticeably lighter than those from elsewhere in the Pacific. Photos: Hanauma Bay, O'ahu. 60 ft.

THOMPSON'S BUTTERFLYFISH
Hemitaurichthys thompsoni
Fowler, 1923

Neatly clad in conservative gray, these unusual schooling butterflyfish with pointy snouts aggregate in mid-water near dropoffs where they feed on plankton, sometimes forming mixed schools with the Pyramid Butterflyfish. They also aggregate with similarly-colored planktivores, such as Thompson's Surgeonfish and Threespot Chromis, blending in so well as to be completely overlooked. Often, they can be closely approached. Hawai'i is one of the few places where this somewhat rare species can be seen regularly. The scientific name honors John W. Thompson, technician and artist at the Bishop Museum from 1901 to 1928, who prepared beautifully colored casts of many Hawaiian fishes. To 6 in. Hawai'i, Samoa, the Marianas, French Polynesia, and the Line Islands. Photo: Hōnaunau, Hawai'i. 20 ft.

Thompson's Butterflyfish with Pyramid Butterflyfish. Pai'olu'olu Point, O'ahu. 15 ft.   Keoki Stender

53

PENNANT BUTTERFLYFISH *Heniochus diphreutes* Jordan, 1903 [Longfin Bannerfish; Pennantfish]

These boldly patterned butterflyfish are white with two black bars; their soft dorsal and tail fins are yellow, and they sport a long white dorsal pennant. (Rare specimens have a double pennant.) They school along current-swept dropoffs, usually at depths of 40 ft. or more, and feed on plankton. A large school of these fish makes one of the prettiest underwater sights in Hawai'i. To top it off, they will sometimes approach and surround a diver. Occasionally, especially during the summer, they enter shallow enough water to be seen by snorkelers. Small juveniles remain near the bottom, typically gathering around isolated outcroppings. Subadults often shelter in heads of Antler Coral *(Pocillopora grandis)*. Schooling planktivorous butterflyfishes are believed to spawn in groups at dusk. The author once saw a large number of these fish gather in a milling ball at Molokini Islet, Maui, just before sunset on the day after the new moon in July; running low on air, he was unable to witness what subsequently happened. The superficial resemblance between these fish and the Moorish Idol (p. 195) is striking, but they are completely unrelated. To about 8 in. Indo-Pacific. Photos: (upper) Hanauma Bay, O'ahu. 20 ft. (lower) Lāna'i Lookout, O'ahu. 35 ft.

Subadults sheltering in Antler Coral. Mākua, Oʻahu 40 ft. ▲

Juveniles. Mākua, Oʻahu 50 ft. ▼

Rare double pennant. Mākua, Oʻahu 30 ft. ▼

CARDINALFISHES
(Apogonidae)

Cardinalfishes are small to mid-size carnivores, usually nocturnal, and common in all warm seas. They have two dorsal fins, large eyes, and a large mouth. Most Hawaiian species are plain, although many Indo-Pacific cardinals display attractive patterns of stripes or spots. (The Banggai Cardinalfish from Indonesia, *Pterapogon kauderni,* is one of the most beautiful fishes in the sea.) Some cardinalfishes are reddish, possibly the reason for the common name. After dark, many species develop an iridescent sheen.

During the day cardinalfishes typically rest quietly under ledges, in holes, and in caves, often in groups. Smaller individuals aggregate more densely. Some species outside Hawai'i hover over coral heads or shelter in thickets of coral—sometimes in great numbers. All disperse at night to feed on plankton, small crustaceans, or fish. Almost all cardinalfishes are mouthbrooders: females lay globular masses of eggs which males take into their mouths, holding them until they hatch. During this time a male's mouth appears overfilled and unable to close completely.

Although cardinalfishes are a large family with about 250 species worldwide, they are represented in Hawai'i by only ten, four of them endemic. Omitted here is the normally deepwater Phantom Cardinalfish *(Lachneratus phasmaticus),* which was discovered in the back of a totally dark cave in Kona at a depth of only 10-15 ft. The Hawaiian name for cardinalfish is **'upāpalu.**

a) daytime coloration

IRIDESCENT CARDINALFISH · **'upāpalu** · *Pristiapogon kallopterus* (Bleeker, 1856)
At night these cardinalfish show considerable blue-green iridescence (however, some other Hawaiian cardinalfishes do also). By day large adults are plain light brown with darker edged scales; smaller specimens usually have a darkish stripe running through the eye and ending in a black spot on the base of the tail. The leading edge of the first dorsal fin often has a yellowish tinge. They hover in or near caves and overhangs by day, always near sand, and feed over sand or light colored substrates at night. This is the most abundant shallow-water cardinalfish in the main Hawaiian Islands and a common species throughout much of the Indo-Pacific. To 6 in. Photos: (a) Portlock Point, O'ahu. 30 ft. (b) Pūpūkea, O'ahu. 30 ft. (c) Mākua, O'ahu. 50 ft.

b) nighttime coloration ▼

c) juvenile ▼

BANDFIN CARDINALFISH
Pristiapogon taeniopterus
(Bennett, 1835) · **'upāpalu**

Named for the smart white-edged dark bands on the dorsal, anal and tail fins, this cardinalfish is most strongly patterned at night, when it also shows some bluish iridescence. Common on clear-water coral reefs, it forages mainly over living coral or hard substrate after dark and rests in caves and crevices by day. It occurs off many tropical Pacific islands and a few islands in the southern Indian Ocean, but appears to be common only in Hawai'i. The largest cardinalfish in the Islands, it attains 7 in. The species name means "banded fin." Photos: Kepuhi, O'ahu. 10 ft. (day, above); Kailua Harbor, Hawai'i. 20 ft. (night, below). It is listed in older books as a Hawaiian endemic under the name *Apogon menesemus*.

Bandfin Cardinalfish night coloration ▲

HAWAIIAN SPOTTED
CARDINALFISH · **'upāpalu**
Ostorhinchus maculiferus
(Garrett, 1863)

Rows of dark spots on a light orange-brown body identify these endemic cardinalfish. Adults usually live under overhangs and in crevices at depths of 60 ft. or more, while juveniles and subadults aggregate as shallow as 10-15 ft., often in the open near large underwater objects. At night these fish feed in the water column, most actively near dawn. Like many endemics, they are most abundant in the Northwest Hawaiian Islands. The species name means "spotted." To 5 ½ in. Endemic. Photos: (a) Midway Atoll. 30 ft.; (b) Ulua Beach, Maui. 45 ft.

a) male incubating eggs in his mouth ▲

b) juveniles ▼

BAY CARDINALFISH
Foa brachygramma (Jenkins, 1903)
[WEED CARDINALFISH]

Abundant along quiet protected shores, this cardinalfish hides during the day in seaweed, rubble, and dead coral in densities of up to six per square yard! It also enters brackish areas and even fresh water. Gray-brown with dark edges to its scales, and with a rounded tail fin, it resembles no other Hawaiian cardinalfish except possibly the rarely-seen Waikīkī Cardinalfish (below). To about 2 ½ in. Endemic. Photo: Kewalo, O'ahu. 2 ft.

WAIKIKI CARDINALFISH
Apogonichthys perdix (Bleeker, 1854)

Seen only at night, when it becomes highly iridescent, this cardinalfish is best identified by its rounded tail fin, which is often reddish. (Note that the Bay Cardinalfish, above, also has a rounded tail fin.) It lives in holes and under ledges in isolated coral heads and boulders from the shallows down to at least 60 ft. In areas seasonally affected by large waves, however, it lives at 60 ft. or below. Emerging only in almost total darkness, it hovers in midwater not far from its hole feeding mostly on small planktonic crustaceans. The species name means "partridge." A previous name was *Apogon waikiki*, thus the common name. To about 1 ½ in. Indo-Pacific. Photo: Ka'a'awa, O'ahu. 2 ft. (night).

HAWAIIAN RUBY CARDINALFISH
Apogon erythrinus Snyder, 1904

Never seen by day, this common cardinalfish emerges at night to actively patrol a small territory around its crevice or hole. It feeds on small crustaceans and always orients itself with its belly toward the rocky substrate, be it horizontal or vertical, seldom straying more than an inch away. Its organs and vertebrae are clearly visible through the translucent, reddish body. This Hawaiian endemic has three close relatives (including a Marquesan endemic) inhabiting various parts of the Indo-Pacific. Older books may call it *A. coccineus* (a valid name, but now confined to an Arabian cardinalfish). The Greek word *erythros* means "red." To about 2 in. Endemic to the Hawaiian Islands. Photo: Pūpūkea, O'ahu. 30 ft. (at night)

DEETSIE'S CARDINALFISH
Apogon deetsie Randall, 1998

Named for University of Hawai'i zoologist and cardinalfish expert E.H. "Deetsie" Chave, this cardinalfish is seen only on the darkest nights in the farthest recesses of caves. Sightings are few. When illuminated it immediately seeks shelter. Translucent reddish in color, it has a forked tail fin with two beautifully rounded lobes. To about 3 in. Known so far only from Hawai'i and the Tuamotu Islands of French Polynesia. Photo: Waimea Bay, O'ahu. 30 ft. (at night)

TRANSPARENT CARDINALFISH
Pseudamiops diaphanes
Randall, 1998

Transparent except for its spinal column and silvery internal organs, this tiny cardinalfish occurs principally in caves, where it is seen only after dark hovering well off the bottom. On moonless nights one is occasionally glimpsed over the reef. Male cardinalfishes generally incubate the female's eggs in their mouths until they hatch, but the crew of Mike Severns Diving (Maui) discovered that the egg mass of this tiny species dangles from the male's mouth like a long beard! Apparently it can incubate more eggs that way, and the fish is so secretive that the exposed eggs remain safe. To about 1 ½ in. Endemic. Photo: Hōnaunau, Hawai'i. 20 ft.

EVERMANN'S CARDINALFISH
Zapogon evermanni
(Jordan & Snyder, 1904)
[ODDSCALE CARDINALFISH]

This uncommon cardinalfish is seen in the far recesses of caves, usually at night, almost always swimming upside down on the ceiling. Identify it by the bright white spot just behind the second dorsal fin. The overall color is brownish red. A dark stripe runs from the snout through the eye to the gill cover. It has a forked tail fin with two rounded lobes and the top of the head is oddly flattened. The name honors American ichthyologist Barton W. Evermann (1853-1932). This fish inhabits both the Indo-Pacific and Western Atlantic, the only cardinalfish known to do so. To about 6 in. Photo: Palea Point, O'ahu. 30 ft. (swimming upside down)

Gray Chubs · **nenue** · not at all shy · Midway Atoll. 20 ft. (p. 62)

Most chubs are medium-size, gray, heavy-looking fishes with oval bodies, small pointed mouths, and large tails. Called **nenue** in Hawaiian, they school in shallow rocky areas where they feed on marine plants. In the days of sailing ships they would often congregate around the rudders of ships in harbor to feed on algae and perhaps wastes thrown overboard, earning themselves another common name, rudderfish.

Chubs of the genus *Kyphosus*, to which most Hawaiian species belong, have unusually long digestive tracts and use bacterial fermentation to extract maximum nutrition from their diet of seaweed. It is perhaps no surprise, then, that they love the easy, concentrated goodness of fish food. If food is offered, these greedy characters will swarm around snorkelers and waders, often becoming pushy and aggressive. If it is not offered quickly enough they sometimes, in their excitement, nip hands. In the days when fish feeding was allowed at Hanauma Bay, O'ahu, the chubs there were sometimes dubbed "Hanauma Bay pirhanas."

The four most common Hawaiian chubs often occur together and can be difficult to tell apart. The Gray Chub and the endemic Bicolor Chub are so similar that ichthyologists long considered them a single species. The family Kyphosidae includes about 47 species worldwide; six occur in Hawai'i, and five are illustrated here. Omitted is the Japanese Nibbler *(Girella leonina),* known in the Islands from only a few sightings at Midway Atoll in the northwestern chain.

HIGHFIN CHUB · **nenue**
Kyphosus cinerascens
(Forsskål, 1775)
[SNUBNOSE CHUB]

Flaring soft dorsal and anal fins and a snub nose give this chub a distinctive profile. There are no faint stripes on the side and body color ranges from light silvery gray to blackish with light flecks (some scales being lighter than others). Highfin Chubs sometimes aggregate in large numbers, but are just as often seen singly or in small groups apparently guarding territories on high outcroppings along turbulent rocky shores. Where they are present the Bicolor Chub (below) is likely to occur too. They sometimes associate with floating objects far from land. The species name means "ashy" or "ash colored." To about 20 in. Indo-Pacific and tropical Atlantic. Photo: Molokini Islet, Maui. 10 ft.

BICOLOR CHUB · **nenue**
Kyphosus hawaiiensis
Sakai & Nakabo, 2004
[HAWAIIAN CHUB]

Museum specimens of this fish resemble those of the common Gray Chub (next page) so closely that ichthyologists did not realize it was a separate species until 2004. Divers and snorkelers, however, can immediately differentiate the two by color pattern—the Bicolor Chub typically darkens the posterior half or third of its body, appearing half dark half light. Sometimes the head area turns dark as well, leaving a broad light band down the center of the body. The back may darken also, leaving only a light belly area. Occasionally the fish becomes very dark, almost black, with a scattering of tiny blue-white spots—a color pattern which might be restricted to aggressive or reproductive males. The Bicolor Chub lives in small groups in the surge zone at the top of reefs and dropoffs and can be found reliably in the same locations over a period of years, thus is probably territorial. It sometimes aggregates with other chubs, especially the Highfin Chub (above), which lives in similar habitat. To about 14 in. Known only from the Hawaiian Islands except for one doubtful record from the Line Islands. Photos: (a) Hanauma Bay, O'ahu. 3 ft. (b) Midway Atoll. 20 ft.

a) typical coloration ▲

b) coloration when aroused ▼

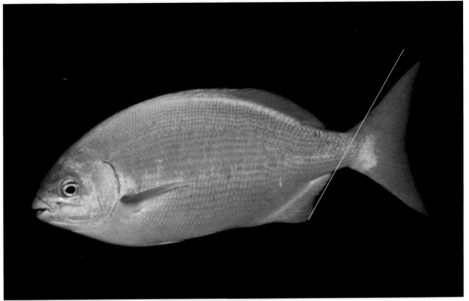

a) normal coloration ▲   b) c) yellow and piebald color variants ▼

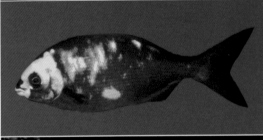

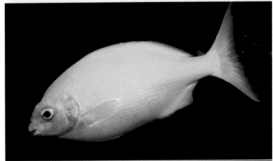

d) coloration when aroused

GRAY CHUB · nenue
Kyphosus sectatrix Linnaeus, 1758
[BERMUDA CHUB, RUDDERFISH]

Hawai'i's most common chub, this fish is bluish gray, often with a pale line following the curve of the back. Faint longitudinal stripes follow the scale rows. It resembles the Brassy Chub (next page), but the anal fin often bears a rounded lobe. A line projected along the margin of the anal fin will not intersect the tail fin. Occasional individuals are yellow, white, or multicolored. In old Hawai'i a yellow **nenue** was regarded as "queen" of the school, but these color variations are not known to have any social signficance. On the other hand, aroused individuals—perhaps dominant males interacting with females—occasionally turn very dark with highly contrasting white spots (see photo at bottom left). The Brassy Chub and the Highfin Chub can put on similar displays.

Gray Chubs live along exposed rocky coasts, often roam in large schools, and do not appear to be territorial. They are not shy, and where common are hard to miss. At Molokini Islet, Maui, the popular dive site Enenue has been named after them. The species occurs worldwide in warm seas, and in the Western Atlantic is called Bermuda Chub. Maximum length is about 20 in. In Hawai'i this fish has been known by a number of different scientific names including *Kyphosus sandwicensis*, *K. pacificus*, and *K. bigibbus*. Photos: (a) Hanauma Bay, O'ahu. 5 ft. (b, c) Lehua Rock, Ni'ihau. 30 ft. (d) Five Fathom Pinnacle, south of Ni'ihau. 50 ft. (see also p. 60)

BRASSY CHUB · nenue
Kyphosus vaigiensis
(Quoy & Gaimard, 1825)
[LOWFIN CHUB]

To differentiate this species from the similar and perhaps more common Gray Chub (previous page), project a line up from the margin of the anal fin. In the Brassy Chub the line will intersect the tail fin, in the Gray Chub it will miss it. Other characters to look for: 1) faint brassy yellow marks about the mouth, eyes and at the edges of the gill covers (brighter in small individuals), and 2) a slightly striped appearance due to prominent rows of scales. While grazing, these fish display faint, evenly spaced pale round spots on their backs and sides; if aroused they intensify these spots. (The Gray Chub and the Highfin Chub can do the same.) Look for Brassy Chubs near the turbulent surge zone where small individuals occur singly or in groups. They also school, sometimes mixing with the more common Gray Chub. The species name is from the Indonesian island of Waigeo. To about 20 in. Indo-Pacific and tropical Atlantic. Photos: Hanauma Bay, O'ahu. 3-10 ft.

a) typical coloration ▲

b) coloration when aroused ▼

RAINBOW CHUB *Kyphosus ocyurus* (Jordan & Gilbert, 1881) [Bluestriped Chub]

These beautiful chubs are dull yellow-green with two bright blue stripes running the body's length, one along the curve of the back. The underside is white. Unlike others of their kind, they are plankton-eaters. They sometimes congregate around floating logs or other objects, far from land. Rare in Hawai'i, they apparently drift in as waifs from the Eastern Pacific, where they occur from California to Ecuador. Waifs also turn up on occasion in Guam, the Mariana Islands, and even Japan. The species name means "sharp" or "swift." A breeding population appears to exist in the Marquesas and Tuamotu Islands of French Polynesia. To about 15 in. Photo: Nuku Hiva, Marquesas. 30 ft.

CUSK EELS and PEARLFISHES
(Ophidiidae and Carapidae)

Bearded Cusk Eel · **puhi palahoana** · Mākaha, Oʻahu. 15 ft.

Cusk eels, or brotulas, belong to the order Ophidiiformes and are thus not true eels. Pearlfishes are also members of this order. Both are secretive eel-like fishes with long continuous dorsal and anal fins which typically merge at the tail to form a tapering point. Pelvic fins are lacking except in a few species, in which they are reduced to filaments. Most cusk eels live deep within the reef, and most pearlfishes inhabit the body cavities of invertebrate animals. Some pearlfishes leave their hosts at night to feed, others are parasitic, feeding on their host's inner organs; a few live freely.

Two cusk eels (out of at least 135 species worldwide) and four pearlfishes (out of about 31 worldwide) occur in shallow Hawaiian waters. One cusk eel and two pearlfishes are illustrated here. Other shallow-water Hawaiian species, almost never seen, include the cusk eel *Brotula townsendi* (distinguished by orange margins on its dorsal and anal fins) and two pearlfishes, *Onuxodon parvibrachium* (shelters in bivalves) and *Encheliophis gracilis* (inhabits sea cucumbers and feeds on their internal organs).

BEARDED CUSK EEL · **puhi palahoana** · *Brotula multibarbata* Temminck & Schlegel, 1846

This fish resembles a cross between an eel and a catfish. Its short, eel-like body is dark grayish brown. Sets of white sensory barbels sprout from the snout and chin. The chin has white markings. Its dorsal and anal fins have a narrow white border and are continuous with the tail fin, which tapers to a point. This is the only commonly-seen cusk eel in Hawaiʻi. Night divers occasionally glimpse it in the open, but seldom far from a hole or crevice to which it immediately retreats when a light is shined on it. Occasionally one can be spotted by day, resting far back in a dark cave or deep under a ledge. The species name means "many-bearded." To about 24 in., although usually less than half that size. Indo-Pacific. Photo: Pūpūkea, Oʻahu. 20 ft. (night)

FOWLER'S PEARLFISH *Onuxodon fowleri* (Smith, 1955) [KEELED PEARLFISH]

Members of the family Carapidae are often called pearlfishes because some live in pearl oysters. They also inhabit the body cavities of other invertebrate animals such as sea cucumbers, sea stars, and tunicates, wriggling into their hosts tail first. Mostly transparent, with a dark smudge on the tail, Fowler's Pearlfish rests by day in large bivalves such as the Black-Lipped Pearl Oyster *(Pinctada margaritifera),* pen shells *(Pinna* spp.), or rock-oysters *(Spondylus* spp.). It swims freely at night, perhaps feeding on small crustaceans and bristle worms. Mated pairs may inhabit the same host. The name honors American ichthyologist Henry W. Fowler (1879-1965), principal author of *Fishes of Oceania*, an enormous multivolume compendium published by Honolulu's Bishop Museum between 1928 and 1949. Two other fishes in this book were named after Fowler, a scorpionfish and a snake eel. To about 3 ½ in. Indo-Pacific. Photo: Kea'au, O'ahu. 50 ft. (at night)

CUSHION STAR PEARLFISH
Carapus mourlani (Petit, 1934)

Transparent with numerous small dark spots, this pearlfish shelters in sea stars and sea cucumbers by day and feeds at night on small fishes and crustaceans. (The fish pictured opposite was actively foraging over sand.) Its favorite host is reported to be the Cushion Star *(Culcita novae-guineae).* It also inhabits the Crown-of-Thorns Star *(Acanthaster planci)* and the Knobby Star *(Pentaceraster cumingi).* Apparently it rarely inhabits sea cucumbers; out of 122 examined off O'ahu (mostly *Holothuria atra*), only 2 contained a pearlfish.   To about 7 in. Indo-Pacific and Eastern Pacific. Photo: Pūpūkea, O'ahu. (at night)

Jerry Kane

One of the most unusual features of pearlfish anatomy is the placement of the anus near the head. This allows the fish to excrete wastes while remaining mostly inside its host, thereby minimizing exposure to predators.

Viviparous brotulas

Viviparous brotulas (family Bythitidae) resemble cusk eels but give live birth to their young, unusual among marine fishes. Out of eight known Hawaiian species, two have been seen on rare occasions by divers exploring dark caves. One of these, discovered and photographed in a Kona lava tube by Kendra Ignacio and Marc Hughes in 1998 (pictured at right), was new to science. Three of the others are known only from single specimens that were found floating at the surface after large lava flows from the 1950 eruption of Mauna Loa entered the sea. Little is known about these rare fishes.

Grammonus nagaredai
photo: Kendra Ignacio.

Hawaiian Sergeants · **mamo** · possibly Hawai'i's most abundant reef fish · Palea Point, O'ahu. 15 ft.

Damselfishes are small, sometimes colorful fishes with moderately deep, laterally compressed bodies, a single dorsal fin, a forked or almost forked tail fin, and one pair of nostrils instead of two. Few species exceed 6 in., most are smaller. They are abundant in shallow tropical habitats and a coral reef without them would seem empty. In Hawai'i, small fishes aggregating above coral heads are almost sure to be damsels. So are the small, drab, aggressive fishes common on reef flats, in rocky shallows, and in tide pools. The ubiquitous sergeants are members of this family, as are the striking clownfishes which inhabit and protect stinging sea anemones in other parts of the Indo-Pacific.

In general, damsels are either plankton-eaters or algae-eaters. The plankton-eaters typically aggregate over the reef in loose groups while the algae-eaters are solitary inhabitants of shallow rocky areas where algal growth is heavy. Some algae-eaters "farm" their algae patches by weeding out undesirable growths. Most algae-eaters feed secondarily on small invertebrate animals and/or organic detritus, thus are really omnivores.

Some damselfishes have an immunity to the stinging cells of sea anemones. Most famous are the clownfishes (or anemonefishes) popular among aquarists. The only Hawaiian example is the Hawaiian Dascyllus (p. 77), juveniles of which occasionally live symbiotically in the sand-dwelling anemone *Heteractis malu*.

The damselfishes form one of the largest fish families, with about 355 species. Seventeen occur in Hawai'i and all are shown here except the deepwater *Chromis struhsakeri*, which is never seen by divers. Only the largest Hawaiian damselfishes have Hawaiian names, probably because the others were not important for food.

Damselfish reproductive behavior is easy to observe. The male prepares a nest site, typically by fanning sediments from bare rock and/or nibbling away algae and other growths, then displays to attract a female, often with a series of up-and-down loops called "signal jumps" which may be accompanied by sounds, color change, or both. The female lays her eggs directly on the substrate, the male following closely behind to fertilize them. The male then guards the nest for several days, often driving away other fish (or divers) that get too close, fanning the eggs to keep them oxygenated, and picking away debris or diseased eggs. After hatching, larvae enter the plankton, eventually settling out in an appropriate environment to transform into juveniles. Juveniles of many species are more brightly colored than adults.

HAWAIIAN SERGEANT · **mamo**
Abudefduf abdominalis
(Quoy & Gaimard, 1825)

It is not even necessary to enter the water to see these common and attractive damsels—the young, yellowish with five black bars, often occur in tide pools. Adults vary from brassy green to yellow with five vertical black bars which are widest and darkest along the upper back. The bars may shorten, lighten, or almost disappear. The ground color, too, may lighten or darken, and the abdomen may develop subtle yellow striping. The most distinct color changes occur during spawning and nest-guarding. Plankton-eaters, Hawaiian Sergeants spend much of their time swarming high in the water to feed, usually over a specific area of the reef where they shelter and reproduce. When disturbed (or when a dark cloud passes over the sun!) they dive as one for cover, but soon rise again to resume feeding. In addition to plankton, they also consume algae or almost anything else they can find. These fish can also be abundant near the bottom where they nest, spawn, and guard their purplish-red patches of eggs (usually deposited in crevices between boulders or under ledges, but when necessary, on flat hard bottom). Other Hawaiian names are **mamamo** and **maomao**. The species name means "abdomen" or "belly." The name "sergeant" is shared by several Indo-Pacific and Atlantic species of the same genus and is probably American in origin, as sergeants in the British Army wear a crown instead of stripes. To almost 10 in., but usually smaller. Endemic. Photos: (above) Kahe Point, O'ahu. 15 ft. (below & next page) Midway Atoll. (Keoki Stender)

Reproduction

Hawaiian Sergeants reproduce all year, with most activity taking place from January through June when the water is coolest. Males form colonies of up to 120 simultaneously nesting individuals (2-30 are more typical). After preparing a nest site, a male attracts a female by assuming nuptial colors (dark or light steel blue, sometimes with pale yellow bars) and performing maneuvers such as head-down hovering, rapid looping, and zig-zagging. If a female is receptive, the two swim upward side-by-side and may "kiss" for 1-2 seconds at the apex before returning to the nest and tightly circling each other. Egg-laying and fertilization may take up to 2 hours, the male continually breaking off to drive away egg-predators and "streakers" (non-nesting males which try to dash in and release their sperm nearby). A male may spawn with multiple females over the course of 1-3 days, resulting in up to 11 batches of purplish red eggs in one nest. The color of each batch varies with age. Eggs hatch in 5-9 days.

Keoki Stender

67

Hawaiian Sergeants spawning. The female, left, is laying eggs. Keoki Stender

Feeding frenzy! A male Hawaiian Sergeant tries to defend his nest against egg raiders. Note his coloration.

Come and get it!

Hawaiian Sergeant eggs are a significant food source on the reef. The nests of reproductive males contain large purple-red egg patches laid on bare rock—a conspicuous fat and protein treat for any fish able to get at them. Typically located on smooth crevice walls, in the spaces between boulders, or on flat hard bottoms, the nests are each guarded by a single male, which vigorously drives off all intruders, or tries to. (A male may spend up to 90 percent of daylight hours in nest defense!) Although effective against individuals, a defending male Sergeant is no match for an attacking swarm of Milletseed Butterflyfish, Raccoon Butterflyfish, or Black Triggerfish, which can easily overwhelm it. Such attacks often happen when a diver is nearby; presumably the close presence of such a large animal upsets the male Sergeant, giving egg predators the edge. Milletseed Butterflyfish know this and may follow divers considerable distances until a Sergeant nesting area is reached. Once a Milletseed attack has begun, wrasses, other butterflyfishes, triggerfishes, filefishes, and even other Sergeants join in, creating a colorful feeding frenzy which lasts several minutes or more. The frantic male darts back and forth trying to repel the raiders, often intensifying or changing his colors as he does so. The swarm, having eaten its fill, eventually moves on. Usually plenty of eggs are left and the Sergeant resumes his duties. One can only wonder why Sergeant eggs are so conspicuous while most damselfish eggs are hardly visible. Perhaps they play some important role in the ecology of the reef that benefits the Sergeants indirectly. Photo: Palea Point, O'ahu. 30 ft.

INDO-PACIFIC SERGEANT
Abudefduf vaigiensis
(Quoy & Gaimard, 1825)

Although the most abundant sergeant in the tropical Indian and Pacific Oceans, this species was unknown in Hawai'i until about 1990. Now common in the Islands, it is breeding side-by-side, and sometimes with, the Hawaiian Sergeant. Bright yellow on the upper sides, it has broad black bars which are typically wider and extend further down the body than those of the Hawaiian Sergeant. Colors are heightened on reproductive males and bluish tones may appear. Juveniles often aggregate under floating objects such as lost fishing nets, which may be how the species arrived here. It is one of the four most common fishes associated with flotsam in the Western Pacific. (The others include the Rainbow Runner and the Bigeye Trevally, pp. 178-9.) To about 8 in. Indo-Pacific. Named for Waigeo, an island in Indonesia. Photo: Kahe Point, O'ahu. 15 ft.

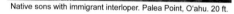

Native sons with immigrant interloper. Palea Point, O'ahu. 20 ft.

Hybrid sergeant. Lahaina, Maui. 30 ft.

A new look?

In 2007, Karen Maruska and Kimberley Peyton confirmed that the endemic Hawaiian Sergeant and the immigrant Indo-Pacific Sergeant are interbreeding. This could have big implications. The traditional **biological species concept** holds that geographical variants of the same basic organism belong to the same species if they can interbreed and produce fertile offspring. Under this concept, the Hawaiian Sergeant and the Indo-Pacific Sergeant could represent a single species.

However, the more recent **phylogenetic species concept** holds that because geographical variants of the same basic organism have taken separate evolutionary paths, they are separate species regardless of whether or not they can interbreed. Under this concept, the Hawaiian and Indo-Pacific Sergeants are two species.

Whichever side you take, questions remain: Will the two remain distinct, producing occasional hybrids, or will they merge completely? If they merge, will they create a new species? In that case, would abdominalis be declared extinct? What might a new species look like? If the above right photo is any guide, the appearances of the two would blend about 50/50.

a) typical adult coloration ▲

b) male guarding eggs ▼

c) subadult ▼

BLACKSPOT SERGEANT · kūpīpī
Abudefduf sordidus (Forsskål, 1775)

This large solitary damselfish is common in areas of moderate surge around rocks and boulders down to about 10 ft. Its color varies from yellowish gray with six broad brown bars to brown with six to seven narrow light bars. The colors can lighten or darken, but a black spot is always present on the upper base of the tail, thus the common name. While establishing a nest, courting, and spawning (a period of about 36 hours), males become black with seven highly contrasting narrow white bars (see next page). They can be extremely aggressive at this time. A day or so after spawning the male's contrasting colors become muted as it guards the newly fertilized eggs (center photo this page). Juveniles and subadults, common in tide pools, have indistinct bars and a yellow wedgelike mark on the back. This coloration sometimes persists into adulthood. Omnivores, these damsels will eat algae, crabs, sponges, molluscs, and anything else they can find. They are known to live at least 9 years in the wild. The species' name means "dirty," probably referring to its coloration. To about 9 in. Indo-Pacific. Photos: (a) Hanauma Bay, O'ahu. 3 ft. (b) Pūpūkea, O'ahu. 8 ft. (c) Makapu'u Point, O'ahu. Tide pool.

Blackspot Sergeant reproduction

Frank G. Stanton, who spent many hours observing Blackspot Sergeant reproductive activity, discovered that males nest in loose colonies and establish their own nesting territories from which they aggressively drive away other males. For a period of approximately 36 hours while establishing a nest, courting, and spawning, they undergo a striking color change, becoming black with seven highly contrasting narrow white bars. They can be extremely aggressive at this time and it is unclear whether the conspicuous coloration is advertising nest defense or attracting mates—probably it accomplishes both. Upon seeing a female nearby, a courting male rapidly zigzags toward her swimming first on one side, then another. Other males in the vicinity may do the same. The successful suitor leads the female back to his nest where he swims around her in a figure-eight pattern and produces faint pulsed sounds. If she enters his nest, both take turns swimming with pelvic fins pressed against the substrate. This mock spawning may continue for 20 minutes. If the female pauses or tries to leave, the male resumes his figure-eight pattern and produces more pulsed sounds. When actual spawning begins the sounds cease. A day or so after spawning the male's black and white color pattern becomes muted, and in 2-3 days his coloration is back to normal. The inconspicuous eggs hatch in 5-6 days. Several clutches may be deposited in one male's nest by different females over a few days. Nests containing eggs are seldom attacked by other fish.

AGILE CHROMIS
Pycnochromis pacifica (Allen & Erdmann, 2020)

The Agile Chromis is brown with a lavender tinge, especially around the gills. The top of the head is yellowish brown and there is a large dark spot at the base of the pectoral fin. These fish typically hover several feet above the coral, sometimes in loose groups, and are most common along outer reef slopes at depths of 30 ft. or more. They are particularly abundant along the Kona Coast of the Big Island. While courting, spawning, or guarding eggs, males become noticeably pale except for the yellowish brown area at the top of the head. To about 4 ½ in. Pacific Ocean. Photos: (a) Hanauma Bay, O'ahu. 60 ft. (b) Ho'okena, Hawai'i. 25 ft.

a) typical colors ▲

b) ▼ male in nuptial colors, female below

Nuptial colors

Most male damselfishes modify their color patterns during nest preparation, courtship, spawning, and nest guarding. These nuptial color changes can be extreme or subtle (examples of each on this page). The majority of species probably use the same basic color change to signal all phases of the reproductive cycle, but a few display different color patterns for different phases, such as spawning and nest guarding. In many cases a male can "turn off" his nuptial colors almost instantaneously.

a) normal colors ▲   b) male nuptial colors (note white eye) ▶

The genus Chromis, *largest in the damselfish family, constitutes about 25 percent of all damselfish species and about half of the Hawaiian ones. Chromises are small to midsize plankton-eaters. Typically aggregating in large numbers over the reef, they are among the most numerous of reef fish. In most species, thin filaments trail from the tips of the forked tail fin.*

CHOCOLATE DIP CHROMIS
Pycnochromis hanui
(Randall & Swerdloff, 1973)

The popular name perfectly describes this small fish, which is chocolate brown with a brightly contrasting white tail. (Many Indo-Pacific chromises have a similar pattern, including the species, below.) It frequents ledges, walls and the sides of coral heads, seldom straying far from cover. If threatened, it retreats into the coral. It may be solitary or form loose groups. During courtship and spawning (occurring most often during February and March) males develop bright white eyes and become pale on the sides. The species name **hanui** is an old Hawaiian name for an unknown damselfish. To 3 ½ in. Endemic. Photos: (a) Hanauma Bay, O'ahu. 30 ft. (b) Mackenzie State Park, Hawai'i. 60 ft.

WHITE-TAIL CHROMIS
Pycnochromis leucura (Gilbert, 1905)

Similar to the Chocolate Dip Chromis (above) but darker brown, appearing almost blue-black underwater, this small damselfish typically occurs at depths greater than 80 ft., sometimes in large aggregations. Yellow pelvic fins provide positive identification. Often a yellow mark also occurs near the base of the pectoral fin. Likely places to see this species are Molokini Islet, Maui, the reef slopes off the Kona Coast of the Big Island, and the Wai'anae coast of O'ahu. To about 3 in. Indo-Pacific. Photos: (opposite) Hōnaunau, Hawai'i. 90 ft. (below) Ka'ohe Bay, Hawai'i. 80 ft.

OVAL CHROMIS *Chromis ovalis*
(Steindachner, 1900)

These endemic damselfish are abundant in many areas, typically swarming high in the water over rocky or coral bottom to feed on plankton. When not feeding they sometimes form dense schools (see next page). Adults are brassy yellow-green but appear grayish at a distance. During spawning season (February through May), males establish temporary spawning territories and nest sites on the bottom. At this time they usually develop two broad blue-white bars, a blue-white tail, and yellow pelvic and pectoral fins. Oval Chromis are most plentiful at depths of about 20 to 130 ft, often mixing with the Threespot Chromis (p. 75). The two species are similar in many ways, with the Oval Chromis dominating the shallows and the Threespot Chromis more prevalent in deeper water. Juvenile Oval Chromis, which start to appear on the reef as early as February, vary from silvery blue with a yellow back and dorsal fin to almost all yellow, often with an iridescent blue stripe above the eye (see next page). Newly settled juveniles sometimes shelter among the spines of sea urchins. To 7 ½ in. Endemic. Photos: (a) Lāna'i Lookout, O'ahu. 30 ft. (b) Portlock Point, O'ahu. 40 ft. (c) Maui (Mike Roberts).

a) normal colors ▲

b) male nest preparation, courtship, and spawning colors ▲

c) male nest-guarding colors

Oval Chromis reproduction

During the spawning season (roughly January through May), many rocky bottoms in Hawai'i become alive with male Oval Chromises establishing temporary spawning territories and clearing nest sites within them. It takes them three or four days to do so. Nests are in the open and spaced a few feet apart. At this stage males take on nuptial colors (blue-white dorsal and tail fins, dark soft dorsal and anal fins, yellow-orange pelvic and pectoral fins, and, usually, two broad blue-white bars on the body) and defend their territories against other Oval Chromis males. When a male's nest site is ready he performs a series of "signal jumps" to attract a female, swimming rapidly up into the water at an angle, then abruptly returning to the nest site. If interested, a female will follow a displaying male to his nest and begin laying transparent, almost invisible eggs, quivering as she does so. The male, also quivering, follows to fertilize them. Every so often he swims up over the nest to detect and drive away any potential intruders. It takes several sessions each lasting from 30 seconds to several minutes for the female to deposit all her eggs. Between sessions she moves slightly away and rests. When done, she leaves and the male fiercely protects the eggs, often driving away much larger fishes and even attacking divers who get too close. At this time the male may become almost silvery blue suffused with orange around the mouth, and sometimes with orange on the lower sides, and along the margin of the dorsal fin as well. Stan Swerdloff, who observed courtship, spawning, and nest-defense at dozens of sites, reports: "Nest defense was so successful that I did not observe a single instance of egg predation during three spawning seasons." The eggs hatch in about three days.

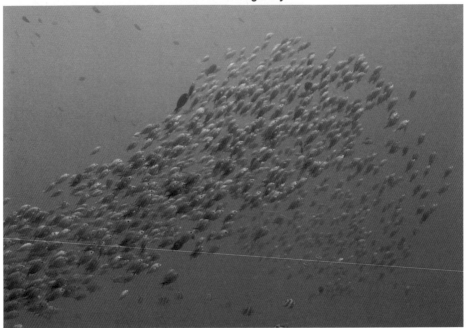

Oval Chromis occasionally swarm off the bottom in large schools. They are not feeding and the purpose of the behavior is not known. Lāna`i Lookout, O'ahu. 40 ft.

Oval Chromis juveniles are variable in color. In addition to the patterns above, they can also be almost entirely yellow or silvery blue. (left) Hanauma Bay, O'ahu. 45 ft. (right) Ka'ohe Bay, Hawai'i. 30 ft.

a) adult ▲

b) aggregation ▼

c) juvenile ▼

THREESPOT CHROMIS *Chromis verater* Jordan & Metz, 1912

This distinctive damselfish is usually dark gray or black with three white spots near the base of the tail. It can lighten or darken the spots, or make them disappear. Sometimes the entire body turns silvery gray. Similar in size and habits to the Oval Chromis with which it often mingles (see previous page), it even prefers the same types of planktonic organisms (pelagic tunicates when available, otherwise cope-pods, which constitute the bulk of both fishes' diets). The two differ, however, in habitat preference: the Threespot is most abundant in deeper water, down to about 500 ft., while the Oval Chromis usually remains above 130 ft. Juvenile Threespots, which occur at 80 ft. or more, often at the bases of dropoffs, have light gray bodies with dark dorsal, anal, and pelvic fins. To 8 ½ in. Endemic. Photos: (a) Hanauma Bay, O'ahu. 40 ft. (b) Midway Atoll. 80 ft. (c) Hōnaunau, Hawai'i. 80 ft.

Threespot Chromis reproduction

To attract a mate during spawning season (late November to June), a male Threespot Chromis often lightens his body while leaving his fins dark (see left photo), a color pattern resembling that of juveniles, and also the Hawaiian Dascyllus. He prepares a nest on a smooth horizontal rock surface, either in the open or under an overhang, if necessary fanning away quantities of sand to make a saucerlike depression 2-3 ft. in diameter. While guarding the inconspicuous whitish eggs he sometimes darkens his white spots. Milletseed Butterflyfish and others sometimes raid Threespot Chromis nests. Photos: Palea Point, O'ahu. 50 ft, 40 ft.

BLACKFIN CHROMIS *Pycnochromis vanderbilti* (Fowler, 1941)

These small attractive damselfishes aggregate above coral heads at depths of 10 ft. or more, sometimes in great numbers, disappearing into crevices if approached. They are yellow with gray-blue stripes and a dark blue-black anal fin. The lower edge of the tail fin is also black. The species is named for Mr. & Mrs. George Vanderbilt, wealthy sponsors of a 1937 scientific expedition to the Pacific on the schooner *Cressida,* during which over 10,000 fish specimens were collected. To 2 ¾ in. Restricted to islands of the tropical Pacific. Photo: Pūpūkea, O'ahu. 30 ft. (The very rare Midget Chromis, below, is similar.)

MIDGET CHROMIS [DWARF CHROMIS]

Pycnochromis acares (Randall & Swerdloff, 1973)

Except for localized population blooms, such as in 2017, this damsel is extremely rare in Hawai'i. However, it is common at Johnston Atoll, south of the Islands, and its larvae probably drift in occasionally from there. It is typically seen schooling with the similar Blackfin Chromis. Unlike the Blackfin, its tail margins are yellow and it lacks faint stripes on the side, To 2 ¼ in. Central and Western Pacific. Photo: Guam (Robert F. Myers).

Robert F. Myers

a) subadults in Antler Coral

HAWAIIAN DASCYLLUS · 'ālo'ilo'i · *Dascyllus albisella* Gill, 1862 [HAWAIIAN DOMINO DAMSELFISH]

When young, these perky, deep-bodied damselfish typically shelter in small heads of branching Cauliflower Coral *(Pocillopora meandrina)*, hovering above to feed on plankton. The smaller they are, the closer to the coral they remain. Tiny juveniles will also shelter in Finger Coral *(Porites compressa)*, long-spined sea urchins of several species, Red Pencil Urchins, Crown-Of-Thorns Sea Stars, the sand-dwelling anemone, *Heteractis malu,* and (rarely) behind the head of a moray eel. Subadults and adults generally live in large heads of Antler Coral *(Pocillopora grandis)*. Many adults, however, leave their coral head entirely to live openly on the reef. These fish occur as deep as 150 ft. and may rise as much as 50 ft. above the bottom to feed.

Juveniles are black with a porcelain-white patch on each side. (Tiny ones have a third light blue spot on the forehead.) As they grow, the head and fins remain dark but the sides bleach somewhat and the white patch becomes less distinct. Adults can lighten or darken considerably. When spawning, for example, their sides become bright white, while the head, pelvic, anal, and tail fins remain dark gray. When feeding, their coloration is similar but the scale edges darken. At night, or when agitated they almost revert to their juvenile colors, becoming black with a bright white patch on the upper side. Hawaiian Dascyllus are common at snorkeling depths only in well-protected locations, such as Kāne'ohe Bay, O'ahu. In places exposed to even moderate wave action one must dive to 20 or 30 ft. to find them.

This fish belongs to a species complex of similar Indo-Pacific damselfishes, the most widespread of which is the Threespot Dascyllus *(D. trimaculatus)*. The Hawaiian Dascyllus appears to be the only one of this group in which juveniles usually settle out in branching corals; juveniles of the other species (with the possible exception of the poorly-known Marquesan Dascyllus, *D. strasburgi*) are usually symbionts of large anemones.

The Hawaiian name means "bright and sparkling." The species name is from *albus* ("white"). To 5 in. Endemic. Photos: (a) Mākaha, O'ahu. 30 ft. (b) Kāne'ohe Bay, O'ahu. 10 ft.

b) juveniles in Finger Coral ▶

Hawaiian Dascyllus reproduction

Hawaiian Dascyllus reproductive behavior is especially easy to observe. A male clears a nesting site near or on the bottom, then courts a female by bleaching his body bright white and performing a series dips (rapid downward rushes while turned on the side). Dips are often accompanied by chirplike sounds, easily heard by divers. If a female responds, he leads her to the nest where she lays tiny, transparent, almost invisible eggs, quivering as she does so. He follows close behind to fertilize them. This sequence occurs a number of times until all eggs are deposited. The female then leaves or is driven away and the male defends and cares for the eggs, often picking at them or aereating them with sideways flutters of his body. When chasing away other fish (or divers!) the male makes popping or chirping sounds similar to those made while courting. More than one female may lay eggs in a single male's nest, but all eggs in a nest are laid on the same day and hatch in about four days. Most nesting takes place from May to August and spawning typically occurs in the morning. Spawning is synchronized: Dascyllus in a given area spawn on the same day at about 6-day intervals. Increases in water temperature stimulate increased spawning. A male at Molokini Islet, Maui, first noticed because of a distinct bite mark, defended the same nesting territory for nine years before disappearing!

male at bottom of "dip" ▲

▼ male and female spawning

BRIGHT-EYE DAMSELFISH
Plectroglyphidodon imparipennis
(Vaillant & Sauvage, 1875)

These tiny grayish yellow damsels defend very small territories, usually in small depressions along the top of the reef in shallow water. Their eyes, although bisected by a dark bar, nevertheless appear bright yellow-white. The base of the tail is faintly yellow. They feed almost entirely on small, bottom-dwelling invertebrates. During very low tides they are often confined to tide pools. They also occur down to at least 30 ft. The scientific name derives from *impar* ("unequal") and *penna* ("fin"). To about 2 ½ in. Indo-Pacific. Photo: Pūpūkea, Oʻahu. 5 ft.

BLUE-EYE DAMSELFISH *Plectroglyphidodon johnstonianus* Fowler & Ball, 1924

These are yellowish gray, with bright blue eyes and blue margins on the dorsal and anal fins. The rear of the body is darker on some individuals. They live among the branches of living coral (in Hawaiʻi, *Pocillopora* or *Porites*), feeding largely on coral polyps. Heads of Antler Coral *(Pocillopora grandis)* usually contain a Blue-Eye Damsel. A study in Kāneʻohe Bay, Oʻahu, showed that a typical colony of Cauliflower Coral *(Pocillopora meandrina)* does not provide enough energy to sustain one fish but that two or more colonies are sufficient. In Kāneʻohe Bay they spawn most frequently from September to October and again from February through May. Males create a nest site by killing a patch of coral on one of their coral heads. Blue-Eye Damsel territories often lie within the larger territory of a pair of less aggressive Multiband Butterflyfish (p. 43). They frequently chase the Multibands, but do not bother to chase other butterflyfishes of similar size that do not feed on coral. The author once photographed one of these damsels cleaning an Orangespine Unicornfish which returned multiple times to the damselfish's coral head. The species name is from Johnston Atoll, south of the Hawaiian chain. To 4 ½ in. Indo-Pacific. Photo: Hōnaunau, Hawaiʻi. 40 ft. (in *Porites compressa* and *P. monticulosa*).

a) adult ▲   b) juvenile ▲   c) male guarding eggs ▲

HAWAIIAN ROCK DAMSELFISH *Plectroglyphidodon sindonis* (Jordan & Evermann, 1903)
These endemic damsels are dark purplish brown with two narrow light bars. They inhabit the shallow surge zone down to about 15 ft. and because of their habitat are seldom noticed. If you find one, look around for the Gargantuan Blenny (p. 18)—the two often occur together. Juveniles, which often occur in tide pools, have a dark spot edged in white on the soft dorsal fin. The species feeds on algae, detritus and small invertebrates. Egg patches are laid in the open on vertical rock surfaces. Males become bright white dorsally during bursts of extreme aggression, as when chasing away other males while spawning. The scientific name honors zoologist Michitaro Sindo, who discovered this fish for science near Kailua, O'ahu, in 1901. To 5 in. Endemic. Photos: (a) Pūpūkea, O'ahu. 5 ft. (b) Mackenzie State Park, Hawai'i. 8 ft. (c) Lāna'i Lookout, O'ahu. 15 ft. (January)

PHOENIX ISLAND DAMSELFISH
Plectroglyphidodon phoenixensis
Schultz, 1943

Extremely rare in the Hawaiian Islands, this damselfish sports three slightly curved pinkish bars on a brown body, and broad black bar before the tail. It inhabits the surge zone of rocky shores exposed to moderately strong waves at depths of 3-9 ft., feeding on algae, coral, and the zoanthid *Palythoa caesia*. It is known principally from sightings of 13 individuals near Hekili and Papawai Points, south Maui, in 1988-89. Although some were paired, suggesting reproduction, all but one were gone by 1992. The survivor later disappeared as well. A lone individual was reported off Ka'a'awa, O'ahu, in 2004, and another was seen at French Frigate Shoals. In 2008 several individuals were spotted along the Kona coast of the Big Island. This Indo-Pacific species apparently drifts in as a waif to the Hawaiian chain on rare occasions, perhaps from Johnston Atoll. To about 3 ½ in. Photo: Ali'i Villas, Kailua-Kona, Hawai'i. 6 ft.

a) adult

HAWAIIAN GREGORY *Plectroglyphidodon marginatus* (Jenkins, 1901) [formerly PACIFIC GREGORY]

This drab, blackish or brownish gray damselfish has bright lemon-yellow eyes and, often, a patchy, unkempt appearance due to some scales being lighter than others. Common in Hawai'i, it prefers areas with moderate to low wave activity and feeds primarily on green filamentous algae. Each individual maintains an all-purpose territory (containing shelter and a nesting site as well as food), which it boldly defends against all other algae-eating fishes. The territory extends about 2-4 ft. in all directions from the shelter hole and is usually defined by natural formations such as coral heads or clumps of weed. (Containing more algae than surrounding areas, these territories are occasionally discernible to humans.) Like similar Indo-Pacific and Caribbean damsels, the Hawaiian Gregory "farms" its patch of filamentous algae by removing undesirable coralline algae. It also eats small invertebrates living in its algal farm.

As anyone who has watched a Hawaiian Gregory can attest, this pugnacious little fish will unfailingly attempt to drive any other herbivore from its algae patch. It does not waste energy by attacking carnivores such as wrasses, but experiments show it can learn to recognize and attack algae-eating fish species it has never encountered before. A male Hawaiian Gregory will also defend its territory against males of its own species. When displaying aggression to another male, it darkens its yellow eyes (see next page). Juveniles, bluish black with a pale yellow tail, appear during

b) juvenile

the summer months, often on wave-scoured reef flats. Those under 1 in. have an iridescent blue-purple streak along the top of the head and margin of the dorsal fin. To about 6 in. Endemic, but closely related to the Pacific Gregory (*P. fasciolatus*) found elsewhere in the Pacific. The Hawaiian species has a subtly different color pattern, including a black spot between the 2nd and 3rd dorsal spines visible only when the dorsal fin is raised. DNA studies confirm it to be a distinct species, previously placed in the genus *Stegastes*. Photos: (a) Kahe Point, O'ahu. 15 ft. (b) Ali'i Beach Park, O'ahu. 10 ft.

Keystone species

The feisty Hawaiian Gregory is a surprisingly important member of the reef community. Where it is abundant, this small fish can alter the local behavior of herbivores such as Brown Surgeonfish, Convict Tangs, and Yellow Tangs, forcing them to feed in schools instead of individually. (Only by schooling can the other herbivores overwhelm the Gregory's defenses.) It can also cause the Fourspot Butterflyfish to feed at night instead of during the day. More importantly, however, Hawaiian Gregories increase both the biodiversity and algal productivity of the reef. Experiments off O'ahu show that intense parrotfish and surgeonfish grazing prevents some algae species from growing anywhere except within Pacific Gregory territories. Furthermore, these territories may be almost the only places where certain rare corals grow! Another study in Kāne'ohe Bay, O'ahu, showed that young coral growth was highest on the windward edge of a patch reef where Hawaiian Gregory territories are most common. Finally, research on the closely related Pacific Gregory (S. fasciolatus) in Australia and Papua New Guinea showed that algal communities inside Pacific Gregory territories, and those of similar damselfishes, were up to 3.4 times as productive as those outside. Organisms with a disproportionate influence on an ecosystem—such as these territorial damselfishes—are sometimes called "keystone" species. Their removal often produces many unintended and unforseen consequences. Photo: Pūpūkea, O'ahu. 15 ft.

Oh, those dark eyes

Like many territorial fishes, Hawaiian Gregories must defend their turf against rival members of their own species. This is true of juveniles as well as adults. A 1968 study at the Hawai'i Institute of Marine Biology showed that rival juvenile Gregories often play "chicken" using a combination of two signals: raising the dorsal fin to indicate fright, and darkening the yellow eyes to gray to indicate aggression. "Fights" can take place without any physical contact, the winner being the one who displays to the other with the highest aggression indicator (the darkest eyes) and the lowest fright indicator (lowest dorsal fin). In adulthood, however, when reproductive success is at stake, dark eyes are not enough—rival males actually chase and bite one another. They also use a particularly nasty behavior called head-scraping wherein two fish approach each other head on, position themselves side-by-side, flare out their gill covers, then swim backwards rapidly. The object is to scrape the opponent's eye with a row of short sharp spines on the edge of the gill cover. In this case, darkening the bright yellow eyes might make it harder for the rival fish to orient itself properly, lessening its chance for successful attack. Interestingly, when attacking other species of fish, Gregories do not darken their eyes.

Hawaiian Gregory spawning

Naturalist Judith Garfield of San Diego writes: "I was freediving around Black Rock in Ka'anapali watching Hawaiian Gregories at a depth of about 10 ft. when I noticed a male swimming in acrobatic loops within his territory. He appeared to be carrying out spawning behavior. He rubbed his entire underside in a wiggling motion on the coral rock area. Was he fertilizing eggs? I saw no female. I moved in to see if I could see eggs or any evidence of a nest. Nothing. Furthermore, I did not hear any clicking or other sounds during his loopy swimming or as a warning for me to keep my distance. I retreated to a respectful distance and watched. I was rewarded. Shortly thereafter, a female swooped in and rubbed her underside, also in a wiggling motion, against the same area as the male. She must have been laying eggs. During this time of several seconds, the male nervously swam around, guarding his clutch and looking for interlopers. The female then dashed out of the nest and, without delay, the male fertilized the eggs as described above. Because these tiny eggs are transparent and the coral is white, I could see no evidence of an egg mass. However, because of my experience observing the nesting Garibaldi, a California damselfish, and its bright-yellow eggs, I noticed the distinctive behaviors of the two Hawaiian damselfishes immediately.

DARTFISHES and WORMFISHES
(Ptereleotridae and Microdesmidae)

Indigo Dartfish · often in pairs · Mākua, O'ahu. 40 ft. (next page)

Dartfishes and wormfishes are small slender plankton-eaters related to gobies. Typically living over mixed sand and rubble, they hover above the bottom and dive headfirst into burrows when approached. Dartfishes (family Ptereleotridae) have two dorsal fins and wormfishes (family Microdesmidae) have a single long dorsal fin. Dartfishes often hover a foot or more over the bottom and shelter in natural crevices or holes made by other animals, whereas the sinuous, almost eel-like wormfishes seldom rise more than a few inches from the bottom and inhabit burrows which they construct themselves. Two dartfishes and one wormfish occur in Hawai'i. The name "dartfish" probably derives from the 2nd dorsal and anal fins, which resemble the fins on a dart when flared.

FIRE DARTFISH
Nemateleotris magnifica
Fowler, 1938 [FIREFISH]

These beautiful little fish are pearly white, flushing pink at midbody and becoming progressively darker red toward the tail. They sport a greatly elongated first dorsal fin which they frequently flick up and down. In mature adults (seldom seen in Hawai'i), the leading edge of this fin is red. In subadults (as shown here), the fin is completely white. Preferring patches of rubble at depths of at least 50 ft., Fire Dartfish are uncommon in the Islands. Seen mostly in the summer, they appear to be more numerous in some years than in others. In warm Indo-Pacific waters they grow to about 3 in., but in Hawai'i, perhaps at the limit of their temperature range, they seldom attain that size. It may be that the species does not reproduce here. Indo-Pacific. Photo: Molokini Islet, Maui. 50 ft.

INDIGO DARTFISH
Ptereleotris heteroptera
(Bleeker, 1855)
[Spot-Tail Dartfish]

These pencil-thin fish hover a few inches to several feet over patches of sand or rubble feeding on drifting plankton. They vary from light greenish blue to bluish white and have a pearly sheen. The tail fin, which is sometimes yellowish, contains a dark streak, often faint. When approached too closely they dive headfirst into their burrows, usually under a piece of rock. Adults usually pair; juveniles swim in groups. These fish are seen most often at depths of 30 ft. or more, occasionally in as little as 20. They prefer areas with some current. To almost 5 in. Indo-Pacific. Photos: (a) Mākua, O'ahu. 50 ft. (b) Mala Wharf, Maui. 30 ft.

a) adult ▲

b) juveniles ▼

CURIOUS WORMFISH
Gunnellichthys curiosus
Dawson 1968

Light iridescent blue with an orange stripe along each side, these attractive slender fish swim just above the bottom in a sinuous manner, almost like little eels. Small ones might be mistaken for the more common Gosline's Fang Blenny (p. 23) except for the prominent black spot on the tail. Curious Wormfish typically live over mixed rubble and sand bottoms at 40 ft. or more, usually in pairs or small groups. When threatened they dive headfirst into their holes. (Blennies, by comparison, wriggle in tail first.) To about 5 in. Indo-Pacific. Photo: Mākua, O'ahu. 50 ft.

DRAGONETS and TRIPLEFINS
(Callionymidae and Tripterygiidae)

Dragonets are small bottom-dwelling fishes found most often on sand, rubble, or mud, but sometimes on hard substrate. Most are well camouflaged and some bury themselves when threatened. All have flattened triangular heads, high bulbous eyes which move independently, and little pointed snouts. Their bodies are wider than they are high. All species lack scales and have a strong spine on the gill cover. Few exceed 3 in. Dragonets typically propel themselves with short, forward "hops" using their pelvic fins. They subsist on small invertebrates, and their manner of feeding has been compared to the pecking of a bird. Some are sluggish, but most, when threatened, dart away quickly. Dragonets are typically drab and blend well with the substrate, but males of many species have an oversized dorsal fin, colorful or strikingly patterned, which they raise when they want to be visible, such as in courtship and in aggressive or defensive displays. A few dragonet species (not found in Hawai'i) are conspicuously patterned and colored; some of these, such as the paisley-patterned Mandarinfish (Synchiropus splendidus), secrete distasteful mucus which protects them from predators. Out of about 150 known Indo-Pacific dragonet species, eight are recorded from the Islands (seven of them endemic). Five shallow-water species likely to be seen near reefs are illustrated here, but only one, the Longtail Dragonet (next page), is large enough to be noticed with any frequency. The small size of the others, their excellent camouflage, and their tendency to bury in the sand, keep them hidden from all but the most observant divers and photographers. Usually, they are noticed only when they move.

Triplefins are small blenny relatives similar to dragonets in size, shape, and lifestyle. As the name implies, their dorsal fins are separated into three sections. Some call them "three-fin blennies." Triplefins scoot about on the substrate, usually on or under rocks and boulders, in rubble, or in weedy areas. Cryptically colored or partially translucent, they are seldom noticed (except in New Zealand waters, where they attain their greatest abundance, diversity, and size). Out of about 145 known triplefin species, one occurs in Hawai'i.

male

ORNAMENTED DRAGONET *Callionymus comptus* Randall, 1999
This dragonet is most easily recognized by a series of six roundish orange-brown spots on the side and a first dorsal fin with a dark posterior. In males a yellowish stripe runs the length of the side under the six orange-brown spots. This yellowish stripe is bordered by irregular small blue spots. The side of the head of males is yellowish with irregular pale blue lines. The Ornamented Dragonet lives at depths of 10 to at least 100 ft. on sand, rubble, or hard substrate partially covered with sand. The species name means "ornamented" or "adorned" To about 1 ½ in. Endemic to Hawai'i. Photo: Mākua, O'ahu. 45 ft. (male)

a, b) males ▲▼

D.R. Schrichte

LONGTAIL DRAGONET
Callionymus decoratus (Gilbert, 1905)

This large dragonet lives over sand and can sometimes be seen along protected beaches, foraging in waters a few inches deep. It also occurs to depths of over 300 ft. Tan to almost black and finely spotted to match sand and rubble, it can bury itself if alarmed or when resting. Most remarkable is its tail fin, which in males is longer than the body. Females, generally much smaller than males, have a tail only half the length of the body. Juveniles have a distinct black spot at the rear of the first dorsal fin. To almost 12 in. Endemic. Photos: (a) "Kahala Barge," O'ahu. 90 ft. (b) Hanauma Bay, O'ahu. (D.R. Schrichte) (c) Mākua, O'ahu. 45 ft.

c) female ▼

FRINGELIP DRAGONET
Draculo popognathus (Gosline, 1959)

These dragonets live in sand near the surf line along moderately exposed shores, down to about 8 ft. They remain buried up to their eyes and are almost impossible to see except for their frequent short swims over the sand, perhaps to feed on suspended food particles. They are whitish with scattered brown spots and blotches. The dorsal fin of females is mostly black, but that of males is pale. A fringe on the lower lip keeps sand out while they "breathe." To about 1 ¼ in. Endemic. Photos: Ho'okena, Hawai'i. 8 ft.

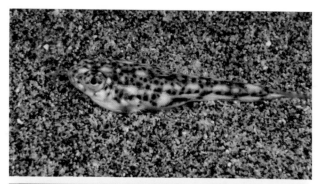

EXCLAMATION POINT DRAGONET *Synchiropus corallinus* (Gilbert, 1905)

These small dragonets are tan to reddish and finely mottled with numerous small pale spots. Four irregular dark blotches lie along the top of the back, the first beneath the first dorsal fin and the last above the base of the tail. A row of irregular dark-edged white dots runs along the lower side. Males have blue lines and spots on the face and an elongated first dorsal fin which, when erected, displays a pattern of vertical lines with dots underneath, like exclamation marks!! Females have low first dorsal fins which are usually unadorned but may be partly or entirely yellow. To about 1 ½ in. Western and Central Pacific. Photo: Mākua, O'ahu. 45 ft. (male)

a) male displaying ▲

b) female ▼

ROSY DRAGONET
Synchiropus rosulentus
Randall, 1999

This dragonet was named for a row of seven orange-pink blotches on its side, often indistinct. These blotches, if visible, may be linked along the top with an orangish line. Males have blue lines on the head which continue down to the pectoral fin, where they are interspersed with yellow. They also bear two hard-to-see black spots above the base of the pectoral fin. The elongated first dorsal fin of males, when raised, displays conspicuous vertical marks similar to those on male Exclamation Point Dragonets (previous page). Females, less colorful, have a low unadorned first dorsal fin. Look for these small fish on mixed sand and rubble, or hard substrate covered with a thin layer of sand at depths greater than 15 ft. They can be common on flat ledges along vertical walls. You probably won't see them until they move. To about 1 in. Endemic. Photos: Mākua, O'ahu. 45 ft.

a) male ▲

b) female ▼

HAWAIIAN TRIPLEFIN
Enneapterygius atriceps
(Jenkins, 1903)

Common but rarely noticed, these small fish can be found in moderately exposed areas from tide pools down to at least 75 ft, often on or under rocks. Males have a greyish body with irregular reddish markings and the lower 2/3 of the head is usually dark. Females lack both the reddish tint and the dark coloration on the lower head. To almost 1½ in. Endemic. Photos: (a) Lāna'i Lookout, O'ahu. 30 ft. (b) Hanauma Bay, O'ahu. 3 ft.

Ken Longenecker and Ross Langston studied the life history of Hawaiian Triplefins in Kāne'ohe Bay, O'ahu, finding that they prey on tiny bottom-dwelling invertebrates and live only about 100 days. Why study these seemingly insignificant fish? There are lots of them and they form an important part of the food chain. For example, they were the 2nd most abundant prey items found in the stomachs of Blue Goatfish (see pp. 143, 153)

EELS
(Muraenidae, Congridae, Ophichthidae)

Snowflake Moray · **puhi kāpā** · lacks sharp teeth · Mākua, Oʻahu. 30 ft. (p. 95)

Eels are a specialized group of fishes adapted to life in crevices, holes, and sand. Their long, snakelike bodies typically lack scales and paired fins, which would only impair movement in narrow spaces. Eels form the order Anguilliformes, which contains 15 families and many hundreds of species. Only conger eels (next page), moray eels (p. 93), and snake eels (p. 116) are likely to be encountered by divers or snorkelers in Hawaiʻi. In old Hawaiʻi all were known as **puhi**. Many secondary names are recorded but it is no longer always clear to which species they apply.

In old Hawaiʻi some eels were relished as food and considered "choicer than wives." Others were revered as **ʻaumākua**, the physical embodiment of certain family gods. Fierce warriors were sometimes compared to "sharp-toothed eels" and when trouble was brewing thoughts were said to "wiggle like an eel."

Conger Eels and Garden Eels (family Congridae)

Congers (subfamily Congrinae) are nocturnal eels, unusual in possessing small pectoral fins. Remaining hidden by day, they swim openly at night in search of sleeping fish or other prey. They have tiny teeth. Out of 12 Hawaiian species (most from deep water), three are illustrated below. Two are fairly common and the other quite rare.

Garden eels (subfamily Heterocongrinae) have an entirely different lifestyle. Active by day, they dwell in burrows and colonize sandy areas, usually where there is some current. There are a number of similar Indo-Pacific species, including one in Hawai'i.

LARGE-EYE CONGER
Ariosoma marginatum
(Vaillant & Sauvage, 1875)

These silvery eels have unusually large eyes. Active only at night, they retreat under the sand by day (although the head may remain visible) and occur from the shoreline to beyond 1,000 ft. At night they swim openly, but when approached will back tail first into the sand, leaving their heads protruding at a 45 degree angle. If further pursued they vanish entirely. Look for them in sand patches; they can be fairly numerous. The species name refers to a blackish margin on the dorsal and anal fins. To about 15 in. Endemic. Photo: Pūpūkea, O'ahu. 20 ft. (at night)

Mike Severns

BARRED CONGER
Ariosoma fasciatum (Gunther, 1871)

This rare, sand-dwelling eel is marked with spots on the head which change to irregular and incomplete bars on the back and sides. It uses its stiff tail tip to wriggle backward into the sand. If you find one, congratulate yourself—few divers have ever seen this animal. Only five museum specimens exist, one each from Madagascar, Sulawesi, Marshall Islands, French Polynesia, and Hawai'i. Formerly *Poeciloconger fasciatus*. It attains about 2 ft. Photos: Molokini Islet, Maui. 70-110 ft. (Mike Severns)

Mike Severns

daytime coloration (but rarely seen swimming by day)

nighttime hunting coloration

HAWAIIAN CONGER · **puhi ūhā** · *Conger marginatus* Valenciennes, 1850 [WHITE EEL]

   Plain brownish gray by day (except for the black margin on the dorsal and anal fins), these large eels assume a pattern of broad light and dark bands when they hunt at night, often for sleeping fish. A fold of skin along the mouth resembles a mustache. Research shows that Hawaiian Congers forage within a well-defined home range but do not necessarily hunt every night. They typically have several refuges in which they hide during the day, which they may share with other animals. Occasionally their hideaway is betrayed by a bladelike tail carelessly protruding from a hole in the reef. At some popular dive sites these eels have been tamed and will accept food from divers. For many years this eel was considered a subspecies of the Mustache Conger (*Conger cinereus*); it is now recognized as an endemic Hawaiian species. To about 5 1/2 ft. Indo-Pacific. Photos: (top 2) Hanauma Bay, Oʻahu. 8,15 ft. (bottom) Pūpūkea, Oʻahu, Oʻahu. 20 ft. (at night)

HAWAIIAN GARDEN EEL *Gorgasia hawaiiensis* Randall & Chess, 1979

These strange eels live by the thousands along sandy bottoms, usually at about 60 ft. or more, stretching up out of their holes and facing into the current to feed on drifting plankton. When approached, they withdraw gradually into the sand. Cautious, slow-moving divers, however, can enter a garden of waving eels along a mysterious slope which beckons temptingly down into the blue abyss. Watch your time and your depth while visiting the garden eels! Look for them at the "'Ewa Pinnacles" and the "Corsair" off O'ahu, at Molokini Islet, Maui, and almost anywhere along the Kona Coast of the Big Island, where in some areas they occur as shallow as 35 ft. The species attains about 2 ft. and is endemic to the Islands. Photos: (above) "Corsair" wreck. Moanalua Bay, O'ahu. 110 ft. (below) Molokini Islet, Maui. 80 ft. (David B. Fleetham)

David B. Fleetham

Garden eels in depth

A colony of Hawaiian Garden Eels studied down to the 130-ft. level at Puakō, Hawai'i, covered about 13,000 square meters and averaged 2.3 eels per square meter—a total of about 29,900 eels! But that's only the beginning—the colony continued downslope to an undetermined depth. The eels at 130 ft. seemed largest and their burrows were farthest apart. Stomach analysis showed that this colony fed mostly on copepods. To capture an eel for study, a noose at the end of a fishing rod was placed over a burrow entrance. When the eel emerged it was "looped" and pulled out. Great care had to be taken not to let the eel's tail touch the sand again. If it hit sand, the eel would dig back down with amazing speed and escape. Little is known of the social organization of these fish, but at Puakō during September 1985 many of the burrows at 80 ft. were distinctly paired and about 6 in. apart. Two burrow pairs were investigated. Eels from one were male and female, from the other both male. Burrows were easy to locate because they were edged with dark brown sand containing high numbers of diatoms.

In a similar Red Sea species, *Gorgasia sillneri*, large dominant males live in the center of the colony while smaller individuals are relegated to the edges. These Red Sea garden eels are preyed upon by snake eels, lizardfishes, and razor wrasses. During the reproductive season, male-female pairs move their burrows within an inch or two of each other. When ready to spawn they entwine their bodies with their urogenital pores close together, and remain exposed in this position for up to 9 ½ hours!

Yellowmargin Morays · **puhi paka** · named for the yellow-green margin on the tip of the tail · "'Ewa Pinnacles," O'ahu. 50 ft. (p. 103)

Moray Eels (family Muraenidae)

Great favorites of divers, morays are among the most easily observed members of the reef community. They peer from their holes watching the underwater world go by, while their thick muscular bodies remain securely hidden. Morays often hold their mouths open, displaying needle-sharp teeth. Their necks may swell and pulse rhythmically. To humans this appears menacing, but the eels are only pumping water over their gills—their way of breathing. Morays have no scales or paired fins, which would only impede them in tight spaces. Like most fishes, they have two pairs of nostrils, but the nostrils of the first pair are set in tubes at the tip of the snout. Sometimes those of the second pair are in tubes as well, above or behind the eyes.

Although many morays can be seen by day, most feed primarily at night. All are predators of fish and/or invertebrate animals, usually crustaceans. In the early morning or late afternoon some species may emerge to hunt, undulating across the sand or twisting and turning among the rocks and coral. A few will also enter tide pools or slither across wet rocks. But for every moray seen, many more remain hidden; the majority of species probably spend the greater part of their lives within the recesses of the reef. Morays are usually dull in color, marked with blotches and speckles. Some, however, such as the Snowflake, Dragon, and Zebra Morays, have attractive patterns.

Morays are perhaps best known for their wicked teeth and supposedly nasty dispositions. In the wild, however, most morays pose little threat. Although alarming eel stories are common in older books, recent investigators agree that almost all documented attacks occurred after an eel was hooked, speared, molested, or fed. It is foolish, however, to stick one's hands into crevices and holes that may contain eels. It is also risky to swim close to large eels if you are carrying speared fish, or if you smell of fish. In such circumstances these animals may strike. Even small morays can inflict considerable damage to tendons and nerves; their backward-pointing teeth make extraction of a hand or finger difficult. If you are bitten, don't jerk your hand back in alarm but wait for the eel to let go by itself—admittedly easier said than done!

Dangerous or not, moray eels accustomed to divers may grow tame enough to be stroked and handled. It is best, however, to leave them alone. Feeding eels is a bad idea because eels accustomed to being fed will sometimes bite divers who have no food to offer.

Not all morays have sharp teeth; some—the Snowflake and Zebra Morays, for example—possess grinding plates or blunt pebblelike teeth which they use to crush the shells of invertebrates. They can do the same to a human finger. Large morays can contain lethal doses of ciguatera toxin, making them dangerous to eat. This poison, which often accumulates in predators of algae-eating reef fish, causes abdominal pain, nausea, vomiting, and strange neurological symptoms such as reversal of hot and cold.

Morays appear to be more numerous in Hawaiʻi than in many other Indo-Pacific locations, possibly due to the lack of native shallow-water groupers and snappers which might compete with them. About 200 species of morays are known worldwide. They fall into two subfamilies, the morays proper (Muraeninae), which have a dorsal fin running most of the length of the body, and the snake morays (Uropterygiinae), which have practically no dorsal fin. Morays have a long-lasting larval stage and are therefore well represented in Hawaiʻi with 42 species—more than any other fish family except the wrasses. Eighteen species of morays likely to be seen by divers and snorkelers are described below, including one endemic. (Three other endemic morays are known, but they are deep-dwelling, rare, or confined largely to the cooler waters of the northwestern chain.)

Morays bite twice ...

Most predator fishes ingest their prey by rapidly opening their mouth—water rushes in, carrying the prey with it. Moray eels, however, just aren't built for this. To ingest their prey quickly, they use a second set of movable jaws hidden deep in their throats. A moray first seizes and grips a prey animal with the sharp teeth of its main jaws, often taking a few moments to rotate and position it just so. Then it launches a pair of inner "pharyngeal" jaws forward into its mouth from within its throat. These snag the prey with curved, backward-pointing teeth and drag it down the gullet. In this manner an eel's hapless victim is bitten twice and swallowed before it knows what happened.

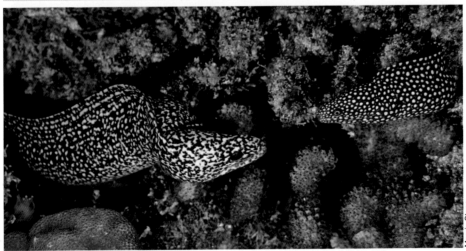

Stout Moray (left, p. 102) and Whitemouth Moray (right, p. 106). Kahe Point, Oʻahu. 10 ft.
Two of Hawaiʻi's most common morays, they can be similar in appearance.

SNOWFLAKE MORAY · **puhi kāpā**
Echidna nebulosa (Ahl, 1789)

These attractive eels have a pale snout and whitish body marked with black speckles and several indistinct rows of irregular dark blotches. In juveniles (often seen in tide pools) the blotches are solid; in adults they contain white or yellowish centers, producing a sort of tie-dyed effect. Snowflake Morays often forage in the open by day and are easy to spot. A small jack or goatfish may follow. They also hunt at night. These eels have pebble-like plates instead of sharp teeth; feeding primarily on invertebrates (especially crabs), they use their blunt dentition to crush the shells of their prey. The author once saw one eat a large, noxious fireworm. This is one of comparatively few morays known to start life female, changing later to male. The species name means "misty" or "cloudy." To almost 30 in. Indo-Pacific and Eastern Pacific. Photo: Mākua, O'ahu. 30 ft. (see also next page and p. 89)

Old Hawaiian records are puzzling: some early physical descriptions of **puhi kāpā** *match the Snowflake Moray, but emphasize that it was an aggressive fighter eel that would even venture onto land to attack. (In fact, the great warrior, King Kamehameha I, was nicknamed* **puhi kāpā**.) *However, the Snowflake is docile, at least toward humans. Likely, some early chronicler confused* **kāpā** *with* **kāpa'a**. **Puhi kāpa'a** *was the Hawaiian name of the Peppered Moray (p. 110), a large, bold, shoreline eel which will actually slither out of the water to capture crabs on the rocks.*

Love, or war?

Within the moray family males and females are usually separate, although some species change sex or are hermaphroditic. Observations of courtship and spawning are rare and usually incomplete, the divers either arriving late on the scene or disrupting the proceedings. By piecing together various partial accounts it would seem that, in at least some species, a pair of eels leave their holes and approach each other, raise the fronts of their bodies, open their mouths in a wide gape, flare their dorsal fins, and then entwine. Still wrapped around each other, they may either fall back to the bottom or hover vertically over the reef for a time before pressing their abdomens together, releasing their gametes and separating. Other morays, however, apparently spawn in groups, sometimes at the surface.

In July, 2005 Matthew Parry and his wife witnessed two Snowflake Morays doing something like this off Pūpūkea, Oʻahu. The eels might have been mating, but more likely they were fighting over a mate, or over territory. Matthew writes: "Swimming at about 30-35 feet we noticed something strange about 30 feet ahead. We swam closer and the object resolved into two E. nebulosa biting each other and twisting around about 10 feet up off of the bottom. The two eels would wind around each other mirroring the other's movements but keeping a space of about an inch or two between them and opening their mouths at one another (not typical moray breathing but the jaws spread and held wide open). Intermittently one or the other would bite and hold on and the eels would thrash quite violently. I noticed fairly large chunks or rips in their bodies, which can be seen on most of the photographs as white cuts. The eels would swim back down to the bottom and continue to attack each other. When one eel got a solid hold on the other both would pull into a knot and pull their heads through the back end of the knot as leverage. I can't be certain but one eel seemed to be more aggressive. The eels continued to face off and bite each other a foot or two off of the bottom (at this point I can't be sure that our presence wasn't bothering them in some way). We watched this occurrence for six or seven minutes without any decrease in the intensity of the eels' interaction. The eels were very violent with lots of thrashing and tearing and bits of eel being torn loose. In some of the pictures you can actually see other fishes circling around that were feeding on scraps of eel that had gotten ripped loose. We did not see any release of eggs nor sperm. Both eels were about the same size and when one would break away from the fight it didn't withdraw very far, not more than a foot or so. Being fairly low on air and still far from our exit point we left them to their devices." Photos: Matthew Parry

a) small adult ▲

b) c) mature adults ▼ ▼

BARRED MORAY · puhi leihala
Echidna polyzona
(Richardson, 1844)

When small, this secretive moray is light brown marked with conspicuous dark bars. One bar goes through the eye and terminates on the lower jaw as an elongate spot; another runs from the top of the head down over the corner of the mouth. As the eel grows, the bars become less distinct and the spaces between them tend to fill with spots and streaks. The elongate spot on the lower jaw and the dark mark at the corner of the mouth, however, generally remain visible. Large adults are almost uniformly mottled brown with remnant bars near the tail tip. Like others in the genus *Echidna*, this moray has blunt conical teeth and feeds primarily on crustaceans, mostly at night. Along calm shorelines small individuals sometimes forage in only inches of water. The Hawaiian name means **lei** of **hala** *(Pandanus)* fruits, seemingly in reference to the color of younger eels. To about 24 in. Indo-Pacific. Photos: (a) Pai'olu'olu Point, O'ahu. 15 ft. (b) Hanauma Bay, O'ahu. (D.R.Schrichte) (c) Molokini Islet, Maui. (Mike Severns).

D.R. Schrichte

Mike Severns

97

a) small adult

b) large adult

Keoki Stender

c) juvenile

(d)

DRAGON MORAY · puhi kauila
Enchelycore pardalis (Schlegel, 1847)

Remarkable for its appearance, the Dragon Moray has long nasal tubes over its eyes, like horns. Its jaws, full of needle-sharp teeth, are so curved they cannot close completely. Vivid spots and streaks complete the picture of this unusual, secretive creature. It feeds primarily on fish and emerges most frequently at night. Unfortunately it becomes brownish after dark, and less colorful. In Hawai'i the species is most common in the northwestern chain. In the main group it is rare, or at least rarely seen. Alternate Hawaiian names are **puhi 'o'a** and **puhi ao.** The species name means "leopard." To about 3 ft. Indo-Pacific. Photos: (a) Lāna`i Lookout, O'ahu. 70 ft. (b) Midway Atoll, 80 ft. (Keoki Stender) (c) Pūpūkea, O'ahu. 15 ft. (d) Waikīkī Aquarium.

Scott Michael writes, "The threat display of the Dragon Moray is spectacular. It will open its jaws as wide as possible, laterally flatten the gill region, cock its head to one side, and erect its dorsal fin. I have seen other morays nearly as long as the Dragon flee when threatened by this menacing-looking beast."

a) nighttime coloration ▲

b) daytime coloration ▲

VIPER MORAY · **puhi kauila** · *Enchelynassa canina* (Quoy and Gaimard, 1824)

These evil-looking eels are reddish brown during the day and gray at night. Their hooked jaws (containing some of the longest, sharpest teeth in the moray family) meet only at the tips, giving the appearance of a perpetual snarl. Like many morays, they sometimes occur in pairs. Viper Morays are seldom encountered by divers and snorkelers, which is perhaps just as well: attaining at least 5 ft., they are one of the largest and potentially most dangerous of Hawai'i's eels. They feed on fish and octopus. The species name means "dog-like," in reference to the sharp teeth. Western Pacific to Eastern Pacific. Photos: (a) "Manta Ray Bay," Kona Coast, Hawai'i. (at night) 50 ft. (b) Pai'olu'olu Point, O'ahu. 30 ft.

ZEBRA MORAY · **puhi**
Gymnomuraena zebra (Shaw, 1797)

Chocolate brown encircled by over 100 yellow-white stripes, Zebra Morays sometimes forage in the open by day and are easy to spot. They have blunt, pebblelike teeth and feed chiefly on crabs, which they crush and swallow whole; if unable to crush the carapace of a large crab they will eat just the legs and claws. Although lacking sharp teeth, they are not harmless; a Honolulu aquarist bitten on the finger describes the experience as "painful, like a vice." The sole species in the genus, it is one of comparatively few morays known to change sex, female first, male later. To 5 ft., but usually smaller. Indo-Pacific and Eastern Pacific. Photos: (top & middle) Kahe Point, O'ahu. 20-30 ft. (bottom) Pūpūkea, O'ahu. 50 ft.

WHITEMARGIN MORAY · puhi
Gymnothorax albimarginatus
(Temminck & Schlegel, 1846)

This eel is usually tan to almost white with 4-5 indistinct pale spots surrounding pores along the lower and upper jaws. The name comes from narrow white margins on the dorsal and anal fins (not present at the beginning of the dorsal). The Whitemargin Moray is most common in the Northwestern Hawaiian Islands. In the main islands it is rare. A researcher, bitten by one at Midway Atoll, experienced unusual pain that traveled up her arm, suggesting that this eel could be venomous. To about 3 ½ ft. Western Pacific. Photos: (above) Magic Island, O'ahu. 20 ft. (right), Midway Atoll. (Keoki Stender)

SLENDERTAIL MORAY · puhi
Gymnothorax gracilicaudus
Jenkins, 1903

This small, pencil-thin moray emerges only at night. The gray-brown back is marked with irregular dark bars. A touch of lavender graces the gill opening. The underside is white. It attains about 12 in. and is one of the comparatively few morays known to change sex, female first, male later. Western and Central Pacific. Photo: Mākaha Caverns, O'ahu. 25 ft. (at night). Similar Hawaiian species include the Lipspot Moray (*G. chilospilus*), and Kidako's Moray (*G. kidako*), both very rare in the main islands.

a) ▲

b) ▲

c) ▲

d) ▼

STOUT MORAY · **puhi**
Gymnothorax eurostus (Abbott, 1860)

This relatively short stocky moray is highly variable in color, ranging from almost solid brown, through brown covered with irregular light spots and marks, to white with a few dark spots and marks. It sometimes resembles the Whitemouth Moray (pp. 94, 106), but it lacks the bright white inner mouth. It feeds primarily on fish, crustaceans, and cephalopods, generally at night, but has been observed striking opportunistically at small fish that swim close to its hole by day. Although this is the most abundant shallow-water moray in Hawai'i, it is inconspicuous due to its relatively small size and retiring nature. The species name means "stout" or "strong." To almost 2 ft. Indo-Pacific, but only in cool subtropical waters. Photos: (a) Yokohama Beach, O'ahu 25 ft. (b) Magic Island, O'ahu. 20 ft. (c) South Point, Hawai'i. 30 ft. (d) Mākaha, O'ahu. 40 ft. (e) Mākua, O'ahu. 30 ft. (see also p. 94)

e) ▼

YELLOWMARGIN MORAY · puhi paka
Gymnothorax flavimarginatus
(Rüppell, 1830)

These big eels are typically light yellowish brown, finely mottled with darker brown; some are very dark. There is always a dark blotch over the gill opening. The tip of the tail is narrowly edged in yellow or, more commonly, green, hence the name. Yellowmargins occupy large deep holes in the reef, sometimes with cleaner shrimps and Bicolor Anthias (p. 161). They have been known to follow divers carrying food or speared fish. They will attack prey, such as an octopus, in broad daylight, with wrasses hovering nearby to get any stray bits (see next page). The name **puhi paka** means "fierce eel" and Hawaiians of old were very careful where this eel was concerned—a large one thrashing about in a fishing canoe undoubtedly commanded respect. Despite this, these eels often seem docile, sometimes accepting food and even stroking from divers. It is best, however, to leave them alone. To 4 ft. Indo-Pacific and Eastern Pacific. Photo: (top) Honolua Bay, Maui. 30 ft. (opposite) Mākua, Oʻahu. 100 ft. (see also pp. 93, 104)

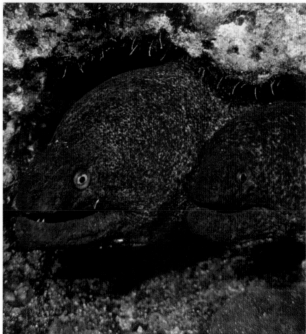

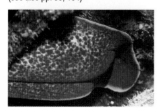

In September 2000, dive guide Kiwini Hall and his customers watched large Yellowmargin Moray attempting to eat an 18-inch baby Whitetip Reef Shark that had been resting on the bottom at Molokini Islet, Maui. Starting from the head, the eel swallowed all of the shark except for the tail. It tried for about 10 minutes to get the rest in, then gave up and regurgitated its victim. The shark lay on its back for a few minutes, seemingly stunned, then righted itself and swam away!

Yellowmargin gallery

Yellowmargin Moray threat display

An octopus meets its end in a flurry of ink and tentacles

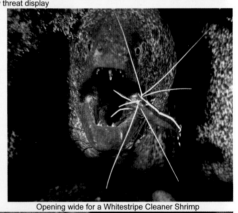

Opening wide for a Whitestripe Cleaner Shrimp

With cleaner shrimp *Urocaridella* sp.

a) large adult

b) smaller adult   Victoria Martocci

GIANT MORAY · puhi · *Gymnothorax javanicus* (Bleeker, 1859)

Attaining 8 ft. with a weight of over 80 lbs., this is the largest of all morays. (Unconfirmed reports exist of 10-foot specimens weighing an estimated 150 lbs.!) The head is brown speckled with dark spots which become larger, more irregular, and farther apart toward the rear of the body, especially on younger individuals. There is a large dark mark at the gill opening. This is a bold eel which eats mostly fish. The large adult in the photo above attacked the hand of a diver who swam by its hole. Two hours of surgery were required to repair the damage. (The diver had previously been spearing and handling fish.) At Johnston Atoll, University of Hawai'i researcher Richard Brock saw a 4½ foot *javanicus* attack and drive off a 5-foot Gray Reef Shark, inflicting a 4-inch wound on its side. (The shark had approached bait set out for the eel.) The Giant Moray is opportunistic, and will consume almost anything on occasion. Bird feathers, an orange, and pieces of metal were among the items Brock found in the stomachs of these eels. Most hunting occurs in the late afternoon or evening, but daytime strikes also occur. As apex predators, Giant Morays accumulate large quantities of ciguatera toxin, making them one of the most virulently poisonous fishes to eat. Out of 48 fish species fed to mongooses in an experiment at Enewetak Atoll, *javanicus* flesh consistently caused the most severe reactions. Indo-Pacific and Eastern Pacific. Common at Johnston Atoll, but rare in Hawai'i. Photos: (a) Nuku Hiva, Marquesas. 30 ft. (b) "First Cathedral," Lāna'i. 50 ft. (Victoria Martocci)

DWARF MORAY · puhi
Gymnothorax melatremus
Schultz, 1953 [PENCIL MORAY]

Fully grown, this tiny moray attains no more than 12 in. It is yellow to yellowish brown with a dark gill opening. The sometimes bluish eyes contain a distinctive dark vertical bar. Although fairly common in Hawai'i, it is secretive and seen infrequently. In his tireless examination of even the least significant fishes, Dr. John E. Randall of Honolulu's Bishop Museum has found that specimens from Hawai'i consistently have more vertebrae than specimens from other locations. The Dwarf Moray ranges throughout the Indo-Pacific, and as far east as Easter Island. Photo: Pūpūkea, O'ahu. 60 ft.

typical dark coloration

WHITEMOUTH MORAY · puhi ʻōniʻo · *Gymnothorax meleagris* (Shaw & Nodder, 1795)

This is one of the most commonly seen morays in Hawaiʻi. Its inner mouth is entirely bright white, thus the name, and the stocky head and body are light or dark brown covered with white dots. Unusual specimens may be light with dark reticulations or completely dark brown, but regardless of body color, the tail is always tipped with white. This eel often holds its mouth wide open, perhaps in a threat display or to attract prey, making for easy identification. Feeding on fish and crustaceans, it forages in the open during the day, often in the early morning, poking its snout briefly into crevices and holes or disappearing entirely into the reef only to emerge in a few seconds somewhere else. Other predators may accompany it (see next page). When the eel enters a cavity at the base of a coral head, the other fish sometimes cover the exits to catch any escaping prey. All parties seem to benefit from this (see p. 158). The species name means "guineafowl" or "spotted." The Hawaiian name means "spotted." To almost 4 ft. Indo-Pacific. Photos: (above) Hanauma Bay, Oʻahu. 30 ft. (below left) Kīhei, Maui (William Stohler). (below right) Pūpūkea, Oʻahu. 30 ft.

rare color variant

typical light coloration

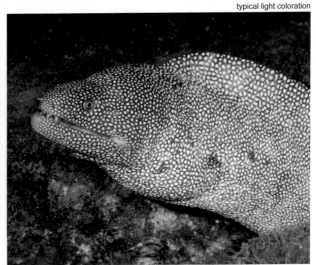

William Stohler

Unlike most Hawaiian morays, the Whitemouth hunts by day. Other predators often accompany it, typically jacks, goatfishes, and groupers attracted by the chance of nabbing prey animals flushed by the eel. The phenomenon is called "associative hunting" or "cooperative hunting." Photos: Pai'olu'olu Point, O'ahu. 50 ft. (see also p. 158)

Whitemouth Morays will sometimes stand upright, mouth agape, with only the lower portion of the body anchored in the reef. They will retreat somewhat at the approach of a diver, but resume their vertical stance when the diver withdraws. Could they be advertising for a mate? Or a hunting partner? Or are they just making a territorial statement? Another reef mystery. Photo: Kahe Point, O'ahu. 40 ft.

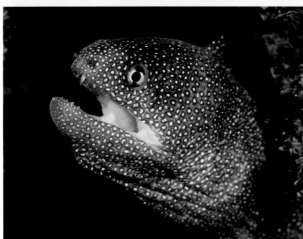

YELLOWMOUTH MORAY · puhi
Gymnothorax nudivomer
(Gunther, 1866)

Once they open their mouths these eels are unmistakable—the interior is bright yellow. (The color might be a warning to potential predators that their skin secretes toxic mucus, see below.) Their brown bodies are covered with dark-edged white spots which become larger and more conspicuous toward the tail. In Hawai'i these eels prefer depths of over 100 ft. and are seldom seen. The species name is from *nudi* ("bare") and *vomer* (a bone on the roof of the mouth). To 3 ft. Indo-Pacific. Photos: (above) "Airplane," Pokai Bay, O'ahu. 100 ft. (bottom) Mākua, O'ahu. 90 ft.

Dr. John Randall of the Bishop Museum discovered this eel's poisonous mucus while handling a specimen from the Waikīkī Aquarium. His hands, which had a number of coral cuts, began tingling. Tasting the mucus, he found it without flavor and odorless. A sample given to the University of Hawai'i made freshly isolated frog muscle turn milky white and caused disintegration of the cell membranes. It was later determined, however, that the poison is quite slow to act. For that reason, and because it does not taste obviously bad, the mucus might have little deterrent effect against predators. (For that matter, though, how many enemies would a big eel like this have?) Perhaps the toxic mucus acts chiefly to deter parasites, but in that case, why the bright yellow mouth? The resemblance of this eel to the Whitemouth Moray, which is not known to be toxic, could be relevant. Perhaps both use the bright mouth to attract potential prey.

a) typical medium size adult ▲

YELLOWHEAD MORAY · **puhi ʻou; puhi ʻapo** · *Gymnothorax rueppellii* (McClelland, 1844)

This eel is seen most often hunting in the open at night, although it is sometimes active by day. Its gray-brown body is encircled with broad bands of lighter gray, but very large individuals, such as the one pictured below, are solid brown without bands. In all specimens the top of the head is yellow. (The more common Undulated Moray, p. 112, sometimes has a yellowish head, but never has bands on the body.) The scientific name honors German naturalist and explorer Eduard Rüppell (1794-1884).The Hawaiian name **puhi ʻapo** (the modifier means to "catch" or "grasp") was coined in 1978 by Mary Kawena Pukui (1895-1986). "Aunty" Kawena was for many years the foremost authority on Hawaiian culture. Her *Hawaiian Dictionary*, compiled with Samuel H. Elbert, made possible the successful revival of the Hawaiian language. To almost 3 ft. Indo-Pacific. Photos: (a) Kahe Point, Oʻahu. 40 ft. (b) Pūpūkea, Oʻahu. 50 ft.

b) large old adult ▼

PEPPERED MORAY · **puhi kāpaʻa** · *Gymnothorax pictus* (Ahl, 1789)

This moray usually inhabits waters less than 30 ft. deep in a variety of habitats including large tide pools, brackish anchialine ponds, harbors, and turbulent rocky shores. It is a bold, active eel which feeds mostly on crabs and will occasionally launch itself up on the rocks, clear of the sea, to catch them. (Careful observations reveal that it usually misses.) Most specimens are whitish, densely speckled with small black spots and marks. Some, principally from the east side of the Big Island, are brown or almost black, and were for many years considered a separate species under the name *G. hilonis*. To about 3 ½ ft. Indo-Pacific and offshore islands in the Eastern Pacific. Photos: (above) Lānaʻi Lookout, Oʻahu. 15 ft. (below) Pohoiki, Hawaiʻi. 10 ft.

According to chroniclers of Hawaiian lore, the great warrior-king Kamehameha the First, who unified the Hawaiian Islands, was nicknamed **puhi kāpā** after a fierce fighter-eel of the same name. This savage eel, it was said, would attack readily and could actually leave the water in pursuit of prey. But according to Pukui & Elbert's authoritative Hawaiian Dictionary, **puhi kāpā** refers to the small, inoffensive Snowflake Moray (p. 95), which even lacks sharp teeth! It seems likely that some writer or chronicler long ago confused "**puhi kāpā**" with "**puhi kāpaʻa**." The latter is the Hawaiian name for the Peppered Moray, which is especially common on the Big Island where Kamehameha was born and raised.

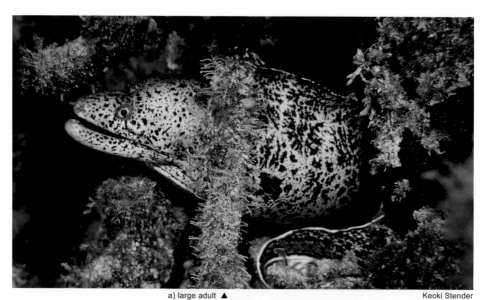

a) large adult ▲   Keoki Stender

STEINDACHNER'S MORAY · **puhi**
Gymnothorax steindachneri
(Jordan & Evermann, 1903)

Most abundant in the northwestern chain, this endemic moray is rare in the main Hawaiian islands, where it is known to date only as far south as O'ahu. Its light brown body is covered with irregular dark markings and spots. Dark lines along the throat, dark marks along the mouth (often near its corner), a large dark spot over the gill opening, and a narrow white margin on the dorsal and anal fins are identifying features. The species name honors 19th century Austrian ichthyologist Franz Steindachner (1834-1919), who traveled the world collecting, describing, and naming fishes. To at least 2 ft. Endemic. Photos: (a) Midway Atoll. 40 ft. (Keoki Stender) (b) Palea Point, O'ahu. 85 ft. (c) "Haleiwa Trench," O'ahu. 3 ft.

b) c) small adults ▲ ▼

a) dark coloration

UNDULATED MORAY · **puhi lau milo**
Gymnothorax undulatus
(Lacepède, 1803)

This moray has narrow jaws full of long sharp teeth, including a row down the center of the mouth. The body varies from dark brown with light speckles and irregular vertical lines or netlike markings to the reverse—almost white with irregular brown blotches. (The light coloration is seen most often at night.) The top of its head frequently has a greenish yellow tinge. It occurs from scuba-diving depths to shoreline waters only a few inches deep. Although most active at night, it will also feed by day. One of the commonest Indo-Pacific morays, it is also one of the nastiest; do not attempt to play with it or feed it. In old Hawai'i it was particularly relished as food. The Hawaiian name means "leaf of the **milo** tree." To 3 ½ ft. Indo-Pacific and Eastern Pacific. Photos: (a) Kawaihoa (Portlock) Point, O'ahu. 30 ft. (b) Mākua, O'ahu (at night).

b) light coloration (seen mostly at night)

Kepuhi, O'ahu. 30 ft.

Mahi wreck, O'ahu. 80 ft.

Pūpūkea, O'ahu. 45 ft.

Young specimen moving in the open by day. Hanauma Bay, O'ahu. 3 ft.

113

Fit to be tied

A moray eel generally swallows its prey whole. If it catches a fish or crab too large to ingest, it will try shaking it or suddenly rotating its body to break off a piece. If that doesn't work, or if resistance is too great, it often has a final trick—it loops itself into a knot to constrict its victim and gain additional purchase. Using its tail, the eel forms a sort of double loop that travels forward the length of its body. Passing over the eel's head, the coil tightens around the prey, enabling the eel to pull back and tear off a mouthful of flesh. This behavior has been documented in morays of the genera Echidna and Gymnothorax. Here an Undulated Moray eats a Yellow Tang. Morays fighting with each other will also knot themselves to gain purchase (see p. 96). Photos: Kona, Hawai'i (Kendra Ignacio)

photos: Kendra Ignacio

Fish in your face

It's puzzling, but small fishes do not always seem to be afraid of morays. Butterflyfishes, surgeonfishes, damselfishes, and perhaps others will sometimes back up to an intruding moray and flutter a tail fin literally in its face, or turn broadside to it, completely blocking its view. Here, a Bluestripe Butterflyfish displays laterally in front of a small Stout Moray (p.102.) In a related tactic, schooling surgeonfishes and damselfishes will "mob" a moray that has caught one of their number, much as small birds mob a marauding hawk. Instead of scattering, as one might expect, the fish "dive bomb" the eel and harrass it unmercifully. In Hawai'i, Convict Tangs have been seen to do this.

TIGER SNAKE MORAY · puhi
Scuticaria tigrina (Lesson, 1828)

Secretive and nocturnal, this eel has a light gray or brown body covered with round dark spots of varying sizes. Despite its name it has no stripes. (In the 19th century when it was named, any large cat, including a leopard, was called a tiger.) The name, however, is apt for another reason: the Tiger Snake Moray is a voracious predator of other eels, which it catches and swallows whole (see below). Snake morays (subfamily Uropterygiinae) are characterized by short dorsal and anal fins confined to the tip of the tail. Out of 12 snake morays in Hawai'i, the Tiger is the only species seen with any regularity. The less common Large-Spotted Snake Moray (bottom of page) is almost identical in appearance. To 3 ft. or more. Indo-Pacific and Eastern Pacific. Photo: Pai'olu'olu Point, O'ahu. 80 ft.

A Tiger Snake Moray attacks a Slendertail Moray (p. 101), which it will swallow whole   Kendra Ignacio

LARGE-SPOTTED SNAKE MORAY
Uropterygius polyspilus
(Regan, 1909)

This seldom-seen eel has large, dark brown spots on a tan body, and closely resembles the Tiger Snake Moray (above). However, its bulb-like posterior nostrils (above the eyes) are much larger than those of the Tiger Snake Moray, and its snout is shorter. For those into the fine details, the anus is located about two thirds of the distance from snout to tail tip, instead of about half way in the Tiger. This eel is encountered both during the day and at night; little else is known about it. To about 28 in. Indo-Pacific. Photo: Kailua-Kona Harbor, Hawai'i. 30 ft. (at night).

Magnificent Snake Eel · Hawaiian endemic · Portlock Point, O'ahu. 25 ft. (p. 117)

Snake Eels (family Ophichthidae)

Slender and snakelike, snake eels have a pointed tail, a long low dorsal fin running the length of the body, and sometimes a small pair of pectoral fins. (True sea snakes, extremely rare in Hawai'i, have a paddle-like tail, and no fins at all. See p. 365.) The tails of snake eels are often stiff at the tip, enabling them to wriggle backwards into the sand. There are many snake eel species worldwide with about 17 known from Hawai'i. Six are endemic. More secretive in general than moray eels, most Hawaiian snake eels are never seen by divers or snorkelers. Six are shown here. The family name derives from *ophis*, the Greek word for snake.

HENSHAW'S SNAKE EEL *Brachysomophis henshawi* (Jordan & Snyder, 1904)

This ugly customer remains buried in the sand near the edge of the reef with only the top of its pinkish tan to red head showing. With opaque-looking eyes set near the tip of its snout, it lies in wait for fishes or crustaceans to pass within striking range. After catching its prey, the monster drags it under the sand to consume it. Powerful jaws, a muscular body and fast reflexes make it a formidable predator. (In the Red Sea, the similar Stargazer Snake Eel, *B. cirrocheilos,* preys on garden eels, possibly by "swimming" under the sand and seizing them from below. Perhaps Henshaw's Eel does the same—garden eels often occur in its habitat.) Henshaw's Snake Eel is most reliably seen at night. By day it usually exposes only the tip of its snout. At least one diver in Hawai'i has been seriously bitten by an unseen eel, likely this species, while lying on the sand taking a picture. Although once considered endemic to Hawai'i, where the first scientific specimen was obtained, Henshaw's Eel is widespread in the Indo-Pacific. It was confused for some years with the similar Crocodile Snake Eel *(B. crocodilinus)* which does not occur in Hawai'i. The name honors Henry W. Henshaw (1850-1930), biologist, anthropologist,and landscape photographer, who lived in Hilo in the early 1900s. To about 3 ½ ft. Photo: Molokini Islet, Maui. 80 ft. (at night)

FRECKLED SNAKE EEL
Callechelys lutea Snyder, 1904
[YELLOWSPOTTED SNAKE EEL]

These odd snake eels are seen in loose sand, their heads protruding several inches above the bottom. Yellowish white with small black spots, they blend in well and are easy to overlook. Their constant, almost frenzied gulping creates continual puffs of sand next to their gill openings. Although their long slender bodies remain buried by day, these eels have been captured swimming at the surface at night, attracted by lights. The species name means "yellow." Believed to attain at least 5 ft. Endemic. (This eel's Indo-Pacific sister species, *C. marmorata,* has recently been discovered to also occur in Hawai'i. It has many dark spots on the belly, where as *lutea* has few or none.) Photo: Kahe Point, O'ahu. 30 ft.

When a disturbed Freckled Snake Eel withdraws, it "swims" backwards under the sand in sinusoidal curves, its progress easily followed by watching the surface sand cave in behind it as it moves. The sinusoidal tracks thus created, along with dimples made where the eel surfaced, remain visible for hours or days as long as the sand is not disturbed by surge.

SADDLED SNAKE EEL
Leiuranus semicinctus
(Lay & Bennett, 1839)

Broad black saddles on a white body distinguish this eel from all others in Hawai'i. It generally inhabits reef flats where it feeds on small fishes and crustaceans, but is rarely seen. If threatened, it burrows back rapidly into the sand with its stiff tail tip. It is sometimes mistaken for the Banded Sea Snake *(Laticauda colubrina),* which does not occur in Hawai'i. Indo-Pacific. To about 2 ft. Photo: Koloa Landing, Kaua'i. 20 ft. (Kent Backman)

Kent Backman

MAGNIFICENT SNAKE EEL
puhi lā'au
Myrichthys magnificus (Abbot, 1861)

White with large round or oval dark spots, these eels sometimes emerge in the late afternoon or evening to nose about the bottom, probing into holes along the reef for crustaceans, small fishes, or carrion. Occasionally several hunt together. Even so, they are infrequently seen. The species name, *magnificus,* means "magnificent," or "splendid." The Hawaiian name means "stick," "pole" or "male erection." Endemic to Hawai'i (with a sister species, *M. maculosus,* elsewhere in the Indo-Pacific). To about 2 ½ ft. Photo: South Point, Hawai'i. 25 ft. (see also previous page)

FOWLER'S SNAKE EEL *Ophichthus fowleri* (Jordan & Evermann, 1903)

Few divers have seen this rare animal, which, like many snake eels, usually remains buried by day with only its head showing. It is light brown with many round spots and about 16 diffuse saddles on the back. The dorsal fin is high and there are small, well-developed pectoral fins. In the past it has been confused with three similar Indo-Pacific snake eels, *Ophichthus erabo* and *O. bonaparti,* (neither of which occurs in Hawai'i) and *O. polyophthalmus* (below). The name honors American ichthyologist Henry W. Fowler (1879-1965). This eel attains about 40 inches and is known only from the Hawaiian chain. Photo: Mākena, Maui. 80 ft. (Mike Severns)

LARGE-SPOTTED SNAKE EEL
Ophichthus polyophthalmus
(Bleeker, 1853)
[MANY-EYED SNAKE EEL]

This handsome and very rarely seen snake eel is brownish to cream and covered with many dark-edged gold spots which get larger and farther apart toward the rear of the body. It is reported to inhabit rubble or gravel near reefs but has also been seen and photographed partially buried in loose sand some distance from any hard substrate. Like most snake eels, it is most likely to be seen at night, but it sometimes emerges on dark cloudy days. The species name means "many eyes" in reference to the spotted pattern. To about 13 in. Indo-Pacific. Photo: Mākena, Maui. 110 ft. (Mike Severns)

PENCIL SNAKE EEL
Apterichtus klazingai
(Weber, 1913)

No larger than a pencil point sticking out of the sand, this tiny, sharp-snouted snake eel with spots on the head is an unusual find for snake eel aficionados and quite difficult to spot. A similar pointy-nosed species, the Yellowtail Snake Eel *(A. flavicaudus),* is yellowish and slightly larger. To 10 in. Indo-Pacific. Photo: Ho'okena, Hawai'i. 40 ft.

FILEFISHES
(Monacanthidae)

Hawaiian Fantail Filefish ·'ō'ili 'uwī 'uwī · territorial or sexual display· Mākua, O'ahu. 20 ft. (p. 123)

Filefishes, like their relatives the triggerfishes, possess a stout dorsal spine which they raise when threatened or aroused. Although this spine often bears tiny thornlike spikes that make it rough and file-like, the common name "filefish" more likely derives from the sandpaper texture of the fish's skin, caused by fine but rough scales. Filefishes have narrow, compressed bodies and small mouths with strong biting teeth. They swim by rippling their soft dorsal and anal fins and can move backward or forward with equal ease. Although they lack pelvic fins entirely, many have a movable stub called a pelvic rudiment (visible in the photo above) that extends down when they erect their dorsal spine. In general, filefishes are omnivorous. Some can change color quickly to match their surroundings.

The order Tetraodontiformes, to which filefishes belong, includes other odd reef fishes such as boxfishes, puffers, triggerfishes, and ocean sunfishes (molas). The family name, Monacanthidae, means "one spine." (Actually, many filefishes have two dorsal spines, but the second is always minute.) The Hawaiian name, 'ō'ili ("sprout" or "come up"), probably refers to the frequently raised first dorsal spine. Seven filefish species occur in Hawai'i; two are endemic and all are shown here.

Robert F. Myers

UNICORN FILEFISH *Aluterus monoceros* (Linnaeus, 1758)

Rare on Hawaiian reefs, the oddly-shaped Unicorn Filefish is a pelagic drifter that turns up in the Islands from time to time. Although similar to the more common Scrawled Filefish (next page), it lacks the blue scribblings and long tail fin. To about 30 in. It is reported to occur in all warm seas, but is not yet recorded from French Polynesia, and there is only one record from Micronesia. Photo: Shedd Aquarium, Chicago. (Robert F. Myers)

feeding on fish eggs

D.R. Schrichte

SCRAWLED FILEFISH · loulu
Aluterus scriptus (Osbeck, 1765)
[BROOMTAIL FILEFISH]

This bizarre fish has an amazingly compressed bluish white body covered with short blue lines and spots that resemble scribblings. The tail fin can account for a third or more of the total body length, the lower jaw juts forward, and the hairlike dorsal spine is scarcely visible even when raised. The body can darken rapidly to a mottled camouflage pattern. Scrawled Filefish occur singly or in small groups, in the open ocean as well as close to shore. They feed in part on jellyfish and other reef animals indigestible to most other predators, such as fire corals and zoanthids of the genus *Palythoa* (which contain palytoxin, one of the most deadly poisons in nature). They are omnivores, however, and will take what they can get, sometimes hovering around foraging Eagle Rays, for example, to nab exposed sand-dwelling invertebrates. In old Hawai'i this fish was used in sorcery to cause death. The Hawaiian word **lou** means "to hook," and the name **loulu** also refers to a group of endemic, greenish white palms (*Pritchardia* spp.), the fanlike leaves of which resemble this fish's tail fin. The scientific species name means "written upon." To 30 in. All warm seas. The similar Unicorn Filefish (previous page), very rare in Hawai'i, lacks the blue scribblings and the long tail fin. Photos: Hanauma Bay, O'ahu. 30-50 ft. (bottom photo by D.R. Schrichte).

BARRED FILEFISH · 'ō'ili
Cantherhines dumerilii (Hollard, 1854)

These large filefish are brownish gray with faint vertical bars. A tuft of orange-yellow spines (longer in males) sprouts at the base of the tail, also orange-yellow. Equipped with powerful jaws and strong teeth, they feed in part on living coral and can sometimes be heard crunching upon it, much like parrotfishes. They often travel in pairs, warily tilting their backs toward divers as they swim. Some pairs become noticeably tinged with yellow, possibly when courting or mating. Juveniles, almost never seen, have many white spots. The species is named for French naturalist Auguste Duméril (1812-1870). To about 15 in. Indo-Pacific and Eastern Pacific. Photos: (top and center) Hanauma Bay, O'ahu. 8-10 ft. (bottom) Kahe Point, O'ahu. 40 ft.

▼ juvenile

Night divers off Kīhei, Maui, once reported seeing several Barred Filefish asleep in Antler Coral, each grasping a branch in its strong jaws, presumably to keep from drifting away. Three other filefish species, including the Scrawled Filefish (previous page), are also known to bite onto fixed objects at night. The behavior is called "mooring" or "parking."

SQUARETAIL FILEFISH · 'ō'ili lepa
Cantherhines sandwichiensis
(Quoy & Gaimard, 1824)

Immediately recognizable, this dark gray filefish has a prominent white spot at the top of the tail base. Orange pectoral fin rays contrast nicely with the dark body. The back edge of the tail may also be orange. The tail is more squared off than other Hawaiian filefishes, giving rise to the common name. The Hawaiian name, **lepa** ("flag-bearer" or "flagpole"), refers to the particularly long dorsal spine. Juveniles sometimes show a honeycomb pattern. The Hawaiian Islands were called the Sandwich Islands by early Europeans, hence the scientific name. First discovered in Hawai'i and long considered a Hawaiian endemic, this filefish is now known also from French Polynesia To about 7 in. Photo: Palea Point, O'ahu. 30 ft.

a) normal coloration ▲   b) camouflaged ▼

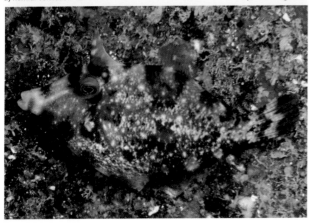

SHY FILEFISH · 'ō'ili
Cantherhines verecundus
(E.K. Jordan, 1925)

This grayish filefish lacks distinguishing marks but usually changes rapidly to a mottled camouflage pattern when approached. Individuals living in *Halimeda* algae may be bright mottled green. The skin is covered with short, hairlike appendages. Appropriately named, this fish seldom strays far from cover, and is uncommon at most dive sites. The species name means "bashful," "shy." To about 6 in. Endemic (with a sister species, *C. fronticinctus*, elsewhere in the Indo-Pacific). Photos: (a) Kawaihoa (Portlock) Point, O'ahu. 20 ft. (b) Kea'au, O'ahu, 50 ft.

122

YELLOWTAIL FILEFISH · ʻōʻili
Pervagor aspricaudus
(Hollard, 1854)

Members of the genus *Pervagor* usually have a colorful tail fin that they can spread like a fan. This small, shy species is gray-black with a bright yellow-orange posterior and tail. Although common in some areas, it quickly retreats into a hole or crevice when approached, often before a diver even sees it. If excited or agitated it can take on a mottled coloration. It is an Indo-Pacific species, but occurs mainly in cooler waters well north or south of the equator. To 7 in., but usually smaller. Photo: Mākua, Oʻahu. 30 ft.

HAWAIIAN FANTAIL FILEFISH · ʻōʻili ʻuwī ʻuwī · *Pervagor spilosoma* (Lay & Bennett, 1839)

These filefish are yellow or whitish marked with dark spots. The fanlike tail is bright orange with a black margin. Blue markings about the mouth, throat, and spiny pelvic rudiment further adorn them. They frequently pair off in a head-to-tail position, raising and lowering their yellow dorsal spines and spreading their colorful tails in some sort of territorial or sexual display (p. 119). Varying in abundance from year to year, they are uncommon to moderately common most years and live near the bottom feeding on algae, detritus, and small invertebrates. In bloom years, however, as from 1985-1988, they are superabundant and feed on plankton in midwater. At such times they take on an unattractive pale coloration and may die off by the thousands, washing up on beaches. In old Hawaiʻi this was said to portend the death of a chief. Their dry bodies were sometimes used as fuel. Fishermen hate these blooms because game fish gorge on the ever-present filefish and lose interest in bait. If removed from the water Fantail Filefish make a small noise, hence the Hawaiian name ʻuwī ʻuwī, meaning to squeal. The species name means "spotted." To 7 in. Endemic. Photo: Lānaʻi Lookout, Oʻahu. 35 ft.

FLAGTAILS
(Kuhliidae)

Flagtails at Honolua Bay, Maui. What species are they? Probably Hawaiian Flagtails, but it's hard to tell for sure.

Flagtails are a small family of silvery perchlike fishes with moderately deep bodies and a single dorsal fin. In many species the tail fin is banded, hence the common name, but only juveniles have banded tails in Hawai'i. These fish usually rest in tight schools during the day, typically above the reef in areas of heavy surge, but also in caves. At night they disperse to feed on planktonic crustaceans. Juveniles occur in tide pools, along shallow sandy shores, and in brackish areas.

Known in Hawaiian as **āholehole**, flagtails have long been prized as food. According to an 1893 Hawaiian newspaper, when a chiefess in Hilo yearned for the "fat **āholehole**," runners brought them to her from the Wai'ākōlea fishpond in Puna, 30 miles away, still alive in their wrappings of seaweed. "Because the chiefess had a craving," it reported, "the distance was as nothing." In old Hawai'i, names were often significant on several levels. For example, the word **hole** means "to strip away" and the **āholehole** was prepared for eating by gripping the dorsal fin with the teeth and pulling the body away. These fishes were sometimes used in ceremonies for the "stripping away" of evil spirits. Early Caucasian settlers, with their white skins, were sometimes called **āhole** (not to be confused with **haole**, meaning "foreigner").

Two species of flagtails inhabit Hawai'i's waters, one of them endemic. The two are so similar that the second species escaped scientific detection until 2001. For more on this story, see p. 126.

HAWAIIAN FLAGTAIL · āholehole · *Kuhlia xenura* (Jordan & Gilbert, 1882)
    By day, these silvery fish form dense stationary schools, often near the tops of reefs or along dropoffs in areas of heavy surge where turbulence and fine bubbles screen them from predators. They also aggregate in caves and crevices where there is turbulence. Subadults will school in very shallow water along protected sandy beaches and in stream mouths. At Honolua Bay, Maui, they congregate near submarine freshwater springs. Resting schools often occupy the same location year after year, although they sometimes shift locations temporarily. At night the fish disperse to feed on plankton. Adults are silvery, sometimes with an olive or bronze tinge along the back, and occasionally with bronze patches on the side. The young have banded tails, but are otherwise plain (in contrast to young Zebra-Head Flagtails, below, which have black reticulations on the head). Juveniles are abundant in tide pools and will enter brackish water; sometimes they penetrate some distance up streams. In old Hawai'i only the young were called **āholehole**; adults were simply **āhole**. To 12 in. Endemic. Photo: Palea Point, O'ahu. 10 ft. (Identified on the basis of the slightly concave head profile, lacking in adult Zebra-Head Flagtails.)

ZEBRA-HEAD FLAGTAIL · āholehole
Kuhlia sandvicensis
(Steindachner, 1876)
    As adults, these fish are almost identical to the Hawaiian Flagtail (above). Only juveniles in tide pools (illustrated at right) are easy to identify; their heads are whitish with wide black reticulations on the upper surface that extend rearward as two black lines on either side of the dorsal fin. The rear tip of the soft dorsal fin is bright white. These markings fade in adults, although dark reticulations sometimes persist under certain lighting conditions. Unlike juvenile Hawaiian Flagtails, juvenile Zebra-Heads do not actually enter freshwater streams, though they do occur near stream mouths. To 12 in. Central Pacific. Photo: Subadult. Whittington Beach Park, Hawai'i. 1 ft.

A tale of two species

Until recently only one flagtail species was believed to occur in Hawai'i. In the late 1990s, however, aquarium collector Darrell Takaoka noticed that there seem to be two types of juveniles in tide pools. Some have black reticulations on their heads, whereas others have plain heads. He took specimens to Dr. John E. Randall at the Bishop Museum, who determined that the "zebra-head" flagtails represent a species not previously known to occur in Hawai'i. Investigating further, Randall and his wife found that the scientific names of both species had been mixed up. The correct scientific name of the less-common "zebra-head" species—Kuhlia sandvicensis—was the name in current use for the more-common "plain-head" species. The correct name for the common "plain-head" flagtail turned out to be Kuhlia xenura, a name long forgotten in the annals of ichthyology. Further confusing the issue, the zebra-headed sandvicensis (which might be expected on the basis of its name to be endemic to Hawai'i) was found to be widely distributed in the Central Pacific, while K. xenura was found to be endemic.

Meanwhile, a biology student at Louisiana State University, Lori Benson, was hot on the same story. In 1999, while doing research in Hawai'i for her PhD thesis on flagtails, she was tipped off by local fishermen that there were two types of āholehole, one with bigger eyes than the other. Suspecting two species, she procured specimens and submitted tissue samples for DNA sequencing. In 2001, however, while Benson's studies were being completed, Randall and Randall published their results in the journal Pacific Science. Benson's PhD Thesis was submitted in 2002. Both studies were completely independent, and each contains useful ID information not present in the other. Is this the end of the flagtail story? Possibly not. Giant āholehole, up to 17 in. long, occasionally turn up in fish markets. Perhaps these represent a third Hawaiian species.

Hawaiian Flagtails *(Kuhlia xenura)* identified on the basis of olive patches and reddish color on edge of eye.

How can I the two species apart?

It's very difficult, unless you want to count scales, fin rays and gill rakers. Even then, the differences are slight. Underwater, adults of the two species appear virtually identical, although under certain lighting conditions faint dark reticulations can sometimes be seen on adult Zebra-Heads. Hawaiian Flagtails (Kuhlia xenura) are reported to be more abundant than Zebra-Head Flagtails (K. sandvicensis).

Theoretically, adults of the two species can also be differentiated by the characters below:

1) **color**: In strong light, the Hawaiian Flagtail often has an olive or bronze tinge along the back, and sometimes bronze patches on the side, whereas the Zebra-Head is more silvery on the back and whitish below. Also, in the Hawaiian Flagtail the upper edge of the eye reflects a reddish color in strong light. (see photo above)

2) **dorsal head profile**: the Zebra-Head Flagtail has a straight dorsal head profile whereas the Hawaiian Flagtail has a slightly concave dorsal head profile.

3) **eye size**: The Hawaiian Flagtail has a slightly larger eye in relation to the length of the head.

FLATFISHES
(Bothidae, Samaridae, Soleidae)

Flowery Flounder · **paki'i** · prefers hard substrate but sometimes lies on sand or gravel (p. 128)

Every habitat has its specialists, and flatfishes are masters of the sand or gravel seabed. Their greatly depressed, oval bodies lie almost flush with the bottom. Virtually invisible to predator or prey, they wait patiently for the small crustaceans or fishes on which they feed. Flatfishes begin life as normal fish, with eyes on either side of the head. As they grow, one eye actually migrates over the top of the head, eventually joining the other on the opposite side. During this process the fish starts leaning over, eventually ending up flat on the sand with the blind side down.

The underside of most flatfishes is white; the upper side is usually speckled or mottled to match the substrate. They are able to fine tune this pattern for almost perfect camouflage. To make doubly sure they are not seen they can partially cover themselves with sand, the eyes protruding like little periscopes.

Flatfishes are so strange and different that they constitute their own order, the Pleuronectiformes. There are many species, including the enormous Barn-Door Halibut of northern seas, which can grow to 7 ft. in length and weigh hundreds of pounds. Most flatfishes dwell in temperate waters or on deep muddy bottoms and are unlikely to be encountered by snorkelers or divers. Of the seven flatfish families, only the left-eyed flounders (Bothidae), the tropical right-eyed or slender flounders (Samaridae), and the soles (Soleidae) are seen regularly in Hawaiian reef environments. How to tell the families apart? Facing the fish head on, left-eyed flounders have eyes to the left of the mouth, whereas soles and right-eyed flounders have eyes to the right of the mouth.

Underwater, flatfishes can usually be approached closely. A flounder, if disturbed, will often take off rapidly in a cloud of sand. Sometimes it will swim ten feet or so in a straight line, land, then flutter backward into the settling sand, which partially covers it. Thus the creature ends up well-hidden several feet from where you expect it. Flounders are not always ambush predators. They will sometimes follow hunting packs of goatfish, along with jacks, trumpetfish, groupers, scorpionfishes, and others, to take advantage of small prey animals flushed from the substrate. They will also associate with Kona Crabs *(Ranina ranina)*.

Hawai'i has 13 left-eyed flounders (seven from deep water), at least two right-eyed flounders (one from deep water), and three small soles. Seven species are shown here. The Hawaiian name for flatfishes is **pāki'i** ("fallen flat" or "spread out").

An old story relates that Moses once tried frying a sole in oil. He browned one side nicely, but the oil ran out and he threw the half-cooked fish back into the sea. Miraculously, it sprang back to life. Ever since, flatfishes have been brown on one side and white on the other. A Red Sea species (Pardachirus marmoratus), still called the Moses Sole, secretes a milky fluid containing a remarkably effective shark repellent. The active ingredient is similar to household detergent. Some other soles are known to secrete toxins as well.

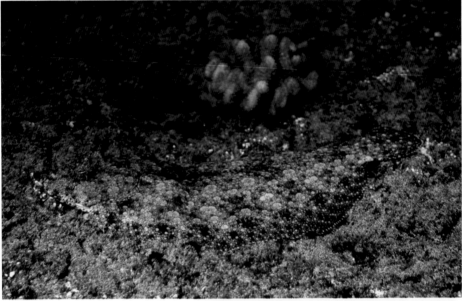

a) Flowery Flounder camouflaged on bottom ▲

b) same fish swimming - long pectoral fin shows it to be male ▼

FLOWERY FLOUNDER · **pāki'i** · *Bothus mancus*
(Broussonet, 1782) [PEACOCK FLOUNDER]
Family Bothidae

The most common large flatfish on Hawaiian reefs, the Flowery (or Peacock) Flounder almost always lives on or near hard bottoms. (The similar Panther Flounder, next page, prefers sandy bottoms.) It is pale to light brown covered with blue flowerlike spots and rings of various sizes, and often displays a row of three dark blotches, the one nearest the tail very small. Other dark spots and smudges may appear as well. <u>The distance between the eyes is about 1-3 eye diameters</u>, with the eyes of males being further apart than those of females. Males have a greatly elongated pectoral fin which they raise when courting a female. The species name means "wounded" or "hurt." To 19 in. Indo-Pacific and Eastern Pacific. Photos: Lahilahi Point, O'ahu. 20 ft. (see also previous page)

PANTHER FLOUNDER · pākiʻi

Bothus pantherinus (Rüppell, 1830)
Family Bothidae

This flounder lives over sand, sometimes close to the reef, but often well away from it. It greatly resembles the Flowery Flounder (previous page), but the distance between the eyes is about 1 eye diameter at most. It is also slightly smaller and somewhat paler, better to match the substrate on which it lives. Males have more widely spaced eyes than females and extended pectoral fin rays that they raise in courtship displays, revealing a finely patterned membrane between the rays. To about 12 in. Indo-Pacific. Photos: (top) Lānaʻi Lookout, Oʻahu. 30 ft. (center) Pūpūkea, Oʻahu. 70 ft. (bottom) Kahe Point, Oʻahu. 70 ft.

Diving far out in the sand off Kahe Point, Oʻahu, I saw a Panther Flounder with what appeared to be a large fish hook in its mouth. Moving closer, I saw that it had caught a small snake eel. As soon as the flounder saw me approach, it sucked the eel right in like a strand of spaghetti!

▲ male courtship display

HAWAIIAN DWARF FLOUNDER
Engyprosopon hawaiiensis
Jordan & Evermann, 1903
Family Bothidae

These tiny flounders live on sand bottoms at depths of 3 ft. or more and are almost impossible to see until they move. To about 3 in. Endemic. Photo: Kahe Point, O'ahu. 30 ft. (Two other dwarf flounders also occur on sand bottoms in Hawaiian waters: the endemic *Engyprosopon xenandrus* has widely spaced eyes and is seen at 40 ft. and deeper, while *E. arenicola* lives in the surge zone.)

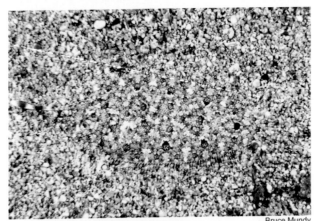

FEATHER-FIN FLOUNDER
Asterorhombus filifer Family Bothidae
Randall & Hensley, 2003

The first dorsal fin of this flatfish is modified into a featherlike appendage (just visible at left of photo). It inhabits sandy areas down to at least 150 ft. In females the eyes are right next to each other, but in males there is a slight space between, less than the diameter of an eye. The purpose of the unusual first dorsal fin is not known. However a close relative not found in Hawai'i, the Angler Flatfish (*A. fijiensis*), has its first dorsal spine modified into a fishing apparatus similar to that of most frogfishes. To about 4 ½ in. Indo-Pacific. Photo: Pūpūkea, O'ahu. 40 ft. (Bruce Mundy)

Bruce Mundy

THREESPOT FLOUNDER *Samariscus triocellatus* Woods, 1966 Family Samaridae

This small right-eyed flounder is hard to find but fun to watch. Usually encountered in sand near or under ledges, it is typically seen creeping slowly forward by means of slow, almost peristaltic waves progressing down its dorsal and anal fins. While creeping it waves its erect pectoral fin back and forth like a lure. The reason for this behavior is not known. The fish is easily recognized by three dark spots with yellow centers on the center of the upper side. The two spots nearest the tail are the most conspicuous. It sometimes rests on near vertical surfaces. To about 3 in. Indo-Pacific. Photo: (left) Lānai Lookout, O'ahu. 30 ft. (right) Mākua, O'ahu. 50 ft.

BOREHAM'S SOLE
Aseraggodes borehami Randall, 1996
Family Soleidae

This small sole is light brown with numerous irregular small white spots and lines. It lives in silty sand under ledges and in caves down to at least 100 ft., often in groups. It may bury itself shallowly by day, but even while resting on the surface, a thin layer of sand usually adheres to its upper side, obscuring the markings. The name honors American businessman and philanthropist Roland S. Boreham Jr. (1924-2004) who gave generously to many charitable and educational institutions and had a particular interest in ichthyological research. Endemic. To about 5 in. Photo: Mākua, O'ahu. 30 ft.

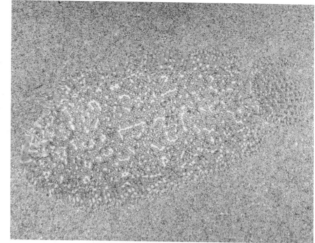

HOLCOM'S SOLE
Aseraggodes holcomi Randall, 1996
Family Soleidae

This small sole is light brown with numerous irregular dark-edged white markings. It lives from the shallows down to at least 90 ft. on sand or gravel bottom The 2-inch specimen at right was in 3 ft. of water on a reef flat at night. The name honors O'ahu diver and photographer Ronald R. Holcom, who discovered and captured the first specimens. Endemic. To about 5 in. Photo: Punalu'u, O'ahu. 3 ft. (Keoki Stender)

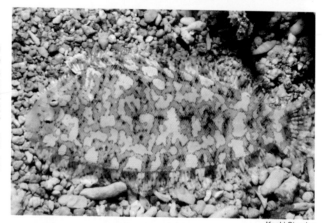

Keoki Stender

THERESE'S SOLE
Aseraggodes therese Randall, 1996
Family Soleidae

Common but rarely noticed, these tiny nocturnal soles lie buried in sand by day, often in caves and under ledges. They emerge at night to hunt, lying flattened and almost invisible against rocky walls. They are tweedy brown with irregular light mottlings and darker splotches. A freshly dead Therese's Sole fed to a jack was immediately spat out, indicating that the species probably secretes a toxin making it unpalatable to predators. The name honors Therese Hayes, longtime Hawai'i diver and naturalist. To about 3 in. Endemic. Photo: Pūpūkea, O'ahu. 30 ft.

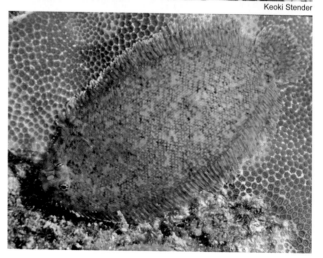

Kendra Ignacio

Three Commerson's Frogfish, probably one female and two males waiting to spawn. Kona, Hawai'i. (p.134)

Frogfishes are the ultimate sedentary predators. Barely recognizable as fish, they sit for long periods in one spot, blending in perfectly with the reef or mimicking brightly colored sponges and other growths. Their pectoral fins grasp the substrate like hands or feet, and can be used (with the help of a joint) to clamber about. Their first dorsal spine resembles a slender, almost invisible fishing rod; a fleshy lure at the tip mimics a fish, worm, or other creature. The spine and its lure (called the illicium and the esca, respectively) normally lie back along the top of the head. At the approach of potential prey the frogfish flicks the "rod" out over its enormous upturned mouth and wiggles or waves the lure. A fish attracted by the ruse soon finds itself inside the frogfish, whose mouth can expand twelve-fold to accommodate guests of any size. Frogfishes engulf their prey in about 6 milliseconds—far too quickly for the eye to follow. This enables a camouflaged frogfish to capture another fish without others nearby ever noticing.

Surprisingly, these awkward lumpy fishes are jet propelled. Although poor swimmers in the normal sense, some (if not all) species can gulp water through their large mouths and eject it under pressure through small, round gill openings set far back on the body behind the pectoral fins, or in one case behind the anal fin! By this means, perhaps aided by currents and surge, they can "fly" considerable distances. A Commerson's Frogfish perched on the top of a ledge can spread its pectorals like small stiff wings, drop its pelvics like landing gear, and glide about 20 ft. to a perfect touchdown.

Frogfishes rely almost entirely on camouflage for protection; they can inflate with water when molested, but have no sharp spines and are not poisonous. They are not often seen by snorkelers, although in calm harbors and lagoons they sometimes enter very shallow water.

The order Lophiiformes, to which frogfishes belong, includes a variety of bizarre animals such as goosefishes, monkfishes, and anglerfishes. Most are from deep water and all use a fishing rod and lure apparatus (often with luminescent "bait") to attract prey within striking distance of a capacious mouth. There are about 44 frogfish species worldwide. Eleven inhabit Hawai'i's reefs and a twelfth pelagic species sometimes drifts in with floating seaweed or debris. Seven frogfishes are shown here. Not pictured are: the Tailjet Frogfish *Antennatus analis* (about 2 in. long), which has its gill openings back near the tail above the anal fin; the possibly endemic *A. duescus* (about 2 in.), known from only three specimens dredged from deep water in 1902; the Coinbearing Frogfish *A. nummifer* (about 4 in.), which almost always has a dark round spot (the coin) below the dorsal fin; tiny Randall's Frogfish, *Antennarius randalli* (about 1 ¾ in.), usually dark with white speckles; and the Lined Frogfish *Antennatus linearis* (about 2 in.), brown with many white encircling lines.

Frogfish love

Two or more frogfish seen in close proximity are probably courting or about to spawn. Usually the female swells noticeably several days prior to spawning. A male Commerson's courts his mate (usually the larger of the two) by flaring his fins, waddling towards her with a jerky motion, and pushing against her with one pectoral fin. (One or more males, perhaps rivals, are often present too. John Earle reports, "I have seen at least seven together, like a living rock garden.") Generally the female does little in response, and the frogfish sit together for a time. Later her mate begins to nudge her swollen abdomen, and eventually the two swim upward to spawn. Several days later the two are usually still together and after about a week the process starts all over again. (Thanks to Kendra Ignacio for the above description.) At the time of spawning the female ejects a large, gelatinous, curled-up raft of eggs that the male promptly fertilizes. The raft, containing as many as 300,000 eggs, floats to the surface and uncurls over a period of hours or days. Larvae remain for a month or two in the plankton before settling to the bottom to mature.

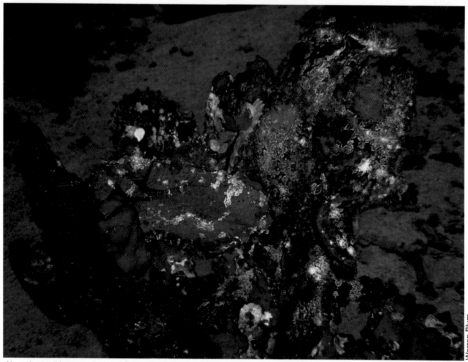

Warren Blum

Almost impossible to see, three red Commerson's Frogfish perch in a black coral stump covered with red sponge. As on the previous page, the group probably consists of one female and two males waiting to spawn. Mākena, Maui. (p. 134)

a) adult ▲

COMMERSON'S FROGFISH
Antennarius commerson
(Latreille, 1804) [Giant Frogfish]

This is the frogfish encountered most often in Hawai'i. The largest of all its kind, it can be brown, yellow, orange, red, pink, whitish, green, black, or mottled, and is frequently covered with scab-like patches and small growths. Juveniles are often bright yellow, apparently mimicking a yellow sponge. In captivity these fish have been observed to change color over a period of days or weeks. A large, impossibly bright orange specimen displayed for years in a small stand-alone tank at the Waikīkī Aquarium turned plain brown when moved to larger quarters. Commerson's Frogfish are territorial, and often remain in the same general area for months or years, typically in the vicinity of walls, caves and undercuts. They may either perch openly, resembling a lump on the reef or a coral head, or flatten themselves against a rocky wall, blending with the growths on it. Their lure (esca) is a scarcely visible small tuft. The species name honors French naturalist Philibert Commerson (1727-1773). To about 12 in. Indo-Pacific and Eastern Pacific, but apparently absent (or overlooked) at many Pacific islands. Photos: (a) Lāna`i Lookout, O'ahu. 30 ft. (b) Portlock Point, O'ahu. 30 ft. (c) Palea Point, O'ahu. 40 ft. (see also pp. xi, 132, 133)

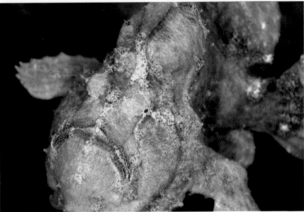

b) adult swimming ▲

c) juvenile ▼

Commerson's Frogfish. Kaiwi Point, Hawai'i   Jerry Kane   Commerson's Frogfish. Magic Island, O'ahu

HAWAIIAN FRECKLED FROGFISH
Antennatus drombus
Jordan & Evermann, 1903

Few divers or snorkelers realize that Hawai'i has an endemic frogfish. Small, uncommon, and well camouflaged, it is rarely encountered. Brown, reddish brown, or gray, it is usually covered with small dark splotches (the freckles), which are especially visible on the fins. It is similar to *A. coccineus,* a species widespread in the Indo-Pacific, and is listed as that species in some older books on Hawaiian fishes. It differs mainly in the number of rays in the pectoral fin: *drombus* has 12, whereas *coccineus* has 10. To about 4 ½ in. Photo: Waikīkī Aquarium. (Fish collected at the Lāna'i Lookout, O'ahu. 30 ft.)

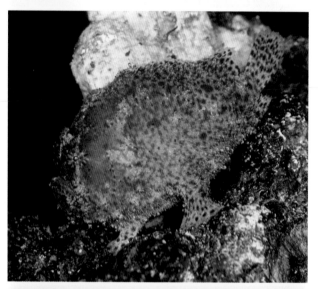

WARTY FROGFISH
Antennarius maculatus
(Desjardins, 1840)

Named for its bumpy, warty skin, this frogfish is typically whitish, yellowish, or pinkish with highly contrasting, dark scablike patches and spots that often form saddles in front of the soft dorsal and tail fins. Its color is variable, however, and the fish can be dark or even black with light spots. The lure sometimes resembles a small fish, complete with a tiny eyespot. Juveniles, which are conspicuously colored and sit out in the open, are often called Clown Frogfish. The species is rare in Hawai'i, known to date only from a few photographs taken off the Kona coast of the Big Island. To about 4 ½ in. Indo-Pacific. Photo: Lembeh Strait, Indonesia.

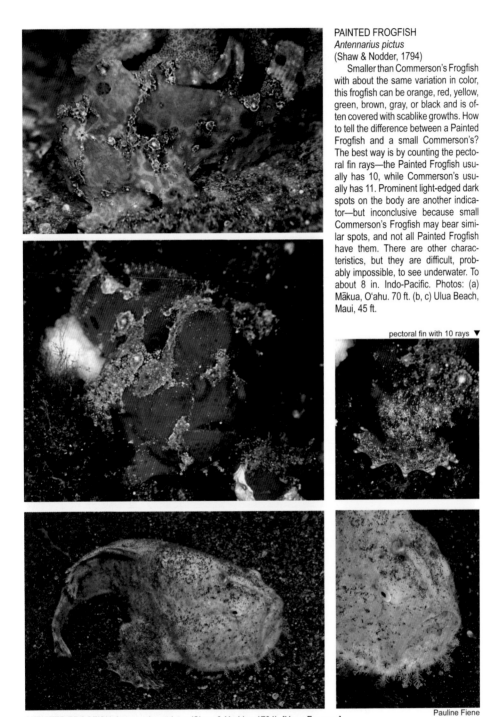

PAINTED FROGFISH
Antennarius pictus
(Shaw & Nodder, 1794)

Smaller than Commerson's Frogfish with about the same variation in color, this frogfish can be orange, red, yellow, green, brown, gray, or black and is often covered with scablike growths. How to tell the difference between a Painted Frogfish and a small Commerson's? The best way is by counting the pectoral fin rays—the Painted Frogfish usually has 10, while Commerson's usually has 11. Prominent light-edged dark spots on the body are another indicator—but inconclusive because small Commerson's Frogfish may bear similar spots, and not all Painted Frogfish have them. There are other characteristics, but they are difficult, probably impossible, to see underwater. To about 8 in. Indo-Pacific. Photos: (a) Mākua, Oʻahu. 70 ft. (b, c) Ulua Beach, Maui, 45 ft.

pectoral fin with 10 rays ▼

Pauline Fiene

STRIATED FROGFISH *Antennarius striatus* (Shaw & Nodder, 1794) [HAIRY FROGFISH]
A large lure with 2-7 fleshy wormlike appendages identifies this frogfish. Greatly variable in color, it typically lives on soft bottoms among algae, sponges, and other growths and often bears dark slanting striations and elongate spots, thus the common name. Some individuals grow long hairlike filaments to help them blend in. In part because of its habitat, it is a very rare find in Hawaiʻi. To about 9 in. Indo-Pacific and tropical Atlantic. Photos: Maʻalaea Bay, Maui. 30 ft. (Pauline Fiene)

RETICULATED FROGFISH *Antennatus tuberosus* (Cuvier, 1817) [BANDTAIL FROGFISH]

John E. Randall

Typically sheltering deep within branching corals, sometimes in pairs, this small frogfish often has a pinkish face resembling coralline algae. Dark brown reticulations on the cream or yellowish body give it its name. Color is variable, however. White individuals with red pectoral tips, and completely tomato red individuals have been reported. The reticulations may be absent, but all fins except the dorsal have a dark brown bar. Like other frogfishes of the genus *Antennatus,* its wormlike "fishing rod" (illicium) lacks a lure. To about 3 ½ in. but usually smaller. Indo-Pacific. Photos: Mākua, O'ahu. 40 ft., Kahe Point, O'ahu. 30 ft.

SARGASSUM FROGFISH
Histrio histrio (Linnaeus 1758)

Mottled yellow and black, these unusual frogfish are found worldwide in floating seaweed, typically sargassum, in which they are almost perfectly camouflaged. They also occur in floating debris, such as fishing nets, and are seen inshore only when their "home" drifts close to land. Over 50 juveniles were once found off O'ahu in a floating net. Juveniles may be entirely black or yellow. Bigger ones will eat smaller ones in a heartbeat. They are not safe, even in their net home, if other Sargassum Frogfish are present. The genus and species names both mean "actor." To about 7 ½ in. Photo: Kona, Hawai'i, (in drifting net).

Kendra Ignacio

Luring behavior

Frogfishes usually lure only when they see or sense potential prey, doing so in bouts of about 10-30 seconds both by day and night. The motion of the lure, even if not visible after dark, can probably be sensed by prey animals. The exact way it is moved, whether waved, jerked, shaken, etc., appears to be specific to the species of frogfish. Some frogfishes have obvious lures, but those of Hawaiian species are inconspicuous, thus luring behavior is rarely noticed in Hawai'i. Photo: Mike Roberts. Ulua Beach, Maui. 45 ft. (Painted Frogfish)

Mike Roberts

137

GOATFISHES
(Mullidae)

Square-Spot Goatfish · **weke'ā** · often rest on bottom by day. Pūpūkea, O'ahu. 20 ft.

Goatfishes are among the first fishes seen by a snorkeler finning over the sandy bottom. They are easily recognized by their barbels, reminiscent of a goat's beard, with which they busily "taste" the sand for worms, molluscs, and other invertebrates. Some use their barbels to flush shrimps, crabs, or even fish from crevices in the reef. When not feeding they tuck these append-ages up out of sight. All goatfishes have a forked tail and two dorsal fins. Many can change color dramatically in seconds, and their resting colors may differ from their active colors. Variable, yet looking much alike, goatfishes are sometimes difficult to identify underwater. Most are bottom dwell-ers, but several of Hawai'i's most abundant species school in midwater during the day.

Despite the obvious similarity between members of the family, there is no general Hawaiian name for goatfishes. Some species, especially those with one or more body-length stripes, are known as **weke** ("to open") and were sometimes used in religious ceremonies when an "opening" or "releasing" was required. **Weke** under 7 in. are called **'oama**. Other goatfishes are known as **moano**. Still others have individual names. All are prized as food. In the words of an old chant: "Delicious, delicious is the fish of the sea, the **moano** of the yellowish sea, delicious, delicious."

Goatfishes are sometimes called "surmullets," the family name coming from the Latin *mullus* ("mullet"). Ten native species inhabit Hawaiian waters, two of them endemic. One of the latter, the Yellowbarbel Goatfish *(Parupeneus chrysonemus),* is a deepwater species seen by divers only in the northwestern chain. It is not illustrated here. An eleventh species, the Yellowbanded Goatfish *(Upeneus vittatus),* was reported from Kāne'ohe Bay, O'ahu, in the early 1980s. It was probably introduced accidentally from the Marquesas Islands in 1955 and may no longer survive in the Islands.

a) foraging

SQUARE-SPOT GOATFISH · **weke'ā** · *Mulloidichthys flavolineatus* (Lacepède, 1801) [YELLOWSTRIPE GOATFISH]
This common goatfish is most easily recognized by a squarish black spot on the side which is embedded within a yellow stripe running from head to tail. The black spot, often intense while the fish is feeding, may fade or disappear when it is resting or schooling. The yellow stripe may also fade. These fish feed both by day and by night. During the day they often aggregate at predictable spots on the reef, either hovering in midwater or lying on the sand. When schooling with the black spot "turned off," they can be difficult to distinguish from the Yellowfin Goatfish (next page). The whitish body color and whitish fins are an indicator, although there always seem to be a few Square-Spots with slightly yellowish fins in every school. These fish never turn pink or red, as Yellowfin Goatfish sometimes do. They will occasionally enter brackish water. The species name means "yellow stripe" and the Hawaiian name means "staring **weke,**" perhaps in reference to the black spot. To 16 in. Indo-Pacific. Photos: (a) Hanauma Bay, O'ahu. 3 ft. (b) Kahe Point, O'ahu. 15 ft. (see also previous page)

Studying goatfishes in Kāne'ohe Bay, O'ahu, Kim Holland discovered that the daytime schooling sites of Square-Spot Goatfish remained the same for 1½ years, and probably much longer. At sundown the fish dispersed, each moving rapidly to a nighttime foraging area to feed, chiefly on polychaete worms. Individual fish migrated up to 600 yards to the same feeding area each night, always taking the same route out and back. They returned just before sunrise. However, informal observations by Cory Pittman at Olowalu, Maui, suggest that during the day Square-Spots alternate between periods of active feeding and resting, and at night "sleep" on the bottom, their color changing to a mottled cream and brown pattern. Why do some feed by night and others by day? We still have much to learn about these common fish.

b) schooling by day with the black spot "turned off"

a) resting in the open

YELLOWFIN GOATFISH · **weke ʻula** · *Mulloidichthys vanicolensis* (Valenciennes, 1831)
    When in the open during the day, these goatfish have whitish bodies with some yellow along the back, yellow fins, and a yellow stripe from eye to tail. The yellow stripe may be bordered faintly with blue. They feed only at night, resting by day in tight schools that hang almost motionlessly in midwater, usually at the same spot on the reef year after year. They also congregate in caves and under ledges, where they often turn entirely pink or red (including the yellow stripe and fins). When posing to be cleaned by wrasses they typically take on the darker red color, perhaps to make parasites stand out. They also turn reddish when taken from the water, thus the Hawaiian name, meaning "red **weke**." (The Square-Spot Goatfish, on the previous page, never turns red.) These goatfish will sometimes enter brackish water. The species name is from Vanikoro in the Solomon Islands. This goatfish is the Indo-Pacific member of a circumtropical species complex. The others are *M. dentatus* of the Eastern Pacific and *M. martinicus* of the Western Atlantic. To 15 in. Indo-Pacific. Photos: (a) Hanauma Bay, Oʻahu. 25 ft. (b) "Five Graves," south shore Maui. 20 ft.

b) resting in a cave

PFLUGER'S GOATFISH · **weke moelua; weke 'ula** · *Mulloidichthys pflugeri* (Steindachner, 1900)

When swimming off the bottom these large goatfish are gray; when resting on the bottom, or actively foraging, they are reddish orange, often with broad light bars. They sometimes swim in midwater, and at such times, because of their size, gray color, and forked tails, they resemble Gray Snappers (p. 277). Uncommon, these fish prefer depths of about 40 ft. or more, although they are sometimes seen in as little as 15 ft. They forage both individually and in roving schools that may include jacks, Bandtail Goatfish (p. 146), and no doubt other species as well. Occasionally they overturn rocks (sometimes larger than you think possible) to get at what is underneath. Attaining about 20 in., this is Hawai'i's largest goatfish (note size relative to other fish in the bottom photo). Indo-Pacific. Photos: Kahe Point, O'ahu. 20-30 ft.

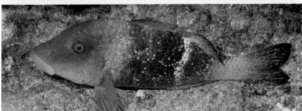

ISLAND GOATFISH · munu
Parupeneus insularis
Randall & Myers, 2002
[DOUBLEBAR GOATFISH]

Variable in color, this solitary goatfish is perhaps most easily identified by its convex dorsal profile, thick lips, and the rounded margins of its tail fin. The head is slightly indented in front of the eye. The body can be pale gray, reddish, purplish, or bluish. When swimming, the fish usually has a broad light bar down the center of the body and a less conspicuous one before the tail fin, but sometimes the posterior bar is brightest. The tail fin is usually dark with a light blue margin. Preferring shallow habitats where coral is sparse, this goatfish feeds both day and night primarily on crabs, shrimps, small octopuses, and small fish. Before 2002 it was known as the Doublebar Goatfish and bore the now-invalid scientific name *Parupeneus bifasciatus*. To 13 in. Central Pacific, from the Marianas to Hawai'i, and from Samoa to Pitcairn (with close relatives in the Western Pacific and Indian Ocean). Photos: Hanauma Bay, O'ahu.

BLUE GOATFISH · moano ukali ulua · *Parupeneus cyclostomus* (Lacepède, 1801) [YELLOWSADDLE GOATFISH]
A bluish body and a yellow saddle above the tail base make this an easy goatfish to identify. Unusual for a goatfish, it eats mainly small fish. An all-yellow color variant, fairly common elsewhere in the Indo-Pacific, is extremely rare in Hawai'i. The species name means "round mouth." The Hawaiian name **moano ukali ulua** means "goatfish with jack following" (see below). To 20 in. Indo-Pacific. Photo: Molokini Islet, Maui.

Kendra Ignacio

A moveable feast

Blue Goatfish are unusual in that they primarily eat small fishes, extending their exceptionally long barbels forward to flush their prey from cracks and crevices. (The tiny Divine Dwarf Goby, p. 153, appears to be their favorite.) They often work the bottom in groups and are sometimes followed by a gaggle of hungry camp followers and hangers-on, all hoping to feed on prey animals the goatfish stir up. Kendra Ignacio writes: "We see the groups of blue goats hunting here in Kona all the time. Most common companions are the young jacks—bluefin trevally. But we will see a whole host of other fish with them. To name just a few—peacock groupers, whitemouth morays (those two, of course, hunt together also), trumpet-fish, cornetfish, flounders, various wrasses, ta'ape, octopus (although we usually only see them hunting with a single blue goat), and one of my all-time favorites, a devil scorpionfish hopping along after the hunting pack! Very cool stuff!"

It works the other way, too. A subadult goatfish, as a feeding strategy, will closely follow a wrasse of similar size, modifying its colors to match. Because most wrasses do not eat fish, small fish do not seek cover when the wrasse approaches, and the goatfish is sometimes able to nab a meal from behind. But the wrasse probably benefits too by eating small invertebrates disturbed by the goatfish, and sometimes the wrasse follows the goatfish, or waits for it. ▶

Following a Pencil Wrasse. Hanauma Bay, O'ahu. 45 ft.

Rare color variant. Molokini Islet, Maui   Pauline Fiene

Following a Shortnose Wrasse. Kahe Point, O'ahu. 15 ft.

following an octopus ▼

MANYBAR GOATFISH · **moano**
Parupeneus multifasciatus
(Quoy & Gaimard, 1824)

These common goatfish are grayish, reddish, or purplish, usually with two broad light bars that become bright white when the fish are swimming. When they rest, the posterior bar (or sometimes both bars) may darken or disappear and the pelvic and anal fins may take on beautiful shades of magenta and blue. In color, these are among the most highly changeable goatfishes. The photographs at left of the same individual were taken several seconds apart, a camera flash triggering the change. Common on Hawaiian reefs, Manybar Goatfish often roam in small groups, feeding mostly on crabs and shrimps. Individuals will sometimes follow a foraging Whitemouth Moray (p. 106) or octopus, presumably to nab small animals it flushes out. Spawning, both in groups and pairs, occurs at dusk usually from March to July. Males swim high in the water, as much as 40 ft. above bottom with body darkened and tail fin bright white to attract females. The species name means "many bars." The Hawaiian name means "pale red." **Moano** were said to become red by eating the red blossoms of the **'ohi'a lehua** tree. To 11 in. Pacific Ocean. Photos: (top) Hanauma Bay, O'ahu. 10 ft. (middle 2) Magic Island, O'ahu. 30 ft. (bottom left) Lāna'i Lookout, O'ahu. 30 ft.

juvenile ▼

WHITESADDLE GOATFISH · kūmū · *Parupeneus porphyreus* (Jenkins, 1903)

This is Hawai'i's only endemic shallow-water goatfish. It can be grayish purple, greenish, or reddish, but almost always has a small white spot, or saddle, above the base of the tail. Pale streaks along the body above and below the eye are another identifying feature. It feeds at night and is often seen resting by day, alone or in small groups. Juveniles sometimes occur in tide pools. Highly valued in ancient times, this fish was sometimes used in offerings calling for a pig, when a pig was unobtainable. It was forbidden to women, as was pork. The name **kūmū** also means master; when a student attained full mastery in any endeavor a **kūmū** was often offered. The species name means "purple." To 15 in. Endemic. Photos: (top) Hanauma Bay, O'ahu. 5 ft. (bottom) Honolua Bay, Maui. 20 ft.

In 1960 the endemic Whitesaddle Goatfish or **kūmū** *was reported to be the most common goatfish in Hawai'i. By the early 1980s it was no longer seen in any numbers. A high market price is the most likely reason for its decline, but the introduced Bluestripe Snapper (p. 278) is often blamed as well. Brought in from the Marquesas in 1958, the snappers have undergone a population explosion in Hawai'i. They are commonly said to prey upon juvenile* **kūmū** *and to compete with adults for food, but this may be largely an urban myth—careful studies by James Parrish and Brett Schumacher at the University of Hawai'i have failed to show a strong or even conclusive connection between the two species.*

145

SIDESPOT GOATFISH · **moano**
Parupeneus pleurostigma
(Bennett, 1830)

These goatfish are among the easiest to identify. Whitish, grayish, or pinkish overall, they usually have an elongated black spot on the upper side with a round white patch behind it. These marks often intensify while the fish are swimming, the white patch seeming almost to glow from within. When the fish are stationary, however, the marks can almost disappear. Juveniles and small adults often forage in groups, sometimes with the Manybar Goatfish. The species name means "side spot." The Hawaiian name means "pale red." To 13 in. Indo-Pacific. Photos: (top) Moku Manu, O'ahu. 50 ft. (others) Mākua, O'ahu.

juveniles ▼

BANDTAIL GOATFISH · **weke pueo** · *Upeneus taeniopterus* Cuvier, 1829 [NIGHTMARE WEKE]
This is the only native Hawaiian goatfish with a banded tail. Two stripes run the length of the body, one brown and one yellow. The barbels are lemon yellow. It forages in tight groups along shallow sandy bottoms near the shoreline down to at least 30 ft. and can often be seen in only inches of water, sometimes followed by a small jack. Occasionally it mixes with Pfluger's Goatfish (p 141). Look for it at Hanauma Bay and Kailua Bay, O'ahu, and at Honolua Bay on Maui. The 5-6 tail bands on each lobe of the tail fin resemble the bands of the **pueo** or Hawaiian owl, hence the Hawaiian name, meaning "owl goatfish." To about 12 in. Indo-Pacific. Photo: Honolua Bay, Maui. 5 ft.

The brain of this fish is sometimes toxic; if eaten it can cause disturbed sleep and hallucinations. In old Hawai'i, offerings to Pahulu, King of Ghosts, were believed to prevent ill effects. For this reason these fish were sometimes called **weke pahulu.** *Today, some people call them "Nightmare Weke."*

GOBIES
(Gobiidae)

Hawaiian Shrimp Goby · sets up housekeeping with a shrimp · Olowalu, Maui. 70 ft. (p. 154)

Gobies form by far the largest family of marine fishes. There are almost 2,000 described species with more being found each year. The typical goby is a small, blunt-headed, somewhat elongated bottom-dwelling fish with two dorsal fins. (The similar blennies have one long dorsal fin.) The pelvic fins of most gobies are fused into a single appendage resembling a suction cup with which they can cling or perch. Few gobies exceed six inches, and most are probably shorter than one. The smallest have adult lengths of about 2/5 in. (1 cm.). Due to their small size and secretive lifestyles, many goby species are never seen by divers and snorkelers.

Some gobies construct their own homes by digging burrows or excavating spaces under stones, using their large mouths to carry rocks and sand. Many species, including the endemic Hawaiian Shrimp Goby (p. 154), inhabit burrows excavated by snapping shrimps. Some live on the surfaces of living corals and others spend their entire lives hidden within the interstices of the reef. A few swim freely. The remarkable mountain-climbing **ʻoʻopu alamoʻo** *(Lentipes concolor)*, a freshwater Hawaiian endemic, scales the rocky sides of waterfalls to reach the headwaters above. (Scientists have found it above thousand-foot Hiʻilawe Falls, the highest free-falling cascade in Hawaiʻi.) The mudskipper gobies of Asia have adapted to life on exposed mudflats and can remain out of the water for hours. Species of cleaner gobies from the Caribbean and tropical Atlantic pick parasites from the bodies and gills of larger fishes, filling, in their home waters, the role of the Indo-Pacific and Eastern Pacific cleaner wrasses. In general, gobies are omnivores. Bottom-dwelling species sift mouthfuls of sand for small animals, algae, or detritus. Free swimmers and some coral-dwelling gobies pick plankton from the water.

Gobies are known in Hawaiian as **'o'opu**. In addition to the **'o'opu kai** (marine gobies), there are four species of **'o'opu wai** (freshwater gobies), three of them endemic. Once abundant, freshwater gobies were highly regarded as food. Today they are uncommon, principally inhabiting the few streams that remain relatively pristine. Two species however—the Hawaiian Blackbar Goby *(Eleotris sandwicensis)* and the Flathead Goby *(Stenogobius hawaiiensis)*—also thrive in brackish ponds such as those at Hapuna Beach or 'Anaeho'omalu along the Kona coast of the Big Island.

Twenty-nine species of marine gobies (at least ten endemic) are known in Hawai'i. Sixteen are included here. Omitted are the Noble Goby *(Priolepis eugenius),* the Petite Goby *(P. farcimen),* the Rimmed-Scale Goby *(P. limbatosquamis)*—all secretive relatives of the Golden Green Goby (p. 152)—the Red Earth Dwarf Goby *(Trimma milta),* the Onescale Dwarf Goby *(Trimma unisquamis),* Susan's Pygmy Goby *(Eviota susanae)*—all similar in size and habits to the Divine Pygmy Goby (p. 153)—the shallow-water, mud-dwelling Speartail Goby *(Oxyurichthys lonchotus),* the introduced Mangrove Goby *(Mugiligobius cavifrons),* which lives in brackish water, and various other small and cryptic species known primarily from scientific collections made with fish poison.

The word "goby" derives from the Greek name *kobios* (a gudgeon, or small freshwater fish).

HALFSPOTTED GOBY
Asterropteryx semipunctatus
Rüppell, 1830

Abundant in the coral rubble of silty, well-protected lagoons, bays, and reef flats, these gobies usually perch in front of small holes into which they vanish when alarmed. Kāne'ohe Bay, Ala Moana Beach Park, and Hanauma Bay, O'ahu, are good places to see them. Their dark gray bodies are peppered with tiny blue spots, especially on the lower half (thus the common and species names). The first three dorsal spines are usually prolonged into filaments. These gobies bob up and down rhythmically when they detect a predator, such as a lizardfish, or when they sense an injured goby nearby. Bobbing may have a dual function, both telling the predator "I see you" and warning other gobies of danger. To about 2 ½ in. Indo-Pacific. Photos: Kāne'ohe Bay, O'ahu. 2 ft.

Sneaky love ...
Mature female Halfspotted Gobies have one to seven yellow spots on the base of the tail. While studying the species at the University of Hawai'i, Lisa Privitera discovered similar spots on small males, but not on large ones. Small males, she suggests, may be mimicking females in order to "sneak" close to a spawning pair and release their own sperm.

female? ▲   Keoki Stender

TIDE POOL GOBIES · 'o'opu 'ohune
Bathygobius spp.

Three similar species of gobies inhabit shoreline pools in Hawai'i—the Cocos Island Frill Goby *Bathygobius cocosensis* (Bleeker, 1854), the Cheekscaled Frill Goby *B. cotticeps* (Steindachner, 1879), and the Whitespotted Frill Goby *B. coalitus* (Bennett, 1832). Almost identical in appearance, the three are almost impossible to tell apart in the field or even from photographs. Their generally dark colors blend well with Hawai'i's black volcanic rock, but they can lighten to match other backgrounds. Light or dark bars often develop, helping to break up the outline of the fish. All are predators of small invertebrates. Of the three, the Whitespotted Frill Goby is most abundant in the higher pools, and is probably seen most often. All four of the photos presented here could well be of that species. The Whitespotted and Cheekscale gobies grow to at least 4 in. The Cocos Island goby probably does not attain more than 3 in. All three are found throughout the Indo-Pacific. Photos: (top and immediately below) Makapu'u, O'ahu. (two center photos) Sandy Beach, O'ahu.

BARRED TIDE POOL GOBY
Kelloggella oligolepis (Jenkins, 1903) ▶

These small slender gobies live in the highest pools along rocky shorelines. Mature males have distinct bars and are readily distinguishable from females and young individuals. A single "big" male usually occupies the deepest hole in the pool; females and juveniles skitter about in the shallows. Males sometimes darken and develop iridescent blue markings on the dorsal fin, possibly courtship coloration. To about 1 in. Endemic to Hawai'i. Photos: Punalu'u, Hawai'i.

male ▲   female ▲

WIRE CORAL GOBY *Bryaninops yongei* (Davis & Cohen, 1968)

Wire corals (*Cirrhipathes* and *Stichopathes* spp.) are unbranched, whiplike relatives of black corals that usually grow off rocky walls in areas with some current. Many wire corals harbor a pair of these minute fish, which use their host as means to venture safely out into the water to feed on passing plankton. Their backs are transparent with seven brownish or yellowish bars. The lower half of the body is greenish brown. A light internal line is visible above the spinal column. Several juveniles and a pair of small shrimps, *Pontonides ankeri,* may be present on the wire coral as well. If you find a wire coral colony with gobies, look for a band cleared of living tissue where the fish lay their clear eggs. The species name honors pioneer British zoologist Sir Charles Maurice Yonge (1899-1986). To about 1 1/3 in. Indo-Pacific. Photo: Mākua, O'ahu. 80 ft.

GORGONIAN GOBY
Bryaninops amplus Larson, 1985

Outside Hawai'i, this goby generally lives on gorgonian sea whips. In the Islands, where suitable gorgonians do not occur, it lives on man-made objects, such as old tires or buoy lines, as well as on wire corals. It resembles the Wire Coral Goby (above) but grows to a larger size, is more orange in color, has a more pointed snout, and lives in groups as well as in pairs. Where wire corals are abundant, gobies often move from one coral to another, darting quickly across the intervening space. To about 2 in. Indo-Pacific. Photo: Mākua, O'ahu. 100 ft.

BLACK CORAL GOBY
Bryaninops tigris Larson, 1985

These gobies live in bushes of black coral (*Antipathes* spp.) They are difficult to find and photograph because most black coral bushes harbor no gobies, and within those that do, the tiny fish are superbly camouflaged. (Look for pairs of bright golden eyes.) Like other gobies in the genus *Bryaninops*, they feed on passing plankton by darting briefly off their host into the water. If disturbed, they jump from branch to branch like little monkeys. To about 1 in. Indo-Pacific. Photo: Molokini Islet, Maui. 95 ft. Note the eggs under the goby. (Jeff Kuehn)

Jeff Kuehn

150

TWOSPOT SAND GOBY *Coryphopterus duospilus* Hoese & Reader, 1985 [HAWAIIAN SAND GOBY]

Small brown and white spots scattered over a translucent grayish body help this goby to blend into the sand. The dorsal fin, usually raised, is marked with two faint black spots; a black line extends from the first of these onto the back. These fish usually occur individually or in small groups at the edge of the reef on silty sand. They shelter under rocks or coral and seldom venture far from cover. Some specialists place this fish in the genus *Fusigobius*. To 2 ½ in. Indo-Pacific. Photo: Kahe Point, Oʻahu. 50 ft.

HAWAIIAN EYEBAR GOBY *Gnatholepis knighti* Jordan & Evermann 1903

This goby is one of two in Hawaiʻi with dark bars through the eye. Its dark bars do not meet at the top of the head. It has scattered dark and white specks on the body and a row of smudgy dark spots along the lower side. There is a tiny, scarcely-visible round yellow spot above the pectoral fin base. It lives in groups on silty sand at the bases of walls or coral heads, usually at depths above 40 ft., and darts into crevices when alarmed. Like some other gobies, it bobs rhythmically up and down when it senses a predator. This probably warns nearby gobies of danger and may also signal to the predator "I see you. Don't waste your energy, and mine, by launching an attack." In Australia gobies of this genus in general are called "weeper gobies." To about 3 in. Endemic to Hawaiʻi. Photo: Mākua, Oʻahu. 25 ft.

SHOULDERSPOT GOBY *Gnatholepis cauerensis* (Bleeker, 1853)

This goby and the Hawaiian Eyebar Goby (above) are easily confused. It has fine dark lines along the side instead of rows of dark spots, and the eye bars meet at the top of the head. The yellow spot on the shoulder is vertically elongated and slightly larger than that of the Eyebar Goby. The Shoulderspot Goby generally lives slightly deeper than the Eyebar Goby, usually at 40 ft. or below, and of the two is the one seen more frequently by scuba divers. To about 3 in. Indo-Pacific. Photo: Waimea Bay, Oʻahu. 50 ft.

CLOUDY GOBY *Opua nephodes* E.K. Jordan, 1925

Not often seen by snorkelers or divers, this goby lives on muddy or silty bottoms away from reefs, either in highly protected areas such as Kāne'ohe, O'ahu, or at sufficient depth offshore to be protected from surge. It is grayish with many brown dots and some smaller white spots. <u>Some of the brown dots coalesce to form "dashes" in a line along the center of the side.</u> It is often encountered in groups, occasionally in large aggregations, and is sometimes associated with burrows made by other animals. To about 2 in. Possibly endemic. Records from the Marshall Islands and Palau need to be verified. Photo: Kahe Point, O'ahu. 70 ft. Previously placed in the genus *Hazeus*.

GOLDEN GREEN GOBY *Priolepis aureoviridis* (Gosline, 1959)

This secretive goby dwells in crevices and holes, almost always clinging upside down to the ceiling. Orange-yellow to brownish green, with darker bars ringing the body, it often contrasts nicely with its surroundings. To about 2 ½ in. Hawai'i, Pohnpei, and the Caroline Islands. Photo: Mākua, O'ahu. 40 ft. (Note: The photo is flipped. To view the fish as it was in real life, turn the page upside down!) Three even more secretive *Priolepis* species occur in Hawai'i (see p. 148).

For years the Golden Green Goby was believed to be endemic to Hawai'i. Recently it was found in the Caroline Islands and Pohnpei. Hawai'i's position as endemic marine fish capital of the world has been slowly eroding. Ten years ago the endemism rate for Hawai'i was thought to be about 30 percent. Today it is closer to 25 percent, due primarily to new distribution records such as this. Occasionally, however, the count is boosted, as when a new endemic fish is discovered, or a well-known species such as the Goldring Surgeonfish or Hawaiian Hogfish is divided into two or more regional species, one of which is endemic to Hawai'i. DNA analysis plays an increasingly large role in this. So far, Hawai'i still rules, although Easter Island is close behind with an endemism rate of 22 percent. (see also p. 69)

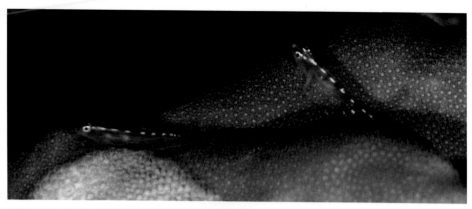

MICHEL'S GHOST GOBY *Pleurosicya micheli* Fourmanoir, 1971

This goby lives on the surface of corals, in Hawai'i usually species of *Porites*. Its transparent body contains an orange-red stripe; in strong light a series of reflective dashes along the top of the spine make the fish appear to glow from within. It has a wide Indo-Pacific distribution and attains about 1 in. Photo: Puakō, Hawai'i. 30 ft. (on Finger Coral, *Porites compressa*). A rarely-seen endemic, Larson's Ghost Goby *(P. larsonae),* duller in color and slightly smaller, also occurs on Finger Coral.

DIVINE PYGMY GOBY *Eviota epiphanes* Jenkins, 1903

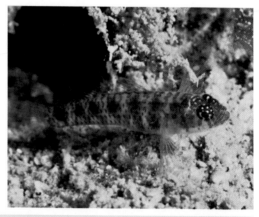

Fully grown, this goby attains scarcely 1 in., and it can mature at less than half that size. Usually it is translucent with reddish or grayish spots and bars, but it can appear bluish green, green, olive brownish, or may be bluish covered with green spots. It inhabits small interstices of the reef from the shoreline down to about 30 ft. in areas with good water movement. For many years this was the only pygmy goby known from Hawai'i. In 1999, however, David W. Greenfield and John E. Randall described two new *Eviota* species from Kāne'ohe Bay, O'ahu: *E. susanae* and *E. rubra*. Later they determined that *rubra* was only a color variant of *susanae*. The reason for the scientific species name, perhaps meaning "divine revelation" is unclear. Known from Japan, Hawai'i, and the Line Islands. Photo: Waimea Bay, O'ahu. 15 ft.

The Divine Pygmy Goby could well be Hawai'i's most abundant fish. Larvae of the genus Eviota *(pygmy gobies) are five times more abundant in Hawai'i's coastal waters than those of any other fish genus. In other words, the number of these tiny gobies within our reefs (2 species known at present) might be truly enormous. If so, they are probably an important part of the food chain, vital to the ecology of the reef. Ken Longenecker found evidence of this when he examined the stomachs of 16 Blue Goatfish (p. 142) and discovered Divine Pygmy Gobies to be by far the most common prey item.*

TAYLOR'S DWARF GOBY *Trimma taylori* Lobel, 1979

Most gobies are bottom-dwellers, but these tiny translucent orange-yellow fish hover in loose groups of sometimes 100 or more under overhangs and in caves. They typically orient to the wall or ceiling. Although common, they are easily overlooked. They feed on planktonic crustaceans, mostly copepods. The name honors marine biologist and author Leighton Taylor, director of the Waikīkī Aquarium from 1975-1986. Ichthyologists enjoy an in-joke here: the gobies have bare heads (i.e. lack scales on the tops of their heads), and Dr. Taylor is not hirsute. Discovered in Hawai'i, Taylor's Dwarf Goby is now known throughout most of the Indo-Pacific. To about 1 in. Photo: Pūpūkea, O'ahu. 70 ft.

HAWAIIAN SHRIMP GOBY
Psilogobius mainlandi Baldwin, 1972

These gobies are light tan with a series of about 10 round, gold-brown patches of various sizes along the middle of the side. Up to seven narrow white bars usually mark the midbody. Adults have scattered iridescent blue spots on the gill covers and sides. Some individuals, probably males, have more blue spots than others. These gobies are symbiotic with either of two similar species of snapping shrimps (*Alpheus rapax* and *A. rapacida*). Goby and shrimp require each other for long-term survival. The almost blind shrimp digs a burrow which it shares with the goby. The goby, with its keener senses, stands guard at the entrance while the shrimp labors underground, clearing and extending passages. The shrimp emerges at intervals, often pushing a load of rubble like a little bulldozer and always keeping one antenna in contact with the goby's tail fin. At the slightest sign of danger the goby twitches its tail, signaling the shrimp to retreat. If danger is imminent, the goby follows, diving in head-first. The burrows are under constant construction and may shift location from day to day. Their entrances tend to enter the sand at an angle and usually have a pile of excavated sand and rubble in front. Shrimp-goby burrows are abundant on shallow reef flats in Kāne'ohe Bay, O'ahu. One can also find them in the Keyhole area at Hanauma Bay, O'ahu, and down to at least 70 ft. in certain calm, protected areas with silty sand bottoms, such as at Olowalu, Maui. Many species of shrimp gobies are known but this is the only one from Hawai'i. The species name honors Gordon B. Mainland who wrote a thesis on Hawaiian gobies in 1939 while at the University of Hawai'i. The goby attains about 2 ½ in., the shrimps about 1 ½ in. The goby is endemic; the shrimps have Indo-Pacific distributions. Photos: (above) Kāne'ohe Bay, O'ahu, 2 ft.; (all below) Olowalu, Maui. 70 ft.

This goby seemed unperturbed as I inched up slowly to it with my giant camera and big double strobes. I waited until the shrimp started to emerge, then snapped a shot.

At the flash of my strobes, the goby retreated slightly, darkened its eye sockets dramatically, and partially raised its dorsal fin. Suspecting a predator, it was probably signaling "I see you, so don't bother to attack." (A predator would presumably lose interest at this point, knowing that an alert goby almost always escapes, and the goby would save itself the trouble of dashing into the burrow.) Meanwhile, the clueless shrimp continued its advance. I snapped another shot.

After the second strobe flash the goby's dorsal shot all the way up, and the fish twitched slightly, signaling the shrimp to retreat. The goby remained on high alert at the burrow entrance until I took this final picture, after which it turned and dived into the hole.

GROUPERS and ANTHIAS
(Serranidae)

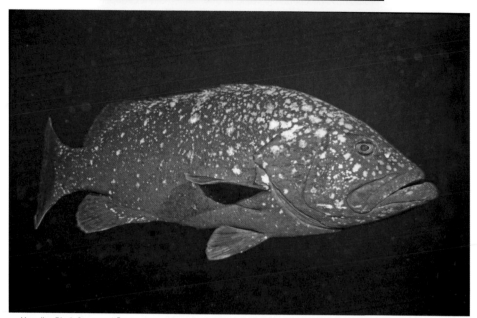

Hawaiian Black Grouper · **hāpuʻu** · enters scuba depths only in the Northwestern Hawaiian Islands · Midway Atoll. 40 ft. (p. 159)

Groupers are large-mouthed, heavy-bodied, bottom-dwelling predators, usually solitary in nature. Anthias, by contrast, are small, delicately colored, social plankton-eaters. Both belong to the large and diverse family Serranidae, along with soapfishes and a few other groups not found in Hawaiʻi.

Groupers (sometimes called sea basses) occur from shallow water to depths of many hundreds of feet. Some grow to enormous size. They have a protruding lower jaw and their tail fin usually has a rounded or straight back edge. Most are blotched, spotted and dull; a few wear bright colors. Groupers seldom chase their prey, relying instead on ambush or careful stalking to get within striking distance. They engulf their prey in a manner similar to many other large-mouthed fish predators, such as scorpionfishes and trumpetfishes. When the prey animal is sufficiently close, the grouper snaps open its large protrusible mouth. Water rushes in, carrying with it the grouper's meal. This operation takes only a fraction of a second and is surprisingly effective. The stomachs of large groupers have been found to contain lobsters, stingrays, porcupinefishes, and sea turtles. The Giant Grouper (p. 159), is probably capable of swallowing a man. Extremely rare in Hawaiʻi, it can attain 9 ft. and weigh almost 900 lbs. The Goliath Groupers of the Eastern Pacific and tropical Atlantic (*Epinephelus quinquefasciatus* and *E. itajara,* respectively) are similar in size and habits.

The larger groupers are known for their curiosity and intelligence. On reefs where they have not been speared or molested they sometimes approach human visitors and may learn to accept food or stroking. They have even been known to identify individual divers (but have also injured divers who neglected them when food was expected). Large groupers have been speared or fished out from many of the world's diving areas. Hawaiʻi is no exception. In 1956 a 354-pound specimen was speared at a depth of 110 ft. in Honokahua Bay, Maui, and in 1958 a 350-pounder was taken at 120 ft. off the south shore of Kauaʻi after a 4-hour fight involving three divers. It exceeded 7 ft.

in length. More recently, in 1989, a 554-pound monster was caught on a handline in Kīhei, Maui. These exceedingly rare fish are found between 15 and 300 ft., usually in or near caves. The species should probably be protected. The economic value of one "tame" Giant Grouper to the dive industry would far outweigh any price it could possibly command in the fish market.

At the other end of the size scale, the delicate and brightly colored anthias, which live in groups, seldom exceed four inches. In other parts of the tropical Indo-Pacific these graceful little fish swarm around shallow coral heads in large numbers. In Hawai'i, however, they occur more sparsely, usually near dropoffs and isolated coral heads at depths of 40 ft. or more, becoming most abundant below 150 ft. Anthias are among the most pleasing and attractive of reef fishes, and Hawai'i is home to a number of species. Most divers, however, have probably never observed them.

The reproductive lives of serranids are interesting—most groupers begin life as females and become male upon attaining a large size. Most anthias remain female for life, living in "harems" dominated by a single male. If the male dies, the top-ranking female reverses sex and takes his place (see p. 162 bottom). Some angelfishes, wrasses, and parrotfishes have similar life histories. Such female to male sex-reversing fishes are known as "protogynous hermaphrodites."

Although the family Serranidae is one of the largest in the fish world, with over 500 species, only 17 are native to Hawai'i, most of them secretive or small and of no commercial value. Ten are described below. Among those omitted are some deepwater anthias and several small perchlets and podges that live within reefs at snorkeling and scuba depths but are never seen alive. Because groupers are an important fishery resource in many parts of the world, the State of Hawai'i introduced three species from the South Pacific in the 1950s. Only one, the Peacock Grouper, has survived to reproduce in Hawaiian waters.

The word "grouper" (from the Brazilian Portuguese *garoupa*) is probably of Native American origin. "Anthias" is a Greek word for an unspecified sea fish, but it would seem to fit. In *20,000 Leagues Under the Sea*, Jules Verne wrote: "I observed some fine anthiae.... Their name signifies flower, and they justify their appellation by their shaded colors, their shades comprising the whole gamut of reds, from the paleness of the rose to the brightness of the ruby, and the fugitive tints that clouded their dorsal fin."

Bicolor Anthias fighting · Mākua, O'ahu. 50 ft. (p. 161)

juvenile ▲

PEACOCK GROUPER · **roi** · *Cephalopholis argus* Bloch & Schneider, 1801 [BLUESPOTTED GROUPER]

Introduced from Mo'orea, French Polynesia, in 1956, for fisheries purposes, **roi** have become common throughout the Hawaiian Islands, where they continue to be known by their Tahitian name. Often ciguatoxic and dangerous to eat, they are not targeted by fishermen and have undergone a population explosion. Small individuals are dark brown with dark-edged iridescent blue spots. In larger specimens the ground color lightens, the spots fade somewhat, and a series of light vertical bars may appear on the rear half of the body. Sometimes a large pale patch develops under the pectoral fins. These wary fish typically sit on or near a coral head, disappearing into a crevice when approached. They hunt by lying on the bottom and darting forward to catch small reef fishes, particularly juvenile surgeonfishes, and occasionally crustaceans. Sometimes they ambush by hanging motionless in midwater, lunging at passing prey or chasing it a short distance. They will also follow a foraging eel or octopus to capture animals flushed from crevices, or swim with a school of browsing surgeonfishes using them as cover while hunting. Sometimes one or more groupers will repeatedly harrass a stationary eel, presumably to get it moving from hole to hole where it may scare out potential prey. (The Kona coast of the Big Island and Molokini Islet, Maui, are good places to see eel-grouper interaction in Hawai'i.) Studies off Sinai in the Red Sea show that these groupers hunt mostly between 6 am and 8 am and again between 5 pm and 6 pm, and that 6 to 12 percent of their hunting strikes occur in association with other animals. The species is named for the hundred staring eyes of the mythical Greek monster Argus. To about 16 in. Indo-Pacific. Photo: Hanauma Bay, O'ahu. 40 ft. (inset: Ahukini Landing, Kaua'i. 20 ft.)

Peacock Grouper Reproduction

In the Red Sea, males maintain harems of 2-6 females in ter-ritories of up to half an acre which they defend against neigh-boring males. Females hold sub-territories within a male's territory which they defend against each other. Every day starting at dawn a male visits his females in turn. Approaching a female's hiding place, he erects his dorsal fin. The female emerges, erecting her dorsal and lightening to pale white with vertical bars. Then they swim together and rub flanks, after which he departs to the next female. During territorial disputes males may engage in "color fights" by positioning themselves at right angles, darkening, and "flashing" the white bars on their flanks on and off. The loser usually pales to whitish and retreats. If neither submits, the two may physi-cally attack each other. In Micronesia, Peacock Groupers spawn in groups within their territories at dusk. During court-ship, both sexes darken except for a white "keyhole" down the center of the body. Photo: Pūpūkea, O'ahu. 15 ft.

Kendra Ignacio

Cooperative hunting

Hunting associations between animals are not uncommon on the reef. Typically, a small predator follows a larger animal in hopes of nabbing small prey inadvertently flushed by it. Peacock Groupers and Whitemouth Morays, however, have elevated the simple hunting association into a true cooperative venture in which each animal benefits.

1) Hunting partners establish visual contact.

2) They touch noses and go, ensuring that both start at the same time.

3) They swim quickly together to a nearby hole in the coral which has two entrances.

4) The eel slithers into one entrance while the grouper waits outside the other. Prey animals inside will either be caught by the eel or try to escape through the back, where they will be confronted by the grouper. It's a win-win situation.

Sometimes, the situation appears more one-sided. Peacock Groupers are occasionally seen rubbing persistently up against stationary eels, seemingly harrassing them. The eel, in this case, is presumably not interested in hunting. What now? Perhaps the grouper is simply trying to get the eel moving, in hopes that it will inadvertantly flush something from the next hole it enters.

Vicky Newman

GIANT GROUPER *Epinephelus lanceolatus* (Bloch, 1790)

The presence of enormous groupers in Hawaiian waters has long been known, but so rare are these fish that until fairly recently no ichthyologist had never examined one. When a 554 lb. monster was caught from shore near Kīhei, Maui, in 1989, Dr. John E. Randall of Honolulu's Bishop Museum flew over and identified it. Adults are dull yellowish to brownish blotched and mottled with darker brown; the fins bear numerous black spots. Juveniles are brighter yellow marked with three wide irregular black bars. Because of their size, these groupers are rare throughout their range, even in areas that have not been fished. They occur from about 15 ft. to at least 300 ft. and often shelter in caves or under large ledges. The Maui specimen had fed on spiny lobsters and crabs, as well as the octopus that had been used as bait. Sightings by divers in Hawai'i are extremely unusual, and most occur in deep water. Spots where Giant Groupers have been glimpsed include Moku Manu, O'ahu, and Lehua Rock, off Ni'ihau. In June 2006 Vicky Newman took this rare photo of one off Kona. It was 3-4 ft. long. Large adults attain at least 9 ft. with a weight of about 880 lbs. Indo-Pacific. Photo: Kona, Hawai'i. 90 ft. (Vicky Newman)

HAWAIIAN BLACK GROUPER · hāpu'u · *Epinephelus quernus* Seale, 1901

This is the most abundant of Hawai'i's two native groupers (The Giant Grouper, above, is extremely rare). Around the main islands it occurs at depths of several hundred feet, well beyond the range of sport divers. In the Northwestern Hawaiian Islands, where cooler water temperatures prevail, it inhabits shallower water and has even been seen by snorkelers! Adults are almost black with whitish blotches and spots that they can lighten or darken. Juveniles (on rare occasions seen by divers around the main islands) have vertical rows of white spots. Groupers of the genus *Epinephelus* usually migrate considerable distances to spawn in enormous groups but little is known of this species' habits. Studies show that it feeds primarily on bottom-associated crustaceans, fishes and cephalopods. Shrimps of the family Pandalidae are an important food. To about 3 ft. Endemic. Photo: Midway Atoll. 40 ft.

SUNRISE BASSLET
Liopropoma aurora (Jordan & Evermann, 1903) [Sunset Basslet]

This rarely-seen Hawaiian endemic usually occurs below 150 ft. in caves and under overhangs. Its stocky orange-red body, pointed head marked with yellow lines, and flaring yellow-edged fins should make identification easy. Although the species name means "dawn," the common name Sunset Basslet is sometimes used because deep-diver Richard Pyle once wrote an article about one that he saw at sunset. To about 6 in. Endemic. Photo: Molokini Islet, Maui, 180 ft. (A similar Hawaiian basslet, *L. colletei*, is whitish with dark horizontal stripes. It hides deep within coral at depths of 20 ft. or more and is so secretive it is almost never observed alive.)

ELEGANT ANTHIAS
Caprodon unicolor Katayama, 1975

Purplish pink with scattered yellow markings and reddish bars on the rear sides, these anthias-like fish were first seen alive in 1997 when divers photographed a small group on a wreck at Midway Atoll. They appear to match a species previously known only from deep water, the first scientific specimens of which were taken on a seamount near Midway at a depth of 550 ft. The species was named in 1975 but the original specimens have subsequently been lost. Little is known about these pretty and almost never seen fish. To about 12 in. Probably endemic. Photo: Corsair wreck, Midway Atoll. 110 ft.

HAWAIIAN YELLOW ANTHIAS
Odontanthias fuscipinnis (Jenkins, 1901)

Orange-yellow trimmed with crimson and violet, this rare and spectacular Hawaiian endemic was first photographed alive in 1989 at Molokini Islet, Maui, to the surprise of scientists who had always assumed it to live beyond the depth range of scuba divers. It has since been found as shallow as 140 ft. and usually occurs in small groups under ledges along deep vertical walls, typically swimming upside down on the ceiling. Previously placed in the genus *Holanthias* (now restricted to the Atlantic Ocean). To about 9 in. Endemic. Photo: Molokini Islet. 180 ft. (Mike Severns)

Mike Severns

a) male ▲ b) females ▼

BICOLOR ANTHIAS
Pseudanthias bicolor (Randall, 1979)

These are the anthias most often seen by divers in Hawai'i. They are orange on the back and upper side, lavender to whitish below. Males are larger than females and their elongated second and third dorsal spines each bear a small fleshy yellow flap at the tip. Preferring depths of 40 ft. or more, these fish typically live in colonies along walls or around isolated coral heads. Off Mākua, O'ahu, they occur in as little as 15-20 ft., often sharing a crevice or hole with a large Yellowmargin Moray. (p. 103) To about 4 ½ in. Indo-Pacific. Photos: (a) Mākua, O'ahu. 40 ft. (b) Puakō, Hawai'i. 120 ft. (c) Pūpūkea, O'ahu. 70 ft. (see also p. 156)

c) male

a) male ▲   b) female ▼

c) male color variation, or possibly a mature female changing to male ▼

HAWAIIAN LONGFIN ANTHIAS
Pseudanthias hawaiiensis
(Randall, 1979)

Long pelvic and anal fins (especially on males) characterize these small, beautiful, uncommon anthias. Males have a yellow head and a reddish orange body which becomes lavender toward the tail. Small females are mostly yellow on the head and back, with pinkish orange sides, and mature females are almost completely yellow except for magenta spots and lines near the eye. These fish prefer depths of 70 ft. or more, typically living under ledges and often swimming upside down on the ceiling. Groups are usually small, but in certain areas, usually along deep walls exposed to some current, they can occur by the dozen or more. Once considered a subspecies of the Indo-Pacific Longfin Anthias *(P. ventralis)*, this fish now enjoys full species status. To about 3 in. Endemic. Photos: (a) "General Store," south shore Kaua'i. 100 ft. (b) Pūpūkea, O'ahu. 70 ft. (c) "Amber's Arches," Kaua'i. 70 ft.

THOMPSON'S ANTHIAS
Pseudanthias thompsoni
(Fowler, 1923)

These anthias have a lavender streak under the eye and vary from almost entirely pinkish to orange-yellow, the scales prominent due to a yellow spot on each. Males have lavender overtones and can develop beautifully extended tail filaments with lavender margins. These fish usually inhabit ledges and dropoffs at 70 ft. or more and are most abundant in the Northwestern Hawaiian Islands. In the main islands they are seen most often around Kaua'i and Ni'ihau. Further south they are rarely encountered, although rebreather divers have reported them common at 300' and below. Strangely, prior to the 1980s they were the most abundant anthias in shallow water on O'ahu—perhaps warming sea temperatures caused a population shift. The species name honors John W. Thompson, an artist and technician at the Bishop Museum (1901 to 1928) who prepared beautifully colored casts of Hawaiian fishes. Males to 8 ½ in.; females usually half that size. Endemic. Photos: (a) "Black Coral Arch," east shore Kaua'i, 70 ft. (b) Corsair wreck, Midway Atoll. 110 ft.

a) male ▲   b) female ▼

EARLE'S SPLITFIN ANTHIAS
Luzonichthys earlei Randall, 1981

These small slender orange-red anthias with magenta undersides swarm over rubble bottoms by the hundreds, usually below 150 ft. When approached they dive into the rubble. Sometimes (probably while spawning), they form dense "bait balls" near the surface and can be collected with a dipnet from a boat. Honolulu naturalist John Earle used to catch them to feed his pet frogfish, thinking them to be immature Bicolor Anthias (p. 161). Bruce Carlson, who later became Director of the Waikīkī Aquarium, dropped in one day at fish-feeding time and immediately recognized these "feeder fish" as a new species. "Stop!" he cried, and just in time. The species now bears Earle's name. To about 2 ½ in. Indo-Pacific. Photo: Five Fathom Pinnacle, about 20 miles south of Ni'ihau. 80 ft.

163

GURNARDS
(Dactylopteridae)

At least three families of odd bottom-dwelling fishes are called gurnards in various parts of the world. Tropical divers and snorkelers, however, are likely to encounter only the "flying gurnards" (family Dactylopteridae), which have enormous winglike pectoral fins and wide squarish heads completely covered with bony plates. Despite the suggestive name, they move slowly and rarely leave the bottom, except perhaps to spawn. Some ichthyologists prefer to call them "helmet gurnards" because of their armored heads. Although belonging to the order Scorpaeniformes along with the scorpionfishes, gurnards bear no venomous spines. There are seven species worldwide, with one in Hawai'i. The Hawaiian name, **pinao**, also means dragonfly.

ORIENTAL FLYING GURNARD
loloaʻu; pinao
Dactyloptena orientalis
(Cuvier, 1829)
[ORIENTAL HELMET GURNARD]

Flying Gurnards do not fly; they crawl along sandy bottoms using specially modified fingerlike spines on their pelvic fins. They also use these spines to scratch for food, "like a chicken's feet scratching gravel to look for worms," as one writer puts it. Ordinarily, the "wings" (an enormous pair of pectoral fins) are kept folded alongside the armored, box-like body. When alarmed, a gurnard spreads its wings, thereby increasing its apparent size and confusing predators. Small specimens, as pictured here, have eye-like spots (ocelli) on the wings, which might further intimidate predators. On the gurnard's head lies a single black dorsal spine. If spreading its wings doesn't work, the gurnard has a final trick: it raises this spine, or flicks it up and down, and makes a popping sound. Oriental Flying Gurnards are encountered most often in sand adjacent to reefs. They sometimes occur in very shallow water where waders can see them. To 15 in. Indo-Pacific. Photos: Ko Olina Resort, Oʻahu. 5 ft. (see also p. xi)

HAWKFISHES
(Cirrhitidae)

Stocky Hawkfish · **po'opa'a** · Hanauma Bay, O'ahu. 15 ft. (p. 167)

Hawkfishes are small to medium-size predators which typically perch motionless on coral heads or outcrops, waiting for prey. They strike swiftly when a small fish or crustacean passes by, either catching it or pursuing it vigorously for a short distance before returning to their perch. Several species are common in Hawai'i and easy to observe. Characteristic of the family are curious tufts of filaments (cirri) extending from the ends of their dorsal spines.

Hawkfishes live in haremic social groups consisting of a male and one or more females. Some species, perhaps most, are capable of changing sex, males being sex-reversed females. Males are usually larger than females. Around twilight they visit their females sequentially, mating individually with each. If the male dies, the dominant female changes sex and takes his place.

Out of 35 hawkfish species worldwide, six are found in Hawai'i (one of them endemic). All are shown here. The Hawaiian name for hawkfish is **piliko'a**, which means "coral clinging."

TWOSPOT HAWKFISH
Amblycirrhitus bimacula
(Jenkins, 1903)

This small secretive species lives far back in crevices or deep between branches of coral and is seldom seen, although it is possibly Hawai'i's most abundant hawkfish. Look for it at night, when it is most active. It resembles the Redbarred Hawkfish (below) in color and size, but always displays two well-defined, light-edged round black spots, one on the gill cover and another under the soft dorsal fin. To a predator these spots may resemble the widely-spaced eyes of a larger animal, thereby acting as a deterrent. To about 3 ½ in. Indo-Pacific. Photo: "Haleiwa Trench," O'ahu. 15 ft. (night)

REDBARRED HAWKFISH · **piliko'a**
Cirrhitops fasciatus (Bennett, 1828)

One of the most common reef fish in Hawai'i, this perky and attractive hawkfish is usually marked with five broad grayish red to brick red bars on the side and a black spot on the gill cover. It frequently lives deep under ledges or in the entrances of caves and in such dim environments a large diffuse blackish spot often develops at the base of the tail and the body becomes almost uniformly pale. A very similar hawkfish (*C. mascarensis*) occurs in the distant islands of Mauritius and Madagascar in the Western Indian Ocean. The two probably had a widespread common ancestor which died out everywhere else. The species name means "barred." Endemic. To about 4 ½ in. Photos: Pūpūkea, O'ahu. 25-30 ft.

typical coloration ▲

coloration in dim environments ▼

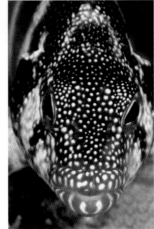

STOCKY HAWKFISH · **poʻopaʻa** · *Cirrhitus pinnulatus* (Bloch & Schneider, 1801)
　　The Stocky Hawkfish perches in exposed rocky areas in shallow water, sometimes wedging its pectoral fins into cracks to stabilize itself in the surge. Its robust, mottled body is blotched with blue, brown, and red, and has three loose rows of white spots on the side. Hawaiian specimens may have more colorful markings on the head than those from other Indo-Pacific locations. The species name comes from *pinna* ("fin"). The Hawaiian name means "hard head." Known to fishermen as "Rockfish," they are easily hooked, but not greatly esteemed. In old Hawaiʻi it was said, "The fisherman who fools around in shallow water takes home a **poʻopaʻa**." To about 11 in. Indo-Pacific. Photo: Hanauma Bay, Oʻahu. 30 ft. (see also p. 165)

LONGNOSE HAWKFISH *Oxycirrhites typus* Bleeker, 1857

   Almost always living in or near black coral (or gorgonians, outside Hawai'i) and usually at depths over 100 ft., the Longnose Hawkfish is an unusual find in the Islands, where most shallow black coral was removed in the early days of scuba diving. It is crosshatched in red and, with its long snout, cannot be confused with any other hawkfish species. Longnose Hawkfish may be seen on Kaua'i at several popular dive sites in as little as 70 ft. The back side of Molokini Islet, Maui, is also home to a few. The species name means "figure" or "shape." To about 5 in. The most widespread species of its family, the Longnose Hawkfish occurs from East Africa and the Red Sea to the west coast of the Americas. Photo: Laupāhoehoe, Hawai'i. 70 ft. (in Feathery Black Coral, *Myriopathes ulex*)

Research in Papua New Guinea shows that Longnose Hawkfish live in groups of a male and one or two females. Each inhabits a separate coral tree. Spawning occurs around sunset, the male visiting his females in their home coral trees, or meeting them at nearby corals.

ARC-EYE HAWKFISH · piliko'a
Paracirrhites arcatus (Cuvier, 1829)

One of the most common reef fish in Hawai'i, this hawkfish has two color patterns: tan to reddish with a broad white stripe on the side, and olive to dark brown with no white stripe. In both patterns there is a red, yellow, and blue arc-shaped mark behind the eye and three short oblique bars on the gill cover. This fish almost always shelters in one of two species of branching corals, Antler Coral *(Pocillopora grandis)* or, more commonly, the smaller, more abundant Cauliflower Coral *(P. meandrina)*. About 99 percent of its daylight hours are spent perched inactively on the coral, or on the substrate nearby. Occasionally, it darts out to strike at prey, usually xanthid crabs or other bottom-dwelling organisms. At the approach of a predator (typically a Yellowsaddle Goatfish or a Bluefin Trevally, or the two hunting together) it retreats into its coral head, nestling deep within the branches. One or two hawkfish usually inhabit a single head; more than two is unusual. To 5 ½ in. Indo-Pacific. Photos: (top) Mākaha, O'ahu. 50 ft. (opposite) Palea Point, O'ahu. 25 ft.

Why two color patterns?

The two color patterns of the Arc-Eye Hawkfish are independent of body size or sex. Research by Edward DeMartini and Terry Donaldson off the Big Island's Kona coast revealed that the white stripe pattern predominates in areas where colonies of Cauliflower Coral are relatively far apart, generally at depths of about 25 ft. or more. Where coral colonies are closely spaced (generally in shallower water), the all-brown pattern is most common. The haremic social structure of this fish may explain these patterns. One or more females live in coral heads within the home range of a larger dominant male. The male regularly visits his females to spawn, generally at dusk. The white stripe probably increases visibility, important for the male when coral heads are widely spaced or light is poor, less important when they are close together or light is good. Because the white stripe also increases the risk of predation, it tends to be absent in environments where it is not needed. For unknown reasons, the all-brown color pattern is more prevalent in Hawai'i than in the rest of the Indo-Pacific.

Refugee camp

William Walsh studied the effects of an unusually strong storm on reefs along the Kona coast of the Big Island. Before the storm, heads of Cauliflower Coral (Pocillopora meandrina) had been abundant on shallow reef flats in his study area, but only scattered heads grew in deeper water. Many of the shallow corals sheltered Arc-Eye Hawkfish. The storm destroyed almost all of the shallow colonies, but left many of the deeper ones intact. After the storm, one of the deeper colonies that had previously sheltered no Arc-Eye Hawkfish became home to 11 individuals!

The colony of Cauliflower Coral at right, photographed at Mākua, O'ahu, was sheltering at least 8 hawkfish. However, there had been no recent storm or destruction of coral. Perhaps it was just a social occasion.

a) adult ▲   b) rare color variant ▼   c) juvenile ▼

Pamela Higgins

BLACKSIDE HAWKFISH · hilu pilikoʻa · *Paracirrhites forsteri*
(Bloch & Schneider, 1801) [FRECKLED HAWKFISH]

    Reddish or black spots densely freckle the front half of this large hawkfish; a broad black band bordered in white marks the upper rear. Some adults are considerably darker than others. A yellow-tailed color variant, very rare in Hawaiʻi, is more common in other parts of the Indo-Pacific. Juveniles are half white, half black (divided lengthwise) with a yellow back. Tiny ones may look somewhat like juvenile Saddle or Bird Wrasses. Juveniles shelter in colonies of Cauliflower or Antler Coral and large adults usually perch in the open. They spawn around dusk. The species is named for the Forsters, father-and-son naturalists who accompanied Captain Cook on his second voyage to the Pacific and Indian oceans between 1772 and 1775. To almost 9 in. Indo-Pacific. Photos: (a,c) Mākua, Oʻahu. 30 ft. (b) Kona, Hawaiʻi (Pamela Higgins). (opposite) Hoʻokena, Hawaiʻi. 30 ft.

INFANTFISHES
(Schindleriidae)

You've seen them—thousands of tiny "fry" hovering over the bottom in a loose cloud. These are not fry—they are fully grown infantfish! (or else mysid shrimp—see blue sidebar). Most fishes hatch from eggs into tiny larvae that are quite different in appearance from adults. Typically, these larvae drift as plankton for a period of time, then settle to the bottom and transform into the more familiar mature form. Infantfish, however, become sexually mature in an infantile larva-like form and never attain a "grown up" fish body. Hawai'i has two known species, both likely endemic. Infantfishes are most closely related to the gobies.

 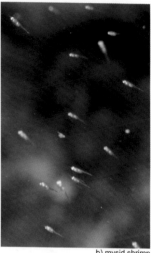

a) infantfish

b) mysid shrimp

INFANTFISHES *Schindleria* spp.
The miniscule fish above, at left, could be either Pietschmann's Infantfish *Schindleria pietschmanni* (Schindler, 1931) or Schindler's Infantfish *S. praematura* (Schindler, 1930). A survey found Pietschmann's Infantfish to be 10 times more abundant than Schindler's, so they are probably the former. Microscopic examination would be needed to confirm this. Both species occur commonly over sand and rubble near reefs, and no habitat difference has been found between them. Their elongate, ribbonlike bodies are transparent except for the head. Neither attains more than 1 in. Both species are probably endemic to Hawai'i. Photos: (a) Haena, Kaua'i. 3 ft. (Larry Basch). (b) Pohoiki, Hawai'i. 50 ft.

Also common in Hawai'i are tiny mysid shrimp that swarm like midges over sand and rubble and are easy to confuse with infantfishes (see photo above, at right). It is not difficult to tell the two apart. Mysids are shorter and stockier than infantfishes, less transparent, and less mobile. Although the two often occur within a few yards of each other, mysids typically remain closer to the bottom, don't swim away as quickly, and are often easier to see.

Smallest fish wars

Are infantfishes the world's smallest fishes? You will have to decide for yourself. For some years the smallest fish (and small-est vertebrate animal) was believed to be Trimmaton nanus, a tiny Indo-Pacific goby that matures at a length of 10 mm (2/5 in.). In 2004, however, the Stout Infantfish (Schindleria brevipinguis) from Queensland, Australia, was hailed as the world's smallest vertebrate. Mature females of this species max out at about 8.4 mm (1/3 in.) and weigh about 1.5 mg (.00005 ounce). Then, in 2006, scientists investigating freshwater peat bogs in Sumatra proclaimed their discovery, Paedocypris progenetica, to be the smallest vertebrate. Females of this tiny carp relative mature at 7.9 mm (1/4 in.). Infantfish promotors countered that weight, not length, should be the deciding factor, and that their infantfish was far lighter than the tiny carp. Meanwhile, frogfish expert Ted Pietsch joined the fray, declaring that a 6.2 mm parasitic male of the deepsea anglerfish Photocorynus spiniceps, was easily the smallest. These minute male anglerfish consist mostly of testicles, attach perma-nently to females vastly larger than themselves, and have almost no independent existence of their own. The other scientists objected, maintaining that it is the smallest species that matters, not just individuals of one sex, especially if parasitic. So, in the end it depends on how one defines "smallest," and whether it is smallest species or smallest animal that counts.

JACKS
(Carangidae)

Bigeye Trevallies · **pake ulua** · rare in Hawai'i · Pai'olu'olu Point, O'ahu. 20 ft. (p. 176)

The jack family includes the jacks, trevallies, rainbow runners, pompanos, leatherbacks, scads, and others. Most are swift, strong-swimming predators which frequent open water near the edge of the reef, but many also occur in shallow water close to shore. They are prized by fishermen for their fighting ability, which can be spectacular. Large jacks have been known to pull a fisherman off his rock ledge into the sea!

Jacks and their relatives are typically silvery on the sides and undersides, and bluish or greenish on the back. This color pattern, common among pelagic (ocean-going) fishes, makes them difficult to see both from above and below. Most have deeply forked tails and deep, narrow, streamlined bodies which vary in shape according to genus. The base of the tail is typically slender and usually reinforced by specially strengthened scales called scutes (easy to see on jacks that have them).

Most jacks feed on fish, typically patrolling the reef in schools, small groups, or as individuals, and relying on superior speed to catch their prey. In the early morning or late afternoon hunting behavior may intensify, the jacks flashing by swiftly and making sudden changes of direction to confuse or isolate their quarry. A study of Giant Trevallies and schooling **nehu** (Hawaiian Anchovies) in Kāne'ohe Bay, O'ahu, showed that single jacks are most efficient at catching isolated prey while groups of jacks are most efficient at catching schooling prey. Typically they break up the school and go after the stragglers. Some jacks, however, feed primarily on the bottom, foraging for crustaceans and other invertebrates, often at night. Smaller members of the family, such as the scads, (**akule** and **'ōpelu**), are schooling plankton-eaters. Night-feeding jacks (or those that feed primarily at dusk and dawn) usually rest by day in semi-stationary schools.

Many jacks can tolerate brackish or nearly fresh water and juveniles and subadults of some species occur in river mouths and estuaries. In the late 1800s field hands on windward Oʻahu sometimes caught huge jacks in rice paddies!

Most jacks are called **ulua** in Hawaiian. Juveniles of about 12 in. or less are **pāpio**. Admired for their vigor and strength, large jacks in olden times were sometimes substituted for a man when human sacrifice was called for. The word **ulua** also became a poetic symbol for "warrior, man, lover, sweetheart," especially in love songs. Women would say "Pull in the **ulua**," meaning "Get your man." The scientific family name comes from *caranga*, a Native American word.

Out of about 140 carangids worldwide, at least 24 are known in Hawaiʻi and 15 are pictured here. One, the Hawaiian Thicklipped Jack (p. 180), is a probable endemic. Among those not shown is *Caranx caballus*, a small schooling immigrant from the Eastern Pacific reported in 1998, apparently erroneously, to have established a breeding population in the Islands. Few have been seen since.

THREADFIN JACK · **ulua kihikihi**
Alectis ciliaris (Bloch, 1787)
[AFRICAN POMPANO]

Juveniles have compressed, diamond shaped bodies with amazingly long filaments trailing from the dorsal and anal fins. Bright and silvery (some call them "mirror fish") they swim near the surface, often in harbors or lagoons, and are believed to mimic venomous jellyfish. As they grow, the body thickens and elongates and the filaments shorten. Fully mature individuals, which lack the filaments entirely, inhabit deep water, often below 200 ft., and are rarely seen by divers or snorkelers. Sightings of juveniles are also out of the ordinary. Very young ones have five dark bars. The scientific name means "hairlike." The Hawaiian word **kihikihi** means "angular," or "zigzag." To about 4 ft. All warm seas. Photos: (a) Maui. (David B. Fleetham) (b) South Point, Hawaiʻi. 20 ft.

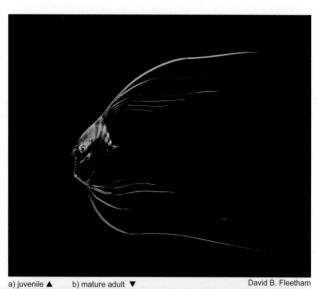

a) juvenile ▲   b) mature adult ▼   David B. Fleetham

173

BARRED JACK · ulua
Ferdauia ferdau (Fabricius, 1775)

Eight to ten dark bars, sometimes faint, identify these jacks. Typically the body is bluish silver, often with tiny, scattered, dark-centered gold spots mostly on the upper sides. Some individuals temporarily darken to almost black. Uncommon in Hawai'i, Barred Jacks usually roam in small schools over sand or rubble bottoms adjacent to the reef. They feed on bottom-dwelling crustaceans and small fishes. Snorkelers at Hanauma Bay, O'ahu, can often see small groups these fish hunting in shallow water, sometimes following foraging bonefish or goatfish. Juveniles sometimes shelter among the tentacles of large pelagic jellyfish. Island Jacks (bottom of page) are similar but lack distinct bars. To about 21 in. Indo-Pacific. Photos: (a) Lāna'i Lookout, O'ahu. 30 ft. (b) Hanauma Bay, O'ahu. 3 ft.

a) adult ▲

b) a juvenile Barred Jack (**pāpio**) follows foraging goatfish in hopes they will uncover something tasty ▲

ISLAND JACK · ulua · *Ferdauia orthogrammus* (Jordan & Gilbert, 1882) [YELLOWSPOTTED JACK]

Silvery, like most jacks, these can be identified by a few oval yellow spots on the side, often with darker centers. Because they sometimes show faint dark bars, they might be confused with the Barred Jack (above), which can also have yellow spots. Small individuals are occasionally seen at snorkeling sites foraging near the bottom in shallow water. Larger individuals school or form small groups in deeper water. This is not a common species in Hawai'i. To 28 in. Indo-Pacific and Eastern Pacific. Photo: Lehua Rock, Ni'ihau. 50 ft.

Giant Trevallies at Midway Atoll. 40 ft. (see next page)   John L. Earle

a) large adult ▲

b) small adult ▼

David R. Schrichte

GIANT TREVALLY · **ulua aukea**
Caranx ignobilis (Forsskål, 1775)
[WHITE ULUA; GIANT ULUA]

The largest of all jacks, these are usually silvery or gray peppered with fine black spots, but can temporarily become almost black. Silvery vertical streaks often mark the back. The steep head profile combined with a black spot at the base of the pectoral fin are identifying features. In old Hawai'i these jacks were admired for their size, vigor, and strength, and came to symbolize a male sweetheart or lover. Today they are the catch fishermen dream about, their profile adorning pickup trucks and T-shirts all over the Islands. As a result, few remain. Maui's Molokini Islet, where they are protected, is one of the few dive sites in Hawai'i where one can count on seeing Giant Trevallies. In the northwestern chain, however, these huge fish still occur in large schools and will approach and surround divers—a heart-thumping experience! Juveniles and subadults often live in river mouths and canals. The species is inappropriately named "low" or "ignoble." The Hawaiian name means "white." In ancient Hawai'i, when a human sacrifice was called for, a large **ulua aukea** was sometimes substituted. Large jacks can be full of ciguatera toxin; be careful before eating them. To about 5 ½ ft. The maximum confirmed weight for this species is 191 lbs. (caught off Maui). Indo-Pacific. Photos: (a) Molokini, Maui. 50 ft. (b) Hanauma Bay, O'ahu. 30 ft. (David R. Schrichte) (see also previous page)

Kings of the reef

*Studies in the Northwest Hawaiian Islands reveal that Giant Trevallies eat 90 percent fish (parrotfishes, **opelu**, wrasses, bigeyes, and eels the most important), a few percent each of crustaceans and cephalopods, and trace amounts of molluscs. These are among the few fishes that consume large adult spiny lobsters. Curious and completely fearless, they have been known to grab and rip away divers' bright snorkel tips and colorful fins. Divers off Molokini Islet, Maui, have seen them rip remoras from manta rays and tear them to bits. An estimated population of 130,000 at French Frigate Shoals is believed to consume about 19,600 metric tons of prey per year.*

Giant Trevally reproduction

In the Northwestern Hawaiian Islands, peak spawning season for these fish is May through August. Reproductive activities observed in the Bohol Strait, Philippines, occurred by day and began with 2-3 males chasing a ripe female 10-12 ft. above the bottom. Eventually the female and one of the males descended to a sandy patch and slowly circled one another, releasing eggs and sperm. At this time they were exceptionally easy to approach. Afterwards the pair moved on, possibly to spawn again somewhere else. During courtship, males developed black coloration on the upper part of the head while females remained uniformly silver-gray.

a) large adult

BLUEFIN TREVALLY · 'ōmilu · *Caranx melampygus* (Cuvier, 1833) [BLUE ULUA]

The most common large jacks in the main Hawaiian Islands, these beautiful predators are bluish white with scattered blue spots on the sides and lovely blue fins. They can alter their color in seconds, however, becoming almost black (see next page). Small individuals (**pāpio**) are more silvery, often with light yellow pectoral fins. Swimming singly, in pairs, or in small groups, these fish typically occur on shallow reefs, sometimes in only a few feet of water. (A study in Kāne'ohe Bay, O'ahu, showed that most remained around the same reefs for at least a year, straying no more than about ¼ mile.) Occasionally they school farther off shore, perhaps to spawn. Active daytime hunters, Bluefin Trevallies are adept at appearing suddenly from around a corner, surprising a fish (sometimes in its own hole), and nabbing it before it can take cover. They will also strike at fish from midwater or from a hidden ambush position. While pursuing escaping prey, these jacks do not hesitate to charge right into or under a coral head, afterwards displaying fresh scrape marks. Some individuals, usually smaller ones, regularly feed in association with eels, octopus, rays, goatfishes, or other species (including human divers!) that flush prey or disturb the substrate while foraging (see pp. 39, 107, 233). A study at Johnston Atoll showed that they turn up regularly at surgeonfish and parrotfish spawning aggregations, striking at prey during both pre-spawning behavior and the spawning act itself. The species name means "black rump." Indo-Pacific to Eastern Pacific. To about 3 ft. Photos: (a, b, c) Hanauma Bay, O'ahu. 3-10 ft. (see also next page)

b) small adult ▼

Important predators

Some scientists consider Bluefin Trevallies to be the most important large daytime fish predators in the Indo-Pacific. An estimated population of 230,000 of these jacks at French Frigate Shoals in the Northwest Hawaiian Islands are believed to consume about 11,000 metric tons of prey per year. Their diet consists of 90% fishes (wrasses, goatfishes, filefishes, damselfishes, parrotfishes, and bigeyes being most important) with lesser amounts of crustaceans and cephalopods, and traces of molluscs.

c) juvenile (**pāpio**)

177

Why do jacks turn black?

While observing group-spawning parrotfish at Johnston Atoll, researcher Gorka Sancho on several occasions saw a large Bluefin Trevally suddenly approach, turn black, and duck under a large table coral nearby. As the parrotfish ascended to spawn, the jack would burst forth and ram through the group, then turn to pursue individual fleeing fish. If another Bluefin Trevally approached the area, the black individual would swim out and nudge its head against the intruder's side. After the nudge, the intruder, which invariably displayed the normal silvery blue coloration, always left peacefully and the black individual returned to its hiding place. Gorka theorizes that black coloration, in addition to concealing the ambusher, signals aggression and temporary "ownership" of the hunting grounds. In support of this, jacks of various species are reported to sometimes turn black when following a ray, an eel, or other foraging fish, presumably to signal that it is "their" fish. Male jacks also turn black during courtship or spawning, perhaps to warn away rival males, impress the female, or both. But it is also quite common to see a black individual simply cruising the reef, often in the company of a normally colored jack. Do both sexes do it? There's still more to learn about why jacks turn black. Photo: Bluefin Trevally, Hanauma Bay, Oʻahu

A black jack scores

While snorkeling in the early morning along the top of the shallow fringing reef at Hanauma Bay, Oʻahu, I saw a free-swimming 4-foot Yellowmargin Moray approaching, closely followed by a big black Bluefin Trevally. So shallow was the reef that the jack's back was almost out of the water. I expected to see some cooperative hunting, but the jack abruptly forsook the eel and darted down into a deep hole in the reef. After a brief flurry the jet black jack emerged with a bright red soldierfish held crosswise in its jaws. Although it lasted only a second, it was one of the most beautiful underwater sights I have ever seen.

BIGEYE TREVALLY · **pake ulua** · *Caranx sexfasciatus* Quoy & Gaimard, 1824 [Bigeye Jack]
These jacks are silvery gray with <u>a black spot on the upper edge of the gill cover</u>. The tips of the second dorsal and anal fins are white and the scutes are dark. They feed primarily on small fish at night, hence the large eyes. By day they congregate in semi-stationary or slowly-circling schools composed of dozens, hundreds, or (outside Hawaiʻi) even thousands of individuals. These jacks may also accompany floating objects far out to sea. (A 1998 study showed that Bigeye Trevally are one of the four most common fish species associating with flotsam in the Western Pacific. Two others are the Rainbow Runner, next page, and the Indo-Pacific Sergeant, p.69.) Bigeye Trevally are now rare in the main Hawaiian Islands, probably because their daytime schooling behavior makes them so easy to spear. The best place to look for them is in marine preserves such as Hanauma Bay, Oʻahu. Pairs spawn at dusk, the male turning almost black. The scientific name means "six-banded" but only **pāpio** (juveniles) display this pattern. Small juveniles are yellow with 5 or 6 dark bars. Juveniles may occur in brackish or even fresh water. To about 3 ft. Indo-Pacific and Eastern Pacific. Photo: Hanauma Bay, Oʻahu. 20 ft. (see also p. 172)

BLACK TREVALLY · ulua lāʻuli · *Caranx lugubris* Poey, 1860

Jacks of the genus *Caranx,* often called trevallies, have prominent scutes—a line of strengthened scales that reinforce the tail. The scutes of the Black Trevally, or Black Jack, are especially easy to see. These jacks vary from almost black to dull gray, but the scutes are always dark. There is a dark spot on the upper gill cover. The species occurs singly or in pairs, typically along steep dropoffs adjacent to deep water. In Hawaiʻi, Black Trevallies are known almost exclusively from the northwestern chain. The photograph at right, taken at Lehua Rock off Niʻihau, is one of the southernmost recorded Hawaiian sightings. To almost 3 ft. Worldwide in warm seas. Photo: Lehua Rock, Niʻihau. 80 ft.

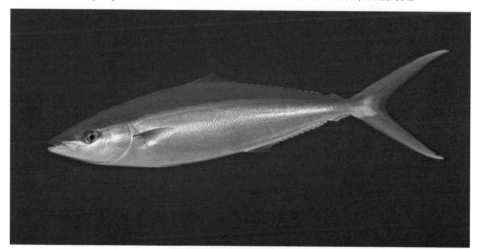

RAINBOW RUNNER · kamanu · *Elagatis bipinnulata* (Quoy & Gaimard, 1825)

These streamlined jacks are round in cross section with a large forked tail. Olive to bluish above and whitish below, they have two light blue stripes running from eye to tail separated by a wider yellowish stripe. They are usually seen adjacent to deep water, often in small schools and occasionally in large ones, and are one of the four fish species most frequently found around floating objects in the Western Pacific. Their principal foods are small fishes that aggregate under those objects and ʻōpelu, or Mackerel Scad (p. 184). Rainbow Runners have been observed swimming close to sharks and scraping themselves against the shark's rough skin, presumably to dislodge parasites (see also p. 184). To almost 4 ft. Indo-Pacific and Atlantic. Photo: Hālona Blowhole, Oʻahu. 30 ft.

GOLDEN TREVALLY · ulua paʻopaʻo · *Gnathanodon speciosus* (Forsskål, 1775) [YELLOW ULUA]

When young these are golden yellow with alternating wide and narrow black vertical bands. Older adults become silvery and their black bands fade or are replaced with spots. Adults, toothless in the upper jaw, feed on deep sandy bottoms and are seldom seen by divers in Hawaiʻi. Even small ones are hard to find. Very small juveniles are pelagic, often accompanying floating objects, large jellyfishes, or large fishes such as sharks, in the manner of the well known Pilot Fish *(Naucrates ductor)*, also a jack. In the latter case they may appear to lead their host by maintaining a position on either side of the snout, but their real purpose is to eat scraps left by the predator when it feeds. The position is safer than it seems; they swim in the predator's blind spot (resulting from eyes placed on either side of the head). The habit of accompanying other animals is not entirely lost with age. In the Marshall Islands adults have been recorded associating with at least three other species of foraging fishes. The species name means "splendid" or "showy." To about 3 ft. Indo-Pacific and Eastern Pacific. Photo: Pacific Beach Hotel aquarium. (Keoki Stender).

HAWAIIAN THICKLIPPED JACK
lehe · *Pseudocaranx cheilio*
(Snyder, 1904)

A conical pointed snout, thick fleshy lips, and an underslung lower jaw characterize these jacks, known locally as "Pig Ulua" or butaguchi. The silvery adults are deep-dwelling and almost never seen by divers and snorkelers except in the cooler northwestern chain. Subadults, however, sometimes enter shallow water around the main islands. They have a yellow stripe from eye to tail and another along the top of the back. Thicklipped Jacks rest in large semi-stationary schools by day, dispersing at night to feed on bottom-dwelling fishes, crustaceans, and cephalopods. In the main islands, where their numbers are few, subadults will sometimes join schools of similarly-colored goatfishes. To 36 in. Probably endemic, but with several very similar species in subtropical waters worldwide. Photos: Midway Atoll. 40-60 ft.

◄ subadults   adults on next page ►

◄ Hawaiian Thicklipped Jacks (see previous page) ▲

LEATHERBACK · **lai** · *Scomberoides lysan* (Forsskål, 1775) [DOUBLESPOTTED QUEENFISH]

Jacks of the genus Scomberoides have long, almost bladelike silvery bodies. They lack scutes and their sides are marked with a series of round spots. This common species has a double row of 6-8 such spots, the lower larger than the upper. The dorsal fin has a conspicuous black tip. The skin is tough and full of embedded needle-like scales; the dorsal and anal spines are venomous. These jacks are seen most often as solitary individuals, but they also swim in schools of a dozen or more. In Kāne'ohe Bay, O'ahu, juvenile Leatherbacks of 1-6 in. have been observed repeatedly striking silversides, mullets, and **nehu** (Hawaiian Anchovies) to feed on scales and skin tissue. When chased, the smaller juveniles dart to the surface and mimic a floating leaf. Adults subsist on small fish, crustaceans, and planktonic organisms. The author has seen them make glancing strikes at sea turtles, large needlefishes, and sharks, when those animals are swimming near the surface. Whether this is for food, to dislodge parasites, or for some other purpose, is open to question, but the recipients of their attentions are clearly annoyed (see also p. 184). These jacks reportedly accompany Humpback Whales wintering in Hawai'i, also for reasons unkown. In old Hawai'i their tough skins were used to make drum heads; more recently they have been used to make fishing lures. To about 28 in. Indo-Pacific. Photo: Hanauma Bay, O'ahu. 5 ft.

GREATER AMBERJACK · **kāhala** · *Seriola dumerili* (Risso, 1810)
    Silvery gray or silvery brown above and silvery below, these predators often have a dark diagonal stripe through the eye. A yellow stripe from eye to tail may or may not be visible. Small juveniles, which typically shelter in floating debris, have five prominent dark bars and a dark diagonal stripe above the eye. Large Amberjacks occasionally enter sheltered bays where snorkelers can see them. At sea they frequently accompany drifting objects. These fish are full of curiosity and will often approach or circle divers, or their bubbles, for a closer look. In Hawai'i they are frequently "hot" (ciguatoxic); take care before eating them. The species name honors French naturalist Auguste Duméril (1812-1870). To almost 6 ft. All tropical seas. Photo: South Point, Hawai'i. 45 ft. (see also next page).

juvenile ▲

ALMACO JACK · **kāhala** · *Seriola rivoliana* (Valenciennes, 1833)
    Like the similar Greater Amberjack (top of page) with which it is easily confused, this silvery predator often has a dark diagonal stripe through the eye and occasionally bears a faint brassy stripe from eye to tail. Its color is more bluish than the Amberjack, its body slightly deeper, and its scales may appear more prominent. Its habits are similar to the Greater Amberjack. It sometimes accompanies "bait balls" as described on the following page and often approaches divers, or their bubbles. Juveniles (inset) have five dark bars and a diagonal eyestripe. Almaco Jacks are commercially farmed off the Big Island's Kona coast and marketed under the name Kona Kampachi. To almost 6 ft. All tropical seas. Photos: (adult) Laupāhoehoe, Hawai'i. 60 ft. (juvenile, inset) courtesy of Kona Blue Water Farms.

Amberjack feeding strategies

In the Hawaiian chain, Greater Amberjacks feed chiefly on Mackerel Scad ('ōpelu) and Bigeye Scad (akule) (p. 184-5). When large "bait balls" of scad form offshore (Bigeye Scads shown here), several Amberjacks are usually in attendance. They accompany the bait ball even if not actively feeding and when hungry punch through the closely packed fish to grab what they can. Greater Amberjacks will also take bottom-dwelling fishes and invertebrates. The young feed on planktonic organisms and on occasion adults may do so too, for they sometimes swim with their mouths agape, presumably to filter tiny organisms from the water with their gill rakers. They are the only known fish predator to do so. Photos: (above) South Point, Hawai'i, 60 ft. (below) Hanauma Bay, O'ahu. (D.R. Schrichte)

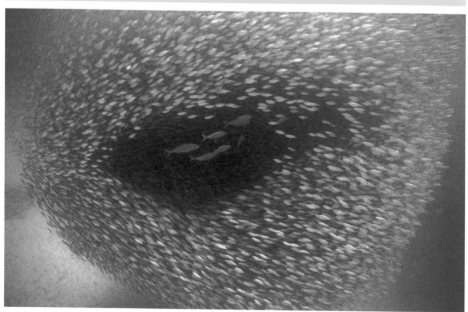

David R. Schrichte

Brian Bronk

'Ōpelu will sometimes "mob" large predators, such as sharks or barracudas, repeatedly striking themselves against the larger fish. Are they dislodging parasites? Or trying to drive the predator out of the neighborhood? Most likely the former, but no one knows for sure. In any case, the recipient is clearly annoyed. Some other members of the jack family behave similarly.

MACKEREL SCAD · 'ōpelu
Decapterus macarellus Cuvier, 1833

'Ōpelu are small schooling fishes of the jack family. Their bodies are round in cross section, tapering evenly at both ends, and they have a dark patch on the gill cover. The tail fins are yellowish. 'Ōpelu are highly prized as food by humans, larger fishes, and seabirds. Frenetically active, they swim high off the bottom picking plankton from the water. Occasionally they descend to the reef to be cleaned by wrasses. Divers usually see these fish in schools of about a dozen to several hundred, but some schools consist of thousands of individuals which appear from above the surface as a dark mass slowly moving through the water. Although schools of juveniles ("bait balls") occur as far as 80 miles from land (preyed upon by tunas, wahoo, mahimahi, and marlin), adults apparently stay within a few miles of shore. Large jacks, such as **kāhala**, herd them into dense balls for their feeding convenience (see pp. 182-3). Fishermen in old Hawai'i trained special barracudas to do the same so they could be easily netted (see p. 11). The Latin species name translates as "happy," or "fortunate," perhaps in reference to the humans who catch them. The English word "scads" is synonymous with "many," as in "scads of people." To about 12 in. All tropical seas. Photos: (above) Magic Island, O'ahu. 25 ft. (center, feeding) Palea Point, O'ahu. 20 ft. (bottom, with Blacktip Reef Shark) Hanauma Bay, O'ahu. 50 ft. (Brian Bronk)

BIGEYE SCAD · akule · *Selar crumenophthalmus* (Bloch, 1793)

Unlike the frenetically active Mackerel Scad (previous page), these schooling plankton-eaters typically rest by day and feed at night. Deeper-bodied than the Mackerel Scad, they have larger eyes and lack the dark patch on the gill cover. Young Bigeye Scads (**halalū**) are common during mid to late summer in some protected areas such as Waimea Bay, Oʻahu, or Honolua Bay, Maui, where they may be attacked by predators such as Bluefin Trevallies, Greater Amberjacks, and even small sharks. When the action gets heavy the school takes evasive action, twisting and turning as one, and producing an unusual tearing or ripping sound underwater. Among the most important food fishes of old Hawaiʻi, they were called **pāʻāʻā** when very small and **halalū** at a size of 6 or 7 in. Their movements are seasonal and adults are usually found offshore. They form massive "bait balls," sometimes in the same location year after year, attracting sharks, amberjacks, and other large predators (see p. 183). In old Hawaiʻi, when people escaped or went into hiding it was said "The **akule** have fled to the depths." The species name (Latin) means "purse-eyed." To about 12 in. All tropical seas. Photo: Honolua Bay, Maui. 5 ft. (The Yellowfin Scad, *Atule mate*—**ʻōmaka** or **makiawa**—which lives in calm bays such as Kāneʻohe Bay and Pearl Harbor, Oʻahu, is somewhat similar.)

WHITETONGUE JACK · ulua lāuli
Uraspis helvola
(Forster & Schneider, 1801)

As adults, these jacks generally live below sport-diving depths. Subadults, however, sometimes come inshore, where they rest by day in almost stationary schools, sometimes intermingling with Bigeye Trevallies (p. 178). They range from silvery gray with seven broad dark bars (darker on the underside) to entirely black. Adults lack bars and are uniform grayish brown to black. The dark mouth is upturned and the tongue, roof, and floor of the mouth are bright white. Small juveniles, yellowish with dark bars, sometimes accompany large pelagic jellyfish or hang about under floats and buoys. The Hawaiian name **lāuli** means "overcast" or "dark." The species name means "honey," probably because of the juvenile coloration. To about 21 in. Indo-Pacific, Eastern Pacific, and tropical Atlantic (St. Helena). Photo: Hanauma Bay, Oʻahu. 20 ft.

subadults

KNIFEJAWS
(Oplegnathidae)

Knifejaws are a small family of subtropical and temperate water fishes with deep narrow bodies and sometimes striking color patterns. They are also called "false parrotfishes" or "beakfish" because their teeth are fused into sharp beaks, used to crush molluscs and other shelled animals. In Hawai'i, knifejaws are most common in the cool waters of the northwestern chain; around the main islands they are rare. Both of the Hawaiian knifejaw species are common in Japan. Most other knifejaws occur in Australia and South Africa, well south of the equator.

a) mature adult ▲

b) young adult ▼

Keoki Stender

BARRED KNIFEJAW
Oplegnathus fasciatus
(Temminck & Schlegel, 1844)

When young these fish are marked with five dark vertical bars on a gray-ish or whitish body. On large adults the body darkens, the bars fade, and a black mask develops over the face. In Hawai'i, the Barred Knifejaw occurs almost exclusively in the Northwestern Hawaiian Islands, where it is less common than the Spotted Knifejaw (next page). In the main islands it is extremely rare. Even so, the author once saw one at Hanauma Bay, O'ahu, swimming among the snorkelers. Hybrids between the two species have been reported. Japan and Hawai'i. To about 2 ½ ft. Photos: (a, b) Midway Atoll, 40-50 ft.

a) mature adult ▲   b) young adult ▼   Keoki Stender

SPOTTED KNIFEJAW
Oplegnathus punctatus
(Temminck & Schlegel, 1844)

When fishermen call the Bishop Museum to report catching a strange fish, this is often what they caught. Younger individuals are light silvery gray with highly contrasting irregular dark spots. Large adults have bright white snouts and dark gray bodies densely covered with tiny black spots (most evident on the head and fins). Spotted Knifejaws shelter by day in caves and under ledges, often in small groups. They are moderately common in the Northwestern Hawaiian Islands and rare in the main islands. Your best chance of seeing one is off Kaua'i or Ni'ihau. On O'ahu, they have been glimpsed at the "Haleiwa Trench" and at Hanauma Bay. To almost 3 ft. Japan and Hawai'i. Photos: (a) Midway Atoll. 40 ft. (Keoki Stender) (b) Hanauma Bay, O'ahu. 70 ft.

LIZARDFISHES
(Synodontidae)

Reef Lizardfish · **'ulae** · swallowing a juvenile Sleek Unicornfish. It took 10 minutes to get it down · Sea Tiger wreck, O'ahu. (p. 192)

Lizardfishes are voracious ambush predators which typically rest motionless on rocks or sand, often blending in well with their surroundings. Propped on their pelvic fins with head tilted up for a better view, they may display a grinning mouthful of teeth as they wait for their next victim to swim by. (Australians, in fact, call them "grinners.") These nasty customers even have teeth on their tongues. They sometimes wriggle into soft bottoms, partially covering themselves. Confident in their camouflage, lizardfishes often allow divers a surprisingly close approach before darting away explosively in a cloud of sand.

Lizardfishes feed mainly on other fish. Some can shoot 6 ft. or more up into the water from the bottom to nab unsuspecting prey. (Next time you encounter a school of silversides or other baitfish near the surface in shallow water, look below for an excited lizardfish maneuvering to strike.) Victims are swallowed whole, usually head first, the needle-like teeth of the lizardfish folding backwards to ease the way. Divers sometimes come upon one of these predators so fat and heavy from a recent meal that it can scarcely swim, or with a fish in its jaws almost too big to swallow.

Lizardfishes look much alike and can be difficult to identify. The general Hawaiian word for them is **'ulae**. Specific descriptors, such as **'ula**, **ā**, and **niho**, were used in ancient times, but it is no longer known to which species they applied. Out of about 50 lizardfish species worldwide, 15 are known from Hawai'i (four from deep water). Ten are pictured here. Among those omitted are the Nebulous Lizardfish *(Saurida nebulosa)*, a shallow-water inhabitant of muddy bottoms almost identical in appearance to the Slender Lizardfish (p. 189), and the Falcate Lizardfish *(Synodus falcatus)*, an endemic lizardfish, known primarily from deep water. Although *falcatus* has been reported once or twice at scuba depths, such sightings have never been confirmed.

ORANGEMOUTH LIZARDFISH
'ulae
Saurida flamma Waples, 1982

Lizardfishes of the genus *Saurida* have thick lips bearing multiple bands of small teeth which are scarcely visible underwater. This species has distinctive red-orange lips that are often barred with white. Three smudgy dark saddles (varying in intensity) mark the back and sides, the first just behind the dorsal fin, the last at the base of the tail. Orangemouth Lizardfish typically lie at the edge of the reef in crevices or under ledges at depths greater than 15 ft. The species name means "fire." The distribution is antitropical: Hawai'i above the equator, Easter Island, and southern French Polynesia below. To about 12 in. Photo: (above) Portlock Point, O'ahu. 20 ft. (opposite) Mākua, O'ahu. 25 ft.

SLENDER LIZARDFISH · **'ulae** · *Saurida gracilis* (Quoy & Gaimard, 1824)

This lizardfish has thick gray lips bearing rows of small teeth, blackish bars or blotches on the side, and the usual three dark saddles (the first just behind the dorsal fin, the last at the base of the tail). Although most common on silty sand and rubble in protected bays and harbors, sometimes in only a few feet of water, it also occurs on reefs. The species name means "thin" or "slender." Indo-Pacific. To 11 in. Photo: Kāne'ohe Bay, O'ahu. 3 ft. (The similar Nebulous Lizardfish, *Saurida nebulosa*, occurs on muddy or silty bottoms. It has almost the same coloration, but shorter pectoral fins and usually fewer pectoral rays.)

TWOSPOT LIZARDFISH · ʻulae
Synodus binotatus Schultz, 1953

Lizardfishes of the genus *Synodus* have no teeth on the lips. This species has a pair of black spots on the tip of the snout. (The larger Clearfin Lizardfish, next page, has six). Blotchy greenish gray (in deeper water reddish), it often displays an almost iridescent or metallic sheen and has a slightly striated appearance. Like many other lizardfishes it may have dark smudgy bars along its back below and behind the dorsal fin. Common, it typically rests on rocks or coral in 30 ft. or less. The species name means "two marks." To 7 in. Indo-Pacific. Photos: (opposite) Kahe Point, Oʻahu. 25 ft. (top) "Haleʻiwa Trench," Oʻahu. 15 ft.

CAPRICORN LIZARDFISH · ʻulae
Synodus capricornis
Cressey & Randall, 1978

First discovered at Pitcairn and Easter Islands, this lizardfish was named for the Tropic of Capricorn due to its southerly distribution. Subsequently it was found in Hawaiʻi. (Species named after a specific place all too frequently turn up later somewhere else!) It is marked with a series of round reddish spots along the side and many narrow reddish bars below, and usually lives at about 80 ft. or more. It is not often seen. To about 9 in. Hawaiʻi, Pitcairn, and Easter Island. Photo: Molokini Islet, Maui. (Mike Severns)

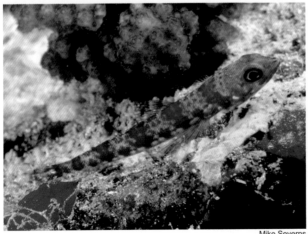

Mike Severns

190

a) adult ▲   b) juvenile ▼

CLEARFIN LIZARDFISH · 'ulae · *Synodus dermatogenys* Fowler, 1912

c)

   This common lizardfish lies in sand or rubble, sometimes buried with only the eyes and tip of the snout visible. The series of 8-9 dark blotches along the side usually have pale centers and may even be ringlike. The spaces between the blotches are wider than the blotches themselves. Six tiny black spots mark the tip of the snout and there is a faint bluish stripe on the upper side. Spawning has been studied at Saipan, Mariana Islands. At dusk, males aggregate on the sand in groups to wait for roving females, which may spawn multiple times with different partners. To about 9 in. Indo-Pacific. Photos: (a) Kona, Hawai'i. 50 ft. (b) Kahe Point, O'ahu. 30 ft. (c) Hau'ula, O'ahu. 5 ft.

HAWAIIAN LIZARDFISH · 'ulae · *Synodus ulae* Schultz, 1953

   These lizardfish have a series of 8-9 blotches along the side that tend to have pale centers and may be shaped somewhat like an hourglass. The spaces between the blotches are never wider than the blotches themselves and there are no tiny spots on the tip of the snout. Like the similar Clearfin Lizardfish (above), they inhabit sand and rubble bottoms near rocks or coral. They are often seen in pairs. Courtship activities include the male chasing the female and flaring his gill covers or circling her. Sometimes the two fight. Afterwards they rest side by side, or the male may lie across the female. At Miyake-Jima, Japan, spawning has been observed at dusk, the pair rising 13 ft. off the bottom to release an immense cloud of gametes. The species name is the Hawaiian word for lizardfish. A common species. To about 13 in. Hawai'i, Japan, Taiwan. Photo: Lāna'i Lookout, O'ahu. 20 ft.

191

LOBEL'S LIZARDFISH · 'ulae
Synodus lobeli Waples & Randall, 1988
This rarely seen lizardfish attains only about 6 in. and lives over open sand far from reefs. Its habitat, small size, and faint blue and yellowish stripes are perhaps the best means of identifying it. The Blunt-Nose Lizardfish (next page) has similar coloration and habitat, but is far larger and more robust. The name honors ichthyologist Philip S. Lobel, who discovered this fish. To about 6 in. Hawai'i and Japan. Photo: Kahe Point, O'ahu. 65 ft.

REEF LIZARDFISH · 'ulae · *Synodus variegatus* (Lacepède, 1803)
This is the lizardfish seen most often by snorkelers and divers in Hawai'i. It prefers rock or coral substrate rather than sand, and is splotched with varying shades of red, or sometimes greenish or grayish brown. A dark central stripe along the side passes through a series of dark spots, some of which may extend upward as saddles on the back. The lips are often banded red and white. The species name means "marked with differing colors." To about 9 in. Indo-Pacific. Photos: (upper) Ka'ohe Bay, Hawai'i, 30 ft. (lower) Hō naunau, Hawai'i. 30 ft. (see also next page and p. 188)

Catch of the day

How often does a lizardfish score? Dive slate and timer in hand, H.P. Sweatman painstakingly observed Reef Lizardfish (Synodus variegatus) at Lizard Island, on Australia's Great Barrier Reef. He found that, on average, these fish shift position every 4 minutes, strike at potential prey every 35 minutes, and miss 89% of the time. This works out to about two fish per day. Even then, not all end up where the lizardfish wants them. The toby at right, for example, has inflated itself, becoming too large to swallow. Life on the reef is not easy, even for a lizardfish.

REDMARBLED LIZARDFISH · 'ulae
Synodus rubromarmoratus
Russell & Cressey, 1979

This tiny lizardfish attains no more than about 3 in. It often lives on hard substrate (sometimes on vertical walls) and is marked with 5 distinct saddles across the back, the first brownish, the others red. It is known from the Western and Central Pacific. Although not rare in Hawai'i, it is rarely noticed due to its small size and excellent camouflage. Photo: Ho'okena, Hawai'i. 80 ft.

BLUNT-NOSED LIZARDFISH · wele'ā · Trachinocephalus trachinus (Temminck & Schlegel, 1846)

This lizardfish has a strongly upturned mouth and is patterned with light blue lines—features unusual enough to earn it a distinct Hawaiian name. Living in open sand, typically far from the reef, it often buries itself up to its eyes, which are set far forward and high on the body. Divers seldom see it—and neither, presumably, does its prey. To 13 in. Indo-Pacific, with similar species in the tropical Atlantic, the Marquesas Islands, and probably elsewhere. Photo: Kahe Point, O'ahu. 40 ft.

MILKFISH
(Chanidae)

The milkfish family consists of a single species. Among the most ancient and primitive of bony fishes, it is classified in the order Gonorhynchiformes, whose members are thought to be related to freshwater minnows and catfishes. Milkfish are one of the most important cultured food fishes in Southeast Asia.

MILKFISH · **awa** · *Chanos chanos* (Forsskål, 1775)

These are large silvery fishes with a small pointed mouth, deeply forked tail, and a single large dorsal fin. Milkfish grow to 6 ft. in length, although 3 ft. is more typical, and often enter surprisingly shallow areas. They can tolerate brackish or even fresh water, but are seen most often swimming over the reef either singly or in groups, occasionally with mouth open. Because of the pointed dorsal fin, snorkelers and divers sometimes mistake them initially for sharks. The resemblance ends there. Lacking teeth, these fish feed by nibbling algal growths and by filtering plankton from the water. Occasionally small invertebrates or fish may be taken. Milkfish spawn in the sea, but their larvae subsequently enter freshwater streams where they can be caught and placed in fishponds. The Hawaiians of old raised Milkfish this way, regarding them as highly as the 'ama'ama, or Striped Mullet (p.200). Small fish were called **pua awa**; medium-sized fish, tender and perfect for eating, were **awa 'aua**; adult fish were **awa**; and very large ones were **awa kalamoho**. The chiefs especially relished well-fattened awa 'aua, often reserving them for their own eating pleasure. The genus and species names mean "open mouth." This fish is widespread in Indo-Pacific and Eastern Pacific. Photo: Palea Point, O'ahu. 10 ft.

How did the milkfish get its name?

I asked the world's expert in these fish, Dr. Doris Bagarinao of the SEAFDEC aquaculture research center in the Philippines. She replied, "When milkfish is cooked, the flesh is milky white and I think, milky delicious. When you make a soup of it, the soup is nearly milky white. Try cooking and eating milkfish. It is delicious! Well, at least, the ones we raise in brackish water ponds."

MOORISH IDOL
(Zanclidae)

The Moorish Idol, sole member of the family Zanclidae, is literally one of a kind. Although related to the surgeonfishes, it lacks scalpels and more closely resembles a butterflyfish in appearance and behavior. A careful observer will note, however, that like surgeonfishes (and unlike butterfly-fishes), a Moorish Idol propels itself largely with its pectoral fins. Evidently, this type of fish has been inhabiting coral reefs for a very long time; a fossil Moorish Idol relative at least 50 million years old has been found at Monte Bolca, Italy. The family and genus names derive from the Greek *zanclon* ("sickle"), in reference no doubt to the somewhat sickle-shaped dorsal filament.

MOORISH IDOL · **kihikihi** · *Zanclus cornutus*, (Linnaeus, 1758)

With their perfect blend of form and color, Moorish Idols are the classic coral reef fish. Living symbols of the exotic un-dersea world, they have light gold bodies marked with jet-black bands, long orange and white striped snouts, and graceful trailing filaments. They typically swim singly, in pairs, or in small schools; occasionally twenty or thirty will band together. To view these fish is always a delight. Common, even in silty harbors, they can often be seen from shore grazing in very shallow water. Although omnivorous, they feed primarily on sponges and probably taste bad, a possible explanation for their approachability and conspicuous coloration. Adults have a thornlike spine in front of each eye, larger in males, giving rise to the species name *cornutus* ("horned"). The transparent planktonic larvae grow to a relatively large size (over 3 in.) before transforming into juveniles and settling on the reef, explaining why small "baby" Moorish Idols are never seen. Newly settled juveniles often band together as they begin to explore their new world, but in the absence of their own kind they will some-times fall in with juveniles of the Pennant Butterflyfish (p. 54), which looks remarkably similar. For such a beautiful and widely distributed fish, surprisingly little is known of its biology and reproductive habits. The Hawaiian name ("curves," "corners," "angular," "zigzag") was applied to a number of fishes, including hammerhead sharks. Moorish Idols are difficult to maintain in captivity, being active and high-strung, hard to feed, and surprisingly aggressive. To about 8 in. Indo-Pacific and Eastern Pacific, but absent from the Red Sea. Photo: Hanauma Bay, O'ahu. 10 ft.

Fishy IQs

The Moorish Idol is the smartest fish on the reef—almost. Roland and Marie-Louise Bauchot examined the brains of 110 species of Hawaiian reef fishes relative to body size, finding that colorful, fast moving fishes tended to have large brains while slower, well-camouflaged, poisonous, or very spiny fishes tended to have small brains. Eels, scorpionfishes and puffers, for example, ranked low, while butterflyfishes, surgeonfishes, and wrasses scored high.

The Bauchots explained their findings thus: Active fishes that roam the reef and/or hold territories need large brains, primarily to avoid predation. Wherever they are, they must always know the locations of the nearest hiding places, and must be able to navigate accurately at speed if chased by predators. To see colors and recognize patterns, they must have highly developed vision centers. If they have haremic or other complex social lives, they must be able to identify individuals of their own species and know their own and others' standings within their social hierarchy. (continued on following page)

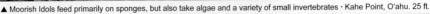

▲ Moorish Idols feed primarily on sponges, but also take algae and a variety of small invertebrates · Kahe Point, O'ahu. 25 ft.

Moorish Idol with rare double streamer · Kepuhi, O'ahu. 70 ft.

A school of Moorish Idols grazing on sponges · Pai'olu'olu Point, O'ahu. 80 ft.

Sedentary or slow moving fishes, on the other hand, usually have passive defenses such as inflation, venomous spines, toxic bodies, and good camouflage, and therefore don't need complex behaviors to avoid predation. These fishes tend to have smaller brains relative to their body weights.

The Bauchots developed a formula that yielded a single "encephalization index" number, a fish IQ of sorts. The Undulated Moray came in lowest at 15, closely followed by the Yellowmargin Moray at 16. Some of the others were (in ascending order): Whitemouth Moray (19); Hawaiian Conger (28); Dwarf Moray (37); Reef Lizardfish (42); Hawaiian Freckled Frogfish (46); Kellogg's Scorpionfish (62); Star-Eye Parrotfish (85); Potter's Angelfish (89); Hawaiian Flagtail (90); Yellowfin Surgeonfish (94); Ewa Fang Blenny, Whitespotted Toby (99); Yellow Tang (101); Hawaiian Dascyllus (102); Saddle Wrasse (105); Hawaiian Sergeant (106); Cornetfish (117); Milletseed Butterflyfish (122); Raccoon Butterflyfish (137); Oval Butterflyfish (140); Arc-Eye Hawkfish (142); Trumpetfish (144); Wedgetail Triggerfish (145); Fisher's Angelfish (146); Elegant Coris (147); Longnose Butterflyfish, Multiband Butterflyfish (149); Belted Wrasse (153); Hawaiian Cleaner Wrasse (155); Sleek Unicornfish (158); Manybar Goatfish (161); Paletail Unicornfish (167); Iridescent Cardinalfish (173); Orangespine Unicornfish (175); Chocolate Dip Chromis, Blue-Eye Damselfish (176); Bluefin Trevally (183); Hawaiian Squirrelfish (194); and the Moorish Idol (199).

So what was the smartest fish on the reef? The drab little Brown Surgeonfish, at 244, won by a very large margin.

MORWONGS
(Latridae)

Morwongs are an unusual group of fishes found in subtropical and warm temperate seas. Their high, laterally compressed bodies are typically marked with bold black diagonal bands, and their small mouths have thick fleshy lips. Bony knobs often protrude above the eyes. Morwongs are related to hawkfishes, and, like hawkfishes, many species have strong pectoral fins which allow them to prop themselves upright on the substrate. They typically feed on small crustaceans and other invertebrates found in sand. Occurring from South Africa to the Pacific coasts of Peru and Chile, morwongs attain their greatest diversity in the cool waters off southern Australia, hence the distinctive aboriginal name. Above the equator they occur in Japan, Korea, China, and, of course, Hawai'i. This type of distribution, known as "anti-tropical," is characteristic of a number of Hawai'i's fishes.

HAWAIIAN MORWONG · **kīkākapu** · *Cheilodactylus vittatus* (Garrett, 1864)
These odd fish have thick reddish lips and bold diagonal black stripes which may serve to disrupt their outline or to make them appear extra-large to predators. Bony lumps and bumps adorn the front of the head. They often prop themselves on the bottom with strong pectoral fins, somewhat like hawkfishes. Unlike hawkfishes, however, they appear to be nocturnal and are probably resting rather than waiting to ambush prey. They feed by pressing their thick fleshy lips to the bottom, sucking in sand and detritus, and filtering out small invertebrates. Although common in the cool subtropical Northwestern Hawaiian Islands, morwongs are rare in the main islands. Divers on Kaua'i probably have the best chance of seeing them. The Hawaiian Morwong is now considered endemic; previously it was lumped together with a similar species from New Caledonia and Lord Howe Island in the South Pacific. Morwongs share their Hawaiian name ("strong **kapu**") with several butterflyfishes. The species name means "striped." To 16 in. Endemic. Previously in the genus *Goniistius*. Photo: Midway Atoll, 40 ft.

MULTILINE MULLETS and THREADFINS
(Mugilidae and Polynemidae)

Mullets were one of the early Hawaiians' most important food fishes. They occur in shallow, often brackish coastal waters and are easily raised in fish ponds. Their long bodies are round or oval in cross section with large scales and two well-separated dorsal fins. They have flattened heads, blunt snouts, and are usually silvery-gray in color. Typically feeding off the bottom, mullets take in sand or mud and filter out the organic material through their gills. Their teeth are minute.

In olden times, enormous numbers of Striped Mullets migrated annually from Pearl Harbor around the southeastern end of O'ahu and up the windward side to Lā'ie, probably to spawn. Starting around October, they returned in March or April. At certain known spots—Black Point was one—the **'anae holo** (traveling mullets) came close to shore and could be seen by the thousands. This phenomenon continued on a reduced scale as late as the early 1960s, but seems now to have disappeared. The annual journey of the mullets inspired many ancient legends and tales. Striped Mullets are also prodigious leapers. After Kamehameha I drove O'ahu's warriors off the precipice at Nu'uanu Pali in 1795, the victors derisively called the site **kaleleka'anae** "leaping place of the mullets." About 70 mullet species occur worldwide, with three in Hawai'i. Omitted here is *Valamugil engeli*, a small, commercially worthless introduction which is proliferating in estuaries at the expense of the valuable **'ama'ama**.

Threadfins are bottom-feeders somewhat similar to mullets. Like mullets, they have two well-separated dorsal fins; their mouth, however, lies well under the snout instead of at its tip. Threadfins get their name from their unusual two-part pectoral fins, the lower part consisting of separate thread-like rays which can be arched forward in contact with the bottom to sense crustaceans, worms and other sand-dwelling prey. When not feeding, the fish fold these rays back against the body. There is one threadfin species in Hawai'i out of about 29 worldwide. Dwindling wild stocks of these locally popular food fish are sometimes enhanced by release of captive-bred fingerlings. In recent years threadfins have been cultured successfully in cages suspended in the ocean offshore.

SHARPNOSE MULLET · **uouoa** · *Neomyxus leuciscus* (Günther, 1872) [Acute-Jawed Mullet]
   Known locally as False Mullet, or False **'ama'ama**, these have a distinctive yellow spot at the base of the pectoral fin and a sharper snout than the Striped Mullet (next page). They typically swim in small fast-moving schools, often grazing directly off the rocky reef rather than foraging on the sandy bottom. The young occur in tide pools. The head, if eaten, is said to cause sleeplessness or nightmares unless an offering is first made to Pahulu, King of the Ghosts. To about 18 in. Pacific Ocean. Photo: Hanauma Bay, O'ahu. 1 ft.

STRIPED MULLET · **'ama'ama**; **'anae** *Mugil cephalus* Linnaeus, 1758 [GRAY MULLET]
These are Hawai'i's largest mullets. Silvery gray with faint stripes along the scale rows, they have blunt snouts and their tail fins are often edged in black. Although common in some marine conservation zones, such as Hanauma Bay, O'ahu, and Honolua Bay, Maui, Striped Mullets are seldom seen at other snorkeling or diving sites. At home in brackish water, they are easily raised in fish ponds. The ancient Hawaiians had different names for each stage of growth: **pua'ama** (finger length), **kahaha** (hand length), **'ama'ama** (8-12 in.) and **'anae** (full sized). Because mullet were highly valued and often reserved for chiefs, overly ambitious persons were sometimes told "Don't strive for the **'ama'ama** fish." (In other words, be satisfied with what you have.) To about 20 in. Found in tropical seas around the world. Photo: Hanauma Bay, O'ahu. 3 ft.

PACIFIC THREADFIN · **moi** · *Polydactylus sexfilis* (Valenciennes, 1831)
This fish is found over shallow sandy bottoms near shore, usually in small groups, sometimes in large schools. Silvery in color, it has a bulbous snout like a cartoon character, an underslung mouth, distinctive swept back fins, and a deeply forked tail. Unlike mullets, **moi** do not swim at the surface. In old Hawai'i large schools were said to foretell disaster for **ali'i**, or chiefs. Recently this species has been successfully mass-cultured in cages suspended offshore. In earlier times it was raised in fish ponds, largely for chiefs. The Hawaiian word **moi** also signified a variety of taro and a variety of sweet potato. The species name means "six threads." To about 12 in. Indo-Pacific. Photos: (above) Honolua Bay, Maui. 4 ft. (opposite, feelers extended) Hanauma Bay, O'ahu. 3 ft.

NEEDLEFISHES and HALFBEAKS
(Belonidae and Hemiramphidae)

Keeltail Needlefish at Hanauma Bay, O'ahu.   David R. Schrichte

Needlefishes are long slender carnivores with pointed needlelike beaks filled with sharp teeth. They live just below the surface and prey on small schooling fish which they catch sideways and swallow whole. Some needlefishes inhabit the open ocean; others live close to shore. Strong swimmers, they can skim over the surface or leap out of the water.

Halfbeaks are similar with only the lower jaw extended. In many species the lower jaw is tipped with red. Some halfbeaks are herbivores, feeding on bits of floating seaweed or other plant material. Others feed on plankton or small fish.

Needlefishes and halfbeaks are both related to the flying-fishes or **malolo** (family Exocoetidae), which are frequently seen by boaters as they skim the surface to escape underwater pursuers. Flying-fishes can skim and glide for distances of at least an eighth of a mile. Columbus was branded a liar when he first described this feat to the royal court of Spain.

Most of these fishes have tail fins with the lower lobe longer than the upper, a modification helpful in propelling them on the surface. Generally, they are silvery below and bluish or greenish on top, a color pattern common among open-ocean (pelagic) fishes that makes them hard to see from both above and below.

Lights attract and excite needlefishes at night. Night divers should keep their lights off until well submerged wherever these fishes are common. If impaled by even a small needlefish, seek medical help. Undetected beak fragments can remain in the wound, causing infection. Large needlefishes, sometimes called "living javelins," have caused serious injuries (see p. 203).

Hawai'i has at least four needlefish and two halfbeak species. Not shown here is the Agujon (*Tylosurus acus*), which grows to 39 in. and sometimes has a rounded keel on the underside of the beak. Needlefishes are known in Hawaiian as **'aha** ("cord"), and halfbeaks are **iheihe** or **me'eme'e**. Juveniles sometimes resemble small twigs floating on the surface. Needlefishes and their relatives belong to the order Beloniformes.

KEELTAIL NEEDLEFISH · 'aha · *Platybelone argalus* (Lesueur, 1821) [FLAT-TAIL NEEDLEFISH]
Schools of these fish, sometimes large, are common at many shallow snorkeling areas. Look for them just under the surface. They have a silvery blue stripe along the side and the lower lobe of the tail fin is about the same size as the upper lobe. (In most needlefishes, the lower lobe is longer.) The caudal peduncle (that part of the fish joining the tail fin to the body) is flattened and bears a prominent keel on each side, difficult to see underwater. These fish seem to rest by day and feed at night. To about 15 in. All tropical seas, with a different subspecies in the Atlantic. Photo: Keauhou Landing, Hawai'i Volcanoes National Park. (see also previous page)

FLATSIDED NEEDLEFISH · 'aha · *Ablennes hians* (Valenciennes 1846) [FLAT NEEDLEFISH; GAPING NEEDLEFISH]
This large pelagic needlefish approaches shore only on rare occasions, perhaps to be cleaned. Its body is flattened side-to-side, thus the common name. It is greenish on the back and silvery on the sides and belly. The sides are marked by dark bars or squarish dark spots, often most visible near the tail. It attains at least 40 in. and occurs in warm seas worldwide. Photo: Magic Island, O'ahu. 10 ft.

CROCODILE NEEDLEFISH · 'aha · *Tylosurus crocodilus* (Péron and Lesueur, 1821) [HOUNDFISH]
Large and heavy-set, with a stout beak and deeply forked tail, this powerful fish grows to more than 3 ft. in length. It swims near the surface along the outer reef and usually escapes the notice of divers except when descending to be serviced by a Hawaiian Cleaner Wrasse (p. 339). Capable of leaping free of the water when frightened or attracted by lights, large needlefish such as this one have injured night divers at the surface and even killed fishermen in boats with their sharp beaks. To 40 in. All tropical seas. Photo: Leleiwi Beach Park, Hawai'i.

The spearer speared

Spearfishing at night at Kahana Bay, O'ahu, in July 2005, 19-year-old Tonga Loumoli saw a 4- to 5-foot slender blue fish swim past, just inches from his mask. Thinking it was a barracuda, he turned his light on it. The fish swam directly at him, stabbing him deeply in the abdomen. "I stood there like two seconds staring, then I felt this tremendous pain in my chest," Loumoli said. " I couldn't speak. It felt like a missile to the chest, or a sledgehammer." The fish wriggled free and Loumoli's quick-thinking buddy Braven Rivera got him to shore and flagged down a passing police car. "By then I didn't have feeling in my right leg and left arm," Loumoli recalled. After hours of emergency surgery for internal bleeding and liver damage, and days in intensive care at Queen's Medical Center, Loumoli was released with a long scar bearing 45 stitches where the surgeons had opened him up. A tiny tooth they found in the wound confirmed that a needlefish had done the damage, probably a Crocodile Needlefish.

Tragedy at Hanamā'ulu

On September 5, 1977, a ten-year-old Hawaiian boy fishing with his father at Hanamā'ulu Bay, Kaua'i, was pulling net when a 3- to 4-foot. 'aha jumped from the water, struck him near his right eye, then fell into the boat. The father, who had been looking the other way, heard the noise and turned to see his son slump to the floor, clasping the right side of his face. He asked the boy what happened. The boy did not answer, but took his hands from his face and showed the father the wound. The father rushed the boy to Wilcox Hospital by truck. During the ride, the boy lost consciousness. He was admitted in a comatose state with paralysis on the right side of the body. Suspecting brain injury, the doctors had the boy flown immediately to Straub Hospital in Honolulu. He never regained consciousness. Becoming progressively weaker, he was placed on a respirator and passed away on September 11. An autopsy showed that the needlefish's beak had penetrated the left side of the brain. The fish was determined to be a Crocodile Needlefish.

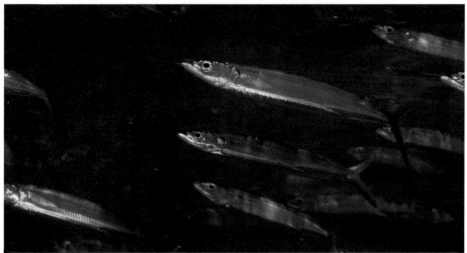

POLYNESIAN HALFBEAK · **iheihe** · *Hemiramphus depauperatus* Lay & Bennett, 1839

Halfbeaks have a stubby triangular upper jaw and a long needle-like lower jaw, thus the common name. They cruise just under the surface much like needlefishes and, at least in Hawai'i, can be distinguished from needlefishes by their slightly deeper bodies. The Polynesian Halfbeak is silvery with sometimes intense blue-green iridescence on the side. Its lower jaw is tipped with red. The dorsal fin originates well forward of the anal fin. To about 15 in. Hawai'i south to French Polynesia. Photo: Hanauma Bay, O'ahu. (David R. Schrichte)

ACUTE HALFBEAK · **iheihe** · *Hyporhamphus acutus* (Günther, 1872)

Slightly smaller and more slender than the Polynesian Halfbeak (above), this fish is silvery on the sides with dark blue-green iridescence on the back. The tip of its lower jaw is reddish on the underside, but the red is often scarcely noticeable. The best way to differentiate it from the Polynesian Halfbeak is by the placement of the dorsal fin. The dorsal fin lies directly above the anal fin. Hawaiian specimens differ slightly from those found elsewhere, earning them the subspecies name *pacificus*. Central Pacific. To about 13 in. Photo: Hanauma Bay, O'ahu.

PARROTFISHES
(Scaridae)

Spectacled Parrotfish supermale, feeding • Hanauma Bay, O'ahu. 15 ft. (p. 208)

With their heavy beaks and typically blue-green bodies, parrotfishes are well named. Like the wrasses, to which they are related, they swim primarily with their pectoral fins and undergo confusing sex and color changes as they mature. Unlike wrasses, parrotfishes are herbivorous. Their teeth are fused into strong, beaklike dental plates which they use to remove algae from nonliving surfaces of the reef. A few species will also feed on live coral. Most parrotfishes merely scrape the thin algal turf from the underlying surface, leaving it intact, but some (generally of the genus *Chlorurus*) can actually dig into the substrate, removing significant amounts of coral or calcareous matrix as well. This scraping and gouging is easily heard underwater. Small wrasses may hover nearby, hoping to catch bits of food dislodged by the giant. Marks on the rock show where parrotfishes have fed. Species which ingest bits of calcareous substrate or living coral grind it finely with special toothlike bones in the throat, extract the organic matter, and expel the remaining fine sand through the anus. (The Hawaiian name for one species means "loose bowels.") Much of the world's coral sand is produced by these fishes.

Parrotfishes can be difficult to identify underwater. They are fast-moving, wary, and extremely variable, yet often look alike. Color patterns can differ radically within a single species, depending on sex and age, and some species can modify their pattern in seconds.

In the Hawaiian language parrotfishes are known collectively as **uhu**. The young are **'ōhua**, and mid-size fish **pānuhu** or **pōnuhunuhu**. In old Hawai'i, parrotfishes were sometimes compared to a sweetheart or lover because of their pretty colors. Eyeing an attractive woman, a man might say "my mouth waters for the parrotfish passing by." Parrotfish behavior, it was said, could tell a fisherman what his wife was doing at home. Hawaiian scholar Mary Kawena Pukui writes, "If the **uhu** capered and frolicked in the water it was a sure sign of too much levity. If two **uhu** seemed to be rubbing noses, it was a sure sign that there was flirting going on at home." A wily person, hard to catch, was called "a slippery **uhu**."

In the descriptions below, references are made to initial and terminal phase fishes. The drably colored initial phase usually consists of both males and females, identical in appearance. In some species, however, the initial phase is always female. When both sexes are present in the initial phase, the two may spawn together in large groups, "capering and frolicking." Terminal phase parrotfishes are always male and usually brightly colored. They hold territories and mate with individual initial phase females. These "supermales" are almost always sex-reversed females.

Small juvenile parrotfishes are often marked with dark longitudinal stripes. They can quickly change their patterns depending on their activity and surroundings, making them especially hard to identify. Eight parrotfishes, including three endemics, inhabit Hawaiian reefs. Not shown is a small species of the genus *Calotomus* that inhabits *Halimeda* seaweed beds.

a) supermale

STAREYE PARROTFISH · **pōnuhunuhu** · *Calotomus carolinus* (Valenciennes, 1840)

Parrotfishes of the genus *Calotomus* have "beaks" composed of many separate teeth partially fused together. They often feed on leafy algae. In this species, magenta lines radiate from the eyes of supermales, providing easy identification. Supermales are grayish green to dark green, often with a broad pale patch on the side and/or irregular pale spots along the back. Initial phase fish (both sexes) are gray-brown, speckled with lighter marks, especially on the back. To 20 in. East Africa to the Galapagos. Photos: (a, b) Hanauma Bay, Oʻahu. 15-20 ft. (c) Palea Point, Oʻahu. 30 ft. (d) Hoʻokena, Hawaiʻi. 35 ft.

b) initial phase (male or female)

c) d) juveniles ▲▼

Tracy Clark

a) supermale ▲

b) initial phase (male or female) ▼

YELLOWBAR PARROTFISH
Calotomus zonarchus (Jenkins,1903)

This unusual parrotfish is uncommon to rare in the main Hawaiian Islands, but fairly abundant in the cooler northwestern chain. Terminal males are gray-brown with a bright yellow vertical bar on the side, usually containing scattered white spots. The size and shape of this bar varies. There are pinkish red marks under the mouth. Initial phase fish are gray with scattered white scales in a pale central bar. The species name is from *zona*, meaning "belt" or "girdle." To about 1 ft. Endemic. Photos: (a, b) Midway Atoll. 40 ft. (c) Lāna`i Lookout, O'ahu. 30 ft.

c) juvenile ▲

Sex change and deception

In most parrotfish species all adults start off in a drab "initial phase" (IP), which is either entirely female or includes both sexes, identical in appearance. Most adults remain in the initial phase for life. The more exclusive "terminal phase" is composed only of large, brightly colored males which derive from sex-reversed IP females. These "supermales" are territorial, controlling all the best spawning sites. Each dominates and defends a harem of females with which he spawns individually. If the dominant supermale dies, the top-ranking female changes sex and takes his place, probably within days. (Note the male "spectacles" developing on the Spectacled Parrotfish IP female/male below.) Meanwhile, IP males must make do by group-spawning with whatever stray and willing females they can find when the lord of the manor is

not looking. Occasionally, a brazen IP male masquerades as a female and sneaks close to a spawning supermale and his mate, releasing his own sperm nearby in hopes of fertilizing some eggs. The enraged supermale immediately gives chase, of course, but probably to no avail. "Sneak spawning" is a common tactic with many fishes and must work at least some of the time, or the behavior would not persist.

a) supermale ▲

b) c) initial phase (male or female) ▲▼

d) subadult. Wai'opae Tidepools, Hawai'i

SPECTACLED PARROTFISH

uhu 'ahu'ula (initial phase)
uhu uliuli (supermale)
Chlorurus perspicillatus
(Steindachner, 1879)

This is the largest of Hawai'i's three endemic parrotfishes. Supermales are deep blue-green overall with a conspicuous dark band (the spectacles) across the top of the snout. In large old individuals the snout becomes big and bulbous. There is a bright yellow mark at the base of the pectoral fin. Initial phase fish (both sexes) are grayish brown with red fins and a broad white band at the base of the tail. They can rapidly display a series of pale blotches along the back. Sometimes body and fins become uniformly gray, lightening almost to white when the fish is displaying aggression. Spectacled Parrotfish are the most abundant parrotfish in the northwestern chain, but are uncommon in the main Hawaiian Islands except in conservation zones or areas with difficult access. Like other parrotfishes, they are easy to spear at night when they sleep. The Hawaiian name for the initial phase means "feather cape parrotfish." The word **uliuli** applied to supermales means "any dark color, including the deep blue of the sea." The species name means "spectacled." To 24 in. Endemic. Photos: (a) Midway Atoll. 40 ft. (b, c) Hanauma Bay, O'ahu. 20-30 ft.

a) supermale ▲

b) initial phase (male or female) ▼

BULLETHEAD PARROTFISH · uhu
Chlorurus spilurus
(Valenciennes, 1840)

A bullet-shape head profile (symmetrical above and below the beak) gives this common species its name. Terminal males are greenish overall, often with cheeks or sides washed with yellow-orange or tan. Their beaks are blue-green. Initial phase fish, which may be either male or female, have white beaks and are grayish in front, becoming dark brown to almost black toward the rear. There is often much red about the mouth. A double row of three or more white spots may mark the side, and a broad white bar (which may contain a dark spot) is often present at the base of the tail. Sometimes the entire tail fin is white. All these bars and spots can appear and disappear quickly. Juveniles are dark with four light horizontal stripes which they can turn on and off. The Bullethead Parrotfish is reported to feed on coral polyps as well as algae. Western and Central Pacific. To about 15 in. Photos: (a, b) Hanauma Bay Oʻahu. 30 ft. (c) Moku Manu, Oʻahu. 50 ft. (d) Pūpūkea, Oʻahu. (*Chlorurus sordidus,* a very similar species, is confined to the Indian Ocean.)

c) initial phase color variations▼

d) juvenile ▲

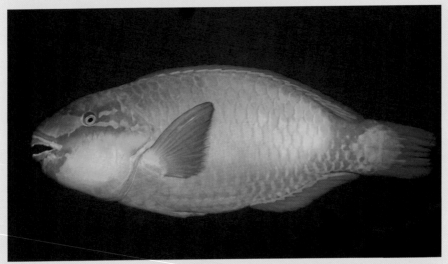

Bullethead show-off

During courtship, which usually begins right around high tide, a supermale Bullethead Parrotfish intensifies his colors, often becoming golden yellow on the sides. Swimming high above the reef, he puts on an acrobatic performance to attract a female, fluttering his pectoral fins while vibrating body and tail, swimming with exaggerated motions, circling, excreting plumes of sand like a sky-writing airplane, and making sudden downward dives. If he attracts a mate, the two spawn one-on-one, rising toward the surface, releasing their gametes, and quickly descending. By contrast, initial phase fish spawn in groups, their bodies often darkening almost to black and their tail fins lightening to white to exhibit maximum visual contrast. Half a dozen or more initial phase males may spawn with a single female.

Bullethead sleeping bag

Many parrotfishes of the genera Scarus and Chlorurus secrete cocoons of mucus around themselves at night. The advantage of this is not yet completely clear, and many individuals sleep without them. Some biologists have suggested that this covering protects the sleeping fish from eels, which hunt by smell during the night; although this remains unproven; others have shown that it does ward off small crustacean or molluscan parasites. One (first-hand?) report calls the mucus "foul-tasting." Another study found antibacterial proteins in the cocoon of a Caribbean parrotfish. To create a cocoon a parrotfish secretes copious mucus from glands in the gill cavity, expelling it through the mouth. Progressing backwards in folds, the mucus takes 30 minutes or more to envelop

the entire fish. Small openings remain at front and back for respiration. Though it may look like a thin-walled balloon due to fine particles adhering to the outside, the perfectly transparent gelatinous covering can be almost 3 inches thick in places. With or without a cocoon, parrotfishes are often such sound sleepers that they can be gently picked up by divers, photographed, and replaced without waking up. At other times, however, merely touching a sleeping parrotfish can cause it to bolt suddenly. Often it will collide with the nearby reef. Best to let sleeping fish lie.

a) b) supermales ▲▼

REGAL PARROTFISH · **lauia**
Scarus dubius Bennett, 1828

Uncommon to rare in the main Hawaiian Islands, this endemic parrotfish is most abundant in the northwest chain. Supermales are yellowish orange with blue bars on the body scales, the orange color being considerably brighter on some individuals than on others. A straight narrow blue line runs from the upper lip to below the eye. The crescent-shaped tail fin contains a wide bright green band. Initial phase adults (both sexes) are reddish to brownish, usually with irregular bars and several narrow pale longitudinal stripes on the belly. The snout in all phases has a parrot-like shape similar to that of the Palenose Parrotfish (next page). Early confusion with that species probably accounts for reports stating *Scarus dubius* to be common in the main islands. The species name means "doubtful" or "wavering." To about 14 in. Endemic. Photos: (a, d) Palea Point, Oʻahu. 20-40 ft. (b, e) Midway Atoll. 40 ft. (c) Hōnaunau, Hawaiʻi. 40 ft.

c) initial phase (male or female) ▼

d) initial phase (male or female) ▼

e) initial phase (male or female) ▼

a) b) supermales ▲▼

c) juveniles ▼

PALENOSE PARROTFISH · uhu · *Scarus psittacus* Forsskål, 1775

The species name *psittacus* means "parrot," and this is the original "parrotfish," described over 200 years ago from the Red Sea by Swedish explorer/naturalist Peter Forsskål. Common throughout the Indo-Pacific, it is probably the most abundant parrotfish in the main Hawaiian Islands. Supermales are green and blue with lavender tints about the head. There may be a yellow spot at the base of the tail and/or a yellow patch covering some or almost all of the side. While patrolling their territories or when chasing rival males they develop a dark blue-black "cap." Initial phase fish (both sexes), often quite small, usually graze the reef in tight schools. They are plain light gray to dark brownish gray often with reddish pelvic fins. The distinctively shaped snout is sometimes paler than the rest of the body, but only in the initial phase. Juveniles look like miniature initial phase fish. To almost 1 ft. Indo-Pacific. Photos: (a) Hanauma Bay, O'ahu. 10 ft. (b) Lāna'i 30 ft. (c) Haleiwa Beach Park. 5 ft. (d) Hanauma Bay, O'ahu. 20 ft.

d) initial phase fish (male or female) ▼

a) supermale

EMBER PARROTFISH · **uhu pālukaluka** (initial); **uhu ʻeleʻele** (terminal) · [REDLIP PARROTFISH]
Scarus rubroviolaceus Bleeker, 1849

This is the largest parrotfish in Hawaiʻi. In areas protected from spearing, such as Hanauma Bay, Oʻahu, these fish glide about oblivious to humans, sometimes in water barely deep enough to cover their backs, turning lazily from time to time to scrape algae from the rock. A Saddle or Christmas Wrasse often follows to nab small creatures dislodged by the grazing giant. Supermales, predominantly light green with blue tints and darker blue marks about the mouth and eye, have a distinctive squarish humped snout. The beak is bluish and usually bears a "mustache" of darker algae. Initial phase fish (both sexes) are typically reddish brown to grayish with numerous short black lines at odd angles on the sides, creating a textured appearance. They may become entirely pale. Both the initial and terminal phases frequently display a distinct bicolor pattern, darker in front, lighter in back. Reproductively active females are reported to further darken the front of the body. The beaks of initial phase fish are reddish to white, often with an algal "mustache." Juveniles are usually greenish brown with rows of indistinct white spots and three conspicuous white stripes. The Hawaiian name for the initial phase means "loose bowels." (Anyone who has seen a parrotfish eject a cloud of sand from its anus knows why.) The word ʻeleʻele applied to terminal males means "black, dark, the black color of Hawaiian eyes." The origin of the English common name is unclear but perhaps to some the pattern on the initial phase resembles loose embers. The species name, meaning "reddish violet," is not much better. To 28 in. Indo-Pacific and Eastern Pacific. Photos: (a, b) Hanauma Bay, Oʻahu. 5-10 ft. (c) Pūpūkea, Oʻahu. 20 ft.

b) initial phase (male or female)

c) juvenile ▲

213

Mystery parrotfish

In 1998 diver Ken Lee speared a colorful 20-inch parrotfish off Sandy Beach, O'ahu. Not recognizing it, he sent it to Dr. John E. Randall of Honolulu's Bishop Museum, who couldn't identify it either. DNA analysis confirmed it to be different from any other known parrotfish, yet the likelihood of a new species of large colorful parrotfish in the Hawaiian Islands seemed remote. Dr. James Nelson, who analyzed the DNA, had suggested it might be a hybrid, but it was not clear from the color pattern who its parents might have been. Dr. Randall published a photo of this mystery fish in Hawai'i Fishing News for July 1999, asking anyone who found another to contact him. When I saw the article I remembered a puzzling parrotfish (upper left) that I had photographed in Hanauma Bay years ago. The photo reminded me of a terminal male Bullethead, but was not quite right. I sent the slide to Dr. Randall, who thought the fish looked like a hybrid between a Bullethead Parrotfish and a Spectacled Parrotfish. Meanwhile Dr. Randall found an unidentified

16-inch female parrotfish specimen in the Bishop Museum which had been obtained from the Honolulu fish market in the 1920s then stored in alcohol and forgotten. Most of the colors were gone, but it had the size and shape of a Spectacled Parrotfish and the scale count of a Bullethead. Finally, in January 2005 Kevin Sakuda speared a 17-inch male **uhu** off Moku Manu, O'ahu, which matched my slide and seemed clearly intermediate between the Bullethead and Spectacled parrotfishes. That seemed to clinch the matter, except that Ken Lee's original specimen didn't closely match my photo or Kevin Sakuda's fish. Dr. Randall finally concluded that Ken's fish was a second-generation hybrid, the result of a half-breed hybrid mating with a pure-blood Spectacled Parrotfish. He announced his conclusions in Hawai'i Fishing News for December 2005 in an article entitled "Mystery Parrotfish Revealed." Still, no one yet knew what an initial phase hybrid looked like. I went through all my parrotfish slides again and found one from Puakō, Hawai'i (lower left) which Dr. Randall thought might also be a Spectacled-Bullethead hybrid. If the theory is correct, the scientific name for these fish would be Chlorurus spilurus x perspicillatus. For a Hawaiian name, how about **uhu kapakahi**?

Algal mustaches: the essential facts

(1) At least twelve species of algae grow on parrotfish beaks, usually at the corners and along the edges bordering the lips. (2) On a large supermale these tufts may stick out half an inch or more on either side, looking amazingly like mustaches. (3) Algal filament length increases in proportion to fish length. Fishermen in Micronesia sometimes express the size of a parrotfish in terms of the length of the tufts growing from the corners of its beak! (4) Five different species of algae were once found on the beak of a single Bullethead Parrotfish, a separate species on each of three dental plates and two others in equal abundance on the fourth. (5) These are ordinary species of algae such as might grow on any exposed part of the reef. (6) Parrotfish beaks are ideal for algal growth because no animals graze there and water flow is constant. (7) The algae don't care what species of parrotfish they grow on, but they don't grow on individuals less than about 7 in. long. (8) Parrotfishes from the same immediate area do not necessarily host the same species of algae. (9) Algae will also grow on porcupinefish beaks.

PIPEFISHES and SEAHORSES
(Syngnathidae)

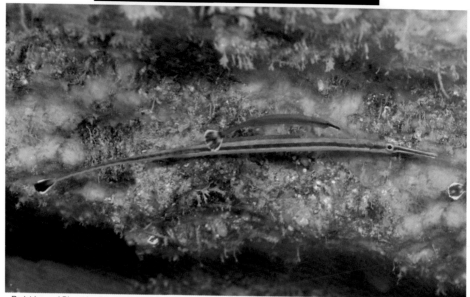

Redstripe and Bluestripe Pipefish at the Lāna'i Lookout, O'ahu. 25 ft. The Bluestripe Pipefish appeared to have been picking at the eggs of the Redstripe Pipefish, which are on its underside (facing up).

Most people are familiar with seahorses. Less well known are their cousins the pipefishes, which are more numerous in Hawai'i, and more frequently seen. Both have tubular snouts, small toothless mouths, and fairly rigid armored bodies segmented into rings.

Distinguishing a pipefish from a seahorse is easy. The head and snout of a pipefish are directly in line with its long slender body, while the head and snout of a seahorse are roughly at right angles to its body. Stockier than pipefishes, seahorses are the only fishes with a prehensile tail. Both seahorses and pipefishes are slow, weak swimmers. Seahorses spend much of their time holding on to plants or other fixed objects with their tails. Some pipefishes hover under ledges or in crevices, others live on the bottom, often hidden in weed or rubble. Both seahorses and pipefishes feed on micro-crustaceans with their elongated tubular mouths. Independently movable eyes help them locate their miniscule prey. A few pipefish species have been observed cleaning other fishes, presumably of parasites.

Because males bear the young, pipefishes and seahorses have been called the answer to a woman's dream. A female lays her eggs on the ventral (belly) side of the male, either on a special brood surface or in a pouch, then leaves. The male incubates them until they hatch (about 10-50 days). During this time the eggs, or the distended brood pouch, are often plainly visible. The young hatch into free-swimming miniature adults. Some authors report that newly hatched seahorses rise immediately to the surface for a tiny gulp of air, which helps them stay upright. If subjected to the stress of capture, a "pregnant" male seahorse will often give birth prematurely.

Pipefishes and seahorses belong to the order Syngnathiformes, which includes other tube-mouthed fishes such as cornetfishes and trumpetfishes. Although they form a large family with over 200 species worldwide, most are rarely seen, being small, cryptic, or well camouflaged. It is possible, for example, to gaze directly at a seahorse a foot or two away and mistake it for a weedy appendage of the reef.

Six pipefishes and three seahorses occur in the Islands. Two pipefishes known only from deep water are omitted here. Because of commercial collecting for the traditional Chinese medicine market, and to a lesser extent for the aquarium trade, there is concern that seahorse populations may be threatened worldwide. On the Big Island of Hawai'i, several non-Hawaiian seahorse species are being raised commercially to help satisfy this demand.

BALL'S PIPEFISH
Cosmocampus balli
(Fowler, 1925)

This endemic pipefish is entirely whitish and spends most of its time hidden in rubble or seaweed along shallow protected shores. Bottom-dwelling pipefish such as this are often somewhat sluggish, but Ball's Pipefish thrashes back and forth vigorously when disturbed, and can move away fairly quickly. Little else is known about the species and very few divers or snorkelers have ever seen it. Named for Yale zoologist Stanley C. Ball (1885-1956). To about 2 ½ in. This individual was found in seaweed at a depth of 8 ft. in front of the Waikīkī Aquarium and photographed later in a tank.

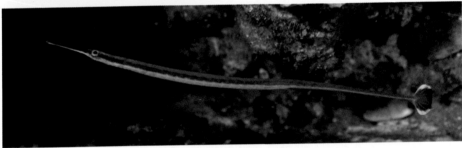

REDSTRIPE PIPEFISH *Dunckerocampus baldwini* (Herald & Randall, 1972) ▲
Hovering far back in caves and crevices, usually at depths of 20 ft. or more, these long slender pipefish are pinkish red with a bright red stripe along the side. Their fanlike tail fins, sometimes spread wide, are orange-red with white edges. These fish occur in pairs or small groups of mixed adults and juveniles. The male often bears several rows of pink eggs on the underside, deposited there by the female. He carries them until they hatch. When close to hatching the eggs turn dark silver. These pipefish sometimes act as cleaners. Diving in a cave at 75 ft., Dr. Deetsie Chave once watched an adult Redstripe Pipefish clean a cardinalfish. It then turned its attentions to a moray eel. Finally the pipefish tried to clean her wrist. Some authorities place this species in the genus *Doryrhamphus*. The name honors ichthyologist Wayne J. Baldwin, who collected the first specimens in 1969. To about 5 in. Long considered endemic, but now known from a few Indo-Pacific localities outside Hawai'i. Photo: "Marty's Reef," Maui. 50 ft. (swimming almost upside-down, oriented to the side of the cave.) (see also previous page)

▼ BLUESTRIPE PIPEFISH (see following page) ▶

◄ BLUESTRIPE PIPEFISH *Doryrhamphus melanopleura* (Bleeker, 1858) (photo on previous page, bottom)
These small pipefish are dusky orange or brown with a dull bluish gray stripe down the body. The fanlike tail fin, brownish orange with a white margin, forms almost a full circle when spread. Usually in pairs, they hover deep within crevices or under ledges, usually at 25 ft. or less, venturing out after dark. They sometimes clean other fish. The conspicuous open tail fin, similar in shape to that of the Redstripe Pipefish (also a cleaner), perhaps advertises that grooming services are available. This pipefish is also reported to bob up and down like a cleaner wrasse to attract customers. The eggs of "pregnant" males, carried in a brood pouch on the underside, may make the belly appear distended. This is a common Pacific pipefish, but seldom seen in Hawai'i unless looked for. To about 2 ½ in. Pacific Ocean. Photo: Mākua, O'ahu. 8 ft. (see also p. 215)

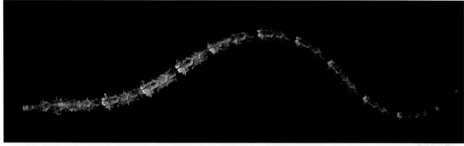

Pauline Fiene

EDMONDSON'S PIPEFISH *Halicampus edmondsoni* (Pietschmann, 1930) ▲
One of the most rarely seen animals in Hawai'i, this reddish pipefish attains about 4 in. (some books say 7 in.) It occurs in tide pools and down to at least 100 ft. in algae or sand. Little else is known of its habits. The name honors Charles H. Edmondson (1876-1970), a prominent marine biologist at Honolulu's Bishop Museum during the first half of the 20th century. Endemic. The individual above was collected in Ma'alaea Bay, Maui, at 55 ft. and photographed later in an aquarium.

FISHER'S SEAHORSE
Hippocampus fisheri
Jordan & Evermann, 1903

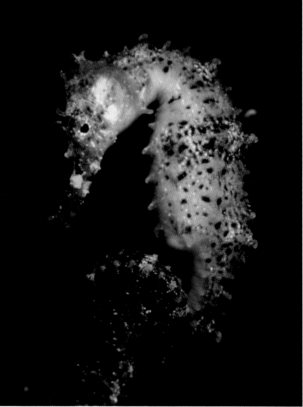

This seahorse has small sharp spines and may be golden orange, red, pink, or yellowish, with blackish mottling. Apparently pelagic, its habits are little known. Of their first specimen, obtained at Kailua, Hawai'i, in 1901, Jordan and Evermann wrote "the species was new to the natives." They later obtained five more specimens in Hilo from the stomach of a dolphinfish, or **mahimahi**. The individual at right, caught in a surface trawl off O'ahu, appears to be *H. fisheri*. Seahorses sometimes found washed ashore after storms are probably this species, as are those occasionally collected by fishermen at night, usually offshore in deep water. In 1999, Karen Brittain of the Waikīkī Aquarium raised several generations of *H. fisheri*. Up to 250 tiny hatchlings were produced every 15 days. Her specimens were red to orange when first captured, but took on a yellow hue after several months in captivity. The species name honors American zoologist Walter K. Fisher (1878-1953) who pioneered the study of Hawaiian sea stars and sea cucumbers in the early 1900s. Endemic. To about 3 in. Photo: surface trawl off O'ahu. (Mike Severns)

Mike Severns

SMOOTH SEAHORSE
Hippocampus kuda Bleeker, 1852

This seahorse lacks spines, thus the common name. Most individuals are blackish or brownish, but white ones have been seen and females are often yellow. Typically occurring in shallow protected embayments, even where the water is brackish, these fish are usually coated with filamentous algae and silt and thus easy to overlook. For many years they were very rare, but around 2005 the species underwent a small population boom, becoming only moderately rare. This is a widespread Indo-Pacific species. DNA studies have shown that the Hawaiian population is an endemic subspecies. Its full name is *Hippocampus kuda hilonis* (after the town of Hilo, where specimens were obtained). To about 7 in. with tail stretched out. Photos: top: Puakō, Hawai`i. 12 ft. left: Lagoon One, Ko Olina Resort, O`ahu. 5 -8 ft.

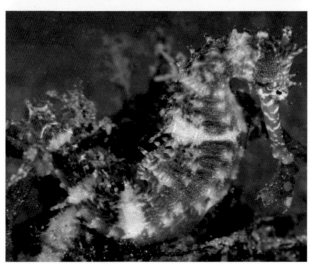

◄ THORNY SEAHORSE
Hippocampus histrix Kaup, 1853

This seahorse has been recorded only once in Hawai`i, off Maui in the 1920s. Someday, it could turn up again. The head and body ridges bear prominent spines and the long snout has a few white bars. (On the other hand, it is possible, even likely, that the specimen was actually the similar *H. fisheri,* previous page.) To 6 in. Indo-Pacific. Photo: Manado, Indonesia.

PORCUPINEFISHES
(Diodontidae)

Giant Porcupinefish · **kōkala** · inflated · "Sea Cave," O'ahu. 15 ft. (p. 221)

The porcupinefishes form a sister family to the pufferfishes (p. 223). Like puffers they can inflate with water into a ball too large to swallow, but unlike puffers they are covered with stout sharp spines. Porcupinefishes of the genus *Diodon* have long spines which lie flat against the body, erecting only when the fish begins to swell. Those of the genus *Chilomycterus*, often called burrfishes, have shorter spines most or all of which are permanently erected. Ichthyologist Robert F. Myers writes "A large inflated *Diodon* is as hard and round as a basketball, and, with 5-7 centimeter spines covering nearly its entire surface, is an impenetrable fortress capable of choking a large shark to death." Even juveniles can do damage: an 8-foot marlin was once found dead with a small inflated *Diodon* lodged in its throat. (Tiger Sharks, however, do prey upon these fish, a feat commanding respect.)

As a second line of defense, porcupinefishes are poisonous. Their internal organs and skin often contain tetrodotoxin, one of the most potent natural toxins known. Other toxins may be present as well. Tetrodotoxin causes paralysis and death by disrupting normal nerve conduction. It occurs in a number of other animals including pufferfishes, blue-ring octopuses, some flatworms, and a freshwater salamander. Bacteria within the animal manufacture the toxin, not the animal itself. If tetrodotoxin is ingested, numbness about the mouth and other unusual sensations typically occur within 10 to 45 minutes. Take any suspected victims to a hospital immediately because death can occur quickly, within 24 hours or less. (see p. 223 for more information on tetrodotoxin). In Hawai'i it is illegal for restaurants to serve porcupinefishes and pufferfishes.

Porcupinefishes tend to be larger than puffers, but resemble them in most other respects. Like pufferfishes, they lack scales and spines in their fins and lack pelvic fins entirely. Their single dorsal fin is set far back on the body above the anal fin. Unlike puffers, however, the pectoral fins are large

219

and fanlike. When porcupinefishes swim they seem almost to waddle. During the day they typically rest under ledges or in caves or hover quietly in midwater, often in loose aggregations. At night they feed on a variety of invertebrates. Their teeth are fused into a strong beak with which they can easily crack mollusc or crustacean shells and rip apart other animals. (Puffers have beaks too, but each half, top and bottom, is split down the center into two parts. This is reflected in their family name Tetraodontidae, which means "four teeth." Diodontidae, the family name for porcupinefishes, means "two teeth" because the top and bottom halves of the beak are not split.) Like pufferfishes, porcupinefishes can blow strong jets of water onto sand bottoms to uncover buried animals. Some scientists believe this to be the evolutionary precursor to inflation: having gained the means to blow water out, it became relatively easy to "blow" it in, and to trap it inside with a one-way valve.

There are about 19 porcupinefish and burrfish species worldwide, with three in Hawai'i. The general Hawaiian name is **kōkala**, a word which also means the thorns on the edge of a **lauhala** (*Pandanus*) leaf or the spines on a dorsal fin. In old Hawai'i, porcupinefishes were revered by some families or individuals as **'aumākua** (family gods or ancestors). If a porcupinefish was caught by such a person, a special chant was recited and it was returned to the sea.

SPOTTED BURRFISH · **kōkala**; **'o'opu hue** · *Chilomycterus reticulatus* (Linnaeus, 1758)
   This uncommon to rare porcupinefish is similar in shape, color, and size to the more abundant Giant Porcupinefish (next page), although it has shorter spines and may have a diffuse dark bar below the eye and similar bars on the sides. The biggest difference, however, is that <u>the spines do not lie back along the body, but are permanently erected</u>, resembling thorns on the stem of a rose. Like others in its family, this fish is most active at night. By day it generally hovers quietly, often in caves and under ledges. Although occurring in warm seas throughout the world, it is most abundant in the cooler subtropics. In Hawai'i it is seen most predictably in the northwestern chain. Around the main islands it is uncommon to rare. O'ahu divers can sometimes find it in some of the large caves along the cliffs of Koko Head, and snorkelers can occasionally see it in Hanauma Bay. To about 22 in. Photos: (top) Kahe Point, O'ahu. 15 ft. (bottom) Midway Atoll.

GIANT PORCUPINEFISH · **kōkala**; **ʻoʻopu kawa** · *Diodon hystrix* Linnaeus, 1758

This is the largest of all porcupinefishes. Its head and eyes are so big that the body may seem flabby and emaciated in comparison. Long backward-pointing spines lie flat along the entire body, erecting when the fish inflates. The back and sides are light gray or brown <u>covered with small black dots</u>. The fins also usually have black spots (generally not true of the Longspine Porcupinefish, next page). There are generally <u>no dark blotches or saddles</u>, but dark marks sometimes appear while the fish is feeding. During the day, solitary individuals typically rest under ledges or in caves, but at certain "traditional" places along the reef a dozen or more may be seen hovering loosely together in midwater year after year. Giant Porcupinefish feed primarily on molluscs, crustaceans, and urchins. Up to a length of about 7 in. they are pelagic (living in the open ocean), thus small individuals are almost never seen on the reef. Although sometimes considered safe to eat, people consuming this fish have on occasion died within an hour. The Hawaiian name means "spiny" and the species name means "porcupine." To 28 in. All tropical seas. Photo: *Mahi* wreck, Oʻahu. 60 ft. (see also p. 219)

"Please be officially advised..."

Divemaster Randy Jordan (of Jupiter Dive Center, Jupiter, Florida) spotted an 18-inch porcupinefish in a hole and tried to coax it out for his customers by stroking its head. The fish didn't budge. Randy then waggled his fingers in front of its face. That worked. In Randy's words, "He launched forward and got hold of my pinkie. Playtime over! Man that hurt. He bit my kevlar-gloved hand like a piranha on a dining mission. When he was ready, he let go. I was in pain, but relieved that my glove wasn't cut. When I took my glove off, I realized half of my finger was still in the glove. The stump that extended from my hand was clouding the water with green smoke.... I grabbed the base of my finger to attempt to stop the blood cloud and was shocked to see the damage inflicted." Due to the severe crushing, doctors were un-able to reattach the finger. Ten days later Randy was back in the water with a whole new philosophy about interact-ing with animals. Now he tells his divers, "Please be officially advised. Do not mess with the animals. It's not good for them and may not be good for you. They will do what they need to do to defend themselves."

LONGSPINE PORCUPINEFISH · **kōkala**; **ʻoʻopu ōkala**
Diodon holocanthus Linnaeus, 1758 [SPINY BALLOONFISH]

These fish are light brown marked with several large dark blotches and bars on the back and sides and many small dark spots. Long, backward-pointing spines lie flat along the entire body, erecting only when the fish inflates. Except for the larger dark blotches (which may be indistinct) and smaller body size, this fish is similar enough to the Giant Porcupinefish (previous page) that ichthyologists once suspected they were variants of the same species. Distinguishing characteristics of the Longspine Porcupinefish include short barbels under the chin and clear fins containing few or no spots. Very long spines on top of the head are another clue. Longspine Porcupinefish are primarily nocturnal. By day they rest on the bottom or hover quietly under ledges or in sheltered areas. (While studying fish sheltering behavior in Kona, William J. Walsh observed a Longspine Porcupinefish using the exact same resting spot on the reef for over seven months.) Both the Hawaiian name and the species names mean "spiny." These fish attain about 15 in., but are usually half that size. They occur in all tropical seas and are generally considered poisonous to eat. Photos: (top) Magic Island, Oʻahu. 25 ft. (right) Palea Point, Oʻahu. 70 ft.

Pushy lovers

In a Japanese public aquarium four or five male Giant Porcupinefish were observed repeatedly nudging a female on the underside, pushing her up to the surface where she released her eggs and the males shed their sperm. Afterward, all rushed back to the bottom. Field observations in the Sea of Cortez show a similar pattern: In a sheltered bay half a dozen pairs spawned simultaneously, males pushing their mates all the way to the surface where the two splashed noisily and vigorously, releasing their gametes. During this time females assumed a distinct white-sided color pattern. Courtship and spawning occurred at dusk or just before first light in the morning and took only three or four minutes.

Spotted Puffer · **'o'opu hue** · almost fully inflated · Midway Atoll. 80 ft.

When it comes to unusual defensive strategies, few fishes outdo the puffers and their close relatives the porcupinefishes (p. 219). Both, when alarmed, distend themselves with water into prickly balloons, becoming difficult or impossible for predators to swallow. If removed from water, they inflate with air, sometimes to the accompaniment of little croaking noises. The most obvious difference between pufferfishes and porcupinefishes lies in their skins—puffers are bristly whereas porcupinefishes are covered with sharp spines.

Inflating into a hard, bristly ball is not a puffer's only defense—many of these fishes are poisonous. The little tobies of the genus *Canthigaster*, some of which have limited powers of inflation, secrete a skin toxin which makes them immediately unpalatable to many predators. More importantly, most puffers accumulate in their bodies a poison called tetrodotoxin. One of the most powerful neurotoxins known, tetrodotoxin is produced by bacteria living within the puffers, not by the fish themselves. Puffers raised in captivity are not toxic until they are fed the flesh of a wild, toxin-producing fish. The poison is typically concentrated in the skin, liver, intestines, and gonads, and affects fish, mammals, crustaceans, and perhaps even insects. (In South Africa, dead puffers rotting on beaches are reported to kill flies by the hundreds!) For humans, one milligram of the substance is deadly. It causes tingling, numbness, and eventual paralysis of the voluntary muscles, including those responsible for breathing. A state of "living death" often ensues wherein the victim retains consciousness while unable to move. (The poison reportedly used in Haiti to create "zombies" contains tetrodotoxin.) True death may occur within 17 minutes to 24 hours. There is no antidote, but artificial respiration (CPR) can keep a victim alive until the effects wear off.

In spite of their toxicity, or perhaps because of it, pufferfishes are delicacies in Japan, where government-licensed "fugu chefs" prepare them safely for the table. The flesh is said to be firm, white, and sweet; the small amount of poison left produces a relaxing warmth or "glow." It is illegal to serve these fish commercially in Hawai'i. Medical researchers have recently found that miniscule amounts of tetrodotoxin, far below the lethal dose, can quickly alleviate certain types of chronic cancer pain that do not respond to morphine or other traditional drugs. Tetrodotoxin may also be useful in treating the withdrawal symptoms suffered by heroin addicts.

Puffers have chunky, scaleless bodies with a single dorsal fin set far back on the body, no pelvic fins, no ribs, and no spines in the fins—characteristics which make it easier for them to inflate. They range in length from a few inches to almost 3 ft. Equipped with sharp beaks, powerful jaws, and strong crushing plates, they are capable of eating almost anything that doesn't swim away, including thick shelled snails, urchins, and coral. They are also capable of delivering a painful bite, or worse (see pp. 221, 226). Puffers are comparatively weak swimmers. Except for the small tobies of the genus *Canthigaster*, most do not appear to have well-defined territories, although they often rest in predictable spots on the reef. Puffers in Hawai'i feed mostly at night, whereas tobies feed by day. Puffers will occasionally blow a jet of water at the sandy bottom to uncover buried prey. This ability is thought to be an evolutionary precursor to inflation. To inflate, puffers close a valve at the intestinal end of the stomach and start to gulp in water. A one-way valve at the stomach entrance traps the water inside. Continued gulping soon fills a special expandible chamber under the stomach, inflating the fish into a hard bristly ball.

Pufferfishes belong to the order Tetraodontiformes, which also includes porcupinefishes, boxfishes, and triggerfishes. The pufferfish family is divided into two subfamilies, the puffers proper (Tetraodontinae, with 95 species worldwide) and the diminutive tobies, also known as "sharpnosed puffers," (subfamily Canthigasterinae, with 26 species). Locally, puffers are sometimes called **makimaki**, a term apparently not used in ancient times and perhaps a corruption of **make** ("death"). In old Hawai'i the fishes called **'o'opu hue** (perhaps a corruption of **ōpūhue**, "calabash" or "gourd"), or **kēkē** ("potbelly") were probably puffers. Most of the small tobies have no known Hawaiian names. Twelve members of the puffer family inhabit our waters, three of them endemic; nine are described below. Among those omitted are the puffer *Arothron manilensis* and the toby *Canthigaster solandri* (both rare waifs), the deepwater toby *Canthigaster inframacula*, and the pelagic puffer *Lagocephalus lagocephalus*, a large open-ocean species that on rare occasions dies by the thousands, washing up on island beaches.

STRIPEBELLY PUFFER · **'o'opu hue**; **kēkē** ▶
Arothron hispidus (Linnaeus, 1758)

Sometimes called the "Stars and Stripes Puffer," this fish has white spots on its back and sides and stripes on its belly (sometimes faint). The body is light greenish brown. At the base of the pectoral fin is a prominent black area surrounded by white rings. This puffer is most common over sand, and often rests on the bottom during the day, seemingly asleep. It also occurs on reefs. A list of its food items resembles a catalog of all organisms in the sea: sponges, hydroids, anemones, zoanthids, corals, polychaete worms, molluscs (gastropod and bivalve), crabs, hermit crabs, brittle stars, sea stars (including the notorious, coral-eating Crown-of-Thorns Star), tunicates, algae (both fleshy and coralline), and detritus. On O'ahu, a great place to see these puffers is around the hot water outlet at Kahe Point Beach Park. A study in Taiwan showed that the skin of this puffer contained an unusually high concentration of toxin, whereas in other puffers tested, the liver, gonads, and intestines were typically the most toxic parts. Eating these fish has caused at least seven deaths in the Islands. It is illegal in Hawai'i for restaurants to serve them, or any other pufferfishes. Numbness or unusual sensations around the mouth are typical first symptoms of poisoning; nausea with no vomiting is also common. Take any suspected victims to a hospital immediately. This fish has survived up to 15 years in captivity. The species name means "bristly" or "rough." The largest puffer in Hawai'i, it grows to about 19 in. Indo-Pacific and Eastern Pacific. Photos: Kahe Point, O'ahu. 30 ft.

SPOTTED PUFFER · **ʻoʻopu hue**; **kēkē** · *Arothron meleagris* (Lacepède, 1798) [Guineafowl Puffer] ▲

This chunky puffer, usually brown or black, is covered with numerous small white spots. Some individuals are all yellow with a few dark spots, or partly yellow, partly brown, with dark or white spots, but these color variants are seldom seen in Hawaiʻi. Unlike most puffers, this fish feeds primarily on coral, preferring species of the genus *Pocillopora*. (Stomach contents of 6 specimens from Hawaiʻi contained 77 percent coral.) It will also consume the usual wide variety of marine invertebrates. Sometimes it hovers head down over sand and squirts jets of water from its mouth to uncover buried animals. Off Panama, a population of these puffers which fed almost entirely on living corals switched to eating sponges, tunicates, and coralline algae after El Niño episodes killed most of the corals. The bristly skin of these fish feels like velcro, especially when the fish is inflated, leading some divers to call them "velcro puffers." However, handling and inflating puffers for amusement is considered bad form, not to mention that the skin mucus of this species can be highly toxic. A study off Baja California, Mexico, found that black puffers contained more tetrodotoxin than yellow ones. In black individuals the intestine contained the most toxin, followed by the mucus, muscle, and liver, whereas in yellow ones the mucus had the highest concentration followed by the intestine, gonads, and liver. The species name means "guineafowl," a dark African bird covered with white spots. To about 13 in. Indo-Pacific and Eastern Pacific. Photo: Hanauma Bay, Oʻahu. 30 ft.

◀ STRIPEBELLY PUFFER (see previous page) ▼

Living dangerously

Entering a restaurant in Kyoto, Japan, with a group of friends, the famous Kabuki actor Mitsugoro Bando nodded and smiled at the other diners who recognized him. The year was 1975, and it was 7:30 on a January evening. The actor and his party were looking forward to a meal of fugu, or pufferfish, a favorite dish of the well-to-do because of its superb flavor and intoxicating side effects. Depending on the amount of fugu toxin consumed, a euphoric state with sensations of warmth is produced, accompanied by a numbness and tingling of the lips, tongue, and extremities. The knowledge that each fish carries a different amount of poison made the meal even more exciting. Laughter and good feeling increased as hot saki combined with the effects of the fugu. By 10:30 when the party broke up, the desired relaxed feeling had taken effect, indicating enough of the fish had been consumed. By 11:00 the actor had returned to his hotel room. Crawling into bed, he spoke briefly to his wife of the enjoyable evening. She protested about the danger of eating fugu but he silenced her. "Everything is fine," he said. "I feel great, just like I am floating on air." At 3:00 AM he awakened to go to the bathroom, but found his legs too numb to carry him. He roused his wife to bring him a glass of water, but his arms failed when he tried to hold it. Alarmed, his wife called for an ambulance, which delivered the great actor to the hospital within half an hour. It was too late, however. Revered as a "living national treasure" by his countrymen, Bando died at 4:40 AM, approximately six and a half hours after dinner. Why did the actor succumb? According to the newspaper account, he daringly ordered the liver and ate four portions, while his friends ate only the flesh. Like many who enjoy living dangerously, Bando played a game of chance against risky odds, and lost. (Adapted from an article by Jean N. Hill in Oceans magazine, March 1982.)

Piranhas of the sea

Sharp beaks and strong jaws enable pufferfishes to attack almost anything. A few Australian species are downright dangerous. In 1979, a little girl bathing near Proserpine, Queensland, lost three toes to a large puffer later identified as Feroxodon multistriatus. Another Australian puffer, known locally as the Silver Toadfish (Lagocephalus sceleratus), is easily provoked into a feeding frenzy by the presence of blood. Under such conditions it will not hesitate to bite a human. Called the "piranha of the sea," it attacks either alone or en masse, chomping out large chunks of flesh and even biting through bone. Where common, it is feared more than sharks. Luckily, none of these puffer species occur in Hawai'i. On the lighter side, schools of the small Banded Toadfish (Torquigener pleurogramma), whose teeth are too tiny to do much damage, will follow spearfishermen and their catch. An Australian diver reports hundreds of these puffers swarming over him after he speared a lobster. They even attacked the spear, and clung to the line with their teeth in such numbers that it resembled a clothesline! Juveniles of the Floral Puffer (below) sometimes behave similarly.

FLORAL PUFFER *Torquigener florealis* (Cope, 1871)

Puffers of the genus *Torquigener* have long sloping foreheads, eyes set high on the head, and prominent "chins." Typically living over sand, they are seldom seen by divers in Hawai'i. This species is marked with a line of orange-yellow spots along the upper side. When alarmed it buries itself loosely, often just up to the eyes. In rare years, juveniles occur in the hundreds or thousands close to shore and will behave much like the Banded Toadfish described above, emboldened by their numbers or hunger, or both. Most perish, and little sign of them remains after several weeks. To about 7 in. Hawai'i, Japan, and the East China Sea. Photo: Kahe Point, O'ahu. 50 ft.

RANDALL'S PUFFER *Torquigener randalli* Hardy, 1983

Although generally dwelling beyond scuba depths, these puffers can occur at 40-50 ft. in well-protected sandy areas. On Oʻahu, Kāneʻohe Bay and the "Haleʻiwa Trench" are good spots to see them. Foraging in groups, they will sometimes follow divers, perhaps to eat animals stirred up by their fins. The odd shape, a conspicuous dark line running along the side, and a dark bar below the eye will identify the species. The name honors ichthyologist Dr. John E. Randall of Honolulu's Bishop Museum, who has discovered, classified, and named more fish species than any other living person. On field trips in his late-seventies he would still do 6 dives a day, then stay up half the night preserving, pinning out, and photographing his finds. One of Randall's young students once tried to match him dive for dive, but soon gave up. To about 5 in. Endemic. Photo: "Haleʻiwa Trench," Oʻahu. 45 ft.

HAWAIIAN WHITESPOTTED TOBY *Canthigaster jactator* (Jenkins, 1901)

Tobies are diminutive puffers, generally less than 4 in. long, with a somewhat elongated snout. This species is brown with numerous white spots (those on the head often showing a slight green fluorescence), and is by far the most common toby in Hawaiʻi. Usually seen in pairs, it occurs on hard substrate almost everywhere, from areas of 100% coral cover to dead silty places where little else seems to live. Some individuals have irregular black marks on the snout, body, and fins—perhaps a disease. Others are so distended with parasitic worms (nematodes) that they appear about to burst (see next page). One study indicated that Hawaiian Whitespotted Tobies feed mostly on green and red algae; another showed sponges to be the main food, followed by algae and tunicates. Aquarists have observed these cute but mischievous puffers stealthily approaching other fishes and nipping their fins, leaving perfect semicircular "cookie-bites" along the edges (see p. 303, bottom photo). They also nip at the skin of resting sea turtles, especially those with tumorous growths, causing the turtles to flinch. The species name means "boaster," or "braggart," no doubt because of the fish's ability to inflate. To about 3 ½ in. Endemic (with two sister species, *C. janthinoptera* in the Indo-Pacific and *C. punctatissima* in the Eastern Pacific). Photo: Magic Island, Oʻahu. 25 ft.

While diving at Pūpūkea, Oʻahu, I saw something strange-looking on the bottom. Investigating, I found a frogfish with its mouth stretched around an inflated Whitespotted Toby. Only the toby's tail was protruding, and the frogfish was dead. I extracted the little puffer, which then swam off. Did the inflation stop the frogfish's respiration? Or was death caused by the skin toxin? In either case, Whitespotted Toby defenses were field-tested and they worked. - John Earle

Whitespotted Toby: social life, parasites, sleep...

Tobies in general are sexually dimorphic (males larger than females) with both sexes defending territories against others of their own sex. Large males hold "super territories" which include the smaller territories of one to four females, and they visit each of their females daily. These females never pair with other males. Each female prepares a nest, often in a patch of algae, and when ready to spawn flexes her tail and/or displays her swollen abdomen to the male (perhaps augmented by a puff or two). Spawning occurs throughout the year with the female depositing her eggs in the nest where the male then fertilizes them. Neither parent guards the nest, but the eggs and larvae of at least one species are unpalatable to predators. If a male is removed, his territory is absorbed into that of a neighboring male, often overnight. The lifestyle of the Hawaiian Whitespotted Toby appears similar. During the course of a science project off Kona, Hawai'i, in 1985, high school students Kim Bruno and Marguerite Nogues observed that Whitespotted Tobies spent most of their time in pairs (although not necessarily next to or very near each other) and swam in a distinct pattern which seemed to mark circular territories that varied in diameter from 3 to 20 ft. The students marked the territory boundaries with shiny new nails and observed that the tobies displayed considerable interest in these foreign objects. On one occasion a toby entered another pair's territory and one of the resident tobies swam out, nipped its side, and chased it away. The tobies spent about 50

percent of the daytime swimming around the territory, 40 percent hiding among the rocks, and 10 percent feeding. During a 1990 study of parasitised Whitespotted Tobies in Kāne'ohe Bay, O'ahu, Robert Reavis and Michele Barrett observed that large normal males controlled territories of about 225 sq. ft. which usually contained 3-4 female territories of about 10 sq. ft. Males spent much of their time following females within their territories. Juveniles, which lurked within adult territories, were mostly ignored or briefly chased by the resident adult. Individuals heavily infested with parasitic nematodes, however, (see photo at right) seldom interacted with other tobies and did not take part in normal toby social or reproductive life. These outcasts ate at twice the rate of normal individuals.

After the excitement of the day, what do Whitespotted Tobies do at night? William J. Walsh, while studying fish sheltering behavior in Kona, noted that a Whitespotted Toby rested at night on one of his polypropylene transect lines spanning a vertical wall. Although the line was essentially uniform throughout its length, the toby rested within an inch of the same precise spot for over two weeks.

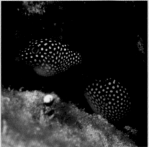

| about to spawn | female laying eggs | male fertilizing eggs |

... spawning

Diving at Mākua, O'ahu, David R. Schrichte photographed a pair of Whitespotted Tobies apparently spawning. The lower fish (presumably male) pursued the upper fish with the swollen belly (presumably female) into a hole (left photo). The swollen fish positioned itself repeatedly in a particular spot and trembled as if laying eggs (middle photo). A totally different pair at Kahe Point, O'ahu, (right photo) seems to show a male fertilizing eggs just laid by a still swollen female.

... sunscreen

Observing a Whitespotted Toby under ultraviolet light, University of Hawai'i researcher Jill P. Zamzow discovered some subtle spots on the fish that were visible only when its mucus was wiped off. The mucus was apparently blocking the ultraviolet light from her lamp. In nature, she surmised, UV-absorbing compounds in the mucus probably protect the fish from the sun's damaging radiation. The UV-blocking capability of Whitespotted Toby mucus turned out to be equal in strength to SPF 15 human sunscreen. Later, Zamzow examined the mucus of 200 Indo-Pacific fish species, finding sunscreen compounds in 84 percent of them. One, the Hawaiian Saddle Wrasse (p. 350), was able to change the SPF factor of its mucus depending on the depth at which it lived!

AMBON TOBY
Canthigaster amboinensis
(Bleeker, 1865)

These tobies vary from light to dark brown, often with ochre-yellow on the upper head, nape and snout. Blue-green lines radiate from the eyes. A fine pattern of dark blue spots and lines adorns the cheeks. The rest of the body is covered with iridescent light blue spots. The base of the anal fin is intense blue. Pairs are frequently encountered in boulder habitat close to shore, but may also be seen in the coral environment. One study shows they feed mainly on coral. Although chunky and rotund, they are fast swimmers and often hard to approach. The species is named for the Indonesian island of Ambon. To about 5 in. Indo-Pacific. Photos: (top) Kahe Point, O'ahu. 15 ft. (bottom two) Mākua, O'ahu. 8 ft.

CROWNED TOBY · **pu'u olai** · *Canthigaster coronata* (Vaillant & Sauvage, 1875)

The three dark saddles on the back of these tobies may have reminded the old Hawaiians of lava flows, for the Hawaiian name means "cinder cone." Yellow dots cover much of their whitish bodies; blue and yellow lines radiate from the eyes. Although common, they prefer depths of 20 ft. or more and are unlikely to be seen by snorkelers. Like many tobies, they usually occur in pairs. To about 5 in. Endemic (with a sister species, *C. axiologa*, elsewhere in the Pacific and another in the Indian Ocean). Photos: (left) Kahe Point, O'ahu. 25 ft. (right) Magic Island, O'ahu. 30 ft.

LANTERN TOBY *Canthigaster epilampra* (Jenkins, 1903)

Iridescent blue-green lines radiate from the eyes and across the yellow head of this beautiful little toby. At a distance, however, the fish is most easily identified by a large dark mark at the base of the dorsal fin. The body is whitish, the tail fin is yellow. It is usually seen singly and, like others of its kind, is probably territorial. Sometimes two males vie for a female, chasing one another up into the water, facing off, swimming in parallel, or circling one another warily. While engaging in these behaviors, each erects a flap of skin along the underside of the body, presumably to enlarge its appearance (as in photo above). Many other tobies do the same. Although generally found at depths of 80 ft. or more, this species occasionally occurs in as little as 20 ft. The caves around Portlock Point, Oʻahu, are a good place to look for it. The species name means "shining." To about 4 in. Western and Central Pacific. Photos: (above) YO-257 wreck, off Waikīkī, Oʻahu. 90 ft. (Jerry Kane). (left) Keaʻau, Oʻahu. 50 ft.

MAZE TOBY *Canthigaster rivulata* (Schlegel, 1850)

This toby is rare in Hawaiʻi. Its head and back are covered with a maze of blue lines. A U-shaped mark around the pectoral fin connects with two irregular dark stripes running back toward the tail, the upper dark, the lower faint. There is a black mark under the dorsal fin. Like most tobies, it erects a flap of skin along its underside when threatened or aroused. Small individuals are reported abundant in shallow water during some years. The species name comes from the Latin *rivulus* ("stream"). Large for a toby, it attains almost 8 in. Indo-Pacific. Photo: Hanauma Bay, Oʻahu, 40 ft.

Coastal Manta Ray · **hāhālua** · "Old Airport," Kona, Hawai'i. 30 ft. (p. 234)

Rays have flattened bodies, great winglike pectoral fins that extend forward and attach to the head, and often a long whiplike tail. Close cousins to the sharks, their skeletons are composed entirely of cartilage, they lack swim bladders, and their skins bear dermal denticles instead of over-lapping scales. The gill slits are always under the pectoral fins. Water is drawn into the gill chamber through openings behind the eye called spiracles, enabling these animals to forage in sand or mud or lie flat on the bottom. The mouth is on the underside (except in manta rays). Rays are carnivores, and most spend their lives on the bottom, sometimes covering themselves with sand. Bottom-dwelling rays swim by rippling their large pectoral fins. Eagle rays, cownose rays, devil rays, and mantas, however, use their triangular pectoral fins like wings, "flying" gracefully high in the water and sometimes leaping into the air.

Male rays use claspers (paired rodlike organs at the base of their tails) to internally fertilize fe-males. The presence or absence of claspers makes it easy to distinguish the sexes. Females gen-erally give birth to fully formed young, which hatch from eggs retained in the body. There are about 450-500 species of rays in ten families, most of which (skates, sawfishes, guitarfishes, various kinds of electric rays, etc.) do not occur along Hawai'i's shores. There are two general names for rays in the Hawaiian language: **lupe**, which also means "kite," and **hīhīmanu**, "magnificent." Along with sharks, ratfishes, and chimaeras, rays fall within the group called "elasmobranchs." Specialists often refer to rays collectively as "batoids."

Stingrays (family Dasyatidae)

Although uncommon at snorkeling and diving sites in Hawai'i, the stingrays are probably the best known group of rays worldwide. These round or diamond-shaped bottom-dwellers bear a venomous barbed spine at the base of a whiplike tail, and can deliver an excruciating and potentially fatal wound. <u>Under no circumstances position your body over a stingray, or attempt to "ride" it.</u> It might drive its spine deep into your chest. To avoid stepping on a buried stingray, shuffle your feet while wading. (In Hawai'i, where stingrays are uncommon, this is normally not necessary.) If somehow you do get stung by a ray, immersing the limb in hot water usually helps to alleviate the intense pain, and is the best first-aid treatment. Do not attempt to remove a deeply embedded spine; get medical attention.

There are about 60 species of stingrays, some attaining a width of 6 ft. and a weight of over 800 lbs. Three species have been recorded from Hawaiian waters, but only the Broad Stingray is shown here. The Diamond Stingray *(Hypanus dipterurus)*, an Eastern Pacific ray known in the Islands from only a single juvenile specimen, differs from the Broad Stingray by having folds or keels of skin running along both the upper and lower surfaces of the long tail instead of the underside only. Also omitted is the unusual sea-going Violet Stingray *(Pteroplatytrygon violacea)*, which occurs offshore and does not normally approach land.

BROAD STINGRAY *Bathytoshia lata* (Garman, 1880) [BROWN STINGRAY]
This is Hawai'i's only common shallow-water stingray. Its roughly diamond-shaped body has convex borders and is slightly wider than it is long. When viewed from above, its front tip is distinctly pointed. The tail is twice the length of the body and a fold or keel of skin runs along its underside. The wide portion of the tail is studded with spiny tubercles. As in all stingrays, a venomous spine sits atop the tail just behind the body. These bottom-dwellers are most common in muddy or silty embayments such as Maui's Ma'alaea Bay and O'ahu's Kāne'ohe Bay, where divers and snorkelers seldom go. They will also live over sand, however, and divers occasionally encounter them foraging adjacent to reefs or lying half-buried, usually at depths of about 50 ft. or more. Occasionally they enter quite shallow water. You can tell if you're in stingray country by the presence of large craters and pits in the sand created by the rays as they excavate for buried prey—perhaps sand-dwelling fishes, worms, crustaceans, molluscs, or echinoderms. To see a large active ray churning up great clouds of sand must be quite a sight. A jack often follows a foraging ray, presumably to nab small escaping animals or perhaps just to get scraps. To at least 5 ft. in width, although 3 ft. is more usual. Indo-Pacific and Eastern Atlantic. Photos: Pūpūkea, O'ahu. 70 ft.

Manta Rays and Devil Rays (family Mobulidae)

These are big free-swimming rays with pointed, triangular wings. Feeding on plankton and lacking a sting, they are considered harmless to humans. Mantas are among the largest of fishes, some reportedly weighing over 3,000 lbs. with a wingspan of 23 ft. or more. Unlike most rays, their mouth is at the front of the body rather than underneath. Devil rays have an underslung mouth and are somewhat smaller than mantas. Extremely rare in Hawai'i, only two species, the Sicklefin Devil Ray *(Mobula tarapacana)* and the Spinetail Devil Ray *(M. japanica),* have ever been seen in the Islands.

The most distinctive characteristic of this entire family of rays, apart from the sheer size of most species, is the strange pair of armlike cephalic flaps which funnel water into the mouth as they feed. The flaps furl up when not in use. When furled they look like a pair of forward-pointing horns, undoubtedly the reason for the name "devil ray." Manta rays and devil rays are generally solitary, though they do congregate to feed in places where plankton is abundant. To a lesser extent, they also gather at certain specific cleaning stations, the locations of which persist over years.

At least two species of mantas are known worldwide, and Hawai'i is one of the easiest places to see them. The Coastal Manta, described on p. 234, is encountered most frequently.

Jerry Kane

PELAGIC MANTA RAY · **hāhālua**· *Mobula birostris* (Walbaum, 1792)

The largest known manta, this species is occasionally encountered in Hawaiian waters. It is more pelagic in its habits than the Coastal Manta, which always remains within a few miles of shore. One individual, for example, was photographed off Kona in 2006 and later off Maui in 2009. No one knows where it was between the two sightings. The Pelagic Manta's back is black, always with white or pale shoulder patches, and often with white wing tips and a white V near the tail. The underside is white with scattered dark spots, but never with dark spots or marks in the "chest" area between the two rows of gill slits. A wide gray margin extends along rear edge of the wings. (Compare with the photo of a Coastal Manta's underside at the top of p. 235.) Also, the mouth area is dark gray or black (best seen from below or when viewed head-on). A few individuals are all black except for a white blaze in center of the underside. Indo-Pacific, Eastern Pacific, and Atlantic. To at least 23 ft. wingtip to wingtip, with anecdotal reports of individuals up to 29 ft. Photo: Kona, Hawai'i. (Jerry Kane)

COASTAL MANTA RAY · **hāhālua** · *Mobula alfredi* (Krefft, 1868)

These huge animals fly continually through the water with graceful beats of their triangular wings, often near the surface. Smaller individuals may even leap free, sometimes cartwheeling, and landing with a great splash. Their back is black, often with white patches or streaks on the shoulders, wings, and tail area (p. 231). Their underside is white or cream with irregular scattered dark spots, each individual having a slightly different pattern. (Unlike the Pelagic Manta, dark spots are almost always present in the "chest" area between the two rows of gill slits on the underside.) The mouth area is whitish or grayish, best seen from below or when viewed head-on. An almost all-black color variation is rare in Hawaiʻi. Because of their size and swimming ability, it was long assumed that all mantas migrate long distances. However, Tim Clark of the University of Hawaiʻi studied Coastal Mantas on the Kona Coast of the Big Island and determined that the population is localized. No Coastal Manta from Kona, for example, has ever been recorded from Maui. Using acoustic tracking technology and visual recognition, he found that these mantas typically ranged 10-20 miles up and down the coast over a 3- to 5-day period and tended to concentrate in several key feeding areas. They usually stayed within about half a mile of shore during the day, but at night migrated offshore as much as 3 miles. Clark hypothesizes that the offshore movement allows the rays to feed on plankton which is migrating upward and inshore during that time. Although generally solitary, mantas will regularly congregate in areas where food is plentiful, providing the basis for a lucrative "manta ray night dive" industry in Kona. *Manta* means "mantle" or "cloak." The species name ("two snouts") and the Hawaiian name ("two mouths") probably refer to the two cephalic flaps extended while feeding. The largest Coastal Manta on record was 18 ft. from wingtip to wingtip. Most individuals are in the 8-12 ft. range. Coastal Mantas occur throughout the Indo-Pacific, but are not known from the Eastern Pacific. Photo: Hanauma Bay, Oʻahu. 10 ft. (see also p. 231)

Manta ray night dive

For many years mantas could be viewed from shore in front of the Kona Surf Hotel in Kailua-Kona, Hawaiʻi, where they congregated every evening to feed on tiny planktonic animals attracted to hotel spotlights. Manta ray night dives in front of the hotel became a specialty of local dive shops. Scuba customers sat on the bottom while snorkelers hovered above, all mesmerized by half a dozen or more big rays looping and somersaulting in the beams of light as they funneled the abundant plankton into their cavernous mouths. The Kona Surf Hotel closed in June, 2000, but another Kona location, Ho'ona Bay, was soon found which offers similar dives, this time using the divers' own lights. Every evening, boatloads of divers and snorkelers at Ho'ona witness one of the most exhilarating underwater experiences in Hawaiʻi. If you go, observe a few basic rules. Scuba divers should sit on the bottom and snorkelers should remain on the surface—the rays need plenty of free space in the water for their acrobatic maneuvers. Also, please refrain from touching the rays, although it may be quite possible to do so. Don't like night dives? A good place to see mantas by day is Molokini Islet, Maui, where these enormous rays regularly visit Hawaiian Cleaner Wrasse stations, usually in the late afternoon, to rid themselves of parasites. They occasionally visit many other dive sites as well.

Manta identification

The irrregular pattern of dark spots and blotches on the white undersides of mantas is unique to each ray and does not change with growth. This allows researchers to identify and name individual mantas, and to track their movements and growth over time. The female Coastal Manta at right was photographed by Tim Clark off Makalea Point, Hawai'i, on May 6, 2003. Tim named her Betsy after his mom, Betsy Clark. He now has extensive tracking data on Betsy, which together with data from other ray sightings helps Tim draw the big picture of manta ray biology and ecology in Hawai'i. You can help! If you have photos of a Hawaiian manta's underside you can try to identify the ray and file a report, using the image database posted at the Manta Pacific Research Foundation website. If your ray is not in the database, you get to add it and name it. It doesn't get better than that! See **www.mantapacific.org**

Tim Clark

Manta love

If you see mantas chasing each other, circling or swimming in single file, romance may be brewing. Free diving off west Maui, photographer Michael S. Nolan observed an 11-foot female Coastal Manta with five smaller males following single-file behind. Sometimes the female led them in a circle. Occasionally she would stop while the nearest male hovered above, resting his unfurled cephalic flaps on her back. Then she would shudder and shoot for the surface, the male would "blanket" her, and the two, pancaked together, would perform beautifully synchronized loops and acrobatics. Although Michael observed this sequence repeated with different males for a period of hours two days in a row, he saw no actual mating. Mating observed off Japan's Ogasawara Islands took place as follows: two 12-foot males chased a 15-foot female for 20-30 minutes, each attempting to bite her pectoral fin. One male succeeded in grasping the tip of her left fin in his mouth, thereby slowing her down. He then positioned himself belly-to-belly under her and inserted his clasper for about 90 seconds. He continued to hold her fin for some time before releasing her. The other male then mated with her in the same way. Both events occurred within three feet of the surface.

© Michael S. Nolan / www.wildlifeimages.net

Jennifer's magic moment

Drift diving off Molokini Islet, Maui, divemaster Jennifer Anderson and two divers had just begun their ascent when something far below caught Jennifer's eye. "After a few moments I made out the white shoulder patches of a manta ray in about one hundred and twenty feet of water," she writes. "I started calling through my regulator, 'Hey, come up and see me!' I had tried this before to attract the attention of whales and dolphins, who are very chatty underwater and will come sometimes just to see what the noise is about. I kept calling to the ray, and when she shifted in the water column, I took that as a sign that she was curious. So I started waving my arms, calling her up to me."

"After a minute, she lifted away from where she had been riding the current and began to make a wide circular glide until she was closer to me. I kept watching as she slowly moved back and forth, rising higher, until she was directly beneath the two divers and me. Looking back to the ray, I realized she was much bigger than what we were used to around Molokini —a good fifteen feet from wing tip to wing tip, and not a familiar-looking ray. I had not seen this animal before.

There was something else odd about her. I just couldn't figure out what it was. Once my brain clicked in and I was able to concentrate, I saw deep V-shaped marks of her flesh missing from her backside. Other marks ran up and down her body. At first I thought a boat had hit her. As she came closer, now with only ten feet separating us, I realized what was wrong. She had fishing hooks embedded in her head by her eye, with very thick fishing line running to her tail. She had rolled with the line and was wrapped head to tail about five or six times. The line had torn into her body at the back, and those were the V-shaped chunks that were missing.

I felt sick and, for a moment, paralyzed. I knew wild animals in pain would never tolerate a human to inflict more pain. But I had to do something. Forgetting about my air, my divers and where I was, I went to the manta. I moved very slowly and talked to her the whole time, like she was one of the horses I had grown up with. When I touched her, her whole body quivered, like my horse would. I put both of my hands on her, then my entire body, talking to her the whole time. I knew that she could knock me off at any time with one flick of her great wing. When she had steadied, I took out the knife that I carry on my inflator hose and lifted one of the lines. It was tight and difficult to get my finger under, almost like a guitar string. She shook, which told me to be gentle. It was obvious that the slightest pressure was painful.

As I cut through the first line, it pulled into her wounds. With one beat of her mighty wings, she dumped me and bolted away. I figured that she was gone and was amazed when she turned and came right back to me, gliding under my body. I went to work. She seemed to know it would hurt, and somehow, she also knew that I could help. Imagine the intelligence of that creature, to come for help and to trust!

I cut through one line and into the next until she had all she could take of me and would move away, only to return in a moment or two. I never chased her. I would never chase any animal. I never grabbed her. I allowed her to be in charge, and she always came back.

When all the lines were cut on top, on her next pass, I went under her to pull the lines through the wounds at the back of her body. The tissue had started to grow around them, and they were difficult to get loose. I held myself against her body, with my hand on her lower jaw. She held as motionless as she could. When it was all loose, I let her go and watched her swim in a circle. She could have gone then, and it would have all fallen away. She came back, and I went back on top of her. The fishing hooks were still in her. One was barely hanging on, which I removed easily. The other was buried by her eye at least two inches past the barb. Carefully, I began to take it out, hoping I wasn't damaging anything. She did open and close her eye while I worked on her, and finally, it was out. I held the hooks in one hand, while I gathered the fishing line in the other hand, my weight on the manta.

I could have stayed there forever! I was totally oblivious to everything but that moment. I loved this manta. I was so moved that she would allow me to do this to her. But reality came screaming down on me. With my air running out, I reluctantly came to my senses and pushed myself away.

At first, she stayed below me. And then, when she realized that she was free, she came to life like I never would have imagined she could. I thought she was sick and weak, since her mouth had been tied closed, and she hadn't been able to feed for however long the lines had been on her. I thought wrong! With two beats of those powerful wings, she rocketed along the wall of Molokini and then directly out to sea!

I lost view of her and, remembering my divers, turned to look for them. Remarkably, we hadn't traveled very far. My divers were right above me and had witnessed the whole event, thankfully! No one would have believed me alone. It seemed too amazing to have really happened. But as I looked at the hooks and line in my hands and felt the torn calluses from her rough skin, I knew that, yes, it really had happened.

I kicked in the direction of my divers, whose eyes were still wide from the encounter, only to have them signal me to stop and turn around. Until this moment, the whole experience had been phenomenal, but I could explain it. Now, the moment turned magical. I turned and saw her slowly gliding toward me. With barely an effort, she approached me and stopped, her wing just touching my head. I looked into her round, dark eye, and she looked deeply into me. I felt a rush of something that so overpowered me; I have yet to find the words to describe it, except a warm and loving flow of energy from her into me.

She stayed with me for a moment. I don't know if it was a second or an hour. Then, as sweetly as she came back, she lifted her wing over my head and was gone. A manta thank-you.

I hung in midwater, using the safety-stop excuse, and tried to make sense of what I had experienced. Eventually, collecting myself, I surfaced and was greeted by an ecstatic group of divers and a curious captain. They all gave me time to get my heart started and to begin to breathe.

Sadly, I have not seen her since that day, and I am still looking. For the longest time, though my wetsuit was tattered and torn, I would not change it because I thought she wouldn't recognize me. I call to every manta I see, and they almost always acknowledge me in some way. One day, though, it will be her. She'll hear me and pause, remembering the giant cleaner that she trusted to relieve her pain, and she'll come. At least that is how it happens in my dreams."

Manta intelligence

Mantas have the largest brain to body weight ratio of any cartilaginous fish. Their brains compare in relative size to those of some mammals and birds. Furthermore, a complex net of arteries and veins surrounding the brain is believed to keep the brain warmer than the surrounding water, unusual in a cold-blooded fish. Some sharks and tunas use the same type of circulatory "net" to keep their muscles 9-18 degrees F. above the ambient water temperature, ready for high power output at any time or place. Similarly, a warmed brain could be useful to maintain alertness and intelligence regardless of water temperature. Just why a plankton-feeding ray needs a large brain is not clear, but in general, warm-blooded animals are thought to have higher intelligence than cold-blooded ones.

John Davies

Manta pit stop

Many mantas pull in to cleaning stations on a daily basis where smaller fish busily work them over, presumably removing parasites. At this station at Molokini Islet, Maui, attendants include Hawaiian Cleaner Wrasses, Blacklip Butterflyfish, and Saddle Wrasses. Other mantas may hover near by, awaiting their turn.

Eagle Rays (family Myliobatidae)

Eagle rays are "flyers" with pointed triangular wings. Although they feed on the bottom, they do not rest there but always soar back into the blue. All are deep-bodied animals with a prominent head which protrudes well forward of the wings. The gill slits and eyes are on the side of the head, unlike those of other rays. A long slender tail often greatly exceeds the length of the body. Most eagle rays have one or more venomous spines on the tail, but swimmers or divers are unlikely to get close enough to be wounded. Out of about 10 Indo-Pacific eagle ray species, one is in our area. Some authorities include manta rays, devil rays, and cownose rays in this family as well.

SPOTTED EAGLE RAY · **hailepo**; **hīhīmanu** · *Aetobatus ocellatus* (Kuhl, 1823)

These magnificent rays can attain almost 10 ft. from wingtip to wingtip. Their back, light brown, gray or black, is beautifully spotted with white. The underside is mostly white, often with a faint mazelike pattern under the wings. The long slender tail can equal three times the width of the body (if not broken or bitten off), and bears 1-5 venomous spines at the base. Under the large protruding head is a wide fleshy lobe somewhat resembling a "duck bill" which helps the ray dig for molluscs and other organisms. When not foraging, Spotted Eagle Rays swim well off the bottom, sometimes in small groups. One of the most beautiful of all underwater sights is a formation of Spotted Eagle Rays flying together in synchrony. In some parts of the world schools of 50 or more have been reported, but such behavior is certainly not common in Hawaiian waters. Occasionally Spotted Eagle Rays will leap from the sea, either dolphin style or by cartwheeling with wings outspread. Leaping by pregnant females is said to facilitate the birth of young. Spotted Eagle rays much like this one occur in warm seas around the world. For many years all were lumped together as one species: *Aetobatus narinari*. However, the various populations host different parasites and their spot patterns and body proportions differ slightly. In 2009, a DNA study confirmed that "spotted eagle rays" in Hawai`i and the Indo-Pacific are distinct from those in the Atlantic and Eastern Pacific. The Hawaiian word hīhīmanu means "lavish," "magnificent," "elegant." In ancient times these powerful animals, which weigh up to 500 lbs., were forbidden to women as food. Photo: "Mahi" wreck, O'ahu. 60 ft.

Eagle Ray factoids

1) Spotted Eagle Rays have one of the largest brain to body weight ratios of any fish.
2) Spotted Eagle Rays are the only members of their family to have multiple spines on the tail.
3) The earliest reference to the native Brazilian name "narinari," from which the original scientific species name was drawn, appears in a book on the natural history of Brazil written by a French monk and published in 1613.

Jerry Kane

Eagle ray feeding

Spotted Eagle Rays feed mostly on molluscs. They will also take worms, crustaceans, echinoderms, and small fish. The mouth of a Spotted Egle Ray contains platelike teeth used for crushing shelled prey. Special papillae on the floor and roof of the mouth separate the broken shell fragments from the edible flesh before it is swallowed. Foraging rays are thought to use electroreceptors to "scan" for buried prey, which they dig out using their shovel-like nose (the "duck bill"). As they dig, sand may be stirred up in clouds or ingested and expelled out the gill slits, enveloping the entire head. Sometimes these rays will overturn large chunks of coral or rock in search of prey. John Earle once watched one chase and consume an octopus which had sought refuge under a coral slab. Pauline Fiene reports seeing a Spotted Eagle Ray dislodge and consume an ark shell (Arca ventricosa) which had been firmly attached to a rock, and Kendra Ignacio reports: "Twice I have seen eagle rays eating Triton's Trumpet shells! I actually have an old (crappy) photo of a ray with the pointy end of the shell sticking out of its mouth! Both times the ray picked up the shell (and these are BIG Triton shells—not babies!) by the bulbous end and proceeded to smash it against rocks to try to break it open. Both times I was not able to see the end result, but it is safe to assume the Tritons got the worse end of the deal!"

Eagle ray reproduction

Spotted Eagle Rays pursuing one another may be about to mate. Writer/photographer Rod Canham describes "a large eagle ray hotly pursued by two smaller ones" at Molokini Islet, Maui. "The male latched onto the larger female and coupled 10 feet in front of us, as the pair rapidly glided out of sight."

Dr. Tim Tricas of the University of Hawai'i observed two episodes of unsuccessful courtship at Enewetak Atoll, Marshall Islands. In the first instance two males swam behind a female on either side, nipping at her posterior margin. The female rose to the surface and vigorously slapped her wings on the water causing the males to back off. When she submerged the males continued to follow and nip. Occasionally one would swim wide circles around her.

In the second episode, Tricas watched as a single male followed a female, periodically gouging her back with his dental plates and attempting to mount her. At each attempt she either shied to one side or surfaced. When she swam at the surface, the male followed either swimming conspicuously from side to side or up and down. Eventually the female left and the frustrated male swam in a wide circle alternately surfacing and diving at a 45 degree angle, his white underside producing bright "flashes" visible even after the outline of the ray disappeared in the distance.

In their book Sharks and Rays of Hawai'i (Mutual Publishing, 2002), Gerald L. Crow and Jennifer Crites write: "In Hawai'i, spotted eagle rays are born in October, November and December in Pearl Harbor and Kāne'ohe Bay, O'ahu, and on the leeward side of Moloka'i. During the birthing process, these rays have been seen leaping from the water and dropping their young in midair." Up to four pups (disc width 10-20 inches) are born per litter.

REMORAS
(Echeneidae)

Also called suckerfishes, these "hitchhikers of the seas" attach to larger animals—typically sharks, rays, turtles, dolphins, and whales—by means of a powerful sucking disk on top of the head. Actually a highly modified first dorsal fin, this disk bears numerous parallel ridges (derived from the spines) which operate somewhat like the slats of a venetian blind to create the vacuum which binds the remora to its host. Some remoras prefer specific animals, such as billfishes or sharks; others are not fussy and will attach to boats, divers, and even other remoras (see below!). These fishes are agile swimmers in their own right, however, and at least one species often lives freely.

Aside from being a drag, remoras do no harm to their larger companions. They may even do some good by feeding on their host's parasites, although these must constitute only a small part of their diet. Remoras attached to large predators undoubtedly nab floating scraps from their messy meals, but these fish also hitch rides on plankton-eating mantas and whale sharks, which presumably leave few pickings. Most likely, remoras feed opportunistically on whatever they can find, including their host's feces, and also use their hosts for transportation and as a home base. The association probably affords them some protection from predators, but there are no guarantees. Divers at Molokini Islet, Maui, for example, have observed large jacks ripping remoras from passing Manta Rays and devouring them. (Remoras attached to passing Tiger Sharks, however, may be less tempting.)

Remoras are related to jacks and dolphinfishes (**mahimahi**). Eight species are known worldwide, with six in Hawaiian waters. The Slender Remora (next page) is the species most likely to be found on smaller reef animals, while the Common Remora (below) favors large sharks. The White Remora *(Remorina albescens),* not illustrated here, is a stout, light colored species which most often attaches to manta rays. The Latin word "remora" means "delay." The Hawaiian name is **omo**.

Marjorie Russell

COMMON REMORA · **omo** · *Remora remora* (Linnaeus, 1758)
These darkish, stout-bodied remoras associate most frequently with large sharks. Divers and snorkelers seldom encounter them in Hawaiian waters, largely because of the scarcity of suitable hosts. This rare photo shows a juvenile remora riding an adult remora which in turn is attached to a Whale Shark (p. 272). Very occasionally these remoras occur on large Manta Rays. The species has a worldwide distribution and attains about 1 ½ ft. Photo: Marjorie Russell. "Monolith," Lāna'i. 35 ft.

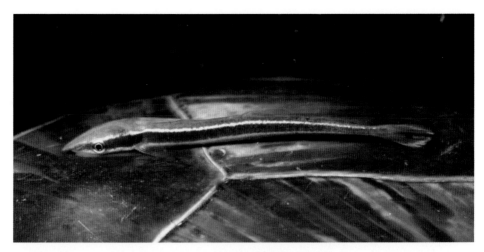

SLENDER REMORA · **leleiona** · *Echeneis naucrates* Linnaeus, 1758 [SHARKSUCKER]
    Easily recognizable by the white-edged black stripe running from snout to tail, these remoras are reported to prefer sharks, but will attach to almost anything that is going their way, as seen here. They have a worldwide distribution, are often free-living, and are the largest species of their family, attaining at least 3 ft. Large adults are almost never seen close to shore in Hawai'i, and juveniles (pictured here) are rare. The genus name is from the Greek *echein* ("to hold") and *naus* ("a ship"). The species name means "pilot." Photos: (above, on turtle) Yokohama Beach, O'ahu. 15 ft. (below, on pufferfish). Ali'i Beach Park, O'ahu. 10 ft. Note that the remoras are upside down, the sucking disk being on top of the head.

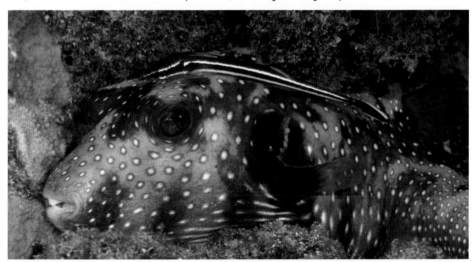

Remoras in legend

"Another inhabitant of these seas drew my attention, and led my mind back to recollections of antiquity. It was the remora, that fastens on to the shark's belly. This little fish, according to the ancients, hooking on to the ship's bottom, could stop its movements; and one of them, by keeping back Antony's ship during the battle of Actium, helped Augustus to gain the victory. On how little hangs the destiny of nations!" Jules Verne - 20,000 Leagues Under the Sea

Fisherman's assistant

In East Africa, and in other parts of the world, remoras are traditionally used to catch turtles and sometimes also large fish. Upon sighting suitable prey from their boat, fishermen release a remora with a line affixed to its tail. The remora swims over to the turtle and attaches itself. Both are then hauled in. Perhaps the remora is then given a reward. When not in action, it is kept in the fisherman's home in a special little wooden "canoe" filled with water.

SANDBURROWERS
(Creediidae)

Sandburrowers are small, elongate, mostly light-colored fishes that spend much of their time buried shallowly in sand, often with eyes exposed. They feed by darting upward to capture passing plankton. Sandburrowers can be abundant, though they are almost never noticed by snorkelers and divers because of their habitat, small size, and protective coloration. Hawai'i has two species.

Robert Whitton

COOKE'S SANDBURROWER *Crystallodytes cookei* Fowler 1923
    These tiny fish are whitish with 11-12 dark markings on the back that extend only a short distance down the sides. (The markings of the similar Elegant Sandburrower, *Limnichthys nitidus,* extend to the center of the body.) Cooke's Sandburrower lives in loose sand exposed to moderate wave action, from the shoreline (including tide pools) down to about 50 ft. During Dave Greenfield's 1990-95 survey of Kāne'ohe Bay, it was the 2nd most abundant fish found. The name honors Charles Montague Cooke Jr. (1874-1948), who discovered the species near Lai'e, O'ahu, probably while collecting shells. Descended from early missonary families, Cooke was a malacologist at the Bishop Museum for 42 years. His mother, Anna Rice Cooke, founded the Honolulu Academy of Arts. To about 2 ½ in. Endemic. Photo: Kahe Point, O'ahu. 15 ft. (Robert Whitton)

SANDLANCES
(Ammodytidae)

The sandlance family contains two dozen or so species, with three in Hawai'i (two in deep water). All live over sand, diving into it headfirst when threatened. Because the tip of the lower jaw protrudes in front of the upper jaw, these elongate fishes can resemble small barracudas.

Richard Pyle

PYLE'S SANDLANCE *Ammodytoides pylei* Randall, Earle & Ida, 1994
    These small slender plankton-feeders form dense schools over open sand away from reefs. When approached, they dive headfirst into the sand. The species is endemic to the Hawaiian chain and has been recorded from O'ahu, Kaua'i, and Midway. The center of population is probably in the Northwest Hawaiian Islands. The name honors ichthyologist and pioneer rebreather diver, Richard Pyle, who photographed this school at Kahe Point Beach Park, O'ahu, at about 25 ft. To about 7 in. The Forktail Sand Wrasse (p.356), is similar in appearance and lifestyle. Photo: Kahe Point, O'ahu. 30 ft. (Richard Pyle)

SANDPERCHES
(Pinguipedidae)

Sandperches are elongated predators which live on rubble or mixed rock and sand bottoms. They prey principally on small crustaceans, fishes, and plankton. Their social structure is haremic, several females maintaining their own feeding territories within the larger territory of a male, who visits each of his females daily. About 60 species are known worldwide, with two in Hawai'i (one from deep water). No Hawaiian name is recorded. Sandperches are also known as grubfishes.

REDSPOTTED SANDPERCH *Parapercis schauinslandi* (Steindachner, 1900)
    These slender fish are whitish marked with several rows of large diffuse red spots. Common on rubble or mixed sand and rubble, usually at depths of 40 ft. or more, they typically perch motionless on small rocky outcroppings and retreat into holes if alarmed. They also hover over the bottom, sometimes 6 ft. or more, feeding on plankton. The species name honors German zoologist Hugo Schauinsland (1857-1937), for whom the Hawaiian Monk Seal (*Neomonachus schauinslandi,* p. 378) was also named. To about 5 in. Indo-Pacific. Photos: (upper and lower left) Kahe Point, O'ahu. 40 ft. (lower right) Mākua, O'ahu. 50 ft.

SARDINES, HERRINGS and SILVERSIDES
(Clupeidae and Atherinidae)

Sardines, herrings, and silversides are silvery schooling fishes found worldwide in tropical and temperate seas. All feed on plankton. Silversides (family Atherinidae) have two dorsal fins and, usually, a silvery stripe running along the side. Their pectoral fins are set high on the body behind the eye. Sardines and herrings (family Clupeidae) have a single dorsal fin, low-set pectorals, and pelvic fins which are often positioned far back on the body. There are 180 or so species of sardines and herrings, with four in the Islands, two of them introduced. About 120 silverside species are known, with one in Hawai'i. Two small silvery schooling fishes not pictured here are the **nehu** or Hawaiian Anchovy (*Encrasicholina purpurea*, family Engraulidae) and the Hawaiian Surf Fish (*Iso hawaiiensis*, family Isonidae). The former inhabits protected bays, estuaries, even fishponds, and is an important baitfish, while the latter, an almost hatchet-shaped silverside relative, usually schools along rocky headlands in turbulent water.

GOLDSPOT SARDINE *Herklotsichthys quadrimaculatus* (Rüppell, 1837) [GOLDSPOT HERRING]
    This is the only sardine common in Hawai'i. It can be recognized by two yellow-gold spots behind the gill covers, one above the other. These fish form dense silvery schools in harbors and protected waters throughout the Islands, but are not often seen by divers or snorkelers. They disperse at night to feed on plankton at the surface. Unintentionally introduced to Hawai'i in the 1970s, these fish probably arrived in the bait well of a fishing boat returning from the Marshall Islands. Another introduced species, the Marquesan Sardine *(Sardinella marquesensis),* was purposefully brought in as a baitfish between 1955 and 1959 to supplement the **nehu,** or Hawaiian Anchovy, whose numbers were declining. The Marquesan Sardine spread through the Islands but never became abundant. After the Goldspot Sardine became established it all but vanished. To about 5 ½ in. Indo-Pacific. Photo: Pūpūkea, O'ahu. 3 ft.

HAWAIIAN SILVERSIDE · 'iao · *Atherinomorus insularum* (Jordan & Evermann, 1903)
These small fish aggregate loosely along rocky or sandy shorelines. At night they feed on plankton at the surface. A silvery stripe topped by a blue-green line runs the length of the body. In ancient times 'iao were said to glow in the dark and the face of a human sacrificial victim was sometimes rubbed with them "so that it shone like the eyes of the maneater shark of the deep." To about 3 ½ in., but usually much smaller. Endemic (with an Indo-Pacific sister species, *A. lacunosus*). Photo: Honolua Bay, Maui. 2 ft.

DELICATE ROUNDHERRING · piha · *Spratelloides delicatulus* (Bennett, 1831) [BLUE SPRAT]
These small fish live along shallow protected reef flats. Snorkelers sometimes see them streaming by in large, dense schools. Silvery with a bluish back, they have two dark streaks at the base of the tail, impossible to see underwater. To about 3 ½ in. Indo-Pacific. Photo: Moku o Loe (Coconut Island), O'ahu. 2 ft. (under pier)

SCORPIONFISHES & CORAL CROUCHERS
(Scorpaenidae and Caracanthidae)

Titan Scorpionfish · **nohu** · camouflage artist · Pūpūkea, Oʻahu. 25 ft. (p. 253)

Scorpionfishes are slow-moving, sedentary carnivores, many with venomous spines that can deliver a painful sting. Some, like the Titan Scorpionfish (above), are masters of camouflage almost impossible to detect; others, such as the lionfishes (next page), have enlarged fins and conspicuous colors that enhance visibility.

Most scorpionfishes fall into the hard-to-detect category. They rely on dull, mottled coloration and irregular-looking, spiny, warty, or tasseled exteriors to escape notice. Many harbor algae and other growths on their skins, the better to blend with their environment. (Some scorpionfishes have the ability to periodically shed these growths along with the outermost layer of skin.) In general, they are nocturnal feeders which use a lie-in-wait strategy.

Scorpionfishes are famous for their stings. If threatened, many bring into play venomous spines on the dorsal, anal, and pelvic fins. In some scorpionfishes the spines are connected to a sac of venom at their base. Once a spine enters the victim's flesh, pressure on it causes the venom to flow up through two grooves and into the wound—a self-administered injection. In others the poison glands lie beneath a sheath of skin covering the spines. In either case, punctures can be extremely painful, causing nausea, cramps and, in the case of stonefishes (mercifully not present in Hawai'i), prolonged suffering and possibly death. Stepping on or touching a highly camouflaged scorpionfish is always a possibility while exploring the reef. Devil Scorpionfish resemble knobs of rock or coral, perfect to hold on to. Lionfishes lurk upside down on the roofs of caves and ledges where careless divers may brush up against them.

If stung, the best treatment is immediate immersion of the affected area in hot, but not scalding, water for 30 to 90 minutes (heat destroys the protein venom). Bleeding should be encouraged and the victim taken for medical care. A study of scorpionfish stings showed that immersion in hot water produced complete symptomatic relief for 80 percent of the victims and moderate relief for 14 percent. Emergency room personnel are sometimes unaware of this simple and effective procedure.

The ornate lionfishes have caught people's fancy and are known by a number of other names, including turkeyfishes, fireworks-fishes, fire-fishes, zebra-fishes and butterfly-cod. The Hawaiians named them **nohu pinao**, after the dragonfly. When a large lionfish glides slowly over the reef, its magnificent fins extended, the effect is majestic. These fanlike fins have several practical purposes: they help corner small fish and crustaceans, they brush the bottom, stirring up the creatures that live there, and they advertise the lionfish's venomous sting to potential predators.

The family Scorpaenidae (one of about 20 families in the order Scorpaeniformes) includes ap-

proximately 350 species worldwide. Most occur in temperate waters where many are important food fishes. Twenty-eight species live in Hawai'i (eleven beyond sport diving depths). Eleven are endemic. Fifteen species are pictured here, along with a scorpionfish relative, the Hawaiian Coral Croucher (p. 259). Among those omitted is the small, cryptic Hairy Scorpionfish *(Scorpaenodes hirsutus)* which seldom emerges from the reef and is almost never seen alive. The general name for scorpionfishes in Hawaiian is **nohu,** the same name used in the South Pacific for the deadly stonefish. In olden times it was believed that the eggs of some **nohu** hatched into sharks.

A pride of lionfish · **nohu pinao** · at South Point, Hawai'i. 40 ft. (see next page)

HAWAIIAN RED LIONFISH · **nohu pinao** · *Pterois sphex* Jordan & Evermann, 1903 [HAWAIIAN TURKEYFISH]

 Striped red and white, this uncommon but fantastic fish has unusually long dorsal spines and enormously extended white spines on the pectoral fins. A pair of antennas rise over the eyes, but are often missing in large specimens. Although similar in appearance to other Indo-Pacific lionfishes, the species is unique to Hawai'i. By day these fish tend to remain in caves and under ledges, often on the ceiling and sometimes in groups. They may frequent the same spot for years. At night they glide forth, with fins extended, hunting for small crabs or shrimps. The spines are venomous; these fish should not be played with or handled. (A Honolulu aquarist, stung on the hand by a similar Indo-Pacific lionfish, *P. volitans*, described the sensation as having his fingers slammed repeatedly with a hammer. For a description of this species' sting, see p. 250.) Unfortunately, many dive sites have been stripped of these fish by over-eager collectors—another good reason to strengthen Hawai'i's system of marine parks. The Hawaiian name means "dragonfly," the species name "wasp." To about 8 in. Endemic. Photos: (above) Pūpūkea, O'ahu. 30 ft. (below left) South Point, Hawai'i. 40 ft. (below right) Lehua Rock, Ni'ihau. 50 ft.

HAWAIIAN GREEN LIONFISH
nohu pinao · *Dendrochirus barberi*
(Steindachner, 1900)
[HAWAIIAN LIONFISH; BARBER'S LIONFISH]

This red-eyed, greenish or reddish brown lionfish is dull compared to its better-known cousin the Hawaiian Red Lionfish (previous page), and more difficult to spot underwater. However, it is much more common. Its pectoral fins, although large and fan-like, lack long showy extended spines. During the day it typically rests between branches of Antler Coral *(Pocillopora grandis)* or along the sides or bases of coral heads, often in sandy or rubbly areas away from the reef. Sometimes half a dozen or more can be found in one isolated coral head. At night it hunts in the open for small crustaceans or fishes, usually with its spot-banded pectoral fins spread wide,

perhaps to help corner prey. The display could also be a warning to would-be predators that the spines are venomous. The species name honors a Captain Barber, on whose ship the Austrian zoologist Franz Steindachner, who first described and named this fish, rode as a passenger around the turn of the century. Steindachner found his tiny specimen by collecting plankton from Barber's vessel. (In case you are wondering, Barber's Point, O'ahu, was named after an entirely different Captain Barber, who wrecked his trading brig outside Pearl Harbor a century earlier. King Kamehameha I salvaged the cannons from this boat and transported them to his fort at Lahaina, Maui.) To 6 ½ in. Endemic. Photos: (top) Mākua, O'ahu. 30 ft. (with Dwarf Moray, p 105). (bottom) hunting at night, pectoral fins spread wide. Koloa Landing, Kaua'i. 20 ft.

DECOY SCORPIONFISH · nohu
Iracundus signifer
Jordan & Evermann, 1903

This unique scorpionfish uses its dorsal fin as a lure to attract prey. A light-edged black spot between the 2nd and 3rd spines resembles the eye of a small fish, the gap between the 1st and 2nd spines looks like an upturned mouth, and the 4th dorsal spine, often elongated, mimics a dorsal fin. When "fishing," the Decoy Scorpionfish snaps and waves its lure in a surprisingly realistic fashion, and the colors of the lure intensify. This fish is seen most often under ledges or in rubble at the base of dropoffs. It is active by day and night. Its venom causes a pricked finger to throb and swell. The species name means "bearing marks." To 5 in. Indo-Pacific. Photos: Mākua, O'ahu. 45 ft.

Stung!

I was leading a dive on Molokini's back wall and began by taking a photographer to a spot where two Hawaiian Red Lionfish had been living for years. One was about 8 in., as big as I've ever seen them get. When we found the big one I placed my open hand close so that it would turn toward the photographer. In an instant it put its head down and lurched forward, sticking its first two dorsal spines into my thumb and index finger. I know it was the first two spines because I saw right away that the skin was pushed back or missing from the tips of those two spines. Pain and swelling began immediately and increased as the dive went on. By the time the dive was ending the pain was excruciating (WAY more painful than bad eel bites). I had heard that hot water is the best first aid treatment, so I crouched in the back of the boat with my thumb and finger immersed in hot coffee, the only hot liquid available. Six hours later the pain was still intense. My hand was swollen like a baseball mitt, and my thumb and finger were still brown from the coffee. It took three days before the swelling was gone. Two weeks later the points of entry were still purple and sore when pressed.

A few years later I was stung by a small Green Lionfish which I didn't even see, but that was nothing in comparison. The pain was minimal and gone within an hour. Maybe it just brushed me, I don't know. Also, I saw a woman stung by a Red Lionfish and she had a reaction to it similar to my Green Lionfish sting—no big deal. So, I don't know whether it was the size of my lionfish, or the amount of venom that entered the wound that made it so much worse than her sting.

– Crystal LaMer

KELLOGG'S SCORPIONFISH

Scorpaenodes kelloggi (Jenkins,1903)

This small, well-camouflaged fish is mottled brown, often with four darker bars along the body and several dark bands radiating from the eye onto the head. Although seldom seen or noticed by divers, it could well be Hawai'i's most abundant scorpionfish. During a 1990-1995 fish survey conducted by David Greenfield in and around Kāne'ohe Bay, O'ahu, it was by far the most common scorpionfish found. The species name honors Vernon Lyman Kellogg (1867-1937), professor of entomology at Stanford University. Kellogg was an active hiker, mountain climber, and officer of the Sierra Club. To about 2 in. Indo-Pacific. Photo: Mākena, Maui. 60 ft. (Pauline Fiene)

Pauline Fiene

CHEEKSPOT SCORPIONFISH

Scorpaenodes evides
(Jordan & Thompson, 1914)

Rarely-seen, this scorpionfish occurs from the shoreline to 100 ft. or more and is most common in the Northwestern Hawaiian Islands. Most O'ahu specimens in the Bishop Museum came from depths of around 80 ft. It is mottled brown, often with a bright red iris. A prominent dark oval spot near the edge of the gill cover gives the fish its common name. Prefers cool subtropical waters. To 8 in. Indo-Pacific. Photo: Midway Atoll. 30 ft. (Keoki Stender)

Keoki Stender

LOWFIN SCORPIONFISH

Scorpaenodes parvipinnis
(Garrett, 1864)

A broad white band covering the front and middle of the body usually identifies this scorpionfish. A second white band may occur at the base of the tail. The body color is orange or brownish red. The white bands are sometimes narrow or faint, but the numerous short threadlike tassels covering the head and body should help to distinguish the fish. In general it is seen only at night, or on the walls or ceilings of dark caves. It is also found in rubble. The species name means "small fin." (The spiny dorsal fin is the lowest of any Hawaiian scorpionfish). To about 5 in. Indo-Pacific. Photo: Hōnaunau, Hawai'i. 40 ft. (night). (bottom) Lāna'i Lookout, O'ahu (in cave)

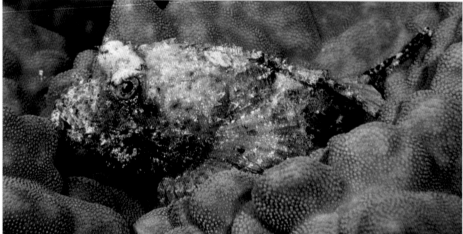

Shortsnout Scorpionfish ▲▼

SHORTSNOUT SCORPIONFISH
nohu · *Scorpaenopsis brevifrons*
Eschmeyer & Randall, 1975

Variable in color, this scorpionfish is every bit as good at camouflage as the larger, more common Devil Scorpionfish (p. 254). Identify it by its smaller size, lack of hump, and peach-pink eye. Because of its short steep snout it might be confused with the Spotfin Scorpionfish (p. 258), but the Spotfin emerges only at night, whereas this fish rests in the open during daylight hours. The species name means "short snout." To about 6 in. Endemic. Photos: (top) Ka'ohe Bay, Hawai'i. 40 ft. (center) Lānai Lookout, O'ahu. 40 ft. (opposite) Magic Island, O'ahu. 15 ft.

TITAN SCORPIONFISH · nohu · *Scorpaenopsis cacopsis* Jenkins, 1901

The largest by far of Hawai'i's shallow-water scorpionfishes, this reddish, or-nately patterned species resembles a living Persian carpet (see p. 246). Like most of its kind, it is an ambush predator which lies motionless on rocks, sand, or even living coral and is easy to overlook. The lower jaw is fringed with orange-red flaps or tassels. The body and fins are covered with short appendages resembling algae or other growths. Its size, its color, the flaps under its chin, and its lack of a hump easily differentiate it from the more common Devil Scorpionfish (next page). The species name comes from the Greek word *kakos* ("bad"). To about 20 in. Endemic. Photos: (above) Pai'olu'olu Point, O'ahu. 80 ft. (middle) Lāna'i Lookout, O'ahu. 20 ft. (opposite) Magic Island, O'ahu. 15 ft.

juvenile

DEVIL SCORPIONFISH · nohu 'omakaha
Scorpaenopsis diabolus Cuvier, 1829

same fish as at top, "flashing" the undersides of its pectoral fins ▲

Common on Hawai'i's reefs, this amazingly well-cam-ouflaged scorpionfish usually sits in the open, its skin texture and color exactly matching the surroundings, whether coral rubble, smooth rounded stones, algae, or silt-covered reef. (It does not generally sit on living coral.) The back is distinctly humped and the undersides of the pectoral fins, normally invisible, sport bright yellow and orange bands. When disturbed, a Devil Scorpionfish will move slightly, flashing the hidden colors. Would-be predators stung once by its venomous spines will remember the "flash" and not repeat the mistake—or perhaps the flash is sufficient warning in itself. (There is also orange around the mouth, visible only when the fish makes an aggressive gaping display or locks jaws with a rival, see p. 256.) These masters of deception harbor algae and perhaps other growths on their skin, the outermost layer of which they shed from time to time. They never fail to fascinate divers and snorkelers alert enough to spot them. Usually only the white crescent of the open mouth or the scallop-like patterning of a spread pectoral fin betrays their presence. Sometimes they occur in only inches of water. Stepping on one, or putting a hand on one by mistake, would be easy, with possibly painful consequences. The sting, however, is relatively mild and certainly not as venomous as that of lionfishes. This fish-eating scorpionfish, like others of its genus, feeds most actively at night, typically moving to the tops of rocks to perch and wait for prey. The Hawaiian name means "streaked," and the species name, "devil." To 12 in. Indo-Pacific. Photos: (top and middle, same fish) Hanauma Bay, O'ahu. 40 ft. (bottom) Lāna'i Lookout, O'ahu. 30 ft

Devil Scorpionfish gallery 1

Clockwise from upper left: Lāna'i Lookout, O'ahu. 40 ft.; Kahe Point, O'ahu. 25 ft. Napili Bay, Maui, 15 ft.; Pūpūkea, O'ahu. 30 ft.; Pūpūkea, O'ahu. 40 ft.; Magic Island, O'ahu. 25 ft.

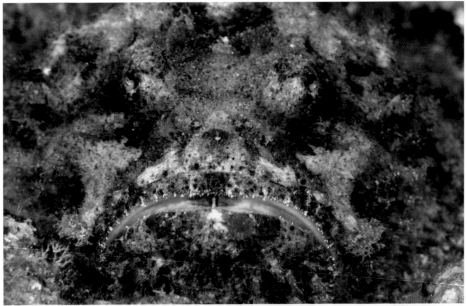

Pūpūkea, O'ahu. 30 ft.

Presumed males fighting. Midway Atoll. 30 ft.   Keoki Stender

Aggressive display. Hanauma Bay, O'ahu. 8 ft.

Scorpionfish tournament

Diving at Mākua, near "pray for sex rock," we followed the reef out and around and noticed an unusual number of Devil Scorpionfish at about 30 ft. We were used to seeing one or two, but there were at least 15 that I counted. There could have been more since they are kinda hard to see, but these guys were very active and easier to spot. We hung out for a bit and ended up watching a few chase each other around. Two at a time, with mouths opened wide, they would "lock" jaws and then push and shove and roll around all over the place till one gave up and left. It was fascinating to watch. This behavior went on for a while with several pairs. The bigger of the two would usually win, but I remember one pair in which the smaller (I thought) of the two won and the big guy left. It was quite a memorable day— like watching elk, or sheep, or medieval jousting. It's the guys, you know? Always the guy thing.
- Lori Kane

SPECKLED SCORPIONFISH
Sebastapistes coniorta
Jenkins, 1903

Look into heads of Antler or Cauliflower Coral and you are likely to see one or more of these scorpionfish wedged deep between the branches. Their light bodies are covered with small dark spots and larger blotches, mimicking the texture of the coral. They leave their refuge at night to hunt. They also occur in caves and tide pools. The species name means "cloud of dust." The largest of several Hawaiian scorpionfish species inhabiting branching corals, they attain almost 4 in. Found only in the Hawaiian Islands. Photo: Pūpūkea, O'ahu. 25 ft. (in Cauliflower Coral, *Pocillopora meandrina*)

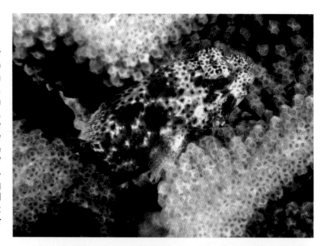

DWARF SCORPIONFISH
Sebastapistes fowleri
(Pietschmann, 1934)

The smallest known scorpionfish, this uncommon species is reddish to orange with very fine white spots. In Hawai'i it is seen most often between the branches of Cauliflower Coral *(Pocillopora meandrina)*, with several individuals often present in the same coral head. It also occurs in coral rubble down to at least 100 ft. It grows to about 1 ½ in. and occurs from the Western Indian Ocean to Hawai'i. The species name honors ichthyologist Henry W. Fowler (1878-1965). Fowler once accompanied Ernest Hemingway on his yacht, later naming an Atlantic scorpionfish after the great writer. Photo: Pūpūkea, O'ahu. 40 ft.

GALACTIC SCORPIONFISH
Sebastapistes galactacma
Jenkins 1903 [MILKY SCORPIONFISH]

This scorpionfish is reddish, often with darker mottlings on the back and upper sides. Two "horns" extend above the eyes, long in some individuals, short in others. The fish is covered with fine white spots and irregular whitish patches, which might have reminded ichthyologist Oliver P. Jenkins of the Milky Way. The species name derives from the Greek "galactos" meaning "milky." The English word "galaxy" comes from the same root. The fish lives in rubble or within heads of branching coral *(Pocillopora* spp.*)*. To about 3 in. Guam, Pohnpei, Hawai'i, and French Polynesia. Photo: Pauline Fiene, "Landing Craft," Maui. 65 ft.

Pauline Fiene

SPOTFIN SCORPIONFISH *Sebastapistes ballieui* (Sauvage, 1875) [Ballieu's Scorpionfish]
    This common shoreline scorpionfish hunts in the shallows at night and hides under rocks by day, preferring depths of less than 15 ft. It also seeks shelter within the branches of Cauliflower Coral *(Pocillopora meandrina)*. Pale greenish or brownish, it is usually faintly mottled with a few dark spots and a row of small tassels along the side. A pair of "horns" may be present over the eyes. (The Galactic Scorpionfish bears similar "horns" but lives in deeper water.) The scientific name honors Théo Ballieu, a French diplomat who served in Hawai'i in the 1870s and collected the first scientific specimens of this fish. The common name derives from a large black spot sometimes present on the rear half of the first (or spiny) dorsal fin, most visible when the fin is raised. To about 4 ½ in. Endemic. Photo: Black Point, O'ahu. 3 ft. (night)

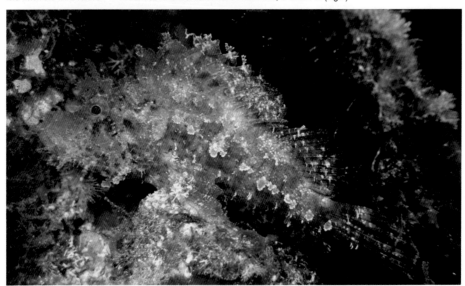

STRANGE-FACE SCORPIONFISH *Rhinopias xenops* (Gilbert, 1905) [High-Eyed Scorpionfish]
    This deepwater scorpionfish occurs within sport-diving depths only in the Northwestern Hawaiian Islands, where cool water temperatures draw it closer to the surface. Even in the northwest chain, however, it is seldom seen. Its color is variable. The original specimen, dredged in 1902 from the Au'au Channel between Maui and Lāna`i at a depth of about 200-250 ft., was brilliant vermilion marked with small purplish spots. Specimens captured in lobster traps near Nihoa Island, were brownish red to greenish yellow with a few moderate-size white spots. The skin, including that on the spines, bears numerous flaps and tassels that break up the fish's outline, helping it to blend in with other growths on the reef. The genus *Rhinopias* contains only 6 species, all rare, and some amazingly ornate. The species name means "strange appearance." To 6 ½ in. Hawai'i and Japan. Photo: Corsair wreck, Midway Atoll. 110 ft.

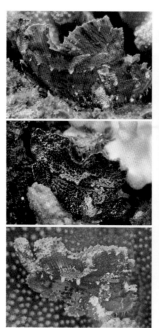

LEAF SCORPIONFISH *Taenianotus triacanthus* Lacepède, 1802 [LEAF FISH]

Flat like a leaf, with sail-like dorsal fin permanently extended, these unusual little fish can be white, pink, red, yellow, brown, black, green, or mottled. By day they typically perch near cracks and crevices or in heads of branching coral, usually head inward. At night they move to more exposed positions. They may wave slightly to and fro like seaweed, even in the absence of surge. Like many others in their family, Leaf Scorpionfish harbor algae or other growths on their skin. When too "fuzzy," they molt, emerging sharp and clean. Molting reportedly begins in the head region, takes less than a minute, and can occur as often as twice a month. Although fairly common in Hawai'i (sometimes in water only inches deep), Leaf Scorpionfish are considered an unusual find in many other parts of the Indo-Pacific. Looking into their eyes is like peering into another universe—try it! The sole species in its genus, the Leaf Scorpionfish attains 4 in. In Hawai'i it is usually half that size. Indo-Pacific. Photos: (right) Kea'au, O'ahu. 50 ft. (upper left, Marjorie L. Awai; lower left, Dan Dickey).

HAWAIIAN CORAL CROUCHER
Caracanthus typicus Kroyer, 1845

Coral crouchers (also called orbicular velvetfishes) are a small family of laterally compressed, disklike fishes which live deep within heads of branching coral. Although related to scorpionfishes, they are not reported to be venomous. Their skin is covered with short hairlike projections (papillae) which produce a velvety texture. The Hawaiian species is violet-gray evenly covered with small red spots. It lives in Cauliflower Coral (*Pocillopora meandrina*) or Antler Coral (*P. grandis*), often in pairs or small groups. Although easy to find, it is difficult to photograph—when disturbed, it just moves deeper into the coral. At night it moves further out on the branches to feed. Endemic (with a sister species, *C. maculatus,* in the Western Pacific). To about 1 ½ in. Photo: McGregor Point, Maui. 30 ft. (in Antler Coral)

Cory Pittman

Galapagos Shark · **manō** · in deep water 3 miles off Hale'iwa, O'ahu. (p. 264)

Sharks are cartilaginous fishes with five to seven exposed gill slits on each side of an elongate body. They generally have a full set of fins—dorsal, pectoral, pelvic, anal, and caudal—and the upper tail fin lobe is usually longer than the lower. Sharks' mouths are almost always on the underside, as are those of their cousins, the rays. Although there are sharklike rays and raylike sharks, the division between sharks and rays is clear: Sharks have pectoral fins originating behind or below the gill slits, while rays have pectoral fins originating above the gill slits and extending forward onto the head.

Sharks (and rays) lack gas-filled swim bladders. Heavier than water, they sink if they stop swimming. This poses no problem to bottom-dwelling sharks, which, perhaps surprisingly, constitute the majority. Sharks which inhabit midwater, however, gain the buoyancy they need from enormous oily livers. This enables them to rise or descend in the water column more rapidly than bony fishes, which regulate bouyancy by slowly changing the amount of gas in their swim bladders. Most of these large active sharks must swim constantly to pass water over their gills and will suffocate if they stop. A few, such as the Whitetip Reef Shark (p. 268) and the Nurse Shark (not found in Hawai'i), can pump water over their gills while resting on the bottom. Sharks typically propel themselves with sinuous sweeps of their bodies and tails, using their stiff pectoral fins for steering and braking. Shark fins are thick and fleshy and do not have the spines and rays typical of bony fishes.

Sharks have keen senses. They can home in on the source of a smell, such as blood, from as far as a quarter mile, and can sense the low frequency vibrations of a wounded and thrashing animal from a mile away. These are detected not by their ears but by a system of special organs corresponding to the lateral line system of bony fishes. At closer range, sharks can sense the weak electrical fields emitted by all living organisms.

Sharks' skins are rough—so rough they were once used like sandpaper. The roughness is caused by tiny embedded dermal denticles, in essence small teeth. Microgrooves in the denticles reduce turbulence and drag, enabling the shark to slip more easily through the water than if it had smooth skin! Denticles also discourage barnacles and algae from growing on the shark. Sharks' teeth, are special dermal denticles enlarged and modified. Arising from the skin rather than the cartilage of the jaw, they can be constantly replaced. New teeth, created on the inside edge of the jaw, move outward on a sort of conveyor belt of tough connective tissue, renewing the outer functional teeth about every 30 days, and as often as every 8 days in some species.

In matters of reproduction sharks (and rays) are surprisingly advanced. Males use paired organs called claspers—the rodlike extended inner edges of the pelvic fins—to internally fertilize females. Claspers are somewhat misnamed in that they do not clasp the female. They are sometimes tipped with hooks or spines, however, to keep them anchored inside the female during mating. The claspers of a mature male shark are fairly conspicuous, making it simple to distinguish the sexes underwater.

While mating, the male typically grasps the female's pectoral fin in his jaws, holding her in place so he can insert his clasper through her cloaca (the single reproductive and eliminative opening) and into her oviduct. In most shark species the young are born alive, having either developed from internally held eggs or directly in the mother's uterus. (Sometimes the largest of the young will eat its smaller siblings while still in the "womb.") Some sharks, however, lay leathery egg capsules, usually on the sea bottom. In either case, infant sharks are fully formed and do not pass through a larval stage as most bony fishes do.

All sharks are carnivores. Although the smaller bottom-dwellers typically subsist on molluscs, shellfish, and other unexciting fare, most of the larger sharks are swift, sleek, streamlined creatures superbly suited to an active predatory life. Few animals, and certainly no other fishes, have so captured the human imagination or excited such admiration and dread.

Sharks in general are known as **manō** *in Hawaiian. In old days, and even into the present, certain individual sharks were believed to physically embody the spirits of certain family ancestors. The haunts of these sharks were known, and they were given regular offerings of food. In return, the sharks were said to protect their caretakers. Not all sharks were sacred; the hunting of large man-eaters called* **niuhi** *(Tiger Sharks and, rarely, Great White Sharks) was a sport especially reserved for chiefs. Large amounts of bait mixed with* **'awa**, *a mildly narcotic root, were fed to the shark from canoes until it became careless enough to be noosed, whereupon the gorged animal was probably turned belly-up—which renders sharks immobile—and brought to shore to be slaughtered for its highly prized teeth. The bait is said often to have consisted of human flesh, left to decompose several days to enhance its appeal. King Kamehameha I, who enjoyed this sport, was said to pen up his victims near the* **heiau** *at Hawi, on the Island of Hawai'i, until he was ready to go fishing. Other shark traditions from old Hawai'i include the riding of sharks by young men—a specialty of O'ahu carried on well into the 1800s—and the existence of tame sharks called* **manō ihu wa'a** *which would swim up and rest their heads on the outrigger of a canoe to be fed. Not all sharks, however, were benign, many were considered evil and greatly feared.*

How dangerous are sharks? The answer can only be: very dangerous—but unpredictably so. Except for the Whitetip Reef Shark and Galapagos Shark (the latter most common in the northwestern chain), sharks in Hawai'i tend to avoid humans. Divers see them infrequently. Many of the species known to attack humans—the Bull Shark, Oceanic Whitetip Shark, Blue Shark, Silky Shark, Silvertip Shark, and Shortfin Mako Shark—are not encountered around Hawai'i's shallow reefs. The Great White Shark, probably the best known and most feared of its family, is a rare visitor from temperate waters. But the Tiger Shark, not uncommon in Hawai'i, has a reputation almost as bad. Between 1900 and 2005 Hawai'i recorded 142 incidents involving sharks, 40 of them fatal. However, these numbers may be misleading in that they include bites sustained by fishermen who had caught sharks, and numerous cases where it is impossible to determine whether the attack occurred before or after the victim's death (which may have been by drowning or other accident). Tiger Sharks are believed to have been responsible for many of these incidents, but Scalloped Hammerheads and Great White Sharks have also been implicated. Typical victims have been surfers, fishermen swept off shore by large waves, and spearfishermen. A few well-publicized attacks have also occurred to shallow-water bathers (see p. 267). Even so, considering the number of people in the water each day, Hawai'i remains a generally safe and shark-free location.

Due to massive and often senseless predation by human beings, coupled with their own slow rate of reproduction, shark populations worldwide have declined sharply. Old-time divers relate that sharks used to be a common underwater sight around the main Hawaiian Islands. This is no longer the case, except in a few specific locations such as Molokini Islet, Maui, and Lehua Rock, Ni'ihau. In the mostly uninhabited Northwestern Hawaiian Islands, however, sharks are abundant and regularly enter shallow water to feed on seabirds and seals.

There are about 370 living species of sharks divided into 19 families. The smallest (not found in Hawai'i) is about 10 in. long; the largest, the Whale Shark (p 272), might attain as much as 60 ft. Although 36 shark species are known from Hawaiian waters, most live in the deep or far from land. The ten most likely to be encountered near shore are pictured below. Rarely seen alive but worth mentioning is the small Cookie-Cutter Shark *(Isistius brasiliensis),* which apparently lures larger fish to the surface at night with a clever bioluminescent display, bites into them, twists its body 180 degrees and excises a perfectly round two-inch plug of flesh.

The word "shark," from the same root as "shirk," originally meant scoundrel or villain. In Hawaiian, the verb **ho'omanō** (literally, "go like a shark") means "to eat ravenously," "to pursue women ardently."

Pilikia at Pearl Harbor

The remarkable story is often told of Pearl Harbor Drydock Number One, which, despite the tearful pleadings of an old Hawaiian fisherman, was constructed between 1909 and 1913 over the home of **Ka'ahupāhau,** *a sacred shark. The fisherman, who had been feeding the shark weekly for many years, predicted* **pilikia** *(trouble) if the site were disturbed. The sacred shark was old, he said, and could no longer feed itself. On Feb. 17, 1913, almost on the eve of its completion, the entire drydock structure collapsed spectacularly. The cause of the failure could not be determined. In 1915 a new drydock was begun at the same spot. At a crucial stage in its construction, a Hawaiian workman, David K. Richards, remembered the old fisherman and his prediction. Feeling uneasy, and doubting that his skeptical* **haole** *boss would understand, Richards asked permission directly from Governor Frear to have the site blessed. Frear readily agreed, and a* **kahuna,** *one Mrs. Puahi, was brought in from Waikīkī. Puahi instructed Richards to make certain offerings at the site between 2 and 3 AM, which he did. When the final pumping out of the drydock was accomplished 20 days later, Richards' boss found a cave underneath containing the 14-foot 4-inch backbone of a large shark. The old lady then came and performed a final blessing, and the new drydock was completed without further incident.*

Oceanic Whitetip Shark *(Carcharhinus longimanus)* · a blue-water shark seen generally only by boaters.   Jerry Kane

Requiem Sharks (family Carcharhinidae)

Requiem sharks are "typical" sharks—sleek powerful swimmers, usually 6 ft. or more in length, and often found near coral reefs and in coastal areas. The majority of sharks known to have attacked humans are requiems, as are the three most commonly-seen Indo-Pacific sharks: the Gray Reef Shark, the Blacktip Reef Shark and the Whitetip Reef Shark. The requiem sharks—called "whalers" in Australia—form the second-largest shark family. (The largest shark family, Scyliorhinidae, is composed of about 100 species of small, harmless, bottom-dwelling, and rather unexciting animals called cat sharks, none of which occur in shallow Hawaiian waters.) Out of 49 species of requiem sharks, 11 are recorded from Hawai'i, and 7 are shown here. Omitted, because rarely seen, are the Silvertip Shark *(Carcharhinus albimarginatus)*, the Silky Shark *(C. falciformis)*, the Oceanic Blacktip Shark *(C. limbatus)*, and the Bignose Shark *(C. altimus)*. The Oceanic Whitetip Shark *(C. longimanus)* is pictured on p. 262. Though never encountered on reefs, this potentially dangerous shark is sometimes seen by boaters offshore.

GRAY REEF SHARK · **manō** · *Carcharhinus amblyrhynchos* (Bleeker, 1856)

These sharks are gray on the back and sides, and lighter below. A dusky margin on the trailing edge of the tail fin helps distinguish them from the Galapagos Shark (next page). Although Gray Reef Sharks generally ignore divers, they are territorial and can be aggressive toward perceived intruders. They often adopt a warning posture well in advance of an attack, humping their back, raising their head, dropping their pectoral fins, and swimming with exaggerated motions. If you see one acting strangely, pause and slowly withdraw, resisting any temptation to take its picture, especially if your camera has a strobe. Cornering the shark or pursuing it, even slowly, are especially likely to provoke an attack. Although one of the more common sharks around Indo-Pacific islands, Gray Reef Sharks are seldom seen in Hawai'i except in the uninhabited northwestern chain, around offshore islands such as Molokini, off Maui, Lehua Rock, off Ni'ihau, and a few select spots off the Kona coast of the Big Island. Large aggregations of pregnant females sometimes occur in shallow water off Ka'ula Rock (south of Ni'ihau), and Johnston Atoll, as well as in the northwestern islands. In Hawaiian waters, most mating and pupping appears to occur between March and July. There is a 12-month gestation period. Gray Reef Sharks feed mostly on fish, but cephalopods are also taken, and occasionally crustaceans. To almost 8 ft. Indo-Pacific. Photo: Five Fathom Pinnacle (about 20 miles south of Ni'ihau). 50 ft.

GALAPAGOS SHARK · **manō** · *Carcharhinus galapagensis* (Snodgrass & Heller, 1905)

Galapagos Sharks are probably the most abundant sharks in the northwestern chain, but are seldom seen around reefs on the main Hawaiian islands. Bold and inquisitive, they are potentially dangerous, especially to anyone carrying speared fish. Although similar to Gray Reef Sharks in appearance, the dusky margin on the back edge of the tail fin is faint or absent. Also, the rear edge of the dorsal fin is straighter than that of the Gray Reef Shark, and tends to form a right angle with the back. Galapagos Sharks eat mostly bottom fish. A threat display similar to the Gray Reef Shark has been reported. To about 12 ft., but in Hawai'i usually a third that size (but see sidebar below). Discovered in the Galapagos Islands, after which they are named, these sharks occur worldwide in warm seas. Photo: Midway Atoll (Keoki Stender). (see also p. 260)

Who will bell the cat?

Diving during our research for a paper on the fishes of Midway Island, we would usually roll over the side of the boat and fin off individually in different directions. Each diver would accumulate four or five small Galapagos shark "diving buddies" which generally kept a respectable distance during the dive. Meeting under the boat for a safety stop, each of us would bring along our shark buddies, which added together made an impressive aggregation. As we left the water one by one, the sharks became progressively bolder, and the last divers out really had their hands full fending them off. Once, as last diver in the water, I found myself at the surface, my back against the side of the boat, kicking off sharks with my fins. The other divers just reached down and hauled me in, tank and all. The Galapagos sharks in the Northwestern Hawaiian Islands and other cool water anti-tropical areas tend to be small and often associate in "rat packs." Galapagos sharks around the main Hawaiian Islands are often much larger, relatively uncommon, and usually solitary. I was once called to identify a large nondescript gray-colored shark that was working a Mafia shake-down racket on East Oahu spearfishermen. Salvatore da Shark turned out to be a huge Galapagos, easily twice as long as any I have seen in the northwest chain. Dr. Jack Randall, of Honolulu's Bishop Museum, has suggested that there may be two species lumped together under the name Galapagos Shark. So the next time you encounter a big Galapagos shark while diving, please do science a favor and snip off a small tissue sample for DNA analysis. - John Earle. Photo: Midway Atoll (John Earle)

Brian Bronk

BLACKTIP REEF SHARK · **manō pā'ele** · *Carcharhinus melanopterus* (Quoy & Gaimard, 1824)

These sharks have distinct black tips or black margins on all fins; those on the first dorsal fin and lower lobe of the tail fin are most conspicuous. Blacktips frequent reef flats, lagoons, and sheltered bays where they feed on a variety of reef fish, typically by rushing at them and chasing them down. Juveniles often cruise the shallows, sometimes in water just off the beach only inches deep. (On Palmyra Atoll, hungry feral dogs have learned to catch and eat these young Blacktips!) Although once a common sight off the main Hawaiian Islands, Blacktips are now scarce, wary, and hard to observe. Lifeguards in their towers occasionally spot them off Waikīkī, and sunrise snorkelers in Hanauma Bay, O'ahu, sometimes see them. Skittish and inoffensive, Blacktips are not considered dangerous, although they have been known to bite waders' feet, apparently mistaking them for fish. (If this happens to you, experts advise to immediately lie down in the water. The shark will flee when it realizes your true size.) The species name means "black fin" and the Hawaiian name means "dark" or "black." To almost 6 ft. Indo-Pacific and Mediterranean (via the Suez Canal). Photo: Hanauma Bay, O'ahu. 50 ft. (Brian Bronk). The similar Oceanic Blacktip Shark, *C. limbatus,* has fewer and less distinct black markings and usually occurs further offshore. (see also p. 184)

▼ SANDBAR SHARK (see description on next page) ▶

◄ SANDBAR SHARK · **manō** · *Carcharhinus plumbeus* (Nardo, 1827) (see previous page)

This shy shark is rarely seen by snorkelers or divers, although fishing records suggest that it is the most abundant near-shore shark around O'ahu, and presumably all the main Hawaiian Islands. Its body, gray or light tan on the back and sides, lacks distinctive markings, but you can easily identify it by its unusually high pointed first dorsal fin, which lies far forward, almost over the pectoral fin. Juveniles have white fin tips and white trailing edges on the fins. On rare occasions boaters and divers encounter aggregations of Sandbar Sharks. Rebreather divers once watched in wonder as about a dozen of these animals milled around at the hot water outfall at Kahe Point Beach Park, O'ahu, at dusk. (Had the divers been exhaling noisy bubbles, the sharks would likely have been frightened away before they were seen.) Another aggregation was observed in the channel between Maui and Lāna'i over a period of months, a bonus for underwater photographer David B. Fleetham, whose dramatic closeup picture of a Sandbar Shark appeared on the cover of Life Magazine. Sandbar Sharks are not known to attack humans. The length record for this species is 8 ft., but in Hawai'i it only attains about 6 ft. Sandbar Sharks eat mostly other fish, supplemented by cephalopods and crustaceans. They occur worldwide in tropical and subtropical seas. Photo: off Hale'iwa, O'ahu. (see also p. 275)

The easiest way to see and photograph wild Sandbar and Galapagos Sharks in Hawai'i is to go on one of the "shark tours" offered by several operators working out of Hale'iwa on O'ahu's north shore. For a price, these folks will take you to a blue-water location three miles offshore where sharks traditionally gather to feed on old bait discarded by crab fishermen. The shark tour operators also chum to ensure the sharks' continued interest. You can watch from topside as half a dozen sharks mill around the stern of the boat, or you can enter a shark cage in the water for an even closer look.

Dennis King

TIGER SHARK · **niuhi** · *Galeocerdo cuvier* (Peron & Lesueur, 1822)

Tigers are among the world's two or three most dangerous sharks. They have wide blunt snouts and dark bars on the back and sides which fade on large adults. Most shark attacks in Hawai'i are the work of these animals. Small Tiger Sharks feed near the bottom at night; larger ones do the same but will also feed near the surface during the day. These opportunistic predators typically consume pufferfishes and porcupinefishes, turtles, lobsters, and other easy-to-catch prey, but sometimes attack dolphins and seals. In late June and July in the Northwestern Hawaiian Islands they wait just off the beaches in broad daylight to feast on albatross chicks that fall in the water while learning to fly. They are also fond of garbage: the stomach of a 10-ft. specimen harpooned in Pearl Harbor in 1931 contained the hind leg of a mule, two bathing suits, a belt buckle, a pint of buttons, two horseshoes, the corner of a wooden soapbox, two small anchors, anchor chain and assorted bolts, nails and copper fittings. Recent evidence indicates that sharks rid themselves of such accumulations from time to time by completely everting their stomachs. Hawaiian Tiger Sharks routinely travel long distances, moving about within home ranges that can include more than one island. Out of eight captured off southern O'ahu and tagged with monitoring devices, six immediately swam approximately 21 miles across the Ka'iwi Channel to the Penguin Banks off Moloka'i. Two of these were subsequently captured again months later near the point of release off O'ahu. Another tagged off O'ahu in 2003 turned up a year later off Baja California, some 3,100 miles away. Tiger Sharks grow to 18 ft., weigh up to 2,000 lbs., and occur worldwide in tropical waters. Human-size prey items, such as dolphins and seals, begin to occur in their diet as they approach 7 ft. in length. Photo: Aliwal Shoals, South Africa (Dennis King)

October 18, 2000

It was a perfect Maui day—clear, cloudless, great water visibility, completely calm. I had snorkeled about a half mile out from the beach near Olowalu on the Lahaina side of the island, about 100 yards past where the snorkeling boats tie up, where the reef falls off to deep blue ocean. I was completely still, resting from the swim and watching a pair of turtles swim serenely below me.

It came out of nowhere—a serious slam on the right side of my back, like I had been hit by a sledgehammer swung by a giant in an epic battle! There was a shaking and release, and my senses were overwhelmed by the sheer force of what turned out to be one strike from an 18-foot tiger shark.

Stunned, I instinctively turned to my right and met the shark head on. We were eye to eye, with not more than six inches separating his nose and my face. His head was huge—wide and large with deep black eyes. We contemplated each other for two to three seconds, a time characterized by absolute other-worldly stillness. I felt a direct transmission of energy coupled with a joyous connection to the animal kingdom. I don't know what happened to the shark, but I definitely was filled full with "shark energy." These moments remain most vivid, even now.

Then I noticed that the water was no longer clear and had a red liquid threading through it. It was obvious that I had been bitten and that the force I had felt was the shark's jaws closing on my midsection. I felt no fear as my known self dissolved into what seemed like a most intimate connection with the ocean and all it holds, has been, and will become.

The shark became very agitated. Thrashing the water, it turned from me and swam away, in the process bucking me up and out of the water! According to my daughter Layla, kayaking nearby, my entire body from the knees up was visible above the surface. She thought I was standing on a coral head and wondered why since I would never do that.

I yelled for help. My friend Ron Bass (a kayak instructor who later said that the water had felt "sharky" that day) and my daughter started paddling towards me. It looked to me like they were coming in slow motion and I wished they would hurry it up. Ron instructed me to hang on to the back of his craft with Layla on guard in the rear with orders to strike with her paddle if the shark returned. At this point, my body began reacting—I was shaken and hyperventilating. Ron and Layla calmed me down and with the help of their soft and kind words, I found the safety of the shore.

During the wait for the ambulance, I felt no pain. I had been bleeding pretty profusely and Ron packed my wounds with his entire store of supplies from his first aid kit (Ron, a onetime emergency room nurse, knew how to handle the situation). The rest of the story is about mending and being sewed and becoming whole again. The lacerations from the bite were five inches deep and ran in a curve from my shoulder blade through my buttock. There was also a front puncture on my right hip where my bone stopped the bite and several of my ribs, also bite stoppers, were broken. I was very lucky that the lacerations missed all organs and arteries. The doctors said that if I had been on my back, I most likely would not have survived.

Three days later, out of the hospital, I went to the beach to put my feet back in the water. It was sort of like "getting back on the horse that threw me." It worked. Later that year I became a certified diver and have since then seen many sharks while diving. There were many personal changes that followed my experience:

· Before the incident I had been a vegetarian for around 10 years. My first meal out of the hospital was the juicy steak I suddenly craved.

· During my yoga practice later that year, I would look down at my hands and they would seem transformed into starfish. In some ways I felt like a sea creature.

· That same year, I had the overwhelmingly strong message to seek western medical attention for Hepatitis C which I had been working on for years with Eastern modalities. I completed a course of Interferon and beat the Hep C, achieving a complete cure.

I credit the shark with opening the channel for that message and others of a more subtle nature. I am grateful for the entire experience as it opened my energy system to many changes. I feel that I have achieved better balance and have been granted a path of growth towards wisdom through my connection to this new energy system.

- Henri Musselwhite

David R. Schrichte

WHITETIP REEF SHARK · **manō lālā kea** · *Triaenodon obesus* (Rüppell, 1837)

This is one of the most common Indo-Pacific sharks, and the only one seen with any regularity on the reefs of the main Hawaiian Islands. The snout is broad, the body grayish brown, the tips of the first dorsal and upper tail fins white. Two short nasal flaps, probably sensory, protrude under the snout. The first dorsal fin is set unusually far back on the body. Whitetips are sometimes encountered swimming over the reef, usually close to the substrate, but most often they are seen resting in caves or far back under ledges. (Individuals have been known to use the same locations off and on for up to 10 years.) In deeper areas they may simply lie on the bottom. Whitetips are among the few large sharks that rest like this. Most need to swim constantly to keep water moving through their gills. Resting Whitetips may appear lethargic, but they are not harmless and should not be trifled with. Whitetips usually hunt at night and are good at nabbing fish and crustaceans from their hiding places in the rocks or coral. Divers at Molokini Islet, Maui, have an excellent chance of seeing these sharks; they also occur at many other sites about the Islands. Although the species name means "fat" (perhaps the first specimen was a swollen female, as in the photo above), the Whitetip is a comparatively slender shark. The Hawaiian name means "white fins." To about 6 ft. Indo-Pacific and Eastern Pacific. Photos: (above) Palea Point, O'ahu. 40 ft. (David R. Schrichte) (below) "'Ewa Pinnacles," O'ahu. 70 ft.

Whitetip identification

Whitetips have a pattern of dark spots on their sides which is unique and which can be used to identify individuals. Nick Whitney of the University of Hawai'i has been collecting photos of Whitetips for his research on the movements and genetic population structure of these animals. If you have a photo of a Whitetip in Hawai'i, visit **www.whitetip.org** and see if you can identify it in the database. You can also submit your photo to help Nick track where sharks have been seen and when.

Whitetip mating

The Whitetip is one of the few sharks that have been observed and photographed while mating. In an event at Molokini Islet, Maui, the male grasped one of the female's pectoral fins in his jaws while inseminating her with his clasper. The act took place in midwater and lasted about 2-3 minutes while the sharks sank slowly to the bottom. In another mating event observed off Kona, two males competed for a female by biting her pectoral fins while a third male hung around waiting his chance. Late term pregnant females are visibly swollen. They bear up to five pups per litter. In some cases the pups remain together for several months after birth. Photo: © SeaPics.com

Whitetip hunting

Rod Canham, in his book **Hawai'i Below**, describes Whitetip Reef Shark octopus hunting behavior: "The shark props its pectoral fins on anything to get leverage, then uses its shovel shaped head to burrow under the rock. With a thrust of its tail upwards, the relentless predator upends the boulder (some unbelievably large), and with a flurry of tentacles, ink, and a gray blur, the victor is off with the spoils, tentacles hanging from both sides of the mouth. Any other shark in the area follows in close rapid pursuit, for morsels that might get away. The successful shark thrusts its head from side to side and rakes the octopus across its tiny teeth, and with a final thrust the octopus is history."

On his website **CoralRealm.com**, Scott W. Michael writes: "I had the opportunity to observe the nocturnal feeding behavior of the Whitetip Reef Shark at Cocos Island, Costa Rica. After dark the diurnally quiescent Whitetip actively moves over the reef, plunging its head into cracks and crevices in search of sleeping fish and octopi. The hungry whitetips would violently twist and turn in their attempt to penetrate deeper into a crevice, with some sharks squirming in to a hole in one side of a coral head only to exit through an opening on the other side. The whitetips also chased and caught Panamic Soldierfish (Myripristis leiognathos) that were feeding over the reef, and snapped at fish that had been stirred from slumber by the sharks' frenetic activity. Although most hunting activity appeared to occur at night, Whitetips also took advantage of unusual daytime feeding opportunities." Photo: © SeaPics.com

Mackerel Sharks (family Lamnidae)

Mackerel sharks are fast-swimming, warm-blooded, pelagic sharks which can maintain a core body temperature as much as 39 degrees Fahrenheit higher than that of the surrounding water. This gives them a metabolic advantage over strictly coldblooded animals. The five known species include various mako sharks and the infamous Great White Shark. All are potentially dangerous.

Piet Strauss

GREAT WHITE SHARK · **niuhi** · *Carcharodon carcharias* (Linnaeus, 1758)

This is perhaps the most-feared large predator on earth. Its heavy body is gray to dark blue-gray above and white below, sharply demarcated between. The snout is conical and pointed, accounting for the Australian common name White Pointer. The tail fin is crescent-shaped (lunate). Great White Sharks are rare in the Hawaiian Islands, with only 10 or 12 confirmed reports in the last 100 years. They are sparsely distributed worldwide in warm temperate and subtropical seas, and are seen most often in cool waters around South Africa, southern Australia, southern California, and other places where they can find the seals and sea lions on which they feed. In 2000 a male tagged off California was tracked by satellite as it migrated 2,280 miles to Hawaiian waters, where it lingered for about 4 months near the island of Kahoʻolawe. Two definite attacks on humans are recorded from Hawaiʻi, one fatal. The Greek word *karcharos* means "sharp pointed" or "jagged," in reference to the sharp, serrated, triangular teeth, prized in ancient Hawaiʻi for making weapons and knives. Largest verified record: 19 ½ ft. (A fossil relative attained an estimated length of 47 ft!) Photo: Gansbaai, South Africa. (Piet Strauss)

Jimmy's great day

Good days on the ocean are not uncommon for me. As the name of my business, Hawaiʻi Shark Encounters, implies, I have a pretty fun and interesting job. Every day, (weather permitting) we take people out of Haleʻiwa, Oʻahu, to view sharks from a shark cage. December 28th, 2005, was looking to be an ideal day. The ocean was like glass and the bright sun seemed to penetrate hundreds of feet down into the blue water. A mix of about 20 Galapagos and Sandbar Sharks were swimming around the cage and putting on a great show.

At about 1:00 pm someone in the shark cage raised his head and shouted something about a giant shark. The last time this happened it was a Whale Shark. Hoping for a repeat, I peered into the water. A massive shape rose up towards the surface. The lack of a square head showed that it was no Whale Shark. The animal was so massive that I believed a small Humpback Whale was paying us a visit. When it was about 20 ft. away Juan yelled "it's a white!" Moments later, I too realized that we were looking at an absolutely enormous Great White Shark! I ran for my camera. (Later I learned that the people in the cage thought the captain was running away in fear, and that they were doomed!)

With video camera in hand, I jumped in the cage. The size of the shark was unbelievable. I opened the small shark cage door so I could hang out and film as the shark made passes around the boat and cage. Right away the shark rubbed its belly against the cage. We could put our hands through the bars and rub its underside. The shark then swam to the boat and rubbed against the hull. We quickly identified her as a female and due to her incredible size wondered if she was pregnant. At one point she swam to the surface and very slowly stuck her head above the water, opened her mouth, and leaned against the cage. The people in the cage were getting the thrill of a lifetime. And so was I!

It was now or never to fulfill a longtime dream. I slipped outside of the cage, and swam out into the blue. Right away the Great White swam slowly towards me. I hung motionless in the water filming her approach. The distance between us got smaller and smaller until only a couple feet of water separated her nose and the port of my camera housing. With an almost imperceptible change of direction, she altered course and passed by me. It was like the side of a bus was going by, so close that I was able to reach out and put my hand on her side.

I cannot explain what it was like to be in such close proximity to what is undoubtedly the most impressive animal, of any kind, I have ever seen, other than it was the greatest experience of my life. Even though I was completely unprotected and armed with nothing other than my video camera, I was not that scared. Of course adrenaline was rushing through me, but I think most of the emotion I was feeling was not fear but the thrill of knowing what sort of images I was getting and just how fortunate I was. Not only was I seeing a Great White in Hawai'i, but it was one so big that even if you were in a Great White Shark hot spot like South Africa, Guadalupe Island, or the Farallons, you would be lucky to see one that big!

For some 45 minutes the shark stayed with us. All of our guests were able to see her from inside the cage and from the boat. We exhausted all our batteries and film and had nothing left. But the shark was still there. We rushed into the harbor and back out, reloaded with fresh guests, batteries, and additional camera equipment, but we never saw the shark again. - Jimmy Hall

Hawai'i Shark Encounters

Whale Shark (family Rhincodontidae)
This family contains the single well-known species on the following page. ▶

WHALE SHARK *Rhincodon typus* (Smith, 1828)

This is the largest fish in the world. It attains at least 49 ft., perhaps as much as 60, and lives for an estimated 100 years or more. To swim with one of these bus-sized giants is a once-in-a-lifetime experience. Typically docile, they pose no threat to humans. Their enormous size aside, they are unmistakable: their dark back, sides, and fins are patterned with light spots and stripes unlike any other shark or large fish. A cavernous mouth stretching the width of the broad flat head is used to scoop up plankton, squid, and small pelagic fishes such as sardines. (Jacks and tunas feeding on the sardines are sometimes ingested as well!) In Hawai'i, Whale Sharks seem to occur most often on the leeward sides of the islands and typically swim at the surface, sometimes fairly close to shore. Although native to all warm seas, these migratory giants are nowhere common. They do congregate regularly at a number of plankton-rich locations in various parts of the world, however, where they can be seen reliably on a seasonal basis. At Molokini Islet, and off Lāna'i they have been encountered more fequently than usual on days when Cauliflower Coral *(Pocillopora meandrina)* spawns. Because of commercial fishing in some parts of the world, Whale Sharks are considered a threatened species. Photo: half mile off Keauhou, Kona, Hawai'i. (Jerry Kane)

Computer aided identification

*The complex pattern of spots on each whale shark's side is unique. Marine biologist Brad Norman teamed up with an astrophysicist and an information systems expert in 2005 to develop software which can identify individual whale sharks from photographs. (Their program uses an algorithm developed for the Hubble Space Telescope to identify star patterns!) With this cutting-edge technology, Norman has established a visual database of whale shark encounters and over 1,000 individually catalogued whale sharks. You can submit your photos. For details, see **photoid.whaleshark.org***

Be careful who you tell...

Dr. Andrew Smith, the South African scientist who originally described and named the Whale Shark in 1828, intended to give it the scientific name Rhiniodon typus. Rhiniodon means "rasp tooth," and Smith chose it because the shark has 300 rasplike rows of minute teeth in each jaw. Before his scientific paper was published, however, Smith wrote a detailed popular article about the huge shark for a local newspaper. The article included the proposed scientific name, but a typesetter mistakenly used a "c" instead of an "i" and the genus name came out as Rhincodon. Months later, after the official scientific description was published, controversy erupted as to which name was correct, Rhiniodon or Rhincodon. Adding to the confusion, alternate names such Rhineodon and Rhinodon somehow appeared in the literature. Finally, in 1984, the International Committee on Zoological Nomenclature put its collective foot down, ruling that the first published name of a new species, if accompanied by a sufficient description, is the correct and final name, period. Thus Rhincodon became official. Since that time, scientists have been careful not to divulge new scientific names to the media, or even their colleagues, until after their official scientific papers have been published.

Hammerhead Sharks (family Sphyrnidae)

There are nine species of hammerhead sharks worldwide with three in Hawai'i. Their odd, blade-like heads probably provide lift as the animals swim forward. They also use the flat lobes for pinning prey, such as rays, to the seafloor. Most importantly, the wide "hammer" bears an array of electrore-ceptor organs on the underside which help locate living organisms under the sand. Hammerheads typically swim over the bottom swinging their heads from side to side ("like metal detectors" writes one author), stopping from time to time to dig out buried rays, fish, octopuses, or crustaceans. Eyes at the tips of the blades give hammerheads a wide field of vision; the great separation of their eyes and nostrils probably enhances depth perception and helps them track odors to their source. Although the design may seem weird, it works: hammerhead sharks are among the most abundant and successful sharks in the sea. NASA has even investigated the odd head design as a model for spacecraft.

Keoki Stender

SCALLOPED HAMMERHEAD · **manō kihikihi** · *Sphyrna lewini* (Griffith & Smith, 1834)
This is one of the most abundant shark species in Hawai'i and, for that matter, the world. The gently rounded front edge of its bladelike head is scalloped with slight indentations, especially in the center. (The Smooth Hammerhead, *S. zygaena*, less common in Hawai'i, has no central indentation.) Seen from the side, the head appears sharply pointed (see next page). Scalloped Hammerheads regularly enter shallow protected bays in the Islands from April to October to mate and give birth. As many as 10,000 pups are believed to be born in Kāne'ohe Bay, O'ahu, each season. About half a yard long, they feed mostly on crustaceans and remain in their natal grounds for perhaps a year, growing and learning to hunt. Adults in Hawaiian waters are believed to feed at sea for much of the year, mostly on squid. Females are 3-4 ft. longer than males. Divers seldom encounter large hammerheads, although schools of 50 or more of these animals have been reported on occasion at Moku Ho'oniki, Moloka'i, and at select spots off the Kona Coast of the Big Island, where sightings of individuals or small groups are not uncommon in some years. Scalloped Hammerheads occur in all warm seas and attain a length of 13 ft. The Hawaiian name means "curves" "corners" "angular" "zigzag." Photos: (above) Sea Life Park, O'ahu (Keoki Stender); (next page, top) pup at Honolua Bay, Maui. 6 ft.; (next page, bottom) Hawai'i Institute of Marine Biology, Kāne'ohe Bay, O'ahu.

Rarer even than the sighting of a Thresher Shark, which I have only seen twice, is an encounter with the Great Hammerhead, Sphyrna mokorran. Years ago in deep water off Mākaha, the Mother of All Hammerheads cruised inexo-rably right past us, utterly dwarfing my 17-ft. Boston Whaler boat. The long sickle-shaped dorsal fin was unmistakable, and the girth of the monster was jaw-dropping. Size matters, and we used to argue how many fully equipped divers could fit inside the beast. To be honest, however, Godzilla Shark had somewhere to go and never even acknowledged our timorous presence. Like the Great Barracuda, these sharks have a bad reputation in the Caribbean, but seem to be relatively benign in the Pacific, which suggests genetic differences. - John Earle

Scalloped Hammerhead pups (see previous page).▼▲ Seen from the side, hammerheads appear to have a sharply pointed head.

Advice to divers encountering a shark

If a shark is sighted, stay calm and maintain your position in as quiet a manner as possible. Most sharks are merely curious and will leave on their own accord. Enjoy your opportunity to see one of nature's most magnificent predators. If you have been spearfishing or abalone gathering and are holding your catch, release the catch and quietly exit the area. It is likely that the shark has been attracted to the sounds and smells associated with your activity and is aroused and interested in consuming your catch. Let it have it—no catch is worth the risk of personal injury.

If a shark begins to get too interested in you by coming closer and closer, the best strategy is to leave the water—swim quickly but smoothly, watching the shark all the time, with your dive partner close at hand. Sharks are less likely to attack a "school" of divers than a solitary individual. If a shark is acting overtly aggressive—making rushes at you, hunching its back, lowering its pectoral (paired side) fins, swimming in a rapid zigzag course, or swimming with rapid up and down movements (sometimes rubbing its belly on the bottom)—try to back up against whatever structure (reef, rock outcropping, piling) is available, thereby reducing the angles with which the shark can approach you. If you are in open water, orient back-to-back with your dive partner and gradually rise to the surface and the safety of your boat. If you are shore diving, gradually descend to the bottom so you can find cover.

Use whatever inanimate equipment (speargun, pole-spear, camera) you have with you to fend off the shark (when diving in known shark-inhabited waters, it is always good to carry a pole or spear for this purpose). If a shark attacks, the best strategy is to hit it on the tip of its nose. This usually results in the shark retreating. If the retreat is far enough away, then human retreat is in order—again, swim quickly but smoothly, watching the shark all the time, with your dive partner close at hand. An aggressive shark often will return, however, and each subsequent hit to the snout will be less effective, so take advantage of any escape opportunities. If you do not have anything to poke with, use your hand, but remember that the mouth is close to the nose, so be accurate!

If a shark actually gets you in its mouth, I advise to be as aggressively defensive as you are able. "Playing dead" does not work. Pound the shark in any way possible. Try to claw at the eyes and gill openings, two very sensitive areas. Once released, do all you can to exit the water as quickly as possible because with your blood in the water, the shark very well could return for a repeat attack. - © George H. Burgess, International Shark Attack File. Florida Museum of Natural History, University of Florida. For more information see ***www.flmnh.ufl.edu/fish/sharks/***

Further advice to divers, or the mouse that roared ...

Barely into our long safety stop following a deep dive off O'ahu, we saw our worst nightmare swim slowly up the anchor line and start circling. But not to worry, I carried a bangstick, and the explosive shell was.....oops, at the bottom of my mesh bag, which was bulging with specimens. Worry! I could see the shell, I could feel the shell, but I could not claw my way through the mesh to retrieve it. My frantic efforts to do so just increased Mr. Tiger's curiousity. The radius of his circling was decreasing. We had many minutes of decompression time remaining and no good ideas. I tried bluffing with my unloaded bangstick, but the big Tiger Shark was decidedly unimpressed. Finally I clanged my steel double tank rig with the bangstick and noted that the shark flinched at the loud reverberating noise. Idea! I charged at the beast clanging like a madman with adrenaline enhanced strength. The Tiger twitched and flinched at the cacophony, and finally when I was just a few feet away, wishing I had a plan B, the huge beast turned and swam off. Years later Dr. Jack Randall of the Bishop Museum and I flew to Maui to test the reaction of sharks in the oceanarium tank there to clanging scuba tanks. They obviously don't like the noise. This may suggest an action when the chips are down and your back is to the wall.... be loud and obnoxious. - John Earle.

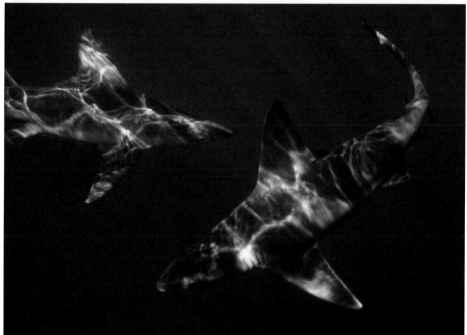

Sandbar Sharks over deep water off Hale'iwa, O'ahu. Note large dorsal fin. (see pp. 265-6)

Bait!

I attached a lift bag to the anchor and sent it up with us so we could decompress without fighting a strong current. Trade winds pushed the boat offshore as we hung on the decompression line like bait, drifting out into the featureless oceanic blue. Passage over the 300-foot drop-off was indicated by the sight of Sleek Unicornfish far below. A large Galapagos Shark rocketed up, made several quick tight turns around us, and plunged back down.

Far off in the clear water, just below the surface, a large silvery orb shone like a planet in deep space. Drifting closer we witnessed a primal sight. Dozens of tuna swiftly circled the ball of baitfish, sculpting a sphere as they snapped up outliers. Seabirds dove into the panicked mass from above. A squad of barracuda, advancing in silver spear phalanx, directly assaulted the planetary surface. Silvery shards of mangled baitfish rained down to be snapped up by half a dozen increasingly agitated Silky Sharks, identifiable by their sleek shape and small first dorsal fin.

Planet Baitfish quickly dwindled and disappeared under this joint onslaught, and the unsatisfied Silkies then turned their attention to us. From 200 feet away, they accelerated like Ferraris and were under the boat in seconds. All but one of us, having clipped our scuba tanks to a line, scrambled frantically to safety over the side of my Boston Whaler. The one diver remaining performed an incredible feat of strength, vaulting directly into the boat while wearing double steel tanks, the pack of Silkies snapping at his heels. - John Earle

275

Bluestripe Snappers · **ta'ape** · introduced species · Kahe Point, O'ahu. 20 ft.

Snappers are perchlike carnivores of considerable economic importance, common on shallow tropical reefs throughout the world. Most species native to Hawai'i, however, inhabit depths greater than 200 ft. These include the **'opakapaka, 'ula'ula,** and **onaga**, some of the Islands' best loved food fishes. The two native shallow-water snappers, solitary predators sometimes known as jobfishes, are not abundant enough to be of major commercial value. To stimulate the fishing industry, three species of reef-dwelling snappers from the South Pacific were introduced to Hawai'i in the 1950s and early sixties. Two, the Blacktail Snapper and the Bluestripe Snapper (p.278) have become common; the third, the Paddletail Snapper *(Lutjanus gibbus)*, is very rare. Unfortunately, the introduced snappers have a low market price and their introduction has been a commercial failure.

Little thought was given in earlier days to the ecological effects of these introductions. Now, decades later, as populations of valuable food fishes such as the Whitesaddle Goatfish (**kūmū**) and deepwater snappers are in sharp decline, the voracious and by now abundant Bluestripe Snapper (**ta'ape**) is often accused of displacing them. The explanation seems reasonable, but careful studies by Dr. James Parrish and colleagues at the University of Hawai'i have failed to verify it. **Ta'ape** do not range as deep as most native deepwater snappers, and in any case have different diets and feed at different times. Investigations into possible competition between **ta'ape** and native shallow-water goatfishes have been less conclusive, but provide no clear evidence of a significant negative effect. Most likely the dwindling catches of goatfishes and deepwater snappers are due to simple overfishing.

About 100 species of snappers are known worldwide, varying in length from about 10 in. to 3 ft. The larger snappers are usually solitary while the smaller species typically school by day, dispersing at night to feed on small fishes and crustaceans. Hawai'i has 14 snappers (including three introduced species); only the four below are likely to be seen by sport divers or snorkelers.

Emperors are a family of mid-size predatory fishes closely related to snappers. They typically have thick lips and molar-like teeth along the sides of their jaws, used for feeding on hard-shelled invertebrates. A few species feed on fish. Like snappers, many emperors are most active at night and rest by day in loose schools. There are about 40 species, with one in Hawai'i.

FORKTAIL SNAPPER · wahanui
Aphareus furca [SMALLTOOTH JOBFISH]
(Lacepède, 1801)

Silvery gray to dark gray with a large, slightly downturned mouth and a deeply forked tail, this solitary snapper typically patrols the reef from a position well off the bottom, often near a dropoff. Some individuals, such as the one pictured here, have bright yellow along the front edge of the head, best seen when the fish is approaching. The species name means "fork," the Hawaiian name, "big mouth." To about 12 in. Indo-Pacific. Photo: Kahe Point, O'ahu. 15 ft.

GRAY SNAPPER · **uku** · *Aprion virescens* Valenciennes, 1830 [GREEN JOBFISH]

This long, powerful, greenish to bluish gray predator has sharp teeth and a large tail fin. The dorsal fin, when raised, reveals an easily seen series of dark marks at the base. It usually swims in midwater, individually or in small groups. Spawning in Hawai'i is from May to October, usually in groups. The species name means "becoming green." To 3 ½ ft. Indo-Pacific. Photo: Hanauma Bay, O'ahu. 20 ft.

*As I was finishing a dive on Molokini's north end, a gray snapper swam underneath me along the bottom, seemingly with some purpose. Suddenly it darted way up to the rim and attacked a cornetfish. The snapper slammed the cornetfish against the bottom until it broke the head from the body, then continued to thrash the body around and use the bottom to get the fish into its mouth. I went over to the cornetfish's head and it was still breathing and the eye continued looking around for several minutes! A few eels were around by then and I ascended and got back on the boat. About five minutes later Tara came upon the scene and two gray reef sharks were circling. She fed the head to an eel which swallowed most of it backwards then spit it out. The thing that amazed me was how the **uku** seemed to have targeted this poor cornetfish from so far away (I'd guess 100 ft.), and of course, how fast it swam, literally like a bullet shooting through the water. I wish there were a way to convey how fast a predatory fish can move through the water. Unless I'd seen it I never would have known it possible. Also, I wouldn't have thought that the **uku** could have even seen the cornetfish from that distance. Maybe the **uku** didn't see it so much as detect vibrations from it being injured or somehow otherwise moving strangely. During the whole encounter the **uku** had an intense mottled coloration that I had never seen before. Afterwards it went back to solid gray. - Pauline Fiene*

BLACKTAIL SNAPPER · to'au
Lutjanus fulvus [FLAMETAIL SNAPPER]
(Forster, 1801)

These snappers are grayish yellow with a red dorsal fin and a black tail which becomes red at the edges. Solitary or in small groups, they rest close to the bottom by day and feed at night. The species was introduced to Hawai'i from Mo'orea, French Polynesia, in 1956, but is not as common as the **ta'ape** (below). Apparently, these fish are wanderers. A few weeks after their original release in Kāne'ohe Bay, O'ahu, **to'au** were captured both in Waimea Bay and off Honolulu, each a good 27 miles away in opposite directions. The species name means "tawny." **To'au** is the Tahitian name. To 13 in. Indo-Pacific. Photo: Honolua Bay, Maui. 20 ft.

BLUESTRIPE SNAPPER · ta'ape
Lutjanus kasmira (Forsskål, 1775)

Yellow with four narrow, dark-edged, blue longitudinal stripes, schools of these showy snappers are a common sight around wrecks and reefs in Hawai'i. Although introduced to Hawai'i from the Marquesas in 1958 for commercial reasons, they have not done well in island markets and are usually regarded by fishermen as a pest rather than an asset. The Tahitian name, **ta'ape**, has come into common use in Hawai'i. To 15 in., but usually smaller. Indo-Pacific. Photo: *Mahi* wreck, O'ahu. 65 ft. (see also p. 276)

In ancient times a public executioner was also called **mū**. *Such a man was sometimes sent to find victims for sacrifice, or for live burial beside the body of a chief. Children, of course, were told that if they were bad the* **mū** *would get them.*

BIGEYE EMPEROR · mū · *Monotaxis grandoculis* (Forsskål, 1775)

These lovely fish have big dark eyes and blunt snouts. They typically hover quietly over the reef facing into the current, either alone or in loose groups. Large adults are entirely silvery gray with tinges of yellow. Smaller adults usually display a pattern of three dark saddles with light narrow bars between, but can take on the silvery gray coloration as well. Juveniles have a permanent, highly contrasting barred pattern and a pointed snout. **Mū** generally feed on sand- or rubble-dwelling invertebrates, using molar-like teeth to crush hard shells. Although most active at night, they also feed by day. To almost 2 ft. Indo-Pacific. Photo: Palea Point, O'ahu. 50 ft. (small adult). Large adult and juvenile on next page.

◀ Bigeye Emperor · **mū** · large adult (see previous page). Molokini Islet, Maui

*The **mū** is the master of motionlessness. Its body seems to be nothing more than a platform for holding its giant eyes as still as possible so that it can detect the slightest movement on the bottom. Once while I was watching one hanging in the water absolutely still, it suddenly swam to the bottom and pulled a large sea hare (Dolabella auricularia) out from under rubble. It chewed the sea hare for quite a while, purple ink coming out the whole time. I have seen them go to the bottom a hundred times and pick up small molluscs that we could never see from that same distance, crushing them, shell pieces spilling out of their mouths. I always go over and catch the pieces to see what it was and to show my divers. I wish I had kept track of all the species I've seen them eating over the years. One day I noticed eleven **mū** swimming together. The lead one had a large Carpilius convexus crab in its mouth. The crab was so big that it took the **mū** a few minutes to crush it and eat it, again with parts falling out of its mouth. Andy had his camera and got a great photo. We don't see the crabs very often, and certainly not out in the open. Where and how did it get it? - Pauline Fiene*

Mū have teeth that resemble human molars. Dr. John E. Randall of Honolulu's Bishop Museum once played a joke on a paleontologist by showing him the jaws of one of these fish, innocently asking what mammal they came from. The paleontologist was baffled. He never suspected they were from a fish.

Juvenile. Pūpūkea, O'ahu. 70 ft.

Bigeye Emperor eating crab. Molokini Islet, Maui

Andy Schwanke

279

SQUIRRELFISHES and SOLDIERFISHES
(Holocentridae)

Hawaiian Squirrelfish and Bigscale Soldierfish · **'ala'ihi** and **'ū'ū** · Portlock Point, O'ahu. 30 ft.

Fishes of the family Holocentridae are small to medium-size nocturnal predators, usually red, with big scales, a deeply forked tail fin, and large dark eyes. All rest by day, usually under ledges and in caves, and hunt freely over the reef at night. The family divides easily into two groups: the squirrelfishes (subfamily Holocentrinae) and the soldierfishes (subfamily Myripristinae).

Squirrelfishes are characterized by one or more backward pointing spines on the gill covers (venomous in some species). Most species are marked with horizontal silvery stripes which follow the scale rows. Approached in their shelters, many squirrelfishes will dash nervously to and fro, and some species make clicking and grunting sounds. Perhaps these behaviors, as well as the dark eyes, gave them their common name. The general Hawaiian name is **'ala'ihi**.

Soldierfishes, by contrast, lack stripes, and have blunter snouts and deeper bodies than squirrelfishes. Most also lack backward-pointing spines on the gill cover. Their name may come from the epaulette-like shoulder bars and the uniform red color, reminiscent of British redcoats. In Hawai'i, soldierfishes are often called by their Japanese name, *mempachi*. The Hawaiian name **'ū'ū** mimics the grunting sounds some make when disturbed.

Both these fishes emerge at dusk to feed; the **'ala'ihi** seeks out crabs and shrimps near or on the bottom, while the **'ū'ū** favors plankton higher up in the water. Their red color is typical of many nocturnal and deepwater fishes, actually making them more difficult to see. Because red wavelengths are rapidly absorbed by seawater, a red fish reflects little light at night or at depth.

Despite their ordinary perchlike appearance, squirrelfishes and soldierfishes do not belong to the order Perciformes with the majority of fishes in this book. Their more primitive anatomy places them in the order Beryciformes, of which they are the only members common on coral reefs. They range in length from about 3 to 18 in. The family name Holocentridae means "all spiny" or "all prickly" (an apt description, if you have ever handled one).

About 20 holocentrids inhabit Hawaiian waters. Some are deep-dwelling or reclusive species seldom seen by divers or snorkelers; 16 are pictured here.

HAWAIIAN SQUIRRELFISH · 'ala'ihi · *Sargocentron xantherythrum* (Jordan & Evermann, 1903)

These are the squirrelfish seen most often by divers and snorkelers in Hawai'i. Common on almost all Hawaiian reefs, they congregate under ledges, in small caves and crevices, and in heads of Antler Coral *(Pocillopora grandis).* They are red with silvery stripes; their dorsal fins are uniform deep red except for the white spine tips and sometimes a few white marks at the base. The Crown Squirrelfish (below) is similar but much less common. To separate the two with certainty look carefully at the two backward-pointing spines on the gill covers: the Hawaiian Squirrelfish has an upper spine much longer than the lower. In the Crown Squirrelfish these two spines are of about equal length. The species name is from the Greek words *xanthos* ("yellow") and *erythrum* ("red"). To 6 ½ in. Endemic. Photo: Lahilahi Point, O'ahu. 20 ft.

CROWN SQUIRRELFISH · 'ala'ihi
Sargocentron diadema
(Lacepède, 1802)

Divers with a practiced eye can distinguish this squirrelfish from the similar and more common Hawaiian Squirrelfish (above) by its stripes, which are more widely and evenly spaced. If the dorsal fin is raised, ID becomes easier: the Crown Squirrelfish has a dark red to blackish red dorsal which contains two disconnected white lines, the frontmost quite conspicuous. Also, the dorsal spine tips are clear, possibly resembling a crown or diadem when the fin is completely raised. At night identification becomes a snap: this fish often develops a white bar at the base of the tail and a white line on the upper rear side. If you are identifying from photographs check the two backward-pointing spines on the gill cover: in this fish they are of almost equal length whereas in the Hawaiian Squirrelfish the upper is much longer than the lower. To 6 ½ in. Indo-Pacific. Photos: (a, b) Town Pier, Kailua-Kona, Hawai'i. 20 ft.

a) daytime coloration ▲   b) nighttime coloration ▼

YELLOWSTRIPE SQUIRRELFISH
Sargocentron ensifer
(Jordan & Evermann, 1903)

This large showy squirrelfish often rests in the open outside its shelter and is always a treat to see. The upper sides and back bear bright yellow stripes which contrast nicely with the red of its body. Preferring depths greater than 60 ft., it is typically solitary and occurs most commonly off Maui and the Big Island. The species name means "sword bearer," referring to a long, backward-pointing spine on the gill cover just behind the eye. To about 10 in. Japan, New Caledonia, Hawai'i, and Pitcairn. Photo: Molokini Islet, Maui. 60 ft. (Mike Severns)

DWARF SQUIRRELFISH · 'ala'ihi
Sargocentron iota Randall, 1998

Named for the smallest letter in the Greek alphabet, this secretive squirrelfish attains a maximum of 3 in. and is seldom seen. Look for it in stands of Finger Coral *(Porites compressa)* at night. With its uniform red color and rounded tail fin lobes, it could be confused with a small Rough-Scale Soldierfish (p. 287), which has similar secretive habits. The latter, however, usually lives in crevices and caves, whereas this species appears to prefer spaces in and around living coral. Central Pacific to the Eastern Indian Ocean. Photo: Kailua Harbor, Hawai'i. 20 ft. (night)

day

night

PEPPERED SQUIRRELFISH
'ala'ihi
Sargocentron punctatissimum
(Cuvier, 1829)

Although seldom seen by day, this small squirrelfish is often encountered by divers at night, especially in waters less than 30 ft. deep. It can be abundant in dark caves and also occurs in tide pools, where it shelters in crevices. Pinkish red with a satiny sheen, it is striped with darker red and peppered by day with small inconspicuous black and silver spots. After dark these spots fade and a pale midbody stripe develops along the side. A white spot may also appear above the base of the tail fin. The red dorsal fin contains a white stripe. To 5 in. Indo-Pacific. Photos: Town Pier, Kailua-Kona, Hawai'i. 15 ft. (lower photo: night coloration)

LONGJAW SQUIRRELFISH · 'ala'ihi · *Sargocentron spiniferum* (Forsskål, 1775) [SABER SQUIRRELFISH]

The largest of its family, this species is easy to recognize: the body is uniform orange-red, the fins (except for the bright red dorsal) are yellowish, and it has a long, sad-looking face. A venomous spine projects back from the lower gill cover. This might have been the species called in old Hawai'i **'ala'ihi kalaloa** ("long-spike 'ala'ihi"). Easy to approach, it is perhaps encountered most often along the Kona Coast of the Big Island at about 50 ft. Although common throughout most of the Indo-Pacific, it is seen infrequently in Hawai'i. The species name means "spiny." To 18 in. Indo-Pacific. Photo: Hanauma Bay, O'ahu. 30 ft.

BLUESTRIPE SQUIRRELFISH
'ala'ihi · *Sargocentron tiere*
(Cuvier, 1829)
[TAHITIAN SQUIRRELFISH]

Iridescent blue-violet stripes gleam lengthwise along the lower sides of this relatively large, uncommon squirrelfish. Viewed from the front, the snout has whitish markings that almost encircle the eye. At night or in dark environments a bright white bar develops down the center of the body and another at the base of the tail. By day this fish remains deep within the reef and is infrequently seen. It prefers depths less than 40 ft. The species name is the Tahitian word for squirrelfish. (Tahiti was where the first scientific specimen was obtained.) To about 12 in. Indo-Pacific. Photos: (a) "First Cathedral" Lāna'i. 30 ft. (b) "Manta Ray Bay," Kona, Hawai'i. 20 ft. (c) Puakō, Hawai'i. 15 ft.

a) daytime coloration ▲

b) nighttime coloration ▼

GOLDLINE SQUIRRELFISH
Neoniphon aurolineatus
(Liénard, 1839)

This uncommon squirrelfish can most easily be distinguished from its near look-alike the Yellowstripe Squirrelfish (p. 282) by the following characters: its yellow stripes occur on both the upper and lower sides, it lacks a long backward-pointing spine on the gill cover behind the eye, and its head bears a pale bar below the eye and another behind it. By day, these fish mill about under ledges and in caves at depths of 80 ft. or more, seldom venturing into the open. The species name means "gold lined." To about 9 in. Indo-Pacific. Photo: *Mahi* wreck, O'ahu. 60 ft.

a) daytime coloration ▲

SPOTFIN SQUIRRELFISH · 'ala'ihi
Neoniphon sammara
(Forsskål, 1775)

This squirrelfish is silvery with brownish red stripes following the rows of scales. The spiny dorsal fin, often raised, contains a dark red spot at the front which continues back as a dark stripe. At night a red stripe appears on the side, the head turns pinkish-red, and the back and upper side become flushed with pink. Sometimes two whitish blotches develop, one midbody over the red stripe and another above the base of the tail. This solitary squirrelfish is absent from many dive and snorkel sites, but where one is found, others are usually nearby. It can sometimes be seen in water only a few feet deep. To 12 in. Indo-Pacific. Photos: (a) "Sea Cave," Koko Head, O'ahu. 20 ft. (b) "Manta Ray Bay," Kona, Hawai'i. 20 ft.

b) nighttime coloration ▼

WHITESPOT SQUIRRELFISH
Pristilepis oligolepis
(Whitley, 1941)

In the main Hawaiian Islands this unusual squirrelfish occurs only below about 300 ft. In the cooler waters of the northwestern chain, however, it can be seen in as little as 30 ft. About 10 rows of prominent white spots readily distinguish it from other Hawaiian squirrelfishes. To about 12 in. Indo-Pacific, but probably restricted to subtropical waters on either side of the equator. Photo: Midway Atoll. 45 ft.

BRICK SOLDIERFISH · 'ū'ū · *Myripristis amaena* (Castelnau, 1873)
This is the only Hawaiian soldierfish whose soft dorsal, anal, and tail fins are plain red without white edges. The pelvic fins, however, bear a trace of white on the leading edge. The body is brick red. It can be abundant in caves and in deep crevices, usually at depths of less than 30 ft. It is commonly seen by snorkelers at Hanauma Bay, O'ahu. To about 10 in. Restricted to the Pacific islands. Photo: Hanauma Bay, O'ahu. 8 ft.

BIGSCALE SOLDIERFISH · 'ū'ū · *Myripristis berndti* Jordan & Evermann, 1903
The largest and most common of the Hawaiian soldierfishes, these fish aggregate in caves and under ledges, sometimes in great numbers. A larger size, larger scales, a shorter shoulder bar, and a strongly projecting lower jaw separate them from the Pearly Soldierfish (below), which can also be abundant in the same shelter. Both species have white on the leading edges of the soft dorsal, anal, pelvic, and tail fins. The first dorsal fin of each shows yellow when raised. The scientific name honors Mr. E. Louis Berndt, inspector of the Honolulu Fish Market in the early years of the 20th century. To 11 in. Indo-Pacific and Eastern Pacific. Photo: Hanauma Bay, O'ahu. 20 ft. (see also p. 280)

PEARLY SOLDIERFISH · ʻūʻū · *Myripristis kuntee* Valenciennes, 1831 [SHOULDERBAR SOLDIERFISH; EPAULETTE SOLDIERFISH]

These soldierfish vary from red to pinkish, often with a satiny or pearly sheen. The leading edges of the soft dorsal, anal, pelvic, and tail fins are white. The shoulder bar is slightly longer and more distinct than that of the Bigscale Soldierfish (above), the scales are slightly smaller, and the lower jaw less projecting. The dorsal fin, when raised, shows yellow. Smaller than other Hawaiian soldierfishes, these fish often seek shelter within the reef rather than in caves and under overhangs. They commonly rest in the open just above the reef during the day at depths of about 15 to 50 ft., sometimes in twos or threes, occasionally in large aggregations. To about 7 ½ in. Indo-Pacific. Photo: Kahe Point, Oʻahu. 20 ft.

Mixed aggregation of Pearly Soldierfish and Bigscale Soldierfish (see previous page).
Both have yellow dorsal fins, but the Bigscale Soldierfish have more prominent scales. Kewalo Pipe, Oʻahu. 60 ft.

WHITETIP SOLDIERFISH · ʻūʻū
Myripristis vittata Valenciennes, 1831

This uncommon soldierfish lacks a dark vertical "shoulder bar" along the edge of the gill covers. The spines of its dorsal fin are tipped with white and the fins have white edges. Uncommon in Hawaiʻi, it frequents crevices and caves along steep dropoffs, such as those at Molokini Islet, Maui, or Lehua Rock off Niʻihau, generally at 100 ft. or more. To about 8 in. Indo-Pacific. The species name means "band" or "stripe"—seemingly inappropriate because this is precisely what the fish lacks. Photo: Molokini Islet, Maui. 160 ft. (Mike Severns)

Mike Severns

YELLOWFIN SOLDIERFISH · ʻūʻū
Myripristis chryseres
Jordan & Evermann, 1903

A brick red to pinkish red body with golden yellow fins (except the pectorals), make these the loveliest of Hawaiʻiʻs soldierfishes. The leading edge of the yellow fins is light iridescent blue. These deep dwellers are only occasionally encountered by divers, usually at depths exceeding 100 ft. but sometimes as shallow as 70 ft. In the Northwestern Hawaiian Islands they occur in as little as 40 ft., probably because the water is cooler. The species name means "golden." To about 10 in. Indo-Pacific. Photo: Molokini Islet, Maui. 120 ft. (Mike Severns)

Mike Severns

ROUGH-SCALE SOLDIERFISH
Plectrypops lima
(Valenciennes, 1831)

This small chunky soldierfish is a uniform pinkish red without markings. Unlike other Hawaiian soldierfishes, its tail fin has rounded lobes. Dwelling in the far recesses of caves and crevices, it is almost never seen by day. Even at night it seldom leaves its cave. Its scales make it rough to the touch. The species name means "file." To about 6 in. Indo-Pacific. Photo: Lānaʻi Lookout, Oʻahu. 30 ft.

In Hawaiʻi, soldierfishes are commonly called by their Japanese name, "mempachi" (sometimes spelled "menpachi"). In local pidgin, to "make mempachi eyes" means to have a blank, dazed, wide-eyed stare.

287

STRIPEYS
(Microcanthidae)

S tripeys and their relatives belong to a small family of schooling fishes which lack a collective common name. Related to both butterflyfishes and chubs, they feed on small bottom-dwelling invertebrates and plankton and are usually conspicuously striped. There are four genera and five species. Most live in the cool subtropical waters of southern Australia and New Zealand.

Three species or one?

The Stripey occurs north of the equator in Hawai'i, Japan, and the China Sea, and south of the equator around Australia, but nowhere between. Most ichthyologists consider it to be a single species, but Australian Rudie Kuiter has tentatively separated it into three: the Northern Stripey (Japan and Hawai'i), the Eastern Stripey (eastern Australia), and the Western Stripey (western Australia). Kuiter does this on the basis of subtle but consistent color differences. Traditionally, ichthyologists have wanted to see some physical differences other than color before declaring a fish to be a separate species, but DNA tests will eventually settle the matter.

STRIPEY
Microcanthus strigatus
(Cuvier, 1831)

With their pointed snouts, disklike bodies, and bold diagonal stripes, Stripeys could easily be mistaken for butterflyfishes. However, they are rarely seen around reefs, preferring quiet murky lagoons, fishponds, harbors, and other places where fresh water mingles with the sea. On O'ahu, look for them in Kāne'ohe Bay and off Hale'iwa Beach Park. On Kaua'i, they are sometimes abundant at Lydgate State Park (near the mouth of the Wailua River). On Maui, they have been seen right along shore at Ulua Beach. Like many of Hawai'i's unusual fishes, Stripeys prefer cool, subtropical waters on either side of the equator, occurring also in Japan, Taiwan, Australia, Lord Howe Island, and New Caledonia—a pattern of distribution known as anti-tropical or anti-equatorial. Some ichthyologists consider the northern Pacific population to be a distinct species. To 7½ in. Photos: (upper) Lydgate State Park, Kaua'i. 3 ft. (lower) Coconut Island Pier, Kāne'ohe Bay, O'ahu. 5 ft.

SURGEONFISHES and UNICORNFISHES
(Acanthuridae)

Surgeonfishes at Pai'olu'olu Point, O'ahu. Four different species.

Fishes of the family Acanthuridae are among the most abundant and prominent fishes on Hawaiian reefs, and probably account for most of the fish biomass in the state. The surgeonfishes (subfamily Acanthurinae) carry two forward-pointing spines at the base of the tail—one on each side. Ordinarily, these "scalpels" lie flat in a groove. A swipe of the tail automatically flips one out, ready for action against enemy or intruder. The unicornfishes (subfamily Nasinae) have fixed bony keels instead of scalpels (those of a Bluespine Unicornfish at right). In either case, the

weaponry is razor sharp. The name "surgeonfish" derives from the deep, painful cuts these fish can inflict on careless humans, typically while being removed from a net or spear. But don't blame the fish; the spines, and the areas around them, are often brightly colored as a warning. Those of at least one species are mildly venomous, causing painful wounds that heal slowly. Snorkelers and divers who keep their distance, however, have little to fear from these fish.

Surgeonfishes and unicornfishes are typically oval or oblong in shape with deep compressed bodies and eyes set high on the head. Their scales are so small as to seem nonexistent. They propel themselves mainly with winglike beats of their pectoral fins, as do wrasses and parrotfishes. The majority are herbivores whose small mouths are adapted for either scraping fine algal growths or cropping leafy algae from the surface of rocks and dead coral. Several surgeonfish species feed primarily on detritus (organic matter that settles to the bottom). Unicornfishes, many of which have a horn on the forehead when mature, are typically plankton-eaters. Some species feed on algae when young and switch to plankton as adults. The change is forced by the continually growing horn, which eventually prevents their mouths from reaching the substrate.

Because marine plants grow best in bright light, most surgeonfishes live in relatively shallow water. Some, such as the mid-size Achilles Tang and Whitespotted Surgeonfish, inhabit the turbulent surge zone where they graze on algal turf growing on hard surfaces. Smaller species such as Convict Tangs and Yellow Tangs generally prefer calmer, often slightly deeper waters, typically browsing on filamentous algae in large mixed schools. Moving together in a group affords protection from predators and enables them to overcome the territorial defenses of other algae-eating fish. Larger species, such as the Yellowfin, Eyestripe, and Orangeband Surgeonfishes, generally live near sand patches where they graze on organic detritus, diatoms, and the almost microscopic algae growing on the compacted sand. The Bluespine and Orangespine Unicornfishes browse on leafy algae. Zoologists call such groupings "feeding guilds." Members of a guild are usually similar. The reef browsers, for example, are small and feed almost continuously, while sand-grazing surgeons are large and spend much of their time resting.

Some acanthurids (Achilles Tangs, Bluespine Unicornfish) remain within relatively small areas of the reef, whereas others (Convict and Yellow Tangs) roam freely. Some commute between nighttime sheltering areas and daytime feeding areas over distances of several hundred yards to a mile. Surgeonfishes and unicornfishes can be surprisingly long-lived. A study of ten common species in Australia revealed lifespans in the wild of 30-45 years with up to 80 percent of growth occurring in the first 4-7 years.

The names "surgeonfish" and "tang" are often used interchangeably, although some authors restrict "tang" to members of the genus *Zebrasoma*. In the Hawaiian language there is no general name for surgeonfishes, but the unicornfishes are all known as **kala**, which also means "thorn." In old Hawai'i, a person who could defend himself well was praised as "a **kala** fish with a sharp tail." The family name originates in the Greek words *akanthos* ("thorn") and *oura* ("tail").

Out of 80 acanthurid species worldwide, 23 occur regularly in Hawaiian waters, two of them endemic. All are pictured here except the deep-dwelling Spotted Unicornfish *(Naso maculatus)*, which occurs at scuba depths only in the Northwestern Hawaiian Islands. To make identification easier in this chapter, species within each genus are grouped roughly by feeding and depth preference instead of alphabetically.

Yellow Tangs cleaning a Green Turtle. Puakō, Hawai'i.   Mike Roberts

ACHILLES TANG · **pāku'iku'i** · *Acanthurus achilles* Shaw, 1803 [ACHILLES SURGEONFISH]

This feisty surgeonfish is bluish black with an orange-red teardrop shaped patch over the scalpel and a white-edged orange-red bar on the tail fin. Bright white marks highlight the mouth, gill covers, and pectoral fins. Common along rocky shores in and just below the surge zone, these territorial fish feed on the thin turf of microalgae covering the substrate. Sometimes they swim in loose groups and, rarely, in schools. Juveniles often shelter singly in beds of Finger Coral *(Porites compressa)* in deeper water than adults. The Achilles Tang belongs to a complex of closely related surgeonfishes, another of which also occurs in Hawai'i (see Goldrim Tang, next page). It is named for the Greek warrior Achilles, who symbolizes youthful grace, beauty, and valor. The orange-red "finger marks" near the tail recall the old story that Achilles' mother held her baby by the heels and dipped him in the River Styx to make him invulnerable. The Hawaiian name refers to a method of scaring fish into nets by slapping and pounding the water. To 10 in. Islands of Polynesia, Micronesia, Eastern Pacific. Photo: Hālona Blowhole, O'ahu. 20 ft.

> *Achilles Tangs spend considerable energy defending their territories against other algae-eating surgeonfishes. In most cases, a short charge and a sudden turn to expose a scalpel does the job nicely. A swarm of algae-devouring **manini**, however, can easily overwhelm an Achilles Tang, whose body and flared fins take on a reddish glow as it darts about, in vain, trying to drive the intruders away. In addition to the reddish glow, an aroused Achilles Tang often develops a whitish patch on the chest and sometimes a white ring around the eye. Photo: Hanauma Bay, O'ahu. 10 ft.*

Achilles Tangs schooling in Hanauma Bay, O'ahu   David W. Schrichte

Color change while being cleaned
Palea Point, O'ahu

Achilles Tang with hybrid (see next page)
Pai'olu'olu Point, O'ahu.

Sparring · Hanauma Bay, O'ahu (see also p. 301)

Juvenile · Pūpūkea, O'ahu

GOLDRIM TANG
Acanthurus nigricans
(Linnaeus, 1758)

These elegant fish live from the surge zone down to about 30 ft., and sometimes deeper. The black body bears small white markings below the eye and behind the mouth. A yellow scalpel, a white tail fin containing a narrow yellow bar, and yellow at the bases of their dorsal and anal fins further distinguish them. When defending their territories they extend these fins, outlining their body with gold. The fins, in turn, are edged with electric blue. When truly agitated, or when being cleaned, the rear third of the body turns yellowish white. This species belongs to a complex of four closely-related surgeonfishes, including the Achilles Tang (previous page). In Hawai'i, beautiful hybrids between the two are occasionally seen. They usually have some orange in the tail and a reduced or absent white mark below the eye. The species name means "blackish." To 8 in. Indonesia to the Eastern Pacific. Photos: (a, c) Palea Point, O'ahu. 25 ft. (b) Puakō, Hawai'i. 15 ft.

a) normal adult ▲

b) Goldrim x Achilles hybrid ▼

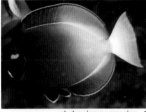

c) showing aggression ▲

LINED SURGEONFISH
Acanthurus lineatus (Linnaeus, 1758)

Striped with electric blue, yellow and black, this spectacular surgeonfish is probably Hawai'i's rarest, recorded only from South Point, Hawai'i, and Hanauma Bay, O'ahu, where one lone individual has been seen off and on for years. Stray larvae evidently drift to Hawai'i from time to time and mature, but the species does not reproduce here. Elsewhere in the Indo-Pacific it inhabits the turbulent surge zone where males hold territories and maintain harems. The scalpels of this surgeonfish are venomous. In many surgeons the scalpels are brightly colored as a warning; in this case the entire fish is the warning! To about 10 in. Indo-Pacific. Photo: Hanauma Bay, O'ahu. 30 ft.

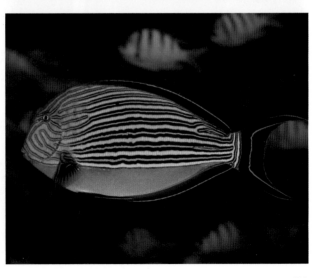

WHITESPOTTED SURGEONFISH ·'api · *Acanthurus guttatus* Forster, 1801 [MUSTARD TANG]

These non-territorial surge-zone fish have an almost circular gray-brown body with a white bar behind the eye and another behind the pectoral fin.The rear half of the body is covered with many white spots, thought perhaps to camouflage them in bubbly white water. The pelvic fins are intense yellow and tail fins are bright yellow and black. A long sloping snout terminates in a thick upper lip. These fish are adept at riding the foamy surge into the shallows to nibble for a few seconds at algae before being swept back into deeper water. Occasionally they graze in large schools. Group spawning, often involving hundreds of fish, takes place at dusk over outcroppings in channels or other areas of current outflow. Spawning coloration is pale or silvery on the sides with faint bars and dots, and dark edges on the dorsal and anal fins. These fish assimilate their algal food inefficiently and their fecal material is thought to contribute considerable detritus to the food web of the reef. The species name means "spotted." To 11 in. Indo-Pacific. All photos: Hanauma Bay, O'ahu.

feeding school ▼   ▼ pale pre-spawning coloration

WHITEBAR SURGEONFISH
māikoiko
Acanthurus leucopareius
(Jenkins, 1903)

Easy to identify, these surgeons have a prominent white bar behind the eye, bisecting the mostly black head. The body is light gray to dark grayish brown with faint lines and spots. A narrow white bar rings the base of the tail. Inhabitants of the surge zone, these fish are sometimes abundant close to shore in bouldery or rocky areas where they browse on algae. They are not territorial and during calm periods may form large feeding schools. Often they mix with Convict Tangs, which usually prefer slightly deeper water. The species name means "white cheek." The Hawaiian name refers to a variety of sugarcane. To 10 in. These fish occur only on subtropical Pacific islands well north and south of the equator, a distribution pattern known as "antiequatorial" or "antitropical" which is shared by a number of Hawaiian fishes. Photos: (right) Hanauma Bay, Oʻahu. 10 ft. (below) Pūpūkea, Oʻahu. 10 ft.

Mixed feeding school of Whitebar Surgeonfish and Convict Tangs

295

CONVICT TANG · manini
Acanthurus triostegus
(Linnaeus, 1758)
[CONVICT SURGEONFISH]

The most widespread and abundant of Indo-Pacific surgeonfishes, Convict Tangs are light greenish or yellowish white with six black bars (the convict's stripes). The Hawaiian population (subspecies *sandvicensis*) has an oblique black bar under the pectoral fin. On protected rocky coastlines these fish are common from the shallows down to about 30 ft. Along more turbulent shores they remain below the surge zone. In either case, they avoid areas where coral cover is heavy. Feeding exclusively on fine filamentous algae, they browse singly, in small groups, or in dense schools, depending on the competition (see sidebar). Juveniles are common in tide pools and inlets, even where the water is brackish. Sometimes they aggregate with small Hawaiian Sergeants. Although **manini** were a favored food fish in old Hawai'i, the popular name has come to mean undersized or stingy, some say through association with the prominent but famously parsimonious Spaniard Don Francisco de Paula y Marin (1774-1837), friend and advisor to King Kamehameha I. In Hawaiian, "Marin" is pronounced "manini." To 10 in. Indo-Pacific and Eastern Pacific. Photos: Hanauma Bay, O'ahu.

*Convict Tangs are not territorial and have small unmarked scalpels, placing them at the bottom of the surgeonfish pecking order. As individuals, they are easily chased from the feeding territories of other fishes. When attacked by a territorial herbivore, such as a Hawaiian Gregory (p. 81), a single **manini** usually escapes upward and then swims slowly 3-6 ft. above the bottom before circling back to the spot where it was feeding. If attacked repeatedly it moves on. While above the reef, however, it is often joined by another **manini** in the same predicament, and in this way a school begins to form. If attacked continually, the school grows large and dense enough (100-300 individuals) to overwhelm the defenders. At this point surgeonfishes of other species often join in, and perhaps a few parrotfishes, wrasses, and even a trumpetfish or two. The wrasses feed on small animals disturbed by the grazers, and the trumpetfish take advantage of the general confusion to nab unwary prey. Thus what started as a few **manini** becomes a large mobile feeding community. (see also p. 298)*

David R. Schrichte

Convict Tang spawning

Like most surgeonfishes, Convict Tangs spawn in groups, usually at dusk and in areas of current outflow such as passes or channels. Often they migrate in great numbers from their shallow feeding grounds to deeper water outside the reef, forming enormous aggregations which constantly swell and pulse with activity. The stripes of males darken and widen before spawning (the effect is like ink spreading on blotting paper) presumably so that females can recognize them. Spawning itself occurs in small break-away groups which swim high into the water, release their gametes, and dash back down to the safety of the crowd. Spawning activity typically peaks just after dark, but has also been observed in the middle of the day. A good time to look for this rarely-seen phenomenon is on an outgoing tide around the full moon, December through July. Photos: Hanauma Bay, O'ahu.

David R. Schrichte

BROWN SURGEONFISH · māʻiʻiʻi
Acanthurus nigrofuscus
(Forsskål, 1775) [LAVENDER TANG]

This common surgeonfish varies from dark brown to light grayish brown with a definite lavender tinge, especially on the fins. There are dull orange spots on the head and two dark spots at the base of the crescent-shaped tail, one above the other. It often feeds in shallow water close to shore and is so unremarkable in appearance that most divers and snorkelers overlook it. Nonetheless, it is possibly the smartest fish on the reef (see pp. 196-7) and is probably the only reef fish to have made headlines around the world (see sidebar below). The species name *nigrofuscus* means "dark brown." The Hawaiian name also refers to a variety of **kalo** (taro). To 8 in. Indo-Pacific. Photo: Kahe Point, Oʻahu. 15 ft. (see also next page)

In March 1993 the media announced that the biggest species of bacteria known to science had been discovered in the gut of this surgeonfish. About the size of a hyphen in a newspaper article, the bacteria apparently aid in digestion.

Brown Surgeonfish driving off maurauding Convict Tangs · note pale aggressive coloration   extreme aggressive display

Browns vs. Convicts

Feeding behavior and ecology of the Brown Surgeonfish vary according to local conditions. Along the gently shelving south shore of Kealakekua Bay, Hawaiʻi, for example, Brown Surgeons are territorial and aggressive. Here, individual fish defend feeding areas primarily against the Convict Tang. Along the Bay's precipitous north shore, however, Brown Surgeons display little territoriality, migrate considerable distances to feed, and often graze in schools—sometimes <u>with</u> *Convict Tangs! Their effect on Convict Tang behavior along the south shore is interesting: where Browns are least numerous, Convicts are able to feed singly; where Browns are moderately common, Convicts can feed only in dense schools, swamping the defenders; where Browns are abundant, Convict Tangs are absent. Photos: Hanauma Bay, Oʻahu, 20 ft. (see also p. 296)*

Fireworks!

Spawning in Brown Surgeonfish occurs around high tide, from approximately February to early September. The fish migrate in single file from various parts of the reef to "traditional" spawning sites, arriving from distances of up to half a mile. Here hundreds or even thousands of fish mill in a dome-shaped aggregation that pulses and swells with activity. Some, probably males, become distinctly pale along the upper back. Periodically a dozen or so excited individuals break away in a group, dash upward, spawn, then return to the safety of the crowd below. Clouds of white gametes released at the apex of their rush resemble fireworks. A good place to see this spectacle on a small scale is over the hot water outfall at Kahe Point Beach Park, O'ahu, where it can be an almost daily occurrence in spring and summer. At other locations, a constant parade of Brown Surgeonfish migrating along the reef in a line can be a sign that it's about to happen. Just follow them. Photo: Hanauma Bay, O'ahu. 40 ft.

Brown Surgeonfish spawning ▲

BLUELINE SURGEONFISH · maiko
Acanthurus nigroris
Valenciennes, 1835

These common reef fish vary from light gray to almost black, always with fine, somewhat wavy blue lines running lengthwise along the body. They sometimes display a white ring around the tail. Like the smaller Brown Surgeonfish (previous page), they have two small dark spots, above and below the base of the tail. They often join mixed feeding schools of other surgeonfishes. Specimens from Hawai'i have higher fin ray and gill raker counts, and a more deeply indented tail fin than similar fish from other parts of the Pacific, and DNA studies have confirmed the Hawaiian population to be distinct. The species name means "blackness." To 10 in. Endemic to Hawai'i (with a similar species, *A. nigros,* elsewhere in the Pacific). Photos: (top) Hōnaunau, Hawai'i. 20 ft. (bottom) Hanauma Bay, O'ahu. 5 ft.

299

YELLOWFIN SURGEONFISH · **pualu** · *Acanthurus xanthopterus* Valenciennes, 1835

Purplish gray to almost black, with yellow and blue banded dorsal and anal fins, these large surgeonfish have deep blue lyre-shape tails, often with a white ring at the base. Three features distinguish them from the similar Ringtail Surgeonfish (below): the outer third of the pectoral fin is yellow, the scalpel is relatively short and surrounded by pale blue, and there is a broad yellow stripe in front of the eye. These fish feed primarily on algae and diatoms growing on compacted sand. They sometimes swim in large schools. Individuals occasionally hover in midwater under resting Heller's Barracudas (p. 12) or pods of resting Spinner Dolphins to feed on excreted wastes. The species name means "yellow-fin." Attaining 22 in., this is the biggest of all surgeonfishes (but many unicornfishes grow larger). Indo-Pacific and Eastern Pacific. Photo: Hanauma Bay, O'ahu. 10 ft.

RINGTAIL SURGEONFISH · **pualu** · *Acanthurus blochii* Valenciennes, 1835

This is the smaller of two surgeonfishes called **pualu** in Hawaiian. It varies from light slatey blue to dark gray, almost black, usually with a white ring around the base of the dark blue tail. The Yellowfin Surgeonfish (above) can look similar. To tell the two apart, note the following features of the Ringtail: the entire pectoral fin is dark, the scalpel is long and not surrounded by pale blue, and there is little or no yellow in front of the eye. Both species feed primarily on the thin films of algae and diatoms growing on compacted sand. Both form large schools on occasion and often swim together. At night or when not feeding, both seek shelter on the reef. The species name honors German ichthyologist M.E. Bloch (1723-1799). To 17 in. Indo-Pacific. Photo: Hanauma Bay, O'ahu. 10 ft.

EYESTRIPE SURGEONFISH · **palani** · *Acanthurus dussumieri* Valenciennes, 1835

These large surgeonfish usually rest by day, typically under ledges or in sand channels. Their <u>bright white scalpels</u> immediately separate them from the Yellowfin and Ringtail Surgeonfishes (previous page), whose scalpels are black. The yellow eye-mark is conspicuous and extends as a band around the front of the head. The overall body color is light yellowish or grayish blue. The lyre-shape tail fin is a beautiful dark blue peppered with round black spots and may have a white or yellow ring at the base. The dorsal fin is yellow with bright blue margins. Large old **palani** have an unusually rounded snout. These fish prefer depths of 20 ft. or more, occur singly or in small groups, and feed over sand on algae and detritus. The Hawaiian name means "stink" because of the strong odor they produce when cooked. Because of the association with bad smell, the word also came to mean "detested person," or "outcast." To 18 in. Indo-Pacific. Photo: "Golden Arches," Kona Coast, Hawai'i. 25 ft.

Shall we dance?

Surgeonfishes are armed with a pair of forward-pointing spines at the base of the tail, one per side. Ordinarily, these knifelike "scalpels" lie flat in a groove. Although a surgeonfish cannot raise or lower them voluntarily, when it flexes its body the spine on the convex side lifts up slightly. In aggressive encounters, therefore, a surgeon will try to sideswipe a rival, bringing the spine tip into contact with its opponent's side. If the tip catches, the rest of the blade swings out, potentially inflicting a deep gash. To avoid this, sparring surgeons often circle each other warily, each trying to maintain a position on its rival's concave inner side, away from the partially exposed spine. Called "carouseling," this is a common avoidance tactic among other types of fishes as well. Photo: "Marty's Reef," Maui. 60 ft.

301

David R. Schrichte

ORANGEBAND SURGEONFISH
naʻenaʻe

Acanthurus olivaceus Forster, 1801

These unusual surgeonfish always have an orange band ringed in blue on the shoulder, and a white bar on the rear margin of the tail fin. The rest of the body can change color rapidly from entirely light olive to entirely dark, although a half-and-half pattern is most common. Tiny juveniles are entirely blackish except for the white bar on the tail. Some turn entirely bright yellow as they grow, and might be confused with Yellow Tangs. The orange band and darker coloration develop as they mature. Orangeband Surgeons graze over both sand and hard reef. They commonly join other surgeonfishes in large mixed feeding schools, or form schools of their own. Individuals often mingle with schools of resting Yellowfin and Square-Spot Goatfish, ready to feed on any wastes the goatfishes might produce. The species name means "olive color." The Hawaiian name refers also to a group of endemic shrubs and small trees, *Dubautia* spp. To 12 in. Pacific Ocean. Photos: (top) Hanauma Bay, Oahu, 40 ft. (middle) Palea Point, Oʻahu. 25 ft. (bottom left) Pūpūkea, Oʻahu. 30 ft. (bottom right) Hanauma Bay, Oahu, 30 ft.

juvenile ▼

juvenile ▼

THOMPSON'S SURGEONFISH
Acanthurus thompsoni (Fowler, 1923)

This small plankton-eating surgeonfish usually swims in midwater either singly or in small groups, occasionally in aggregations of hundreds. It varies from a uniform blue-gray to dark brown, almost black. There is a single black spot above the base of the crescent-shape tail. The species is perhaps most common along the Big Island's Kona Coast, but can be seen at most dive sites. Juveniles occur in beds of Finger Coral *(Porites compressa)*. The name honors John W. Thompson, a technician and artist at the Bishop Museum from 1901 to 1928. (Four Hawaiian fishes are named for Thompson, two of them endemic. He must have been quite a guy!) To 10 in. Indo-Pacific, but with a bright white tail fin outside Hawai'i. Photo: *Mahi* wreck, O'ahu. 60 ft.

a) adult ▲

b) juvenile ▼

BLACK SURGEONFISH [CHEVRON TANG]
Ctenochaetus hawaiiensis Randall, 1955

This unusual surgeonfish is greenish black and covered with closely-set fine longitudinal lines. The dorsal and anal fins are deep and sail-like when extended. Juveniles, often called Chevron Tangs, are cinnamon orange with bluish chevron markings and usually occur between 60 and 100 ft. in areas of heavy coral cover. Adults prefer shallower, more turbulent locations and often occur in pairs or loose groups. The species is uncommon in Hawai'i except on the Big Island, where it can be abundant. To 11 in. Pacific Islands, Pitcairn to Palau. Photos: (a) Pai'olu'olu Point, O'ahu. 20 ft. (b) Hōnaunau, Hawai'i. 60 ft.

303

Surgeonfishes of the genus Ctenochaetus *(the "c" is silent) feed mainly on organic detritus which settles on the reef, rather than on algae. This was discovered after observers noted that territorial herbivores, such as Hawaiian Gregories, do not bother to chase them away. Bristle-like teeth give them the alternate common name "bristletooth."*

b) yellow juvenile (with Yellow Tang below)

a) adult

c) juvenile

GOLDRING SURGEONFISH · **kole** · *Ctenochaetus strigosus* (Bennett, 1828) [GOLDRING BRISTLETOOTH]

A bright gold ring around the eye identifies this attractive fish. Its dark body is marked with many fine horizontal lines; the mouth is surrounded by blue. Juveniles, common in the summer months, vary from the adult coloration to almost entirely ochre or yellow (the latter resembling small Yellow Tangs). In old Hawai'i, these fish were placed under the posts of a new home to ensure good luck. Hawaiians considered their eyes especially beautiful, sometimes calling an attractive person **kole maka onaona** ("sweet-eyed kole"). The species name means "thin" or "meager." The Hawaiian name means "raw" (which is how it was eaten). To 7 in. The Goldring Surgeonfish was for many years considered to have an Indo-Pacific distribution with regional variations. It is now recognized as endemic to Hawai'i, with three similiar species inhabiting other areas of the Indo-Pacific. Photos: (a) Hanauma Bay, O'ahu. 30 ft. (b) Mākua, O'ahu. 30 ft. (c) Pūpūkea, O'ahu. 45 ft.

One of the Goldring Surgeon's most fascinating behaviors is turtle cleaning—at certain "traditional" spots on the reef these fish will eat algae off the shells of any Green Turtles that turn up. Many other surgeonfish species clean turtles as well. Puakō, Hawai'i, is a good place to see this (see p. 290). Photo: Hanauma Bay, O'ahu. 30 ft. (D.R. Schrichte)

a) adults ▲

b) juvenile ▼

YELLOW TANG · lauʻīpala
Zebrasoma flavescens
(Bennett, 1828)

Except for a white tail spine, these beauties are entirely bright yellow. So intense is their color that they are often seen from shore as they browse in the rocky shallows. Underwater, schools of these golden fish flowing over the reef are a sight unique to Hawaiʻi; although ranging as far as Japan and Guam, the species is only abundant here. Juveniles, thin and delicate as wafers, have greatly elevated dorsal and anal fins and are common in stands of Finger Coral *(Porites compressa)*. Unlike adults, juveniles are territorial and aggressive to their own kind. The more easy-going adults browse singly, in small groups, or in schools sometimes containing hundreds of individuals and often including other surgeonfish species. Sometimes they clean sea turtles, a particularly pretty sight (see p. 290). These fish may live 20-30 years! Partly white individuals, perhaps diseased, are sometimes seen. The species name means "yellow," the Hawaiian name, "yellowed leaf." To almost 8 in. Hawaiʻi, Marshall Islands, Mariana Islands, southern Japan. Photos: (a) Midway Atoll. 20 ft. (b) Hanauma Bay, Oʻahu. 30 ft. (c) Molokini Islet, Maui. (see also next page.)

Andy Schwanke

c) partly white individual ▲

305

Yellow Tangs. Hanauma Bay, Oʻahu. 25 ft. (see previous page)

Day and night in the life of a Yellow Tang

Paul Atkins, studying Yellow Tang social behavior at the Univ. of Hawaiʻi, noted that Yellow Tangs in Kāneʻohe Bay, Oʻahu, had tendencies for both social cohesion and aggressive dispersion, and that each tendency was dominant at different times. During the day the tangs' main activity was feeding. At this time they often gathered in groups, and aggression was largely suppressed. This social cohesion was strongest just before sunset and just after sunrise when the tangs moved together from their shallow feeding grounds to their deeper resting areas and vice versa. Not only did they travel together, but upon reaching their shelter areas at twilight they tended to mill about in groups, often around large coral outcrops. Immediately after sunset, however, the tangs' behavior changed dramatically and they began attacking both each other and other fish species. Atkins showed that the onset of this behavior was triggered by light levels and that a fish's aggression was most intense when it was nearest its shelter hole. He also determined that individual tangs often used the same shelter hole night after night and only rarely did two tangs utilize the same hole simultaneously. From this we might infer that during the day it's safer to stay in groups (the social cohesion tendency dominates), but at night it's safest to disperse and hide individually (the aggressive/repulsive tendency takes over).

But having reached their shelters, why would the tangs continue to mill about, exposing themselves unnecessarily to predators? Predators are most active at twilight, and surely, having reached its hole, a fish would be safest if it retired immediately. The answer is probably sex. Atkins noticed that these crepuscular aggregations were often initiated by large males which swam by other individuals already in their shelters and appeared to entice them out. Occasionally Atkins observed courtship and spawning during these crepuscular aggregations. Spawning, he reports, was exclusively at dusk and always in pairs. Atkins made his observations mostly in Kāneʻohe Bay, Oʻahu. William Walsh, observing Yellow Tangs along the Kona Coast of the Big Island, finds a slightly different reproductive pattern. He reports that large males station themselves along the twilight migration route and rise to initiate spawning with individual females as they pass by. Walsh also observes that spawning is always in pairs, never in groups.

Conservation success story

Yellow Tangs are Hawaiʻi's most exported aquarium fish, and one of the most traded animals in the world. As a result, their numbers have declined greatly over the years and large showy feeding schools of these fish started to become rare except in a few marine preserves. Other species are collected as well, of course. Many of them are surgeons, including Achilles Tangs, Sailfin Tangs, Goldrim Surgeons, and Orangespine Unicornfish. In total, hundreds of thousands of Hawaiʻi's prettiest reef fish are shipped out each year. In 1999, to give the targeted species some protection, the State banned the collection of all aquarium fish along nearly 150 miles of the Big Island's Kona Coast. Six years later, the Yellow Tang population off Kona had increased about 50 percent, and counts of the much rarer Chevron Tang (p. 303) had doubled. State biologist William Walsh is now recommending that all islands ban fish collecting along 20 percent of their coastlines. He also recommends statewide bans on a few specific species and perhaps a cap on the number of collectors.

SAILFIN TANG · **māneoneo** · *Zebrasoma velifer* (Bloch, 1795)

Named for their sail-like dorsal and anal fins, these lovely fish are banded with broad bars of brown and white which overlie a fainter pattern of orange-yellow bars. Pale yellow-white dots cover the face, blue surrounds the scalpel, and the tail is mostly yellow. When alarmed, Sailfin Tangs extend dorsal and anal fins, greatly enlarging their apparent size. They eat fleshy algae, and pairs defend a joint feeding territory. When driving away an intruder, they darken until the light bars almost merge with the rest of the body and the light dots on the face stand out. Females within pairs tend to be larger than males. Occasionally they form schools. The solitary and rarely seen juveniles have high, permanently elevated "sails." Juveniles occur mainly in quiet protected areas. Kāne'ohe Bay, O'ahu, is a good place to look for them. The species name means "carrying a sail," and the Hawaiian name translates as "itchy" or "irritating." (Some fishes, when eaten raw, cause an unpleasant sensation in the throat. This may be one.) To 15 in. Indo-Pacific. Photos: (top) Hanauma Bay, O'ahu, 5 ft. (lower right) Kahalu'u, Hawai'i. 2 ft. (lower left) Kāne'ohe Bay, O'ahu. 10 ft.

juvenile ▼

courtship coloration

Sailfin Tangs spawn in pairs, sometimes over their feeding territory. The male initiates proceedings by hanging in midwater over the reef until the female joins him. They then return to the bottom and after some erratic swimming and quivering on the part of the male, both rush toward the surface to release eggs and sperm. During this time both fish darken. The light bars on face and body remain distinct, and the light dots on the face stand out.

307

WHITEMARGIN UNICORNFISH *Naso annulatus* (Quoy & Gaimard, 1825)
   These rarely seen unicornfish vary from light bluish gray to almost black. They have bright white lips and an amazingly long slender horn that may equal the head in length. The rear portion of the tail fin is dark with narrow white stripes. Males sport long white tail filaments. Juveniles and subadults lack horns and resemble juvenile Sleek Unicornfish (next page), but with a white saddle or band at the tail base and a narrow white margin on the tail fin. (Paletail Unicornfish juveniles are also similar, but with more white.) Adults, although considered deep dwelling, have been seen by snorkelers off Kīhei, Maui. To about 3 ft. Indo-Pacific. Photo: Five Fathom Pinnacle (about 20 miles southwest of Niʻihau). 80 ft.

PALETAIL UNICORNFISH · **kala lōlō** · *Naso brevirostris* (Cuvier, 1829)
   These horned unicornfish are gray overall, with a white tail fin that contains a darkish spot. Larger adults have small spots and vertical lines on their sides and may have a broad whitish band behind the head. These fish typically aggregate high in the water, often in the company of Sleek Unicornfish (next page). Young fish, which have a short nub of a horn or none at all, browse on leafy algae in the shallows. As they grow, their horns lengthen, making it increasingly difficult to feed off the bottom. Eventually they move to deeper water and switch to a diet of plankton and occasional bits of drifting algae. The species name means "short-horned," although an old adult's horn may be almost the length of its head. Perhaps the original specimen was not fully grown. The Hawaiian word **lōlō** means "lazy" or "crazy." To 24 in. Indo-Pacific. Photos: (above) Hanauma Bay, Oʻahu. 5 ft. (opposite) Ulua Beach, Maui. 45 ft.

juvenile

GRAY UNICORNFISH
Naso caesius Randall & Bell, 1992

The same size, shape, and color as the more common Sleek Unicornfish (below) with which it may school, this fish varies from dark brown to bluish gray. Occasionally it "turns on" a pattern of vertically elongated spots—the only easy means of identifying it underwater. The species was not described and named until 1992, unusual for a fish of its size and wide distribution. Genetic studies confirm that it is distinct from the Sleek Unicornfish. To about 2 ft. Islands of the Pacific. Photo: Molokini Islet, Maui. 10 ft. (The Spotted Unicornfish, *Naso maculatus*, is somewhat similar, with many small dark brown spots. It occurs only below sport diving depths in the main islands, but in the northwestern chain it rises into shallower water and can be seen by divers.)

Sleek Unicornfish ▲

SLEEK UNICORNFISH · **kala holo**; **'ōpelu kala**
Naso hexacanthus (Bleeker, 1855)

These hornless unicornfish can change almost instantly from a metallic blue-gray to entirely dark. Plankton-eaters, they aggregate in midwater, usually near dropoffs, and can be difficult to approach. They also congregate around cave entrances, perhaps to rest, fleeing upon the approach of a diver. Groups of three or four often descend to be serviced by cleaner wrasses. When being cleaned, a Sleek Unicornfish usually pales to light blue, perhaps making parasites stand out (p. 351). When courting or chasing rivals, large males darken the front of the body and flash several highly contrasting white marks and bars. Spawning aggregations occur in areas of strong currents around the time of high tide. The species name means "six spines." The Hawaiian word **holo** means "swift." To 30 in. Indo-Pacific. Photos: (top) Pai'olu'olu Point, O'ahu. 30 ft. (opposite) Molokini Islet, Maui. 50 ft.

male courtship coloration

309

ORANGESPINE UNICORNFISH · **umauma lei** · *Naso lituratus* (Forster, 1801) [Naso Tang]

Bright orange lips, a graceful curve of yellow from eye to mouth (somewhat like a **lei**), and orange caudal spines identify this attractive hornless unicornfish. Common in shallow water, it feeds on leafy seaweeds, sometimes in schools. Large males have tail streamers. When chasing other fish the body darkens, the dull yellow mark on the forehead intensifies, looking almost like a headlight, and the pectoral fins turn yellow. One observer reports that the body turns sky blue for an instant during episodes of high aggression. The warning best be heeded because the orange, forward-curving tail spines are wickedly sharp (see below). Juveniles are dull in color compared to adults. These fish have been known to live as long as 12 years. The genus name, *Naso*, derives from the Latin *nasus* ("nose") while the species name means "erased" or "blotted out," perhaps in reference to the missing horn. The beautiful Hawaiian name combines **umauma** ("chest") and **lei** ("garland"). To 18 in. Indo-Pacific. Photos: (above) Hanauma Bay, Oʻahu 20 ft. (below top left) Magic Island, Oʻahu. 25 ft. (all others) Hanauma Bay, Oʻahu.

Mona Lisa smile ▲   wicked tail spines ▼

showing aggression ▲   juvenile ▼

BLUESPINE UNICORNFISH · kala · *Naso unicornis* (Forsskål, 1775)
    This is the horned unicornfish most commonly seen by snorkelers. It sports bright blue tail spines and a medium-size horn. (The horn is not long enough to force its owner into a planktivorous lifestyle, as is the case with some other unicornfishes.) Males have tail streamers. Small specimens lack the horn. When feeding it often darkens except for a light, often bluish patch above the pectoral fin, perhaps warning competitors to keep away. This fish is solitary or occurs in small schools, but may form large spawning aggregations in which the presumed males become almost black. In old Hawai'i its tough skin was sometimes stretched over a half coconut shell to make a small knee drum. The Hawaiian name means "thorn." To 27 in. Indo-Pacific. Photos: (above) Kahalu'u, Hawai'i. 3 ft. (below) Magic Island, O'ahu. 15 ft. (below, inset) Pūpūkea, O'ahu. 30 ft. (see also p. 289)

Bluespine Unicornfish aggregating to spawn   ▲ juvenile

311

TILAPIA
(Cichlidae)

Tilapias are a group of hardy, fast-growing freshwater and brackish water fishes native to Africa and the Near East which have been introduced to tropical regions around the world for food and other purposes. Many are, or were at one time, classified in the genus *Tilapia*, thus the common name. All tilapias are members of the enormous freshwater fish family Cichlidae—the second-largest fish family in the world and one of the most diverse. Cichlids are related to marine damselfishes and wrasses and, for freshwater fishes, can be quite colorful. For this reason, and because they provide parental care to their young and are easy to breed, many cichlids are popular in the freshwater aquarium trade.

Over the years, a number of cichlid species have been released by aquarists into Hawai'i's streams and reservoirs, many becoming established to some degree. Most of the tilapias, however, were deliberately introduced beginning with four species in the early 1950s brought in to control vegetation in irrigation canals, for possible use as baitfish, and also for human food and recreation. Of these introduced species, the Mozambique Tilapia *(Oreochromis mossambicus)* was at first the most successful, becoming almost ubiquitous in the fresh and brackish waters of the Islands. Salt-tolerant, it even entered the marine environment to a degree. It has since been largely displaced by the even more hardy and adaptable Blackchin Tilapia (below), which was introduced accidentally in 1965.

BLACKCHIN TILAPIA *Sarotherodon melanotheron* Rüppell, 1852 [SALTWATER TILAPIA]
    These dull silvery or faintly yellowish fish are named for the black coloration often present under the chin. When breeding, males may become darker overall. Originally from brackish estuaries and lagoons of west Africa from Mauritania to Angola, they were introduced to Hawai'i from New York in 1962 for possible use as a baitfish in the tuna fishery. After proving unsuitable, they escaped their holding tanks and spread quickly through the fresh and brackish waters of O'ahu. By the 1970s they were abundant in Lake Wilson in Wahiawā and various other O'ahu reservoirs, as well as in many lower streams and estuaries. Eventually they displaced the Mozambique Tilapia *(Oreochromis mossambicus)* as O'ahu's most common tilapia. Tolerant of high salinities that would quickly kill other freshwater fishes, they have penetrated protected coastal waters around O'ahu and now occur in such places as Pearl Harbor, Honolulu Harbor, the Ala Wai Canal, and along Waikīkī Beach. They seem to be staying close to shore in waters less than about 6 ft. deep and have not invaded the deeper reefs. Most likely they are not reproducing in the marine environment and cannot compete with true marine fish. Hopefully that will not change. A good place to see "saltwater tilapia" is near Kapahulu Groin on O'ahu's Waikīkī Beach, where you can easily spot them from shore as they swim about in small groups. To about 10 in. Widespread throughout the tropics and subtropics in fresh, brackish, and protected marine waters. Photo: Kapahulu Groin, Waikīkī, O'ahu. 3 ft.

Tilefishes, often called sand tilefishes or blanquillos, are a small family of slender elongate fishes that dwell in burrows or mounds which they construct themselves in sandy or rubbly areas. They typically hover several feet over the bottom and retreat to their holes if too closely approached. Small bottom-dwelling invertebrates and plankton are their principal prey. Tilefishes range in size from about 4 in. to 4 ft. Several of the smaller species are quite colorful. Out of about 42 species worldwide, one occurs in Hawai'i.

FLAGTAIL TILEFISH · **maka 'ā** · *Malacanthus brevirostris* Guichenot, 1848 [QUAKERFISH; STRIPED BLANQUILLO]

Often seen in pairs, these lovely bluish white fish swim by rippling their long dorsal and anal fins. They are very fluid in their movements, and can start or stop so abruptly that predators must have great difficulty catching them. They occur mainly on leeward shores in mixed sand and rubble not far from a burrow which they construct themselves using their mouths. Excavated material is usually piled in a mound nearby. If approached too closely they dive headfirst into their burrow. Bluish white overall, they have two black stripes on the tail fin which give them their common name (but see below for an alternate interpretation). The species name means "short snout." To about 1 ft. Indo-Pacific and Eastern Pacific. Photos: (upper) Pūpūkea, O'ahu. 20 ft. (lower) "Marty's Reef," Maui. 60 ft. Do not confuse this fish with the much smaller Indigo Dartfish (p. 84) which shares similar habitat.

As the name "flagtail" suggests, this fish has the amazing ability to hold its head perfectly still while the rest of its body waves behind it like a flag in the wind. - Crystal LaMer

Lagoon Triggerfish · **humuhumu-nukunuku-ā-puaʻa** · (p. 318)

Triggerfishes are named for the unusual arrangement of their first two dorsal spines. The first, thick and strong, can be erected and locked into place internally by the shorter second spine, the lower part of which fits into a groove on the base of the first spine. At the slightest sign of danger, a triggerfish typically dives into a hole or crevice, raises and locks its main dorsal spine, and becomes difficult to remove. In theory, if the second spine (the "trigger") is depressed, the locking mechanism will release, and the surprised triggerfish can be pulled from its refuge. This procedure is not recommended, however, as a surprised triggerfish can deliver a nasty bite.

Triggerfishes have tough skins and small but strong jaws and mouths. Their independently movable eyes are positioned high and about one third of the way down the body, enabling some species to attack long-spined sea urchins. Many are generalist carnivores, feeding on crustaceans, echinoderms, coral, molluscs, or whatever they can find; others are plankton-eaters. All swim principally by rippling their soft dorsal and anal fins, a method that enables them to easily maneuver backwards and forwards in small spaces. They have no pelvic fins, but the pelvic girdle can be extended to make the fish appear larger or to help wedge it securely in a refuge hole.

Demersal spawners, triggerfishes lay and fertilize their eggs on the bottom, and guard them until they hatch (see next page). Although normally wary and shy, they can defend their nests aggressively, charging and even biting humans who approach too close. The Titan Triggerfish (*Balistoides viridescens*) is such a ferocious nest guardian that experienced divers call it, only half-jokingly, the most dangerous fish in the sea. Luckily, it does not occur in Hawaiʻi. However, the Wedgetail or Reef Triggerfish (p. 317), common in the Islands, has occasionally been known to bite humans who encroach on its nest, as have the Pinktail and Lagoon triggerfishes (pp. 315, 318).

Triggerfishes belong to the order Tetraodontiformes, which includes several other curious fish families such as the filefishes, pufferfishes and boxfishes. Of perhaps 20 Indo-Pacific triggerfish species, 10 are known from Hawaiʻi and all are pictured here. In the Hawaiian language, triggerfishes are called **humuhumu** ("to stitch pieces together"), perhaps referring to the geometric patterns of the common Wedgetail Triggerfish.

FINESCALE TRIGGERFISH
Balistes polylepis Steindachner, 1876

Rare in Hawai'i except along the Kona Coast of the Big Island, this species was considered a stray from the Eastern Pacific until an adult guarding eggs (right) was photographed off Kona. Recently, it has been found in the Northwestern Hawaiian Islands and also in the Marquesas. Finescale Triggerfish are gray or brownish, either plain or with interconnected bluish gray markings on the head and body. They have been observed picking up rocks or blowing jets of water into the sand to expose prey. They have also been seen lying sideways, apparently to cover their eggs. To about 30 in. (about twice the length of any other Hawaiian triggerfish). Eastern Pacific, the Marquesas Islands, and Hawai'i. Photo: Kona, Hawai'i (Kendra Ignacio)

Triggerfish nesting

In most bottom spawning fishes, such as damselfishes or blennies, the males prepare the nests and guard the eggs. In triggerfishes the females take this role. Here's why: in most triggerfish species males maintain and guard a harem of females, and each female holds a small territory within the male's larger one. If a male had to guard a nest of eggs he would leave his harem open to the advances of rival males—clearly unacceptable! But even females are at a slight disadvantage when guarding eggs because they also have a small territory to defend. Perhaps for this reason, triggerfish eggs hatch in the shortest possible time. Generally they are laid and fertilized around dawn and hatch the following night.

PINKTAIL TRIGGERFISH
humuhumu hi'u kole
Melichthys vidua (Richardson, 1845)
[PINKTAIL DURGON]

These triggerfish are dark brown with a white tail which often has a pink tinge. The dorsal and anal fins are clear to whitish, beautifully rimmed in black. The pectorals are yellow. Although Pinktail Triggerfish do not school, their habits are otherwise similar to those of the Black Triggerfish (following page). They feed primarily on drifting algae and plankton, but will eat crustaceans, octopus, and even other fish if the opportunity arises. The species name means "widow," the Hawaiian name, "raw tail" or "red tail." To about 13 in. Indo-Pacific and Eastern Pacific. Photos: (right) Hanauma Bay, O'ahu. 50 ft.; (below) Transforming juvenile. Maunalua Bay, O'ahu. 25 ft.

Pinktail Triggerfish are usually skittish and quick to hide. However, females become bold when guarding their eggs (as in photo above), hovering over and around the nest with their dorsal spines erect, sometimes pushing out their pelvic region to increase their apparent size. Divers beware, they often bite!

◀*While transforming from the mostly transparent pelagic larval stage to bottom-dwelling juveniles, Pinktail Triggerfish become bluish with orange-yellow fins. Because they transform at an unusually large size, several ichthyologists have been fooled into describing these transforming juveniles as new species!*

BLACK TRIGGERFISH · **humuhumu ʻeleʻele** · *Melichthys niger* (Bloch, 1786) [BLACK DURGON]

Abundant on many reefs, these triggerfish are black with conspicuous light blue lines along the bases of the soft dorsal and anal fins. When the fish are aroused, iridescent blue lines radiate between their eyes like lines of a magnetic force field. If they become very agitated, their sides turn yellowish, and blue-green lines may form along the entire body. Black Triggerfish aggregate in numbers above the reef to feed on plankton and drifting algae. They will also feed off the bottom, and sometimes descend *en masse* to gorge on Hawaiian Sergeant eggs when the guarding parent is distracted. If threatened, they seek shelter in a crevice or hole. Both the species name and the Hawaiian name mean "black." To about 1 ft. The species occurs in tropical seas worldwide, although significant DNA differences between Atlantic and Pacific fish are likely to be found in future. Triggerfishes of the genus *Melichthys* are also known as durgons. Photo: Hōnaunau, Hawaiʻi. 20 ft.

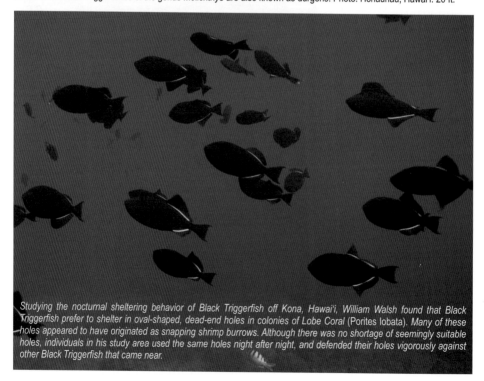

Studying the nocturnal sheltering behavior of Black Triggerfish off Kona, Hawaiʻi, William Walsh found that Black Triggerfish prefer to shelter in oval-shaped, dead-end holes in colonies of Lobe Coral (Porites lobata). Many of these holes appeared to have originated as snapping shrimp burrows. Although there was no shortage of seemingly suitable holes, individuals in his study area used the same holes night after night, and defended their holes vigorously against other Black Triggerfish that came near.

WEDGETAIL TRIGGERFISH · **humuhumu-nukunuku-ā-pua'a** · *Rhinecanthus rectangulus* (Bloch & Schneider, 1801)
[PICASSO TRIGGERFISH, REEF TRIGGERFISH]

Blocks of color, geometrically arranged, give this curiously patterned fish one of its common names—Picasso Triggerfish. A solid black wedge echoed by double gold lines marks the base of the tail. Blue and black bands between the eyes form a colorful "hat." The upper lip is bordered with intense blue and the pectoral fin base is bright red. The independently movable eyes are positioned high and about one third of the way down the body, enabling the fish, in theory, to attack long-spined sea urchins. More commonly, it feeds on small bottom-dwelling invertebrates, and is typically seen pecking briefly at the substrate, then swimming off ejecting a trail of sand and sediment from its gills. Although common on shallow reef flats, it is one of the most difficult reef fishes to approach or photograph. Females guarding eggs are an exception: they will charge an intruding snorkeler or diver, usually turning away at the last second. Occasionally, however, they will actually bite! If you are charged by a triggerfish, back off. Cute juveniles, paler in color, are seen during the summer months. The famous song: "I want to go back to my little grass shack ..." features this fish. In old Hawai'i, dark birthmarks on a child were ascribed to the mother eating **humuhumu** while pregnant. The descriptive phrase **nukunuku-ā-pua'a** means "nose like a pig." (The fish also grunts like a pig when threatened.) The alternate common names "Picasso Triggerfish" and "Picassofish" are loosely applied to several other Indo-Pacific triggerfishes of the same genus. This fish has survived as long as 14 years in captivity, and probably fares similarly on the reef. To about 10 in. Indo-Pacific. Photo: Hanauma Bay, O'ahu. 5 ft. (see also p. ix)

Hawai'i's State Fish: the story

*In 1984 the Hawai'i State Legislature asked the University of Hawai'i and the Waikīkī Aquarium to survey the public and come up with a candidate for a State Fish (there already being a State Bird, the nene, and a State Flower, the hibiscus). Newspapers picked up the story and teachers discussed it in classrooms. Eight candidate species were proposed and a heated pre-election campaign included a rally at the Waikīkī Aquarium during which staff members wearing giant fish costumes moved through the crowd extolling the virtues of their particular fish. Although scientific and cultural experts argued in favor of the **akule** and the endemic freshwater **o'opu**, childrens' **hula** groups dancing to the tune of the famous "little grass shack" song captured the hearts of voters. Out of more than 55,000 votes cast—some from as far away as Maine, Massachusetts, and Arizona—the **humuhumu-nukunuku-ā-pua'a** won with 16,577 votes, followed by the **manini** (8,742), the **lauwiliwili nukunuku 'oi'oi** (8,543), and the **hīnālea lauwili** (6,206). Lesser contenders included the **akule**, **moi**, **'āweoweo**, and **kala**, as well as the **kumu** and the **o'opu**. The story, however, does not end there: Displeased with the election, the experts persuaded the Legislature to limit the **humu**'s term to five years! After its term elapsed, however, few folks noticed and most continued to regard the **humu** as the official State Fish. In 1995 some freshwater **o'opu** enthusiasts proposed their fish as successor, arguing that the State Fish should be endemic to Hawai'i and should have cultural significance. However, the little brown stream fish, once a staple for Hawaiians but now scarce and largely forgotten, captured few imaginations. In 2006 the Legislature renewed the **humuhumu**'s status, and made it permanent.*

LAGOON TRIGGERFISH · humuhumu-nukunuku-ā-puaʻa · *Rhinecanthus aculeatus* (Linneaus, 1758)

Similar to the Wedgetail Triggerfish (previous page), this fish prefers a sandier, weedier habitat and is far less common. It sports a blue hat, yellow lips bordered with blue, and a yellow bridle. A black patch on the side is marked with diagonal white bands. A bullseye-like mark is conspicuous on the fish's back, when viewed from above. Rows of rough, file-like spines at the base of the tail face outward as protection when the fish retreats into a hole (true of all *Rhinecanthus*). Both sexes maintain territories and each male's territory overlaps 2-3 female territories. Pairs spawn around sunrise within a few days of the new or full moon. Females care for the eggs until hatching, which occurs just after sunset on the same day. While guarding eggs these fish can become quite aggressive. To 1 ft. Indo-Pacific. Photo: Hanauma Bay, Oʻahu. 5 ft. (see also p. 314)

> *While snorkeling in about 4 ft. of water, we had the following experience with nest-guarding lagoon triggerfish. First they swam next to us closer than normal. Then they made high speed bluff charges directly at my face. Then they hit my leg, arm, and hand in quick succession. Injury was minor, not more than a pinprick. We were so surprised! - Bruce & Jean Neal*

LEI TRIGGERFISH · humuhumu lei
Sufflamen bursa
(Bloch & Schneider, 1801)
[WHITELINE TRIGGERFISH]

Two curved bands running up from the base of the pectoral fin like strands of a **lei** give this fish its local name. The bands can quickly change from brown to gray or yellow, perhaps to signal their owner's emotional state. The body is grayish-brown and white, washed with yellow on the back. A thin white line runs diagonally from mouth to anal fin. These triggerfish usually forage singly, but pairs are often seen circling or chasing each other in some sort of territorial or sexual encounter, typically high off the bottom with one or both fish making repeated grunting sounds. Females can sometimes be observed guarding almost invisible eggs on the bottom, fanning them every few minutes by fluttering the pectoral fins while in a head-down position. To 8.5 in. Indo-Pacific. Photo: Three Tables, Oʻahu. 35 ft.

BRIDLED TRIGGERFISH
humuhumu mimi
Sufflamen fraenatus (Latreille, 1804)

Uniformly brown to blackish brown, this triggerfish often has a white ring around the tail base. Males, larger than females, have a white or yellow stripe running back from the corner of the mouth, like the traces of a bridle. Both sexes have a band under the chin. The young are light in color with a dark back. Though large, this trigger is exceptionally quick to hide at the approach of divers, sometimes even abandoning its nest and eggs to do so. If disturbed it makes a deep thumping sound. Hawaiians of old considered it a smelly fish, hence the name **mimi** ("urine"). The species name means "bridle." To 15 in. Indo-Pacific. Photos: Mākua, Oʻahu. 30 ft.

a) male ▲   b) juvenile ▲

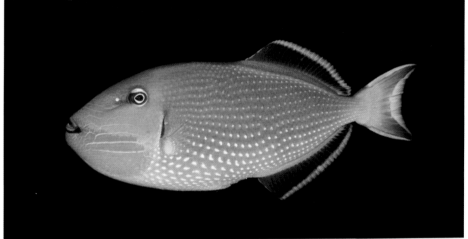

a) male ▲   b) female ▼

GILDED TRIGGERFISH *Xanthichthys auromarginatus* (Bennett, 1832)

All triggerfishes of the genus *Xanthichthys* have a series of longitudinal grooves on the cheek and are usually sexually dimorphic (males and females differ in color or form). Females of this species are gray with a white mark on each scale. Males are similar, but have a beautiful blue patch on the cheek and throat, as well as blue fins edged in gold. Plankton-eaters, they swim in midwater at depths of 30 ft. or more, and are seen most commonly along leeward shores. To almost 8 in. Found in scattered Indo-Pacific localities. Photos: (a) ʻEwa Pinnacles, Oʻahu. 50 ft. (b) Mākua, Oʻahu. 100 ft.

319

a) male ▲

b) female ▼

CROSSHATCH TRIGGERFISH
Xanthichthys mento
(Jordan & Gilbert, 1882)

Preferring deep water, these impressive triggerfish are rare at sport diving depths off the main Hawaiian Islands, but are not uncommon in the northwestern chain. Males have blue grooves on the cheek and a tail rimmed in red; the sides are light yellow, crosshatched in black. Females have yellow instead of red on the tail and are grayish blue crosshatched in black. Underwater naturalist Alex Kerstitch (1941-2001) reported being mobbed and attacked by these triggerfish at Mexico's Revillagigedo Islands. In the Northwestern Hawaiian Islands they sometimes surround divers, but are not known to show aggression. Crosshatch Triggers are mainly encountered in remote, generally subtropical locations such as the Revillagigedo Islands, Pitcairn, Easter Island, Japan's Ogasawara Islands, the Galapagos, and Hawai'i. To about 12 in. Sub-tropical Pacific. Photos: (a) Five Fathom Pinnacle (20 miles south of Ni'ihau). 90 ft. (b) Midway Atoll. 80 ft.

BLUELINE TRIGGERFISH *Xanthichthys caeruleolineatus* Randall, Matsuura & Zama, 1978

This triggerfish was not recorded from Hawai'i until 1993 when a fisherman caught one on hook and line at about 300 ft. Recognizing it as unusual, he gave it to the Bishop Museum where it was identified. Subsequent records have been made from similar depths by rebreather divers off Kahe Point, O'ahu, and the Kona coast of the Big Island. In 1997 diver Mike Severns observed several at 150 ft. off Molokini Islet, Maui, and photographed one of them, establishing that the species does enter scuba depths upon occasion. Males and females have the same color pattern: upper sides yellowish tan and lower sides light gray, the two colors separated by an irregular thin blue line running from the pectoral fin to the tail fin. The diagonal grooves and the cheek are blue. The Blueline Triggerfish is somewhat larger than the others of its genus, attaining about 13 in. It is known primarily from isolated oceanic islands in the Indo-Pacific and Eastern Pacific. Photo: Molokini Islet, Maui. 145 ft.

TRUMPETFISHES and CORNETFISHES
(Aulostomidae and Fistulariidae)

Pacific Trumpetfish · **nūnū** · Makapu'u, O'ahu. 30 ft.

Remarkably elongate, trumpetfishes and cornetfishes are the most common piscivores (fish predators) on Hawaiian reefs. Trumpetfishes are flattened side to side and so stiff that they scarcely bend as they swim. They look wide from the side and slender from above (unless they have just swallowed a meal). Cornetfishes, by contrast, flex back and forth as they swim. Flattened top to bottom, they look slender from the side and surprisingly robust from above

These odd but deadly daytime hunters become especially active in the early morning or late afternoon, carefully stalking small fish and literally sucking them into their tubelike mouths with a sometimes audible "whomp." Their mouths are capable of enormous expansion, permitting them to swallow prey as large in diameter as themselves.

Both belong to the order of tubemouthed fishes, Syngnathiformes, which also includes the pipefishes and seahorses. There are three trumpetfish species and four cornetfish species worldwide, with one of each in Hawai'i. Both received their common names from a fancied resemblance to musical instruments. They are sometimes called flutemouths. The scientific family names derive respectively from *aulos* ("flute") and *fistula* ("pipe"). In Hawaiian they are both known as **nūnū** or **nūhū**.

Bluespotted Cornetfish · **nūnū** · Villingilli, Maldives

PACIFIC TRUMPETFISH · **nūnū** · *Aulostomus chinensis* (Linnaeus, 1766)

Inflexible and sticklike, these elongated predators are usually gray or brown, but may be bright yellow or, less commonly, almost black. When stalking or attempting to blend with the background, gray-brown individuals can rapidly assume pale vertical bars, longitudinal stripes, or both. Longitudinal stripes are most common when the fish is hovering vertically or aligning itself with something long and thin; bars are preferred when it is horizontal. Bars are displayed to signal aggression. Trumpetfish feed mostly on other fish, but also take crustaceans. These sneaky predators ambush or stalk their prey, maneuvering slowly and carefully within striking range, sometimes from an almost vertical position. Their bladelike snout, which resembles the corner tool of a vacuum cleaner, can expand suddenly to engulf a fish the diameter of the predator itself. Trumpetfish swim stealthily by fluttering nearly transparent dorsal and anal fins set extremely far back on the body, out of sight of potential prey. They sometimes hunt by swimming closely alongside a non-predator such as a puffer or parrotfish, using it as a blind, or by skulking alongside a school of browsing surgeonfishes. When swarms of yellow Milletseed Butterflyfish attack a patch of Hawaiian Sergeant eggs, a yellow Trumpetfish will often turn up out of nowhere, taking advantage of its color and the general confusion to nab a small fish. A school of dark surgeonfish, on the other hand, may be accompanied by a black Trumpetfish. While easy to spot from the side, a Trumpetfish is almost impossible to see from the perspective of its prey—head on—allowing the predator to approach within inches. A barbel on its chin may serve as a final lure or distraction before the hapless victim is sucked headfirst into the long expandable gullet. Intent on the hunt, Trumpetfish often allow divers a close approach. If you get near a large one, look carefully for tiny crustacean parasites (probably caligoid copepods) swarming on its sides. To 27 in. Indo-Pacific and Eastern Pacific. Photos: Hanauma Bay, O'ahu. (see also p. 50)

How often does a Trumpetfish score? A study of the Atlantic Trumpetfish (A. maculatus) reported an 18 percent success rate—eight successful strikes in 45 attempts. The Pacific Trumpetfish, shown here with an unlucky Crown Squirrelfish, probably fares similarly. Photo: Hanauma Bay, O'ahu. (David R. Schrichte)

David R. Schrichte

Trumpetfish trumpery

Hanauma Bay, O'ahu, 15 ft. (pretending to be a Convict Tang)

Hanauma Bay, O'ahu, 25 ft. (hiding behind a Barred Filefish)

Pūpūkea, O'ahu, 40 ft. (pretending to be a lobster leg)

How do Trumpetfish do it? During a September dive at Kahe Point, O'ahu, John Earle witnessed a pair perform a leisurely 10-ft. spawning rise. Both were in a vertical position, with the larger twined in a sinuous curve around the smaller. After releasing eggs and sperm they separated and returned to the bottom.

More trumpery

Molokini Islet, Maui, 90 ft. (blending in with Black Coral)

Palea Point, O'ahu, 60 ft. (blending in with butterflyfish)

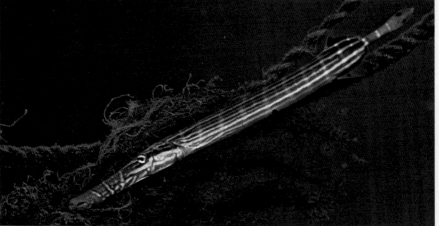

Makapu'u, O'ahu, 30 ft. (pretending to be a rope)

Hanauma Bay, O'ahu, 8 ft. (...not clear on the concept)

BLUESPOTTED CORNETFISH · **nūnū** · *Fistularia commersonii* Rüppell, 1838 [SMOOTH CORNETFISH]

Common on Hawaiian reefs, Bluespotted Cornetfish are encountered both near the bottom and in midwater. They may be solitary or in loose groups. Seen from the side, they look silvery and remarkably slender, but from above appear greenish and surprisingly stout. Ordinarily, the back is marked with light blue lines and dots, but when alarmed or stalking prey, the fish can rapidly assume a pattern of darkish bars. Unique to cornetfishes is a long whiplike filament trailing from the center of the tail fin. The filament bears sensory pores, but little else is known of its function. Unlike trumpetfishes, cornetfishes flex from side to side when swimming. Generally, only the rear third of the body flexes. When slowly stalking, however, they will "cock" themselves in a shallow, spring-loaded "S" shape, then lunge forward and engulf their prey. Cornetfish feed on a wide variety of fish, including, on occasion, spiny venomous lionfish. Sometimes they take squid and even shrimp. Less common on many reefs than Pacific Trumpetfish, Bluespotted Cornetfish grow much larger. They sometimes follow divers, and have even been known to hang around the legs of surfers as they wait for waves. If disturbed while resting at night, a Cornetfish will emit a honk reminiscent of a startled goose. The common name (often misspelled "coronetfish") refers to the cornet, a brass wind instrument something like a trumpet. The species name honors French biologist Philibert Commerson (1727-1773). To 4 ½ ft., including the tail filament. Indo-Pacific and Eastern Pacific. Photos: (above) Hanauma Bay, O'ahu. 3 ft. (below, in strike position with camouflage turned on) Mākaha, O'ahu. 30 ft.

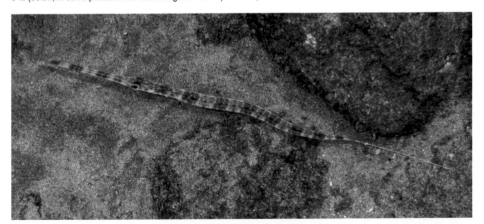

Smooth operator

Recent investigations show that the skin mucus of the Bluespotted Cornetfish contains large numbers of bacteria, many of which produce slippery polysaccharide compounds that reduce friction between the surface of the fish and seawater. Curiously, one of the common names in use for this species is Smooth Cornetfish.

Male Psychedelic Wrasse displaying to one of his females. Pai'olu'olu Point, O'ahu. 70 ft. (p. 329)

No account of coral reef fishes could be complete without the wrasses. Members of this large important family are ubiquitous on tropical reefs. Most have elongated bodies with one continuous dorsal fin, but they vary greatly in size and shape. All are carnivores or planktivores and all swim with winglike beats of their pectoral fins. Some are bold, in-your-face fish that readily approach humans; others keep close to cover and are seldom seen.

Characteristic of the family are bright gaudy color patterns that vary dramatically with age and sex. Because of this, wrasses have been one of the most complex families to classify. In the past, for example, males and females of a single species were often considered separate and were given different scientific names. (This happened with adults and juveniles as well.) We now know that individuals of most wrasse species begin life as females (the initial phase), and that later in life a few transform into males with a different color pattern (the terminal phase). These males are typically larger, more vividly colored, and more active than females. They hold a territory and spawn individually with the numerous females within it. Together, these females constitute a "harem." Should the male "harem-master" die, the dominant female changes sex and takes his place.

It is not always so straightforward. In some wrasse species, chiefly of the large genus *Thalassoma*, the initial phase consists of both females and males. Both sexes look alike, are reproductively mature, and regularly spawn together in a group. Even so, a few of the females will eventually change sex, becoming large gaudy "supermales" that establish spawning territories and mate individually with select females. With a few exceptions, these supermales are always sex-reversed females. Individuals "born" male almost never become dominant and are doomed to a life of mediocrity.

Wrasses have sharp teeth that often project slightly forward and are easily seen. Some have strong molars suitable for crushing hard shells, but most probably prey upon small crustaceans. One

Hawaiian wrasse feeds primarily on fish, several others on plankton. Possibly the most unusual with respect to feeding habits are the small cleaners, which pick parasites and mucus from the skin and gills of other fishes. These "cleaner wrasses" inhabit a specific territory, such as a coral head, and attract attention by swimming with a bobbing motion. Any fish pausing at the cleaning station will get serviced by them; they even enter the mouths of large fishes with impunity.

Most Hawaiian wrasses are small to mid-size, the biggest growing to about 20 in. In 1967, however, a "giant **hīnālea**" weighing 64 lbs. and measuring 3 ½ ft. appeared in a Honolulu fish market. Experts from the Waikīkī Aquarium identified it as a stray Humphead or Napoleon Wrasse *(Cheilinus undulatus)*, an enormous, chunky Indo-Pacific fish that grows to over 6 ft. in length and attains a weight of at least 400 lbs. Although these giant wrasses do not normally occur in Hawai'i, another was reported in 2001 off the Kona Coast of the Big Island at a depth of 120 ft.

During the day wrasses depend on speed and agility to escape predation; at night they seek refuge in holes and cracks, or bury themselves in the sand. A few species spend the night in tide pools. The general Hawaiian name **hīnālea** is applied to most, but not all; many of the smaller wrassses have no known Hawaiian names. In old Hawai'i, a pungent condiment was made using partially decomposed wrasses, crushed **kukui** nuts, and chili pepper; a person with bad breath was sometimes referred to unkindly as "a dish of **hīnālea** sauce."

The family name comes from the Greek name *labros*, also meaning "greedy." The word "wrasse" derives from either the Celtic *urach* or the Cornish *gwragh* (take your pick). With over 460 species in about 65 genera, the wrasses form a very large family, second only to the gobies. Hawai'i has 43 species (more than any other fish family), 19 of them endemic. Thirty-nine are described below. For easier identification, all sand-dwelling wrasses are placed together at the end of the chapter.

Belted Wrasse male. Kahe Point, O'ahu. 15 ft. (p. 347)

a) male ▲

PEARL WRASSE · 'opule ·*Anampses cuvier* Quoy & Gaimard, 1824

This wrasse gets its name from the female color pattern: dark reddish brown with lines of white dots like strings of pearls. Males are green with fine blue lines and marks, especially on the head and tail, sometimes with a light vertical bar on the side that intensifies during courtship. Although seen most often in bouldery areas close to shore, these fish also enter deeper water. Their diet consists mostly of small crustaceans and sometimes polychaete worms. The species name honors French zoologist and statesman Baron Georges Cuvier (1769-1832), who originally described many of the fishes in this book. The Hawaiian name means "variegated in color." The sister species of this endemic wrasse is the widespread *A. caeruleopunctatus*, which occurs almost everywhere in the Indo-Pacific except Hawai'i. To 14 in. Endemic. Photos: (a, b) Hanauma Bay, O'ahu. 3 ft. (c) Kahe Point, O'ahu. 30 ft.

b) female ▲

c) male courtship display ▲

Wrasses of the genus Anampses *have two flattened teeth at the tip of each jaw with which they strike the bottom to dislodge small invertebrates. The forceful blows often make an audible sound. Any sand ingested along with the prey is expelled through the gills. Photos: Pūpūkea, O'ahu. 15 ft.*

a) male ▲

PSYCHEDELIC WRASSE
Anampses chrysocephalus
Randall, 1958
[REDTAIL WRASSE]

This is one of Hawai'i's most distinctive endemic fishes. Males are brown with a splendid orange, blue, and yellow head. Females, dark brown with fine white spots, sport a red tail with a white bar at the base. Subadult females sometimes occur as shallow as 20 ft., but the spectacular males and their harems prefer somewhat deeper water. Females generally forage in a loose school of about a dozen while a lone male harem-master keeps watch from somewhere nearby. If they stray from his territory he brings them back into line, swimming rapidly among them with his dorsal fin raised high and tail fin clamped shut (a posture similar to that adopted by terminal male Saddle Wrasses when patrolling their spawning territories). Psychedelic Wrasses are not abundant, and it is always a treat to see them, especially the males. Neither sex survives long in captivity. The species name means "golden-head." (Look closely at a male and you will see a gold patch on its head above the pectoral fin. When females change into males, this gold patch is the last male color feature to appear.) To 7 in. Endemic. Photos: (a) "Deer Valley," south shore Maui. 40 ft. (b) Palea Point, O'ahu. 40 ft. (c) Kahe Point, O'ahu. 30 ft. (d) Pūpūkea, O'ahu. 50 ft. (see also p. 326)

b) females ▲

c) transitional male ▲

d) juvenile ▲

a) mature male ▲

b) transitional male ▲

c) mature female ▲

HAWAIIAN HOGFISH · **a'awa**
Bodianus albotaeniatus
(Valenciennes, 1839)

This fish is encountered most often as a juvenile or subadult female. Mature individuals of both sexes tend to live deeper than 100 ft., except off Kaua'i and in the northwestern chain where water temperatures are cooler. Juveniles, common in summer, have white tails and mostly black bodies with bright yellow on the upper head and back. As they mature, the yellow fades and the black recedes into a saddle-like spot under the soft dorsal fin, leaving a pale body with dark streaks on the head and many fine longitudinal lines. An elongate white mark under the eye gives the species its scientific name, meaning "white ribbon." Mature males become dirty reddish or purplish gray, often with light patches and dark blotches. The saddle spot may persist in a lighter color, often blue or white. This wrasse feeds mainly on hard-shelled molluscs, also urchins, crabs, brittle stars, and whatever else it can find. For many years it was considered a subspecies of the Saddleback Hogfish *(B. bilunulatus)* of the Western Pacific, which is pinkish instead of a yellowish in the female phase. To 20 in. Endemic. Photos: (a) Midway Atoll, 40 ft. (b) "Sheraton Caverns," Kaua'i. 50 ft. (c) Puakō, Hawai'i. 80 ft. (d) Pūpūkea, O'ahu. 30 ft. (e) Mākua, O'ahu. 20 ft.

d) subadult female ▲

e) juvenile ▲

Hogfishes are "primitive" wrasses distinguished in part by a smoothly curved lateral line with no abrupt turns. The common name comes from a Caribbean species with a piglike snout that it uses to root through sand and rubble. In many hogfish species juveniles act as cleaners.

SUNRISE HOGFISH
Bodianus sanguineus
(Jordan & Evermann, 1903)

Red with a yellow stripe from snout to tail along the upper side, this rarely seen wrasse has a prominent dark spot on the gill cover and another near the tail. It occurs mostly below 200 ft. in the main Hawaiian Islands, although cooler water temperatures in the northwestern chain bring it up to within sport diving depths. The juvenile pictured here was acting as a cleaner, readily servicing larger fish that came to it. Adults are usually in pairs, with one much larger than the other. The species name means "bloody." Adults attain 7 ½ in. Endemic. Photo: Corsair wreck. Midway Atoll. 115 ft.

a) male ▲

b) female (yellow color variant) ▼

c) color variant ▼

CIGAR WRASSE · **kūpou** · *Cheilio inermis* (Forsskål, 1775)
The long slender shape of this wrasse is unique in the family, and it is the only species in its genus. The fish may be light greenish brown, brown, or occasionally yellow. Males have a prominent patch on the upper side composed of irregular white, orange, and black blotches. These fish prefer sandy, weedy or rubbly areas, and feed on a variety of invertebrates. In the Red Sea they have been observed swimming closely alongside large surgeonfishes and other herbivores in order to approach their prey undetected. Trumpetfish often do the same; the similarity in shape, size, and even color of the two is noteworthy. The head lacks scales, thus the species name meaning "bare." To 19 in. Indo-Pacific. Photos: (a,b) Palea Point, O'ahu. (c) Mākua, O'ahu. 45 ft.

331

a) male displaying ▲

b) male at peak display ▲

c) male in typical swimming position ▲

d) female ▼

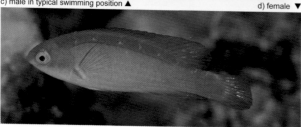

FLAME WRASSE

Cirrhilabrus jordani Snyder, 1904

These striking but elusive fish usually occur at depths over 50 ft. on mixed coral and rubble bottoms. Males are scarlet on the back and tail and yellow on the head and sides. The smaller females have pink sides and a series of faint spots above the lateral line that they can lighten or darken. Males engage in frequent and spectacular territorial and sexual displays, posing with head or tail down, flaring their fins, and flashing a pair of converging blue-white lines along the length of the body. Although absent from most dive sites, Flame Wrasses can be common where the right habitat occurs. Molokini Islet, Maui, is a good place to see them. At night they sleep in a mucus cocoon. The species name honors American ichthyologist David Starr Jordan (1851-1932). To 4 in. Endemic. Photos: (a, b, c) Molokini Islet, Maui. 80 ft. (d) Ka'ohe Bay, Hawai'i. 100 ft.

Wrasses of the genus Cirrhilabrus, *sometimes called "fairy wrasses," are known for their showy territorial and courtship displays during which males extend their fins, intensify their colors, and momentarily "flash" bright blue-white markings. Along with members of the similar genus* Paracheilinus *(not found in Hawai'i), they typically live in and over rubble patches and feed on plankton. Their social organization is haremic (numerous females dominated by a single male).*

a) male ▲

LINED CORIS · **malamalama**

Coris ballieui Vaillant & Sauvage, 1875

Although seldom seen around the main Islands, the Lined Coris is common in the northwestern chain. Females, faded yellow to rose marked with fine horizontal white lines along the scale rows, often have one or more yellow-brown markings on the head and upper side above the pectoral fin. Males at the height of their color are mostly mauve with iridescent blue lines and spots—the only Hawaiian fish to give an overall impression of blue. Their color is variable, though, and they often appear whitish or yellowish with blue lines and spots. Behind the head is a pale region often followed by a diffuse dark band. Lined Corises are sometimes attracted to divers who turn over rocks or otherwise disturb the bottom. At the approach of predators they will sometimes dive into sand. Males maintain harems and are territorial (probably true of most *Coris*). This fish appears to have no close relatives elsewhere in the Indo-Pacific and is considered a relict species. The name honors Théo Ballieu, a French diplomat with an interest in natural history who served in the Kingdom of Hawai'i at the time of King Kalākaua. Two other Hawaiian fishes bear his name as well, a scorpionfish and another wrasse. To 12 in. Endemic. Photos: (a) Moanalua Bay, O'ahu. 50 ft. (b) Kepuhi, O'ahu. 70 ft. (c) Makapu'u, O'ahu. 60 ft. (d) Midway Atoll. 115 ft. (e) Mākua, O'ahu. 50 ft.

b) male color variation ▲

c) mature female ▲

d) small female ▲

e) juvenile ▲

Wrasses of the genus Coris typically inhabit sandy or rubbly areas near reefs, feeding primarily on hard-shelled invertebrates that they crush with their strong teeth. Males usually have a prolonged first dorsal spine that they flick up in display. The genus is unusual in that most of the 25 species are endemic to small island groups or isolated geographic regions. Hawai'i has three.

333

a) female ▲

b) transitional male ▲

Victoria Martocci

c) mature male ▲

d) juvenile, yellow striped color variation ▲

e) tiny juvenile ▲

BLACKSTRIPE CORIS · hilu
Coris flavovittata (Bennett, 1829)
[YELLOWSTRIPE CORIS]

Mature females are white with three black stripes running lengthwise along the upper side. Males, which couldn't be more different, are mottled light blue-green overall. Juveniles are black with four or five white (sometimes, light yellow) stripes. In tiny specimens, the white stripes break up into spots and lines. This endemic wrasse is most abundant in the northwestern chain. In the main islands only subadults and juveniles are seen with any frequency. Large, mature females are uncommon and males are rare. The species name means "yellow striped" (from the unusual yellow-striped juvenile form). The Hawaiian name means "well behaved." Women who ate hilu while pregnant were said to bear quiet, refined children. To 20 in. Endemic. Photos: (a) Portlock Point, Oʻahu. 35 ft. (b) "Knob Hill," Lānaʻi. (Victoria Martocci) (c) Midway Atoll. 45 ft. (d, e) Pūpūkea, Oʻahu. 30-50 ft.

How the hilu got its stripes

An old legend relates that two gods, brothers, each took the form of a hilu. One of them was caught by fishermen and put on a grill. The other brother, taking human form, rescued it and released it into the sea, but not before the fire had seared it with the lengthwise stripes that persist to this day.

a) male (with unusual orange-red tail margin) ▲   b) female ▼

YELLOWTAIL CORIS
hīnālea ʻakilolo
Coris gaimard
(Quoy & Gaimard, 1824)

Females have reddish to greenish bodies speckled with brilliant blue spots, a bright yellow tail, and orange-red dorsal and anal fins edged with electric blue. Males develop a dark greenish tinge, with a light bar at mid-body and rarely a beautiful orange-red margin on the tail fin. Juveniles are bright red with a series of white saddles edged in black. As they grow, the colors change to the adult pattern from the tail forward; the white spot on the snout is the last to go. Juvenile coloration is somewhat fluid and a subadult harrassed by adults can temporarily revert to juvenile coloration. These fish are most common in areas where the coral reef is interspersed with small sand patches. Large adults will overturn surprisingly large rocks in search of the hard-shelled invertebrates upon which they feed. They will take urchins in their jaws and knock them sideways against rocks to remove the spines before eating them. The Hawaiian name means "brain-biting" (the fish was used in the treatment of head diseases). The species name honors Paul Gaimard (1796-1858), naturalist and officer aboard the French ship *Uranie*, which visited Hawaiʻi in 1819. Gaimard helped collect and describe many fishes in this book. To about 15 in. Eastern Indian Ocean to Hawaiʻi. Photos: (a) Kahaluʻu, Hawaiʻi. 5 ft. (b, c) Kaʻohe Bay, Hawaiʻi. 15 ft. (d) Puakō, Hawaiʻi. 40 ft. (e) Hōnaunau, Hawaiʻi. 20 ft. (f) Pūpūkea, Oʻahu. 30 ft.

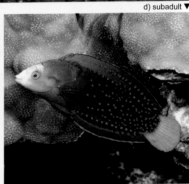

c) female ▼   d) subadult ▼

e) transforming juvenile ▼   f) juvenile ▼

a) male courtship display ▲

b) male courtship display, color variant ▼

c) female ▼

d) subadult ▼

e) juvenile ▼

ELEGANT CORIS
Coris venusta
Vaillant & Sauvage, 1875

These wrasses are common over mixed sand and rock, but their normally drab colors and smallish size attract little attention. During the winter months, however, when most courtship takes place, males spreading their fins in display can be gorgeous. Some are yellow on the head and forebody with blue and pink stripes on the head and rose stripes that break up into blue spots running about halfway down the body. Other males have a darker gray-green body with reddish stripes and chevron-like marks on the back half, and an orangish head bearing narrow green stripes. Females are greenish gray, yellowish, or reddish, with narrow blue and yellow stripes on the head. In females the black spot above the pectoral fin tends to be thicker and less narrowly crescent-shaped than in males. Juveniles and subadults, although highly variable, are usually whitish on the underside below the head. The species is named after Venus, Roman goddess of love and beauty. It belongs to a group of five closely related Indo-Pacific *Coris* species known as the *caudimacula* complex. To about 7 in. Endemic. Photos: (a) Magic Island. 20 ft. (b) Lāna'i Lookout. 30 ft. (c) Mākaha. 30 ft. (d, e) Pūpūkea, 10-15 ft. (all locations, O'ahu)

a) supermale

(b) initial phase (male or female)

(c) juvenile

BIRD WRASSE · hīnālea ʻiʻiwi · *Gomphosus varius* Lacepède, 1801

These unique wrasses have a long curved snout that they use to wrest crabs, shrimps, and brittle stars from crevices in the reef or from heads of branching coral. They also feed off the bottom on other invertebrates and even small fish. Supermales are dark green to intense blue-green with a light green bar above the pectoral fin. Initial phase fish have a whitish head and forebody with an orange-red wash along the top of the snout. The rest of the body is brownish gray darkening to almost black posteriorly, with a dark spot on each scale. Juveniles lack the long snout and somewhat resemble juvenile Saddle Wrasses. Bird Wrasses inhabit shallow reefs, often where Cauliflower Coral *(Pocillopora meandrina)* predominates. The species name means "different," perhaps reflecting the unusual body design. Fast moving and always on the go, these fish are difficult to photograph. Studies suggest that their pectoral finstrokes are amazingly similar to the wingstrokes of insects, and that they truly fly through the water much as insects and bats fly through air. The Hawaiian name refers to the ʻiʻiwi, or Scarlet Hawaiian Honeycreeper, an endemic bird with a long curved bill. To about 12 in. Central and Western Pacific (with a similar species in the Indian Ocean). Photos: (a, b) Hanauma Bay, Oʻahu. 5-10 ft. (c) Aliʻi Beach Park, Oʻahu. 15 ft.

Bird Wrasse love

Bird Wrasse spawning occurs at high tide and is easy to observe. During courtship a supermale intensifies his light green bar, becomes more bluish, and hovers 3-4 ft. off the bottom over a potential partner. To further attract her he periodically flutters his pectoral and tail fins. If ready and willing, she rises to join him and both make a sudden belly-to-belly rush toward the surface to release eggs and sperm. The female quickly resumes her normal activities but the male usually stays high in the water to attract another mate. Bird Wrasses are closely related to Saddle Wrasses and other members of the genus Thalassoma *and Bird x Saddle Wrasse hybrids have been reported.*

a) subadult female ▲

SLINGJAW WRASSE
Epibulus insidiator (Pallas 1770)

The mouths of most predatory and planktivorous fishes project forward when opened, but this wrasse takes the art to an extreme—its mouth "unfolds" into a tube half the length of its own body! It uses this specialized mouth to nab shrimps, crabs and fishes from between branches of coral. The Slingjaw Wrasse is particularly associated with corals of the genus *Acropora*, which in Hawai'i occur only around French Frigate Shoals in the northwestern chain. For this reason, it is extremely rare in the main Hawaiian Islands and probably does not grow to maturity here. (The fish pictured at top was about 6 in. long. See also the Chevron Butterflyfish, p. 48) More slender and deep-bodied than other Hawaiian wrasses, these fish are brownish in the initial phase, or occasionally bright yellow as shown here. Terminal males are darker with a pale head. Full grown adults attain about 12 in. Indo-Pacific. Photos: (a) Hanauma Bay, O'ahu. 15 ft. (b) Jaluit Atoll, Marshall Islands.

b) male ▲

a) male ▲   b) female ▼

c) juvenile ▲

ORNATE WRASSE · la'o
Halichoeres ornatissimus (Garrett, 1863)

These common wrasses are reddish salmon with iridescent green stripes on the face and green spots on the body. The dorsal, anal, and tail fins are bluish with green spots and lines. Females have two prominent black spots in the dorsal fin, males only one, and supermales none. Juveniles are dark reddish brown with light green body-length stripes of varying thicknesses and a pair of light-edged black spots (ocelli) on the dorsal fin. Generally solitary, these fish remain close to cover and feed on a wide variety of small invertebrates. The species name means "ornate," the Hawaiian name, "sugarcane leaf." To 6 in. Endemic (with similar species elsewhere in the Pacific). Photos: (a) Lāna'i Lookout, O'ahu. 30 ft. (b) Ho'okena, Hawai'i. 25 ft. (c) Ali'i Beach Park, O'ahu. 20 ft.

a) adults

HAWAIIAN CLEANER WRASSE *Labroides phthirophagus* Randall, 1958

These little fish glow with color. Adults of both sexes are yellow, blue, and magenta with a broad black stripe that widens from head to tail; juveniles are all black except for an intense blue or purple line along the back. Cleaner wrasses of the genus *Labroides* (five species in the Indo-Pacific) generally make their living by picking external crustacean parasites, dead tissue, and mucus from the bodies of larger fishes. The Hawaiian Cleaner Wrasse does the same, feeding most heavily on mucus. Individuals or pairs of these fish, but sometimes as many as five, establish permanent territories, typically near a prominent outcrop or under a ledge, attracting customers by flaring the tail fin and swimming with a conspicuous up-and-down bobbing motion of the rear body. Fish that come to be cleaned often assume odd postures (typically head up or down and fins flared) as the wrasses work them over. Often, they will change color, becoming either lighter or darker, possibly to make parasites stand out. Multiple fish waiting to be cleaned will sometimes form a line! Occasionally a cleaner will enter the mouth of a large predator with apparent impunity. At night, Cleaner Wrasses often encase themselves in thick mucus, as do some parrotfishes. The mucus is secreted by glands in the gill cover and might have antibiotic properties. The Hawaiian Cleaner Wrasse will not eat in captivity and eventually wastes away. The scarcely pronounceable species name means "louse eater." To 4 in. Endemic. Photos: (a) Hanauma Bay, Oʻahu. 3 ft. (b) Puhi Bay, Hawaiʻi. 25 ft. (c) Hōnaunau, Hawaiʻi. 15 ft. (d) Kahe Point, Oʻahu. 20 ft.

b) subadult ▲   c) juvenile ▼

d) Yellowfin Goatfish posing to be cleaned

Look, sweetheart, no hands!

How does a small fish impress his sweetheart? By riding a bigger fish! Prior to spawning, a male Hawaiian Cleaner Wrasse will sometimes "ride" a Saddle Wrasse that swims through its territory, maintaining a position just over the wrasse's dorsal fin for varying lengths of time. This can be repeated with several passing Saddle Wrasses and seems to be a signal to a nearby female that he is ready to spawn. During courtship, which may commence a week or more before actual spawning, the male circles a swollen female, then displays to her with a series of undulations, leaning away from her and flaring the magenta margin of his tail fin. She responds by contracting her body to form an S-shape (as viewed from above). The two may also chase each other and perform their bobbing dance. When ready to spawn both dart forward or upward a short distance, releasing their gametes in a small milky cloud. A pair may spawn more than once per day. Hawaiian Cleaner Wrasses are reproductively active throughout the year. Photo: Hanauma Bay, O'ahu. (David R. Schrichte)

Hawaiian Cleaner Wrasse factoids

• The Hawaiian Cleaner Wrasse feeds mostly on fish mucus, supplemented by the occasional crustacean parasite. Experiments suggest that, if given a choice, it prefers "cleaning" species of fish with the most abundant or nutritious mucus such as wrasses or parrotfishes. Technically, this makes it more of a parasite than a cleaner!

• As it inspects for parasites, a cleaner wrasse will drag its fins over its customer's body, gently stimulating it. Apparently this feels so good that a customer fish will regularly come to be "cleaned" even if it has no external parasites. On the other hand, the cleaner will occasionally nip a customer, causing obvious pain. Although the customer fish may flinch and swim away, it often returns to continue the session. Perhaps these painful bites occur in the process of removing a parasite, or perhaps the wrasse is feeding on a bit of live tissue.

• Laboratory-reared Hawaiian Dascyllus that have never before encountered a cleaner wrasse, will readily pose to be cleaned when a cleaner is placed in their tank, demonstrating that this behavior is innate, and not learned.

• The ecological importance of cleaner wrasses on a reef is not easy to demonstrate. When all Hawaiian Cleaner Wrasses but one were removed from a patch reef in Kāne'ohe Bay, O'ahu, there was no increase in the number of interactions with the one remaining cleaner. When absolutely all cleaner wrasses were removed from a similar reef, there was no decrease in the number of other fish on the reef and no increase in the number of parasites on those fish.

• Depending on circumstances, subadults can shift between juvenile and adult coloration. Juvenile coloration may protect juveniles from aggression by adults, while adult coloration may attract customers more effectively.

• Juvenile Ewa Fang Blennies often mimic juvenile Hawaiian Cleaner Wrasses, presumably to more easily approach their prey (see pp. 22-23).

• Hawaiian Cleaner Wrasses will sometimes pick at damselfish eggs on rocks within their territories, or growths on the shells of sea turtles. The author once had a hungry pair show considerable interest in his swim fins.

• A few other reef fishes (including juvenile Saddle Wrasses, juvenile Hawaiian Hogfish, Milletseed, Longnose, Blacklip and Pennant Butterflyfish, Redstripe and Bluestripe Pipefish, and, rarely, Bandit Angelfish and Blue-Eye Damselfish) will clean other fish on occasion, presumably removing parasites, but this is strictly part-time (facultative) work. The Hawaiian Cleaner Wrasse is the only full-time (obligate) cleaner fish in Hawai'i.

Cleaner Wrasse gallery 1
(courtesy of Mike Roberts)

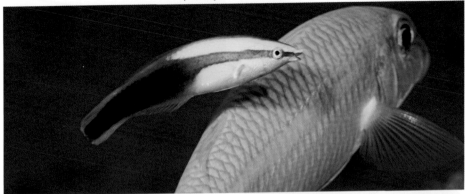

Open for business

Negotiation

Gill job

Root canal

photos & captions by Mike Roberts

Cleaner Wrasse gallery 2

With Achilles Tangs (note color change)

With a Whitemouth Moray

D.R. Schrichte

With an Undulated Moray (ooh that tickles!)

With a Pyramid Butterflyfish (a Thompson's waits in line)

Investigating aurthor's fins

With a Gray Reef Shark

Andy Schwanke

a) male

SHORTNOSE WRASSE
Macropharyngodon geoffroy
(QUOY & GAIMARD, 1824)
[POTTER'S WRASSE]

These handsome wrasses are orange, covered with iridescent blue spots and lines. Although both sexes are similar, male harem-masters are larger and have a more prominent red spot at the front of the dorsal fin. When patrolling their territories or keeping their females in line, males darken, develop a dusky bar down the center of the body, and flick up their dorsal fin to show the red spot. While swimming above their territories at high tide in typical wrasse courtship display, they darken even more, especially at the front of the body, becoming gray with no traces of red color except for the spot on the dorsal fin. Only moderately common, these fish feed largely on marine snails, whose shells they crush with their big molars. In captivity they usually waste away, perhaps because of an insufficient diet. The species name honors the great French zoologist Etienne Geoffroy St. Hilaire (1772-1844). To 6 in. Endemic (with sister species *M. meleagris* elsewhere in the Pacific). Photos: (a) Magic Island, O'ahu. 25 ft. (b-d) Mākua, O'ahu.

b) older juvenile

c) young juvenile

d) male chasing after a straying female

Shortnose Wrasses often swim with their dorsal and anal fins extended, giving them a deep-bodied appearance; because of their shape and color they are sometimes mistaken at first glance for Potter's Angelfish (p. 4). Some people even call them "Potter's Wrasse," suggesting that they mimic the angelfish. However, the two species are rarely seen together and have quite different lifestyles—the wrasse swims openly over the reef whereas the angelfish remains within its small territory and seldom strays far from cover. Mimicry is unlikely between these two species.

a) adult ▲   b) adult color variation ▼   c) juvenile ▼

d) subadult ▼   e) juvenile ▼

Mike Roberts

ROCKMOVER WRASSE *Novaculichthys taeniourus* (Lacepède, 1801) [DRAGON WRASSE]
    Juveniles of this species, often called Dragon Wrasses, are among the most unusual fishes on the reef. Filamentous fin extensions and peculiar swaying and twisting motions help them resemble drifting seaweed. Most are brown with white blotches, but occasional green ones are seen. As they grow, they lose the fin filaments, becoming dark brown with white marks on each scale and a white bar through the tail, and sometimes a pinkish belly. Some, perhaps males, become grayish with a yellow pectoral spot. Large adults spend much of their time nosing about the bottom, often actually moving or overturning rocks in search of invertebrate prey. The species name means "ribbonlike" because of the juvenile form. To 12 in. Indo-Pacific and Eastern Pacific. Photos: (a) Molokini Islet, Maui. 30 ft. (b) Kahalu'u, Hawai'i. 5 ft. (c) Maui. (d,e) Hanauma Bay, O'ahu 8 ft., 30ft.

courting male ▲ (note black on rear lobes of dorsal and anal fins)

RINGTAIL WRASSE · po'ou
Oxycheilinus unifasciatus (Streets, 1877)

Predators of other fish, these large wrasses are typically seen hovering head down several feet off the bottom, ready to strike. They also eat crustaceans and echinoderms. Their color is variable, can change rapidly, and has little to do with sex. They can be dark on the back and light on the underside, uniformly colored, or mottled. A white ring around the base of the tail, usually present (and reported to be wider and more distinct in males), can disappear in seconds. The only constant markings are two narrow stripes from eye to pectoral fin, sometimes faint. In courting males the area inside these double stripes becomes a highly contrasting white or greenish and the rear lobes of the soft dorsal and anal fins darken. This fish has caused ciguatera poisoning in Hawai'i. The species name means "one bar," referring to the tail ring. To 18 in. Central and Western Pacific. Photos: (upper two) Hanauma Bay, O'ahu. 25-30 ft. (opposite) Leleiwi, Hawai'i. 30 ft.

subadult ▲

While diving at Molokini I spotted a Ringtail Wrasse that had caught a Yellowtail Filefish tail first. It seemed to be having trouble swallowing it. The wrasse then rammed the filefish repeatedly against the wall to get it all the way in, and eventually succeeded. - Crystal LaMer

a) male in courtship display ▲

b) female ▼

c) juvenile   Pauline Fiene

TWOSPOT WRASSE · *Oxycheilinus bimaculatus* (Valenciennes, 1840)

Males and females of this wrasse are similar, although males are often light greenish brown, while females are reddish and darker. Both have delicately colored spots and lines, intensified in males during courtship. Males have a distinct wedge-shape tail fin with a backward pointing spikelike projection at the top. In both sexes the tail fin is often held closed, appearing pointed. These wrasses live on rubble and sand bottoms, often near seaweed; they seldom occur over coral. The species name ("two spots") refers to a pair of dark spots, one in the center of the side, the other (rarely conspicuous) just behind the eye. To 6 in. Indo-Pacific. Photos: (a) Mākua, Oʻahu. 40 ft. (b) Magic Island, Oʻahu. 30 ft. (c) "Landing Craft," South Maui. 50 ft. (Pauline Fiene)

Male Twospot Wrasses maintain harems. Patrolling his territory, a male swims rapidly with his pectoral fins, keeping his dorsal and anal fins folded. Finding a female, he stops, turns broadside, and spreads his fins. If ready to spawn, she rises slightly off the bottom. He flutters his fins and both rush upwards to release eggs and sperm.

346

PENCIL WRASSE
Pseudojuloides cerasinus
(Snyder, 1904)
[SMALLTAIL WRASSE]

Males are blue and green, striped lengthwise with even brighter blue and yellow. Females are rosy red. Both prefer depths of 40 ft. or more and occur most often over rubble. Dominant males of this active species keep loosely structured harems and display to their females by flicking the first few rays of their dorsal fin up and down. Although endemic to Hawai'i, it belongs to a species complex that includes 6 similar Indo-Pacific fish. The species name means "cherry color," obviously from the female form. To almost 5 in. Photos: (a) Lahilahi Point, O'ahu. 50 ft. (b) Magic Island, O'ahu. 30 ft.

a) male ▲

b) female) ▼

BELTED WRASSE · 'omaka
Stethojulis balteata
(Quoy & Gaimard, 1824)

Supermales are green with several vivid blue lines on head and body, a broad orange stripe from pectoral fin to tail, and an orange dorsal fin. The top of the head becomes yellow when they are aroused. Initial phase adults (both sexes) are gray stippled with fine white spots, with a bright yellow spot at the base of the pectoral fin. Fast-moving and always on the go, these fish feed on a wide variety of small invertebrates that they pluck from the sand or rubble. As they rise off the bottom a trail of fine sediment often emerges from their gill openings. Following the typical wrasse pattern, they spawn during daytime high tides, typically at the downcurrent ends of reefs. Terminal males spawn individually with females, initial phase adults spawn in groups. These fish do poorly in captivity. The species name means "girdled" or "belted." To almost 6 in. Endemic (with sister species *S. bandanensis* elsewhere in the Pacific.) Photos: (a) Palea Point, O'ahu. 30 ft. (b) Kahe Point, O'ahu. 15 ft. (c) Makapu'u, O'ahu. tide pool. (see also p. 327)

a) supermale ▲

b) initial phase (male or female) ▼

c) juvenile ▼

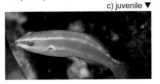

DISAPPEARING WRASSE
Pseudocheilinus evanidus
Jordan & Evermann, 1903

These small wrasses are red with many fine white lines along the length of the body and a blue-white streak under the eye. Sometimes pale bars develop along the sides. They are found in coral-rich areas and seldom stray far from cover. The sexes differ mainly in size, with larger specimens always male. The first scientific specimen was collected from a deep tide pool near Hilo, but normally this shy fish is seen only at scuba depths. The species name means "disappearing," presumably because of the fish's retiring nature. To about 3 in. Indo-Pacific. Photo: Hōnaunau, Hawai'i. 40 ft.

EIGHTLINE WRASSE
Pseudocheilinus octotaenia
Jenkins, 1901

Yellowish tan to pinkish, this wrasse has eight dark lines along its body. A color variation has white lines and rows of dark elongate blotches. (This is the predominant color pattern at some Indo-Pacific localities, such as Christmas Island, Kiribati.) The sexes differ only in size, males always larger. Although this is the boldest member of its genus in Hawai'i, it seldom ventures far into the open. It feeds on crabs and other invertebrates. The species name means "eight lines." To 5 in. Indo-Pacific, with regional color differences. Photos: (upper) Hōnaunau, Hawai'i. 70 ft. (lower) Pu'u Olai, Maui. 45 ft.

typical color ▲

color variant ▼

FOURLINE WRASSE
Pseudocheilinus tetrataenia
Schultz, 1960

These shy beauties are brown with four blue lines on the upper side and a blue-white diagonal streak from the snout to the pelvic fin, which is violet. Divers usually glimpse them only as they dart from one crevice to another. They spawn from approximately December to July during twilight. The species name means "four lines." To 2 ¾ in. Pacific Ocean, but limited to the cooler waters north and south of the Equator (antiequatorial). Photo: Kahe Point, O'ahu. 15 ft.

a) supermale ▲

b) initial phase (male or female) ▼

OLD WOMAN WRASSE
hīnālea luahine [BLACKTAIL WRASSE]
Thalassoma ballieui
(Vaillant & Sauvage, 1875)

Like many Hawaiian endemics, these large wrasses are most common in the northwestern chain. They have little fear of humans and can eat almost anything, including spiny sea urchins. Initial-phase adults (both sexes) are grayish with a thin reddish vertical line on each scale. Terminal males are similar with a darker head, dull blue under the chin, and a black tail. Small juveniles are green, turning yellow as they approach adulthood. The species name honors Théo Ballieu, a French diplomat to the Kingdom of Hawai'i at the time of King Kalākaua. Monsieur Ballieu, who had an interest in natural history, provided specimens, and perhaps hospitality, to the French scientists who named the fish in his honor. Two other Hawaiian fishes bear his name as well, a scorpionfish and another wrasse. The Hawaiian name means "old woman." To about 15 in. Endemic. Photos: (a, b) Hanauma Bay, O'ahu. 3-10 ft. (c) Mākaha, O'ahu. 25 ft. (d) Magic Island, O'ahu. 20 ft.

c) subadult ▼

d) juvenile ▼

At Midway Atoll I once saw a Hawaiian Green Lionfish wandering across the bottom. An Old Woman Wrasse attacked it but the lionfish was too big to fit into its mouth, so other fish joined in and they tore it apart. - Crystal LaMer

No spring chicken
The ancient Hawaiians may have been on to something when they named this fish "old woman." DNA studies reveal Thalassoma ballieui *to be one of the two oldest species in the genus* Thalassoma, *ancestral to Hawai'i's endemic Saddle Wrasse and almost all other species in this large and important genus.*

a) supermale ▲

b) initial phase (male or female) ▲

c) juvenile ▼

SADDLE WRASSE · hīnālea lauwili
Thalassoma duperrey
(Quoy & Gaimard, 1824)

These ubiquitous wrasses occur from the shallows down to about 70 ft. Initial phase adults (both sexes) have a dark blue-green head followed by a band of dull orange that intensifies during spawning. The rest of the body is blue-green with numerous narrow magenta vertical lines. Terminal males have a diffuse white bar behind the orange band and a crescent-shape (lunate) tail fin. They can turn the white bar on and off. Juveniles are whitish with a dark stripe running from snout to the tail. Small adults can revert to juvenile coloration to avoid harassment by larger adults. Adults feed on a wide variety of small invertebrates. The species name honors physicist Louis Isodore Duperrey (1786-1865), 2nd lieutenant aboard the French ship Uranie, which visited Hawai'i in 1819. J.R.C. Quoy and Paul Gaimard, who described and named this wrasse (as well as a great many other fishes and invertebrates), were officers on the same ship. Duperrey later commanded his own scientific expedition around the world. The Hawaiian name means "leaf of the **wiliwili** tree." To 10 in. Endemic. Photos: (a) Hanauma Bay, O'ahu. 25 ft. (b, c) Kahe Point, O'ahu. 15-20 ft.

Saddle Wrasses as cleaners

Juvenile and small adult Saddle Wrasses sometimes establish cleaning stations for other fish, much like those of the Hawaiian Cleaner Wrasse (see next page). They even copy the bobbing "dance" of a cleaner wrasse to entice customers. Although adults rarely if ever clean fish, they sometimes clean Green Turtles by eating tiny parasitic barnacles (Platylepas hexastylos) that grow on the turtles' skin.

Saddle Wrasse juvenile cleaning Sleek Unicornfish at Molokini Islet, Maui

Saddle Wrasse social life and reproduction

Saddle Wrasses on a given reef feed within home ranges that overlap widely. They do not hold permanent territories or form harems or schools. For about two hours around high tide each day, large terminal males gather at traditional spawning sites, usually at the downcurrent ends of shallow reef tops, where they set up temporary territories. Holding dorsal fins erect, tail fins clamped, and brightening their white bar, these supermales actively patrol their turf, chase away rival males, and perform courtship displays. Females migrate from all over the reef to join them. A supermale may dash up and down vertically, loop, circle, flutter his fins or quiver above or around his potential partner, eventually spawning with her in a paired upward rush. Successful supermales spawn with up to 20 females a day; these females spawn at most once a day with any male they fancy, often returning to the same partner. Other females prefer group sex, spawning once a day with up to about

40 small initial phase males in a single upward rush. Group spawning occurs primarily on shallow protected reefs where visibility is poor. To ensure social balance, females change into supermales when they grow larger than a certain proportion of other females within their home range. As far as is known, however, initial phase males never enter the terminal stage.

Group spawning at Puhi Bay, Hawai'i. 25 ft

a) supermale ▲

b) transitional supermale? ▲ Victoria Martocci

c) initial phase (male or female), probably with some Saddle Wrasse ancestry ▲

SUNSET WRASSE
Thalassoma lutescens
(Lay & Bennett, 1839)

This wrasse is evidently named for the warm gold coloration of the initial phase. Large terminal males are brilliant green with a salmon-pink head that bears irregular green stripes. The fins are combinations of yellow, blue, green and pink. Seen in bright sunlight these supermales are breathtaking—the intensity of their color is never adequately caught in photographs. Although rare in Hawai'i, they are common on shallow reefs elsewhere in the Indo-Pacific, and also at Johnston Atoll. In Hawai'i (and at Johnston) they often hybridize with the closely related Saddle Wrasse (previous page). The hybrids themselves are fertile, and it is likely that many if not all Sunset Wrasses in the Islands have "mixed blood." The species name means "yellow" (after the initial phase). To 7 ½ in. Indo-Pacific. Photos: (a) Kealakekua Bay, Hawai'i. 10 ft. (b) "Wash Rock," Lāna'i. 60 ft. (Victoria Martocci). (c) "Golden Arches," Kona, Hawai'i. 20 ft.

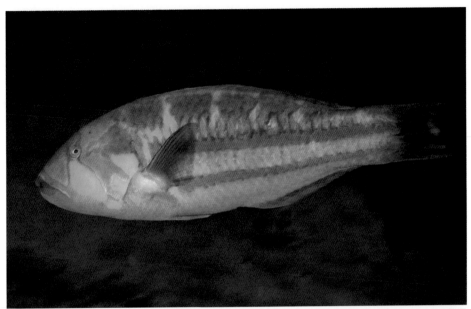

a) supermale ▲

b) initial phase (male or female) ▼

SURGE WRASSE · **hou** · *Thalassoma purpureum* (Forsskål, 1775)

These large, fast-moving wrasses typically inhabit shallow water in areas where wave action is strong, but can venture down to at least 90 ft. Terminal males are green with broad pink marks on the head and ladderlike pink marks on the sides. Initial phase adults (both sexes) resemble large initial phase Christmas Wrasses (page 355) but have a distinctive "Y" or "V" mark between eye and mouth. As a feeding strategy, these fish will sometimes swim briefly alongside a large surgeonfish or parrotfish so as to approach their prey of crabs and fish undetected. They also eat sea urchins, including the thick-spined Red Pencil Urchin. Surge Wrasses are not common in Hawai'i, perhaps because they readily take a baited hook. They are also one of the most difficult Hawaiian fish to photograph. The species name means "purple." To 16 in. Indo-Pacific. Photos: (a) Kahalu'u, Hawai'i. 5 ft. (b) Kahe Point, O'ahu. 10 ft.

*Prized as food in ancient times, **hou** were caught at night in the large tide pools where they sometimes sleep. Old accounts relate that they snore like human beings, and one legend describes them as the "celebrated snoring fish." These nocturnal noises were said to be easy to hear if one approached quietly, making Surge Wrasses easy to catch with torch and spear.*

353

a) supermale courtship display ▲

b) supermale ▲   c) initial phase (male or female) ▼

d) supermale with probable Saddle Wrasse ancestry, courtship display ▼

FIVESTRIPE WRASSE
Thalassoma quinquevittatum
(Lay & Bennett, 1839)

The initial and terminal phases of this wrasse are similar. The head is magenta with curved green lines and stripes and the body is green with ladderlike magenta marks. Around high tide during the day, however, supermales shift into high gear, turning bright yellow on the sides, intensifying the colored stripes on the head, darkening the tips of their pectoral fins, and racing about their comparatively large territories to attract mates and repel intruders such as male Saddle Wrasses (there seldom being other males of their own species to chase). This dramatic color change lasts for the duration of courtship, an hour or more. Males may turn on their yellow sides at other times too. First recorded from Hawai'i in 1980, the species is uncommon in the Islands. Like most other wrasses of the genus *Thalassoma*, it prefers shallow reefs and is not averse to surge. It sometimes interbreeds with the Saddle Wrasse (see photo opposite). The species name means "five stripes." To about 5 in. Indo-Pacific. Photos: (a, b, d) Kahe Point, O'ahu. 10-15 ft. (c) Ho'okena, Hawai'i. 10 ft.

a) supermale ▲   b) initial phase (male or female) ▼

CHRISTMAS WRASSE · 'awela
Thalassoma trilobatum
(Lacepède, 1801)

These fast-moving wrasses inhabit shallow reefs, often in the surge zone, where they feed mostly on crabs and molluscs. Terminal males have bright ladderlike blue-green markings on a reddish body. The brown and green initial phase adults (both sexes) are smaller and drab by comparison. At night these fish sometimes sleep in tide pools, presumably for safety. Juveniles occur in tide pools. Adults spawn daily during daytime high tides. Drab initial phase fish of both sexes aggregate at specific sites, often a large coral head or other landmark, to spawn in groups. Terminal males hold spawning territories scattered more widely along the top of the reef and mate with individual females. To advertise themselves these males intensify their colors, often becoming more reddish and turning their pectoral fins blue-black. They swim back and forth in an excited manner high off the bottom, pausing now and again to flutter their blue-black pectoral fins in an exaggerated and conspicuous display. The Hawaiian word 'awela also means "heated" or "hot." At least nine other Hawaiian names have been applied to this wrasse, some to designate different growth stages. To about 12 in. Indo-Pacific. Photos: (a) Hanauma Bay, O'ahu. 3 ft. (b) Pūpūkea, O'ahu. 10 ft.

Rudie Kuiter

WHITEBANDED SHARPNOSE WRASSE ▲
Wetmorella albofasciata Schultz & Marshall, 1954

This small pretty wrasse hides far back in caves and under ledges, thus is almost never seen. Its brown body is marked with several white lines radiating from the eye, two white bars on the body, and several dark ocelli. To about 2 ¼ in. Indo-Pacific. Photo: Tomini Bay, Sulawesi, Indonesia. (Rudie Kuiter)

FORKTAIL SAND WRASSE
Ammolabrus dicrus
Randall & Carlson, 1997

These small slender schooling fish live over sand away from reefs, feed on plankton, and dive into the sand when threatened. Fast and difficult to approach, they are similar in lifestyle and appearance to Pyle's Sandlance (p. 242). Hawai'i and Wake Island. To about 3 ½ in. Photos: (left) Kahe Point, O'ahu. 30 ft. (below) fright coloration before diving into sand. Pūpūkea, O'ahu. 70 ft.

HAWAIIAN KNIFEFISH
Cymolutes lecluse
(Quoy & Gaimard, 1824)

These pearly white sand-diving wrasses are less deep-bodied than the razor wrasses (next page) that share their habitat. Males have a tiny blue-edged dark spot high on the upper side, about mid-body; females have a dark spot high on the base of the tail. Juveniles, slightly barred and some-times mottled, often have dark spots in both locations. These fish prefer sandy areas with some current not far from the edge of the reef. They typically live in small groups consisting of a male and 3-5 females. To about 8 in. Endemic. Photos: Kahe Point, O'ahu. 25-30 ft.

male ▲   ▼ juveniles ▼

◄ INDO-PACIFIC KNIFEFISH
Cymolutes praetextatus
(Quoy & Gaimard, 1834)

Because of its similarity to the Hawaiian Knifefish (above), this spe-cies went unrecognized in the Hawaiian Islands until 2005. It differs from the latter by having faint gray or brown bars on the rear half of the body and a faint brownish or salmon-pink stripe along the upper back. Males have a light-edged black spot high on the side. Females smaller than about 3 in. have a black spot above the base of the tail fin. To about 8 in. Indo-Pacific. Photo: Mākena, Maui, 100 ft. (Mike Severns).

male   Mike Severns

WHITEPATCH RAZOR WRASSE
laenihi
Iniistius aneitensis (Günther, 1862)

This razor wrasse has a round snow white patch centered on the side. A dark patch precedes it in females, a faint yellow patch in males. Juveniles, often seen nearer to shore than adults, have three dark bands that may fuse together, making them almost all black. As the fish grow, the bands recede to become one to three dark spots along the back. This might have been the razor wrasse known in old Hawai'i as **laenihi kea** (**kea** meaning "white"). To about 8 in. Central and Western Pacific. Photos: (a) Puakō, Hawai'i, 80 ft. (b) Kahe Point, O'ahu. 30 ft.

b) subadult   a) female

BALDWIN'S RAZOR WRASSE
laenihi
Iniistius baldwini
(Jordan & Evermann, 1903)

This seldom-seen razor wrasse has a conspicuous black spot high on the side with a pearly white patch below. The white patch is faintly bordered by yellow, most evident in front. Males may show some red coloration in the black spot. It prefers depths of 70 ft. or more and usually lives far from the reef over somewhat silty sand, thus is not often seen. The name honors illustrator Albertus H. Baldwin of New York (1865–1935), who painted Hawaiian and American fishes in the late 19th century for the scientific publications of ichthyologists Jordan and Evermann. Beautiful fish prints by Baldwin are still available in the antique prints market. To about 9 in. Indo-Pacific. Photo: Ulua Beach, Maui. 50 ft.

Wrasses of the genera Iniistius and Xyrichtys, called razor wrasses or razorfish (and locally, nabeta), live exclusively over open sand. They have high narrow bodies and a bladelike forehead that enables them to knife into the substrate headfirst when threatened. They do not dive in just anywhere, however, but have special "soft spots" where they keep the sand loose and easy to enter. When chased, they will swim to one of these prepared spots (often visible as a circular dimple in the sand with a diameter slightly more than the height of the fish) and dive in. They can "swim" under the sand a short distance, enough to confuse a predator. Most razor wrasses live in colonies consisting of a male harem-master whose territory encompasses the smaller territories of individual females. Juveniles of many species are barred (sometimes all black) and can be difficult to tell apart. The general Hawaiian name for these fishes is laenihi, meaning "sharp forehead." Qualifiers, such as 'ele'ele ("black"), kea ("white"), and nēnē ("chirping") were once used, although we no longer know to which species they applied. Three other genera of sand-dwelling wrasses also occur in Hawai'i (see previous page).

a) typical adult ▲   b) black color variant ▼   c) juvenile ▼

PEACOCK RAZOR WRASSE
laenihi
Iniistius pavo (Valenciennes, 1840)

This common razor wrasse is most easily identified by the long dorsal filament which it can flick up and down. Lightly barred in gray (often with a whitish patch), it has a small black spot high on the side above the pectoral fin. Occasionally all-black individuals are seen (thought at one time to be a separate species). Juveniles vary from almost uniform dark brown or light gray to a barred pattern, but all have a long stem-like dorsal filament projecting forward above the head. Very small juveniles bend and twist as they swim, in wonderful imitation of a drifting bit of leaf or weed. To 12 in. Indo-Pacific and Eastern Pacific. Photos: (a, c) Kahe Point, O'ahu. 30 ft. (b) Mākua, O'ahu.

BRONZESPOT RAZOR WRASSE
laenihi
Iniistius celebicus (Bleeker, 1856)

A large, round, dark spot at midbody and a dark elongated mark near the tail distinguish this species from the similar and more common Blackside Razor Wrasse (next page). The dark spot may include some red, giving it a bronze or reddish tint when seen in bright light. Juveniles look much like miniature adults. Wary and hard to approach, this fish is less territorial than other Hawaiian razor wrasses, with females foraging in loose groups within a home range. It occurs from the western to central Pacific but is rare in Micronesia and spottily distributed in Hawai'i. Among the best places to find it are Kahe Point, O'ahu, and "Black Rock," in front of the Sheraton at Ka'anapali, Maui, where it can be common. To about 7 in. Photo: Kahe Point, O'ahu. 30 ft.

a) female ▲

b) male c) typical juvenile d) color variant

BLACKSIDE RAZOR WRASSE · laenihi · *Iniistius umbrilatus* (Jenkins, 1901) [BLACKBAR RAZORFISH]
This is the most common razor wrasse in Hawai'i. Adults have a black patch on the side with an area of bluish iridescence underneath (most prominent on females). The size of the black patch can vary and is largest in males. Juveniles have three dark bars and remain near the edge of the reef, thus are probably seen more often than adults, which occupy territories over open sand in slightly deeper water. Some juveniles are almost entirely brown or black. Courting males may appear half dark, half light (the dark half in front). The species name means "shadowed" and the Hawaiian name "sharp forehead." The qualifier **'ele'ele** ("black") might have applied to this fish. To about 9 in. Endemic. Photos: (a, b) Ho'okena, Hawai'i. 40 ft. (c) Kahe Point, O'ahu. 20-30 ft. (d) Pūpūkea, O'ahu. 70 ft.

WOOD'S RAZOR WRASSE
Xyrichtys woodi (Jenkins, 1901)
This razor wrasse is pearly gray with a pinkish tinge, especially about the abdomen. The eyes are red. Females have a white patch on the lower side and below it a series of narrow, almost diagonal bars. Juveniles have an orange brown band along the upper back. It usually occurs at 70 ft. or more and becomes increasingly abundant at greater depths. To about 7 in. Endemic (with several antiequatorial Pacific sister species). Photos: (a, b) Kepuhi Point, O'ahu. 80 ft. (c) Kahe Point, O'ahu. 50 ft.

a) female ▲

c) juvenile ▲ b) male ▲

SEA TURTLES
(Chelonidae)

Green Turtle · **honu** · Kahe Point, O'ahu (p. 362)　　　　　　Marcia Stone

The first "walking fishes" are believed to have crawled onto land about 350 million years ago. Over time these animals developed lungs and legs; some evolved into the scaleless amphibians (frogs, toads, and salamanders) while others retained scales and became reptiles. The amphibians remained partially aquatic, but the reptiles mastered terrestrial life and dominated the earth for millions of years as dinosaurs. About 150 million years ago some reptiles re-entered the ocean—perhaps because competition on land became too fierce. Among their descendants are today's crocodiles, sea snakes, and sea turtles. Sea turtles are the only marine reptiles which occur regularly in Hawaiian waters; sea snakes (p. 365) are extremely rare.

Turtles are characterized by a tough shell that protects the entire body—top, bottom, and sides. The shell covering the back is called the carapace, and the shell on the underside is the plastron. Freshwater turtles can retract their heads into their shells, but sea turtles cannot. Sea turtles have flippers instead of legs, and use their front pair to pull themselves through the water breast-stroke fashion. Powerful swimmers, they spend almost their entire lives at sea. Some species undertake migrations of 1,000 miles or more. Like other reptiles, sea turtles breathe air and during normal activity must surface every few minutes; when resting they can remain underwater for over two hours.

A sea turtle's only essential tie to land is reproductive, although Hawaiian Green Turtles often bask on shore. Females of all species return to their natal beach every few years to nest. Laboriously, in the dark of the night, they pull themselves above the high tide line and excavate a shallow body pit by flinging away sand with their flippers, taking several hours to do so. They then scoop out a deep, round egg chamber in the moist sand using their back flippers and drop in 100-200 eggs, one by one. Finally they cover the egg chamber, hide the nest by scattering sand over it, and drag themselves back down to the sea by dawn.

The young hatch in about two months, emerge from the sand at night, make their way down the beach, swim out through the waves, and begin their lives in the open sea. Although this ancient reproductive cycle worked well for millions of years, it leaves sea turtles extremely vulnerable today. All seven of the world's species are in peril. Loss of nesting habitat is the primary cause, as an increasing human population encroaches on or destroys their traditional nesting beaches. Even where they nest unhindered, people dig up the eggs (prized as an aphrodisiac by some cultures), and animals, wild and domestic, prey on the young hatchlings. Under good conditions probably fewer than ten hatchlings in a thousand live to maturity.

Adult sea turtles face new dangers of their own. They sometimes entangle themselves in fishing nets and drown, or die after eating plastic bags and other floating debris, which they likely mistake for jellyfish. Humans in many parts of the world hunt turtles either for meat or for their shells. In recent years numbers of Green Turtles, the most common species, have died from a tumor-causing viral disease known as fibropapillomatosis, which seems to be most prevalent in areas of high human population. Divers and snorkelers often see turtles with tumors on their heads and necks. Happily, some turtles do recover from this disfiguring and debilitating condition,

In most parts of the world, just seeing a sea turtle is a rare experience. Not so in Hawai'i, where Green Turtles are common. These animals will often ignore humans who swim gently or just float in their vicinity. Two species occur in Hawai'i's inshore waters, the common Green Turtle, and the rarer Hawksbill Turtle. The giant oceangoing Leatherback Turtle, which can weigh up to 2,000 lbs., also occurs in Hawaiian waters, but only well offshore. In the Hawaiian language, all turtles are called **honu**.

In the United States, and in the State of Hawai'i, sea turtles are protected by law. It is illegal to catch or harass them. If you see a turtle, swim gently or just float and it will likely ignore you and allow you to get quite close. If you see a resting turtle, do not disturb it. Never pursue or attempt to touch a sea turtle. In particular, "riding" a turtle can quickly exhaust it and prevent it from surfacing to breathe. Imagine someone trying to "ride" you as you try to come up for air!

Green Turtles basking off the Big Island's Kona Coast   Mark R. Rice

GREEN TURTLE · **honu** · *Chelonia mydas* Linnaeus, 1758

Green Turtles are the most widespread and numerous of Hawai'i's marine turtles. Adults and subadults feed mostly on algae and sea grasses, generally grazing along the shore in the early morning and late afternoon. When not feeding they often rest, seemingly asleep. Although active turtles must surface to breathe every few minutes, resting turtles can remain underwater for two hours or more. Green Turtles tend to rest in "traditional" areas, either under ledges and in caves or directly on the reef, where they may create permanent depressions bare of coral. Traditional cleaning areas also exist where turtles come to have surgeonfishes (often Goldring Surgeonfish, but also Brown Surgeonfish, Achilles Tangs, Sailfin Tangs, and Yellow Tangs) eat the algae off their shells. Sometimes Saddle Wrasses will pick commensal barnacles off their skin. Hawaiian Green Turtles are unusual in that they often bask on land during the day. Green Turtles elsewhere in the world rarely do this. Basking behavior is most common in the Northwestern Hawaiian Islands and on parts of the Big Island, such as the black sand beach at Punalu'u. In recent years Green Turtles have started basking at Laniākea on O'ahu's north shore, where visitors can frequently observe them at close range. Basking turtles conserve energy and avoid predation by sharks (generally Tiger Sharks).

When male Green Turtles reach maturity at perhaps age 25, they grow a conspicuous long heavy tail. Immature males and females have quite short tails. In Hawai'i, adult Green Turtles of both sexes migrate periodically to their nesting beaches, which are almost always at French Frigate Shoals, an atoll in the Northwestern Hawaiian Islands. After mating offshore, females crawl up on the beach at night to dig a pit and deposit their eggs. They do not nest every year, but when reproductively active they may nest up to five times in a season. After hatching in about two months, juvenile Hawaiian Green Turtles remain at sea for about 4-6 years feeding on jellyfish and other surface-dwelling animals.

Green Turtles in Hawai'i have been protected under Hawai'i State Law since 1974; in 1978 they were listed as threatened under the federal Endangered Species Act. It is illegal to take or harass them. If you see a turtle, swim gently or just float and it will likely ignore you and allow you to get quite close. If you see a resting turtle, do not disturb it. Never pursue or attempt to touch a sea turtle. Although the dark brown shells of these animals may be greenish from a coat of algae, Green Turtles get their name from the greenish color of their fat, evident to cooks in years past who butchered them for turtle soup, considered a delicacy at the time. These animals reach a length of about 4 ft. but the average adult in Hawaiian waters is probably about 3 ft. Maximum weight is about 400 lbs. The species occurs worldwide in warm seas. The name *mydas* means "wet." Some authors give the subspecies name *agassizi* to Hawaiian Green Turtles, but this is not generally accepted. Photo: Hanauma Bay, O'ahu. 10 ft. (see also pp. 290, 304, 360, and 364 bottom left)

For many years a young turtle nicknamed "Nugget" used to regularly approach divers in Hanauma Bay, O'ahu. Evidently someone had once fed him, and he wanted more. Nugget could be quite a nuisance. Underwater photographer Dave Schrichte relates being pestered by Nugget from behind while he was trying to take a photo of something on the bottom. Ignoring the pesky turtle didn't work—eventually it bit Schrichte's ear, actually drawing blood. Don't feed the turtles!

Large old male Green Turtle · note long tail. Mākaha, O'ahu. 45 ft.

Reef wreckers?

Observing Green Turtles at Honokōwai, Maui, from 1989 to 1999, Peter Bennett and Ursula Keuper-Bennett discovered that these heavy, hard-shelled reptiles can actually reshape the reef. Green Turtles often rest motionless for long periods in specific "home" spots that they probably visit daily. Often, the turtles lie directly on living coral. A dozen or so turtles may use the same area repeatedly, and their daily comings and goings over the years break up and grind down the reef. The turtles also scratch their undersides on coral projections, rub their backs on coral overhangs, and break coral while foraging for food, causing further destruction. Although localized, turtle damage can be severe: sections of Finger Coral beds are flattened and huge Lobe Coral heads are worn smooth and sometimes fractured. Most of the damage seems to have occurred in the last several decades and fish populations in damaged areas have decreased. Are there longterm consequences for our reefs as Hawai`i's beloved turtles continue to multiply?

Taking a breather. Hanauma Bay, O'ahu

HAWKSBIILL TURTLE · **ʻea**; **honu ʻea** · *Eretmochelys imbricata* (Linnaeus, 1766)

Hawksbill Turtles are uncommon in Hawaiʻi. They have narrow pointed bills which are easy to distinguish from the blunter bills of Green Turtles (see below), and the scale patterns on their heads and flippers often seem more conspicuous. Except on very young or very old individuals, the edges of the carapace are slightly serrated due to the large overlapping scutes (scales); the carapace edges of Green Turtles are smoother. In Hawaiʻi, Hawksbills nest principally on the main islands, making them more vulnerable to nest predators and human interference than Greens. Only a handful of their nesting beaches—mostly on the Big Island and on Molokaʻi—remain undisturbed. The nesting season extends from late May through November. Hawksbill Turtles are omnivores, feeding mainly on sponges and other marine invertebrates that grow on hard substrate and using their pointed bills to probe into crevices. They are listed as endangered under the Endangered Species Act and are also protected under Hawaiʻi State Law. It is illegal to take or harass them. Unfortunately, their shells are attractive when polished and in some parts of the world a considerable market exists for "tortoise shell" products such as combs and souvenirs. It is illegal to bring such items into the United States. The species name *imbricata* means "overlapping"—in reference to the scutes (scales) on the carapace mentioned above. The Hawaiian word **ʻea** ("reddish brown") refers to the color of the shell. Adult Hawksbills attain a length of about 3 ft. and weigh up to 270 lbs. Males have longer, thicker tails than females. Hawksbill Turtles range worldwide in tropical seas. Photos: Hanauma Bay, Oʻahu.

Green Turtle (p. 362) · note blunt beak

Hawksbill Turtle · note sharp beak

364

SEA SNAKES
(Elapidae)

Sea snakes, like sea turtles, are reptiles completely adapted for life in the water. All are excellent swimmers, but their laterally flattened bodies and paddle-like tails leave most of them helpless on land. Only a few crawl up on shore, usually to bask or reproduce. Like all reptiles, sea snakes have scales and breathe air. Some can also absorb significant amounts of oxygen through their skins. They swim both at the surface and underwater, some to depths of several hundred feet, and can spend several hours submerged. Sea snakes are extremely venomous, but they rarely bite humans and typically inject little or no venom. Still, they should be given the greatest respect.

Sea snakes occur throughout the warm Indian and Pacific oceans but are absent from Atlantic and Caribbean waters. Out of about 60 known species, the Yellowbellied Sea Snake alone occurs in Hawai'i, but only as a rare straggler. Most specimens are found washed up on land, as in the photo below.

Snake eels, especially the rarely-seen Saddled Snake Eel (p. 117), are sometimes mistaken for sea snakes in Hawai'i, but it is easy to tell the two apart. Snake eels have smooth, scaleless skin, a dorsal fin, and gill openings on the side of the head, while snakes have scaly skins, no fins, and no gill openings. Although the Saddled Snake Eel mimics the common Indo-Pacific sea snake *Laticauda colubrina*, that snake species does not occur in Hawai'i. No Hawaiian snake eel looks anything like the Yellowbellied Sea Snake.

Dick Bartlett

YELLOWBELLIED SEA SNAKE *Hydrophis platurus* (Linnaeus, 1766)

    This is the most widespread snake in the world, occurring from the east coast of Africa all the way to the west coast of the Americas. It lives its entire life in the open ocean and rarely approaches land. In Hawai'i, if seen at all, it is typically found washed up on shore where it is helpless. Fewer than 20 sightings have been recorded. The snake is dark purplish black to brown on the back and yellow on the belly and sides. The greatly flattened tail tip is banded or spotted with the same colors. Some individuals are all yellow or yellow with a black stripe on the back. Most are about 2 ft. long, but large ones can attain 4 ft. Indo-Pacific and Eastern Pacific. Photo: Costa Rica (Dick Bartlett).

Short-Finned Pilot Whale · technically a large dolphin · Kona, Hawaiʻi (p.376)　　Jerry Kane
(The bubbles were blown by the whale.)

Whales and dolphins belong to the order Cetacea, which comprises by far the largest group of marine mammals. Mammals are warm-blooded vertebrates that breathe air, give live birth, produce milk, and grow hair. About 4,000 species exist. The great majority have legs and live on land; a few have flippers and dwell in water. Mammals with four flippers, such as seals and walruses, generally come ashore to rest and reproduce, but those with two flippers, such as whales, dolphins, and manatees, are wholly adapted to life in water and cannot survive on shore. Although a few aquatic mammals inhabit rivers and lakes, most are ocean dwellers.

Hawaiʻi's native mammals are all marine, except for a small land-dwelling bat. Of these, one is a seal, the rest are whales and dolphins. Whales and dolphins are the natural masters of the seas (or would be, without human interference). Powerful swimmers, they propel themselves by flexing their rear body and tail up and down. Some can sustain a speed of 20 mph; others can dive more than a mile deep. Filling their great lungs in one or two seconds through blowholes at the top of their head, many can stay down for at least an hour. They bear live young that they suckle under water with rich milk. To navigate and "see" below the surface most cetaceans (dolphins, porpoises, and toothed whales) detect the reflections from streams of high-frequency buzzes and clicks. Their "sonar" is remarkably effective. Dolphins in captivity can identify and avoid thin wires and recognize small objects previously seen visually. Some cetaceans that lack sonar can "vocalize" in unusual ways. Humpback Whales sing long complicated songs, and Sperm Whales may emit terrible blasts of sound to disable their prey. Cetaceans have large brains and some may be unusually intelligent. A few species seem to enjoy interacting with humans, but in other ways these animals are utter aliens. Land, for example, plays no part at all in their life cycle. Cetaceans, in fact, cannot survive long out of water—the weight of their unsupported bodies fatally compresses their lungs and internal organs.

What makes whales different from dolphins? Basically size—dolphins are just small whales. Porpoises (not found in Hawai'i) are even smaller. Porpoises have chubbier bodies than dolphins and lack their typical beaklike snout. Although the two are distinct, many people mistakenly use "porpoise" for both.

About 80 species of whales and dolphins are known worldwide. Hector's Dolphin *(Cephalorhynchus hectori)* of New Zealand, which is 4-5 ft. long and weighs 75-130 lbs., is one of the smallest. The largest, the Blue Whale *(Balaenoptera musculus),* occurs around the world from the arctic to the antarctic and attains a length of at least 110 ft. with an estimated weight of 200 tons. Far bigger than the largest dinosaurs, Blue Whales are the most enormous animals to have ever lived on this planet. In 1758 the great naturalist Linnaeus, who loved a joke, bestowed upon them the scientific species name *musculus,* which means "little mouse."

Although humans have hunted whales for meat, oil, and bone over at least 1,000 years, it was only recently that serious impacts were made on whale populations. In the 19th and 20th centuries commercial hunters using explosive harpoons and other technological inventions drove the larger species almost to extinction. From 1904 to 1939 whalers slaughtered over half a million blue, fin, and humpback whales in the southern hemisphere alone. In 1966, at the eleventh hour, the International Whaling Commission spared Blue Whales and Humpback Whales, giving them full protection. In 1972 the U.S. Congress passed the Marine Mammal Protection Act, which ended trade in all cetaceans and cetacean products in the United States. Finally, the International Whaling Commission voted to end all commercial whaling at the end of the 1985 season. A few nations such as Japan and Norway continue to ignore or circumvent this ruling.

About 18 whale and dolphin species occur regularly in Hawaiian waters; a few others pass through from time to time. The six illustrated here are the most common; the others are rarely seen.

BALEEN WHALES (suborder Mysticeti)

Whales divide easily into two groups, baleen whales and toothed whales. Baleen whales have two blowholes and curtains of stiff rodlike plates (baleen) hanging from their upper jaw instead of teeth. Frayed along one edge, these plates overlap to form a dense mat with which baleen whales filter their prey from the sea. Fin, Right, and Blue Whales belong to this group, as do Hawai'i's Humpback Whales. Most baleen whales feed on planktonic animals. Some swim slowly, filter-feeding almost continuously; others gulp vast quantities of water into their pleated, expandable mouths, force the water through the baleen plates with their enormous tongues, then lick off and swallow what remains, usually krill (small shrimplike animals) and small fish. In this manner, baleen whales can consume up to four tons per day! The California Gray Whale uses a variation of this technique by sucking up mouthfuls of mud from the sea bottom and filtering out the small animals living in it. A large mouth is most efficient in the filter-feeding game, thus baleen whales are larger than toothed whales. (The Sperm Whale, an enormous toothed whale, is an exception.)

Strangely, ancient Hawaiian lore makes almost no mention of these gigantic animals, so common in Hawaiian waters during the winter months. It may be that Humpbacks began migrating to the Hawaiian Islands only within the last 200 years, not long before the first western whalers arrived.

In the 19th and early 20th centuries Humpback Whales were hunted around the world almost to extinction. To ensure the whales space and quiet in which to rest and reproduce, Congress created the Hawaiian Islands Humpback Whale National Marine Sanctuary in 1992, principally in the waters off Maui, Lāna'i, and Moloka'i, but also off parts of O'ahu, Kaua'i, and the Big Island. In addition, all boats in Hawaiian waters are prohibited from approaching within 100 yards of a whale. Luckily for observers, the whales themselves are under no restrictions and often swim quite close to boats. Humpbacks are the only baleen whales to regularly visit the main Hawaiian Islands.

HUMPBACK WHALE · **kohola** · *Megaptera novaeangliae* (Borowski, 1781) (Family Balaenopteridae)

Humpback Whales are among the biggest in the world, growing to at least 45 ft. with a weight of 40-45 tons. Only Fin, Blue, Right, Bowhead, and Sperm Whales are larger. The genus name *Megaptera* means "big wings," referring to the Humpback Whale's amazingly long, narrow pectoral flippers. These attain about one third its body length—by far the longest pectorals of any whale. The common name refers to the conspicuous way these whales hump their backs just before diving. Some Humpback Whales are completely black, but most have white markings that can vary from a few patches to a completely white underside. The lower side of the pectorals is usually white and the upper side may be white as well. The leading edges of the pectorals bear prominent knobs or tubercles, as do the head and jaws; at least some of these sprout a sensory hair. On average, these whales probably live 30-40 years. Humpbacks have regular migratory patterns, spend lots of time in shallow offshore waters, and are unusually "acrobatic," often breaching, lunging, and splashing at the surface. Regular visitors to many parts of the globe, they are probably the easiest of the world's whales to observe. In the fall and early winter these huge mammals migrate toward the equator from their coldwater feeding grounds near the arctic and antarctic. Often they head for tropical island groups such as Hawai'i, where they mate and give birth. In Hawai'i there is no single mass arrival or departure. Whales come and go throughout the winter breeding season, alone or in small groups segregated by age, sex, and reproductive condition. They begin to arrive from Alaskan waters in November, reach their peak of perhaps 2,000-4,000 animals in February or March, and are mostly gone by late May. The fastest recorded one-way trip—approximately 2,500-miles—took 39 days. Humpbacks in Hawai'i are seen near all the main islands, but occur in greatest numbers in the Penguin Bank area southwest of Moloka'i, and in the shallow waters between Maui, Moloka'i, Lāna'i, and Kaho'olawe. While in the tropics they eat almost nothing, living off energy stored in their blubber. Calves, however, receive up to 130 gallons a day of thick rich milk, squirted into their mouths underwater from their mothers' teats. Mothers and calves usually remain together for at least a year and often swim in close proximity. In Hawai'i, year-old calves are typically weaned during their second winter and by the time they return to Alaska for their second summer they are on their own. While in northern waters Humpbacks gorge mainly on krill and small fish.

In the Islands, Humpbacks are usually observed either as solitary individuals or as pods (groups) of two or three. Occasionally twenty or more are seen together. The larger groups typically consist of a single female and numerous males that often engage in competitive male behaviors such as head rises, head lunges, charges, and physical contact. The most common behaviors, of course, are those performed by all whales: surfacing, spouting, diving, and occasionally breaching. Humpbacks are famous for the lengthy and complex songs (or sound sequences) that males sing during the breeding season, possibly to attract females or to signal competing males, or both. To divers and snorkelers underwater, a whale song sounds like an eerie sequence of moans, snores, "yups," "whoos," "eees," and "moos." Singing whales in a given population all sing the same song. The sequence of repeating patterns evolves slightly from month to month, and after several years it becomes quite different. The song usually lasts 6-18 minutes, but a singing whale may repeat it for hours. When Humpbacks leave Hawai'i, their singing decreases; by the time they reach their Alaskan feeding grounds it has all but stopped. Upon their return to Hawai'i the following winter, the whales start the song again exactly as it was when they left off. Photo: Kona, Hawai'i. (NMFS research permit #587)

The tubercles on the leading edges of a Humpback's pectorals reduce turbulence, helping the whale to make tight power turns. The idea is being used in the design of big windmill blades to increase power at slow speeds and lessen noise.

Whale behavior 101

© Michael S. Nolan / www.wildlifeimages.net

Swimming A small pod of Humpback Whales swimming at the surface. When they sound (dive) they hump their backs conspicuously, hence the common name. As they go down, they lift their flukes for a few seconds above the water.

© Michael S. Nolan / www.wildlifeimages.net

Spouting

Humpback whales typically dive for 10-20 minutes. Upon surfacing they empty their enormous lungs in just half a second. The 300 mph jet of air atomizes any water remaining in the windpipe or above the blow-holes, producing the 20-ft. cloud of spray known as the "blow" or "spout." The subsequent inhalation takes about 2 seconds. After several such breaths the whale is ready to dive again. Photo: West Maui. (Michael S. Nolan)

Breaching

Having launched itself almost entirely out of the water, this whale is about to fall on its back with a colossal splash. It may perform several such breaches in succession. No one knows why whales breach, but it likely has social or communication value. Or perhaps it's just fun! Sometimes whales engage in behaviors similar to breaching, such as head lunging and head slapping, in which they do not launch themselves as completely out of the water. Head lunging and slapping are distinct from breaching and are often performed with another male nearby. They may be forms of male competition or aggression. Photo: West Maui (Michael S. Nolan)

© Michael S. Nolan / www.wildlifeimages.net

© Michael S. Nolan / www.wildlifeimages.net

Pectoral display

Humpbacks often display with their amazingly long pectoral fins. They may raise one of both pecs straight up out of the water as they lie on their back or side. Sometimes they slap them loudly on the surface, or wave them to and fro. Photo: West Maui (Michael S. Nolan)

Fluke display

Humpbacks have huge tail flukes (one third the length of head and body!) that they display in various ways. A whale may assume a head-down position, holding its tail out of the water. Sometimes it will wave the flukes, or slap them forcefully on the surface, creating a great sound and splash. Or it may agitate the water by swishing its flukes vigorously from side to side. The flukes are also displayed briefly just before a whale dives, enabling scientists to identify and track individuals by means of the unique patterns on the underside. Photo: West Maui (Michael S. Nolan)

© Michael S. Nolan / www.wildlifeimages.net

Reproduction

Humpback whales migrate to Hawai'i for the winter, where they mate and give birth. This mother and her newborn calf will probably stay together for about a year, the calf being weaned during its next winter season in Hawai'i. Some mother-calf pairs remain together for two years. Whales with calves tend to prefer nearshore waters and are often accompanied by an adult male "escort." A calf seen off Maui in 1975 was observed yearly until 1988; it appeared to reach sexual maturity in seven years. Photo: Lāna'i. (Michael S. Nolan)

The underwater images I have of Humpback Whales happened by sheer luck. In each case the whales approached my boat while I was either drifting in deep water or at anchor and snorkeling! In the case of the mother and calf images I was actually running a commercial charter when both the mother and calf circled us in 35 feet of water! For 45 minutes she stayed below our boat with her calf right by her side. Male Humpbacks were vying for position to escort her. At one point there were five adult males with the mother and calf, all in less than 40 feet of water! Certainly a day I will never forget! - Michael S. Nolan

TOOTHED WHALES (suborder Odontoceti)

This group includes sperm whales, beaked whales, dolphins, and porpoises. All have have teeth instead of baleen, and one blowhole instead of two. They generally live in groups. Excepting the great Sperm Whale, toothed whales are smaller than baleen whales. Active hunters, they feed primarily upon fish and squid. Out of roughly 70 species of toothed whales in 7 families worldwide, 17 live in or pass through Hawaiian waters regularly, including the Sperm Whale, which is rare. The only toothed whales seen with any frequency in Hawai'i are members of the dolphin family. Beaked whale sightings (see p. 377) are uncommon.

Dolphins (family Delphinidae)

Dolphins can be distinguished from other toothed whales by their distinctive conical teeth. About 37 dolphin species are known, most from 4-12 ft. long. The larger ones, although technically dolphins, are popularly called whales (for example, the Short-Finned Pilot Whale, p. 376). Most dolphins have a beaklike snout and a bulbous forehead or "melon" that is associated with the production of sound. They live in groups and are much given to leaping and frolicking at the surface. When dolphins swim at speed they generally arc in and out of the water—a swimming style called "porpoising" that is faster and more efficient than ordinary underwater swimming. Some dolphins are known for their intelligence. Tales abound of these animals, generally Bottlenose Dolphins (below), interacting with and even aiding humans in various ways. About eleven dolphin species occur in Hawaiian waters, but only the five shown here are seen regularly.

© Michael S. Nolan / www.wildlifeimages.net

BOTTLENOSE DOLPHIN *Tursiops truncatus* (Montague, 1821)

Bottlenose Dolphins are typically 8-11 ft. long, robust, and mostly uniform gray with a dark dorsal fin and light underside. They have a distinct snout, said to have reminded sailors of the business-end of an old-fashioned gin bottle, and a prominent "forehead" or melon. Their face wears the perpetual smile made famous by the TV dolphin, Flipper. These are the animals most likely to come to mind when one thinks of dolphins, and they are widely exhibited in oceanariums. In the wild, Bottlenose Dolphins are primarily coastal, although a deepwater oceanic population also exists. In Hawai'i, they usually travel in small groups of 2-15 animals and are found both in shallow inshore waters and in the channels between islands. Groups tend to remain in particular areas. Bottlenose Dolphins are playful, especially near boats, often riding the bow wave or stealing bait from fishing lines. Divers have seen them toying with large sea cucumbers off Molokini Islet, Maui, lifting them high off the bottom, "tossing" them to and fro, then dropping them, sometimes on the divers! Common along both coasts of the U.S., Bottlenose Dolphins occur around the world in both warm and temperate waters. Because the Pacific population around California and Hawai'i differs somewhat from that in the Atlantic, some authorities recognize it as a distinct species, *Tursiops gillii*. Another regional population in the tropical eastern Pacific is sometimes called *T. nuuanu* (named after the ship that carried the scientist). Most authorities, however, regard all Bottlenose Dolphins as one species. The name "truncatus" means "cut off" and refers to the teeth of the original Atlantic specimen, which were quite worn down. Photo: West Maui (Michael S. Nolan)

Dolphin sonar

As any snorkeler or diver knows, visibility in water is not nearly as good as in air, and it can vary greatly. Sound, however, always travels far and fast underwater. Creating a sound underwater and listening for its echo is a reliable way to sense an object in the water and determine its distance, regardless of the visibility. Humans learned to do this with machines in the last century, calling it "sonar." Dolphins and other marine mammals, as well as bats, have been using sonar, or echolocation, for millions of years, and their abilities are much more sophisticated than ours. Using echolocation, Bottlenose Dolphins can identify thin wires or tiny objects at night and at considerable distances. One experiment in Kāneʻohe Bay, Oʻahu, demonstrated that a captive Bottlenose could detect a metal sphere the size of a tangerine lowered into the water 370 ft. away—a distance greater than the length of a football field. Closer in, at 50 ft., they can tell the difference between a kernel of corn and a BB pellet. With sonar they can identify objects previously seen only visually and may even be able to "see" x-ray fashion inside other animals. Blindfolded, a dolphin can distinguish between two similar-size fish, find an object an inch in diameter in a large tank, and even sense the difference between brass and aluminum.

Dolphin sonar uses a series of clicks. After each click, the dolphin waits for an echo. It then emits another click. The nearer the target, the quicker the echo and the closer together the clicks. It sounds simple, but to humans this all happens incomprehensibly fast and the click trains may sound like buzzing, barking, rasping, or creaking. These clicks, apparently generated in the dolphin's nasal cavity, are beamed or focused quite precisely through the "melon," a pouch of fatty tissue above the beak that serves as an acoustic lens. The dolphin receives the echoes through its upper jawbone, rather than its ears, which are largely vestigial. Sound is transmitted from jaw to brain through fatty tissue similar to that in the melon. The large brain apparently processes these signals instantaneously into some sort of three dimensional image in the dolphin's mind. It is likely that dolphins can also "see" to some extent by using the reflections of ambient sound on their surroundings—that is, without actively producing clicks. Beyond sonar, it is possible that dolphins stun or disable their prey using focused blasts of sound. They also produce all kinds of whistles and other noises, probably for communication.

Dolphin intelligence

Because they are quick to learn, can mimic human speech, and have larger brains than humans, some researchers have speculated that Bottlenose Dolphins have an almost human level of intelligence. Skeptics point out that the large brain, for the most part, provides raw computation power for processing sonar signals rather than conscious intelligence as we normally think of it. However, the complex social interactions of Bottlenose Dolphins must surely rank as "intelligent" (see "The dolphin dark side" below) as must their playful inventiveness. One the best examples of the latter can be observed at Sea Life Park, Oʻahu, where captive Bottlenose Dolphins amuse themselves by swirling water with their fins, then exhaling into the moving vortices to create all kinds of fancy, long-lasting bubble-rings and helices. One dolphin has figured out how to blow two rings then merge them into one; another, in a delicate maneuver, can add more air to an existing ring. Experienced dolphins are able to pass these techniques on to others. Are dolphins self-aware? Recent experiments—also at Sea Life Park—strongly suggest that they can recognize themselves in mirrors. More work is needed in this area. Bright as they are, however, dolphins do not appear to have a symbolic language or the highly developed problem-solving abilities that we recognize as specifically human. On the other hand, dolphins may have well-developed areas of intelligence that are largely alien to ours.

The dolphin dark side

Dolphins are popularly thought of as friendly animals with an almost "spiritual" nature. Some people feel that they emanate uplifting and healing influences. Reports exist of dolphins physically rescuing humans in distress by pushing them ashore or summoning help. These accounts may be true, but dolphins also have a dark side. In Moray Firth, northern Scotland, Bottlenose Dolphins kill smaller Harbor Porpoises with brutal blows of their heads and beaks for no obvious reason, and possibly just for "fun." This unsuspected behavior came to light after more than 100 porpoise carcasses washed up over a period of several years. And Bottlenose Dolphins off Western Australia practice a form of sexual slavery in which "gangs" of two or three males capture a female for a month or so, bullying her, controlling her every move, and allowing her out to feed only under guard. Sometimes these gangs form alliances or "supergangs" to battle other male gangs and steal their captive females. Research shows that the small gangs may be stable for 10-12 years, but the larger alliances are in a constant state of flux. Like humans, dolphins seem capable of a great variety of behaviors, some of them nice, and some not so nice.

Bottlenose Dolphin off Maui — Andy Schwanke

SPINNER DOLPHIN · **naia** · *Stenella longirostris* (Gray, 1828)

Spinners are slender dolphins with a long narrow snout or beak. The back is covered with a "cape" of dark gray or black, the flanks and sides are pearl gray, and the belly is bright white. (Within the Pacific, this three-tone color scheme is seen only around Hawai'i. The same species in the Eastern Pacific tends toward a more uniform gray.) Spinners frequently swim close to shore and are exceptionally active; their leaping and splashing is easily seen from land. The name comes from their trademark behavior: leaping free of the water, sometimes as high as 10 ft., turning several times along their long axis, and crashing back into the sea in a burst of spray. Like all dolphins, Spinners are social animals that swim in groups of about half a dozen to 250 or more. They feed offshore at night, diving as deep as 800 ft. to hunt small fish and squid. By day they enter inshore waters to rest and play (see next page). Sexual differences are not obvious, but males, especially older ones, have a hump on the underside, just behind the anus, and taller, more triangular dorsal fins. Spinners attain about 7 ft. and occur in warm waters worldwide. The species name means "long snout." Photo: Midway Atoll. 10 ft.

© Michael S. Nolan / www.wildlifeimages.net

Why do Spinners spin?

Spinner Dolphins spend about one third of their daytime waking hours performing leaps, spins, and other "aerial" behavior. When spinning they clear the surface by as much as 10 ft., turn on their longitudinal axis several times, and crash back into the sea. Although it may seem like mere frolic and fun, spinning is likely part of a dolphin's "job." In his classic book Dolphin Days, *Dr. Kenneth R. Norris explains that wild dolphins at sea are utterly dependent upon their school—in the vastness of the ocean the school is the only reference point they have, and the only defense against sharks or other predators. Noting that Spinners spin most often at night when the school is most spread out and most active, that they bark sharply before beginning a spin, that they make a loud slapping sound upon re-entry, and that the bubble trail caused by the spinning re-entry creates an excellent target for echolocation, Norris postulates that the leaping and spinning of dolphins in a school mark out the dimensions and changing shape of the school. Spins enable any dolphin in the school to know where all the other dolphins are, even in the dark. A secondary reason for spinning could be the removal of pesky remoras and/or cookie-cutter sharks. Photo: Midway Atoll (Michael S. Nolan)*

A day in the life of a Spinner

Morning

Many people in Hawai'i have watched Spinner Dolphins swimming near shore in the morning, leaping, spinning, and splashing as they go. Having hunted for food all night, they are heading for a resting place—typically a patch of white sand in a sheltered bay or off a sheltered stretch of coast. Here they settle near the bottom, each dolphin just beyond reach of its neighbor's fins, and enter a slow, trancelike swimming state that is probably as close to sleep as they ever get. (Dolphins are thought to sleep one side of the brain at a time, with one eye closed and the other open, ever vigilant for sharks or other predators.) During this lull, which lasts for 4-5 hours from mid-morning until mid-afternoon, the only visible activity is the occasional dolphin rising to the surface to breathe. Spinners need this quiet time. It is important for

dolphin watchers not to disturb them during their resting period.)

Afternoon

Some individuals finish their naps before others. As the afternoon progresses, these early-risers begin a period of play, slapping the surface, leaping, spinning, rushing toward the open ocean and then rushing back, as if to say to the others "Let's get going!" The dolphins still resting near the bottom, however, typically show no interest. Eventually the early-risers give up and descend again for another period of slow trancelike swimming. A bit later they, or maybe another group, try it again, slapping, leaping, spinning, and racing back and forth. Failing to rouse the rest of the entire school, they subside again into rest. Dr. Kenneth Norris, whose 30 years of Hawaiian dolphin-watching provided most of the information presented here, calls this behavior "zigzagging." It continues until the entire school collectively decides that it's time to move, usually in the late afternoon. Norris writes "After zigzagging was complete and the 'decision' had been made to go to sea, one could see a kind of 'joy' sweep over the school. All at once and all together they took off, often enough directly toward the setting sun....leaping high, crashing back into the water, and going twice as fast as before...." As the dolphins raced out to sea, his underwater microphone would pick up "the damnedest cacaphony," "a chorus of squawks, blats, and whistles.... sounds like barking dogs, banjos being plucked, and...cows mooing."

Evening

When the dolphin school reaches the deep water individuals scatter in groups of two or three, spreading out over several miles of sea to hunt. By this time it is dark, but with their sonar they can scan 300 yards in any direction, enjoying a sensory advantage over sharks, their main enemy. The small groups, although widely-spaced, tend to dive and surface at the same time. Spinning intensifies at night and may be one way they keep track of each other (see "Why do Dolphins Spin?" on the previous page). The dolphins feed on deepwater fish and squid at distances of about ½ mile to 5 miles offshore, and sometimes as deep as 800 ft. How do they hunt? Do they herd their prey together? Do they use blasts of sound to disable their prey? No one knows.

Morning again

By early morning, the well-fed Spinners are returning to their traditional resting places near shore. Individuals do not always return to the exact same spots in which they rested the previous day, perhaps because they tend to move some distance along the shore while feeding. Rather, they appear to enter the various resting areas on a first-come-first-served basis. Some Spinners do not enter resting bays at all, but move slowly along shore all day. By mid-morning they settle near the bottom and once again enter their trancelike swimming state. Dolphin watchers should always allow them the space and tranquillity they need for this "quiet time."

PANTROPICAL SPOTTED DOLPHIN
kiko · *Stenella attenuata* (Gray, 1843)

Similar in size and coloration to Spinner Dolphins (not surprising, as they are in the same genus), Spotted Dolphins sport a dark "cape" on the back, a white underside, and a long slender snout. They may or may not be conspicuously spotted, but the tip of the snout is always bright white, providing a good way to identify them. Although fairly common offshore and in the channels between the islands, Spotted Dolphins do not come in close to land as Spinners do. They are fast, active swimmers that travel in small to large groups and frequently leap high from the water but do not spin. In the eastern Pacific they associate with schools of tuna and thousands perish in tuna nets each year. Around Hawai'i they feed primarily at night, diving deep for prey organisms associated with the deep-scattering layer as it rises up to the surface after dark. Pantropical Spotted Dolphins attain about 7 ft. with a weight of about 240 lbs. and are estimated to live about 45 years. The Hawaiian name, probably modern, means "dot" or "spot." Photo: Kona, Hawai'i. (Kendra Ignacio)

Kendra Ignacio

▼ FALSE KILLER WHALE (see next page) ▶

© Michael S. Nolan / www.wildlifeimages.net

◀FALSE KILLER WHALE *Pseudorca crassidens* (Owen 1846) (photo on previous page)

Although growing to about 19 ft. and lacking the typical dolphin beak, these torpedo-shaped animals are technically dolphins. Black with some white or gray on the underside, they faintly resemble true orcas, or Killer Whales (also dolphins), which are very rare in Hawai'i. A backward-sweeping dorsal fin lies almost exactly midway between head and tail. Like most other dolphins, False Killer Whales are highly social and swim actively at the surface, often "porpoising" or arcing almost completely out of the water. (The only other animals of their size likely to be seen in Hawaiian waters are the more robust and comparatively slow-moving Short-Finned Pilot Whales, below, which have a more bulbous forehead, or melon, and a low dorsal fin set forward on the body.) False Killer Whales like to be over deep water and are thus seen only from boats. If they spy a human in the water, they often approach for a closer look. Generally, they feed on large fish and squid, often in the company of other cetaceans such as Bottlenose Dolphins. Sometimes they share their prey with other members of their pod. False Killer Whales have been reported to attack other cetaceans including Humpback Whale calves and even Sperm Whales. They occur in warm waters worldwide and are estimated to live about 60 years. Photo: Michael S. Nolan.

SHORT-FINNED PILOT WHALE *Globicephala macrorhynchus* Gray, 1846

Despite their common name, these cetaceans are actually oversized dolphins. They are completely black except for a white patch on the chin that narrows to a line along the stomach. More apparent is the distinctive bulbous head (the genus name *Globicephala* means "rounded head") and a backward-sweeping dorsal fin set forward on the body. They travel in groups of 20 or more and are not uncommon in the channels between the islands and offshore. Comparatively slow-moving for dolphins, they often lie motionless on the surface when seas are calm, a behavior called "logging." The name "pilot" derives from the closely related Long-Finned Pilot Whale *(G. melaena)* of cold northern seas, that is said to guide fishermen to schools of fish. Another explanation for the name is their strong tendency to stay together and follow a leader or "pilot." Pilot whales are particularly susceptible to mass strandings, that perhaps occur when the leader gets confused and the rest follow blindly behind. However, there are no records of mass strandings in Hawai'i. Male Short-Finned Pilot Whales attain about 21 ft. Females somewhat less. The species occurs worldwide in warm seas. Photo: Kona, Hawai'i (Jerry Kane) (see also p. 366)

Jerry Kane

Beaked Whales (Family Ziphiidae)

The 19 species of beaked whales are among the most numerous but least known of the world's cetaceans. All belong to the family Ziphiidae, which is second in size among the toothed whales only to the dolphin family. Beaked whales are larger than typical dolphins and many, like dolphins, have a beaklike snout. In addition to Blainville's Beaked Whale (below), Cuvier's Beaked Whale *(Ziphius cavirostris)* and Baird's Beaked Whale *(Berardius bairdii)* are also known from Hawaiian waters. Baird's Beaked Whale, however, inhabits only the far northern reaches of the chain. None of the beaked whales are common.

© Michael S. Nolan / www.wildlifeimages.net

BLAINVILLE'S BEAKED WHALE *Mesoplodon densirostris* (Blainville, 1817) Family Ziphiidae

Blainville's Beaked Whales prefer waters over 3,000 feet deep, thus are generally seen only well offshore. Sightings are rare. Mature individuals attain about 14 feet. Adult males have two long prominent teeth on the lower jaw that protrude above the top of the head and are often encrusted with barnacles. The bodies of both sexes are typically covered with light-colored scratches, probably inflicted during mating and fighting. Roundish scars are likely the work of Cookie-Cutter Sharks. These whales have a peculiar way of surfacing that may help to identify them: Kenneth C. Balcomb describes it thus in his book Whales of Hawaii: "upon surfacing the chin and rostrum are thrust vigorously above the water and then rocked back down underwater as the back and dorsal fin appear." These whales travel in groups of 3-7, communicate with clicks and whistles, feed on fish and squid, and remain underwater for 10-40 minutes, spending little time at the surface between dives. Little more is known about them. Their common name honors French naturalist Henri de Blainville (1777-1850) who first described the species in 1817 from its upper jaw bone alone. The scientific name, meaning "dense rostrum," reflects the extraordinary density of this bone, said to be densest of any known animal. Blainville's Beaked Whale occurs around the world in warm termperate and tropical seas. The only other beaked whale likely to be seen around the main Hawaiian Islands is Cuvier's Beaked Whale *(Ziphius cavirostris),* which attains 23 ft. It has a similar light-spotted appearance but lacks a prominent snout.

Drifting with Short-finned Pilot Whales in deep water off the Kona Coast of Hawaii, I had the incredible luck to encounter a lone male Blainville's Beaked Whale. The two teeth erupting from the lower jaw were covered in barnacles. The animal was highly scratched and scarred, probably from fights with other males of it's own species. The whale was not very curious about our small inflatable boat, but was very drawn towards the Pilot Whales logging at the surface nearby. Incredibly, it started to breach! The Beaked Whale came within 50 yards of the Pilot Whales and continued to breach. In total it breached 7 times. These are among the only images of a Blainville's Beaked Whale breaching that are in existence. I couldn't believe the luck! As the Beaked Whale approached the Pilot Whales they started to rouse from their slumber. They did not immediately interact or flee from the Beaked Whale, but they did start to dive as a group. The Beaked Whale swam towards the last of the diving Pilot Whales, but then turned and swam off in a different direction. In all, a very interesting encounter, with an animal that is rarely sighted alive. - Michael S. Nolan.

Hawaiian Monk Seal · **'ilio holo i ka uaua** · hauled out on the beach at Kīhei, Maui

Seals and walruses comprise the **pinnipeds**, a group of streamlined, fur-bearing marine mammals whose four limbs are modified into flippers. (Loosely translated, "pinniped" means "fin-foot.") Pinnipeds spend most of their lives in the water and feed principally on fish, squid, and shellfish. They rest and reproduce on land. Pinnipeds are believed to have evolved from a bearlike ancestor about 23 million years ago.

Out of 37 pinniped species, all but one (the walrus) are seals. Seals are divided into two families, **eared seals** and **true seals**. Eared seals (family Otariidae, which includes the sea lions) have large well-developed front flippers and small rear ones. The front flippers are their main source of propulsion in the water and out, while the rear flippers are used mostly for steering in the water. On land the rear flippers turn forward under the body to help the seal "walk." (Any seal that can walk or prop itself up on its front fins is an eared seal.) Eared seals vocalize by barking and have ears covered with external ear flaps.

True seals (family Phocidae) have large well-developed rear flippers and smaller front ones. The rear flippers provide propulsion in the water, and the front ones steer. This flipper arrangement confers superior swimming and diving ability, but is almost useless on land. True seals cannot walk on their limbs as eared seals do, but must wriggle and flop along shore on their bellies, using an undulating motion of the entire body. True seals vocalize by grunting (sometimes deeply and loudly). Their ears consist of a pair of small holes on the sides of the head. External ear flaps are lacking. The huge elephant seal and the sleek harbor seal are both true seals.

Hawaii's only pinniped, the Hawaiian Monk Seal, belongs to the true seal family. It has two close relatives, the Caribbean Monk Seal (extinct, last seen in 1952) and the Mediterreanean Monk Seal (about 400 individuals as of 2007). Their common name is said to derive from folds of skin around the head that resemble a medieval monk's hood. Monk seals are sometimes regarded as living fossils because they have changed little in the last 15 million years. Time, however, seems to have caught up with these ancient animals; their prospects for survival in the modern world are uncertain at best.

HAWAIIAN MONK SEAL · **'ilio holo i ka uaua; hulu** · *Neomonachus schauinslandi* (Matschie, 1905)

This is Hawai'i's only endemic marine mammal. Adults are 7-8 ft. long and weigh between 400 and 600 lbs. with females typically slightly larger than males. Adults and subadults of both sexes are brown or light gray on the back and sides and lighter underneath; young animals tend to be lighter colored and older adults may become almost black. Newborn pups are black. The species' range encompasses the entire Hawaiian chain (about 1,200 individuals total in 2007), but almost all seals in historic times have resided in the uninhabited Northwestern Hawaiian Islands. In the last 20 years a small breeding population (over 77 seals in 2007) has re-established itself in the main Hawaiian Islands.

Hawaiian Monk Seals are solitary animals; they do not congregate on beaches or in the water as many seals do. They live about 25-30 years, can dive to at least 1,500 ft., and feed on reef fish (including eels), octopus, squid, and crustaceans. When not feeding they spend much time sleeping on shore, either on sandy beaches or rocky ledges. Sometimes they rest in underwater caves, coming up periodically to breathe.

The only natural enemies of monk seals are sharks, with which they have managed to live for millions of years. Coexisting with humans, however, has proved a greater challenge. Seal hunting and other nineteenth century commercial ventures in the Northwestern Hawaiian Islands, followed by military activity during WW II, greatly reduced their numbers. More recently, entanglement in nets and marine debris, and even hooking by longliners, have taken a toll. Hawaiian Monk Seals received legal protection in 1976 under both the Endangered Species and Marine Mammal Protection Acts, and in 2006 the Northwestern Hawaiian Islands, their principal habitat, were declared a National Monument. Despite these efforts, their total population continues to decline. Seals in the northwestern chain are reproducing, but most of their pups fail to thrive after being weaned and appear to be starving. Reasons advanced for this include changes in oceanographic conditions and reduced availability of prey, possibly due in part to competition with fisheries in the area. Wildlife biologists are working hard to understand and reverse this trend. Fortunately, the seal population in the main Hawaiian Islands is growing and the pups are doing well.

Although Monk Seals are not migratory, they sometimes swim from island to island and occasionally venture completely out of Hawaiian waters. Stray individuals have turned up at Johnston Atoll and there have been credible but unconfirmed sightings at Palmyra Atoll in the Line Islands, Bikini Atoll and Mejit Island in the Marshall Islands, and even Wake Island some 2,300 miles from Honolulu. It is possible that the species once enjoyed a much wider geographic distribution, retreated in the face of an advancing wave of humans, and made its last stand in the uninhabited reefs and islands of the northwest Hawaiian chain. The recently devised Hawaiian name **'ilio holo i ka uaua** means "quadruped running in the rough seas." A seldom-used ancient name, **hulu**, means "shaggy" or "furry." Rare mention in the Hawaiian oral tradition suggests that breeding populations in the main islands were extirpated soon after the Polynesian arrival. The current recolonization of the main islands has likely been encouraged by their legal protection and continued efforts to reduce human disturbance. The species name honors German zoologist Hugo H. Schauinsland, who spent three months on Laysan Island in 1896-97 and brought back the seal skins and skulls from which the species was first described. Photo: Kawaihoa (Portlock) Point, O'ahu. 15 ft.

Resting monk seals are easily approached. Unfortunately, if continually disturbed by humans (or dogs) at a particular resting spot, a seal will often abandon that site. Safe, secluded resting places are not plentiful in the main Hawaiian Islands, nor are pups, so it is best to maintain a good distance from all resting seals and give them the solitude they need. It is illegal to harass, disturb, or feed a monk seal and it is recommended to approach no closer than 100 ft., or 150 ft. for mothers with pups. Mothers bond strongly with their pups and will defend them at all cost!

John S. Johnson

Monk Seal reproduction

Most reproduction takes place in the Northwestern Hawaiian Islands and mating occurs in the water. Females usually give birth to a single pup in the spring or early summer. About 3 ft. long when born, and weighing up to about 35 lbs., pups are covered in soft black hair that is replaced by silvery gray hair after several weeks. Mothers nurse their pups for five to seven weeks. Mothers rarely feed during the nursing period and lose a large proportion of their body weight, often appearing thin or emaciated at weaning. During the nursing period pups gain all their nutrition from their mothers' rich milk. A thick blubber layer gives them sufficient reserves after weaning to learn foraging skills on their own, including what to eat, where to find it, and how to catch and eat it. Young females give birth for the first time at an age of five to ten years, continuing the cycle. Photo: O'ahu north shore. John S. Johnson.

Jerry Kane

Threats to monk seals

• Juveniles and subadults have a poor survival rate. They seem not to be getting enough food.

• Predation of juvenile seals by sharks (mostly Galapagos and Tigers) appears to have increased.

• Low juvenile survival means low replacement of breeding females, thus births are declining.

• Breeding females and immature seals are sometimes injured or even killed by over-aggressive males.

• Safe haul-out and pupping beaches are uncommon in the main Hawaiian Islands, increasing the likelihood of disturbance to breeding females.

• Entanglement in abandoned or lost fishing gear and other marine debris kills or injures some seals.

• The small size of the monk seal population and its limited geographic range both increase the chances of devastation by disease and natural disaster.

INDEX